Doo-dah!

STEPHEN FOSTER

and the Rise of

American Popular Culture

Ken Emerson

SIMON & SCHUSTER

SIMON & SCHUSTER
Rockefeller Center
1230 Avenue of the Americas
New York, NY 10020

SIMON & SCHUSTER and colophon are registered trademarks of
Simon & Schuster Inc.

Designed by Karolina Harris

Manufactured in the United States of America

1   3   5   7   9   10   8   6   4   2

Library of Congress Cataloging-in-Publication Data
Emerson, Ken.
Doo-dah! : Stephen Foster and the rise of American
popular culture / Ken Emerson.
p.   cm.
Includes bibliographical references and discography
1. Foster, Stephen Collins, 1826–1864.   2. Composers—United
States—Biography.   3. Music and society.   4. Popular culture
—United States—History—19th century.   I. Title.
ML410.F78E46   1997
782.42164'092—dc21

[B]

96-29816

CIP
MN
ISBN 0-684-81010-7

To Ellen and Maude

CONTENTS

Contents

INTRODUCTION

Early in the evening on January 17, 1992, the day I delivered to my agent the proposal for this book, I boarded the No. 6 subway at Thirty-third Street and Park Avenue in Manhattan. Since I had only one stop before changing trains at Grand Central Station, I stood. At knee-level I heard an eerily familiar melody. Seated before me was a black man who seemed in his late forties, his mustache and goatee a grizzled gray. He was missing several teeth and wearing red sneakers, a dark watch cap, a parka, and a quilted vest that bore the insignia, "World Watch." Between his legs was a white plastic shopping bag that may have held his dinner—or all his worldly belongings.

In a soft, high tenor, almost a falsetto, he was singing "Doo-dah! doo-dah!" It was "Camptown Races," and although his accent seemed Jamaican—Caribbean, at any rate—he pronounced "gwine" as Stephen Foster wrote it almost one hundred fifty years ago: g-w-i-n-e. But instead of singing "Gwine to run all night / Gwine to run all day," he sang "Gwine to *work* all night / Gwine to *work* all day." As he sang "doo-dah!" fat tears ran down his cheeks. He was identifying with the horses rather than the spectators and transforming Foster's frolic into a doleful work song, a deeply personal dirge.

He was doing what Americans—and people all over the world—have been doing with Stephen Foster's songs for a century and a half now: making them their own.

"Oh! Susanna," Foster's first hit song, was published in 1848, the same year as the *Communist Manifesto,* and swept the country and the globe far more quickly. Embroidered with additional lyrics ("I'm going to California, some gold dust for to see"), it became the unofficial anthem of the California gold rush as well as a touchstone of American identity. One "forty-niner" observed in his diary:

I wonder if I am putting it too strongly to say that we American people never really got together until now? Surely there was never such a wide representation as is now seen on these California trails, for here are thousands from perhaps every state. You notice this, for instance, by the curiosity with which Yankees watch and listen to Southerners, or as both of these watch and listen to Missourians and the hill folks of Arkansas. Strange worlds—customs, dress, dialects and manners—here meet together. While travelers from both North and South have visited beyond the Mason and Dixon line, and while minstrel troupes have carried darkey songs far and wide, I think negro melodies never acquired the popularity which is accorded to them here and now. It is not real "darkey" music exactly, I admit; but certainly plantation songs, as written, for instance, by Stephen Foster, are the most popular of all songs among us.[1]

"Oh! Susanna" was translated into Latin (*Heus susanna*) and transformed into a temperance song ("O rum-seller . . ."), even though Foster drank himself to an early grave. Bayard Taylor, a world traveler, reporter and poetaster, heard it sung in Hindu in Delhi and "whistled by a yellowheaded Somersetshire lout, under the broken noses of battered saints in the antique archway of a Norman church." Taylor himself entertained Arabs amid the ruins of Baalbek, in what is now Lebanon, by playing Foster's "Uncle Ned" on his flute.[2]

In 1856, Foster wrote campaign songs for the Democratic presidential candidate, James Buchanan, to whom he was related by marriage. That did not deter Republicans from singing the praises of their man, John Frémont, to the tune of "Camptown Races."[3]

The very next year, a song condensed the chorus of "Camptown Races" ("Bet my money on de bob-tail nag / Somebody bet on de bay") into "a bob tailed bay." The composer was James Pierpont, the uncle of J. P. Morgan, and we now know the song as "Jingle Bells" ("Bells on bob tail ring . . .").[4]

A Democrat, Foster was skeptical, at times even derisive, about the anti-slavery movement. But that did not prevent abolitionists from turning "Oh! Susanna" into "The North Star": "Oh! Star of Freedom, / 'Tis the star for me; / 'Twill lead me off to Canada, / There I will be free."[5]

Even as classical performers—the flamboyant pianist, Louis Moreau Gottschalk, for instance—were working "Oh! Susanna" and "Old Folks at Home" into their barnstorming tours of America, slaves in Georgia were singing "Way down upon de Swanee Ribber," too. A Down East woman teaching music down South heard it "shouted from house to house, from the fields and in the vallies. . . . I find myself often humming the chorus and even dream at night,

> Oh, comrades, how my heart grows weary,
> Far from the dear friends at home."[6]

After the Civil War, the Fisk University Jubilee Singers, the first group to perform black spirituals for concert audiences, sang "Old Folks at Home" as well, and so did black minstrels. William "Billy" Kersands danced "the Virginia Essence"—a soft-shoe precursor, perhaps, of Michael Jackson's "Moon Walk"—to the accompaniment of "Old Folks at Home." ("In the south," another black entertainer wrote, "a minstrel show without Billy Kersands was like a circus without elephants.") When the (African-American) Manhattan Lodge No. 45 of Elks held its annual ball at Madison Square Garden at the turn of the century, the only nonoriginal song the band performed was Foster's "Old Black Joe."[7]

"The well of sorrow from which Negro music is drawn is also a well of mystery," wrote W. C. Handy, the "Father of the Blues," who had often played "Brudder Gardner's Picnic," a medley of Foster songs, when he was a member of Mahara's Minstrels. "I suspect that Stephen Foster owed something to this well, this mystery, this sorrow. 'My Old Kentucky Home' makes you think so, at any rate. Something there suggests close acquaintance with my people. . . ."[8]

Antonin Dvorak thought so highly of "Old Folks at Home" that he conducted his own arrangement of it, with an African-American choir, shortly after the premiere of his *New World* Symphony. Charles Ives had mixed feelings about Dvorak but not about Foster, whose melodies he wove into his Second Symphony, the *Concord* Sonata, and several other works. He once wrote that his bandmaster father, George Ives, had raised him "—and most of the children of [Danbury, Connecticut] for that matter—on Bach and Stephen Foster." Family lore even had it that George Ives fell in with Foster one Saturday night in New York City— an unlikely but not impossible encounter.[9]

While Charlie Ives was attending Yale, ten-year-old Asa Joelson and his brother were singing "anything by Stephen Foster" for spare change in the streets of Washington, D.C. Al Jolson, as he would be known, belted out Foster songs throughout his career and played minstrel leader

E. P. Christy in *Swanee River,* a fanciful 1939 film biography of Foster in which Don Ameche played Stephen. Jolson's very last recording sessions, in 1950, were devoted to eight Foster tunes.[10]

Foster fascinated many of the Jewish immigrants and sons of immigrants who embraced and transformed American popular song in the twentieth century. Not only did Foster symbolize the American identity they were eager to assimilate, but also, as the first American composer to support himself (though not for long and not luxuriously) from the sales of his sheet music, Foster blazed the trail that eventually led to Tin Pan Alley.

Irving Berlin displayed a portrait of Foster on his office wall. Perhaps it was out of gratitude: Berlin's first big hit song, "Alexander's Ragtime Band," paid tribute to the "Swanee River." Not only did it pop the musical question, "Do you want to hear 'The Swanee River' played in ragtime?" but a break in the piano version published in 1911 quoted "Old Folks at Home" and "Dixie" simultaneously. (A later and lesser Berlin song, "Swanee Shuffle," was featured in *Hallelujah,* a 1929 movie musical with an African-American cast, and recorded the same year by Duke Ellington, who turned around and wrote "Swanee River Rhapsody" for his Cotton Club revue, *Blackberries of 1930.*)[11]

A decade after "Alexander's Ragtime Band," George Gershwin and lyricist Irving Caesar stole a page from Berlin's songbook as well as from Foster's and came up with "Swanee" ("How I love you, / How I love you"). When Jolson, having overheard Gershwin play it at a party at the Biltmore Hotel, recorded "Swanee" and added it to his Broadway revue, *Sinbad,* it became Gershwin's first hit and, in terms of sheet music sales, the biggest of his entire career.[12]

In the meantime, Hoagy Carmichael, whose dreamy nostalgia and sentimental stereotypes of Southern blacks are as close as the twentieth century has come to reincarnating Foster, had written his first song, "Riverboat Shuffle," for Bix Beiderbecke's Wolverines. Recalling its composition in his autobiography, Carmichael wrote that he "wondered how Mozart or Bach or Stephen Foster knew they had a live one." One of Carmichael's first recording sessions, with Beiderbecke, Tommy Dorsey and others, included "Toddlin' Blues," which incorporated the "I'm coming" refrain from "Old Black Joe."[13]

Although Tommy Dorsey's band recorded "Old Black Joe" in 1938 and a suave Sy Oliver arrangement of "Old Folks at Home" in 1940, Foster's music seemed to have become a distant echo, inspiring rote invocations of the Swanee River. Foster provided local color, as in Max Steiner's score for *Gone with the Wind,* which quoted ten Foster songs. He also provoked increasing resentment among African Americans. Burlesquing "Oh! Susanna," Fats Waller jeered that the "somethin' " on his knee might be a bottle of gin or (nudge! wink!) even more potent than that. Louis Armstrong made it clear on a recording with the Mills Brothers of "Old Folks at Home" that he was not "longing for de old plantation." "Well looka here," he declared with gleeful defiance, "we are far from home—yeah, man!"[14] Yet one Foster song became a hit for the first time in the early 1940s. A dispute between radio broadcasters and the American Society of Composers, Authors and Publishers encouraged airplay of music in the public domain, whose rights ASCAP did not control. Suddenly "Jeanie with the Light Brown Hair," which had not been particularly successful during Foster's lifetime, became a belated hit.

Another Foster song, "Hard Times Come Again No More," which Dimitri Tiomkin used to evoke the Depression in his score for Frank Capra's *Meet John Doe* (1941), struck a responsive chord once again during the recession in the early 1990s. It was recorded in rapid succession by Syd Straw, the McGarrigle Sisters, Emmylou Harris, Bob Dylan, and Thomas Hampson, and was featured at the beginning and end of Ulu Grosbard's 1995 film *Georgia,* in country-folk and punk-grunge renditions.[15]

Foster's music has cropped up in recent movies as disparate as *Natural Born Killers* and *Little Women,* and in 1994 "My Old Kentucky Home, Good-Night!" was featured in television commercials peddling Toyota Camrys manufactured—where else?—in Kentucky.

Stephen Foster's music, in sum, seems to be all things to all people— from the crowd at Churchill Downs on Kentucky Derby Day to a lone Caribbean immigrant riding the New York City subway—and it has been so for a century and a half. When Thomas Edison demonstrated his tinfoil phonograph at the Smithsonian Institution in 1878, one of his colleagues sang and recorded Foster's "Uncle Ned." Fifty years later, when radio and the Depression drove Edison out of the record business, one of his very last Diamond Discs was a rendition of "Oh! Susanna." No American composer before the twentieth century wrote even half as many songs that are still remembered today. "See, projected through time, / For me an audience interminable," wrote Walt Whitman, who heard America singing. Foster has enjoyed Whitman's wish come true.[16]

Yet almost no one remembers the second verse of "Oh! Susanna," which has seldom been sung in this century:

> I jump'd aboard the telegraph
> And trabbled down de ribber,
> De lectrick fluid magnified,
> And kill'd five hundred Nigga.[17]

No matter how hard you try to distance yourself from those words and put them in some kind of historical context, they still shock and disgust. At least Mark Twain had the decency to reduce the body count in *Huckleberry Finn*. Huck is lying through his teeth as usual, this time to Tom Sawyer's Aunt Sally Phelps, when he attributes his unexpected appearance on foot at the Phelps plantation to a steamboat explosion:

> "We blowed out a cylinder-head."
> "Good gracious! Anybody hurt?"
> "No'm. Killed a nigger."
> "Well, it's lucky; because sometimes people do get hurt."[18]

Scarcely twenty of Stephen Foster's nearly two hundred songs were written in blackface dialect, to be performed *"alla niggerando"* as the sheet music for "Lou'siana Belle" indicated with racist relish. Foster himself became increasingly uneasy about, and eventually abandoned, such dialect, but a disproportionate number of these songs have endured. In addition to identifying with Foster's songs and making them their own, people have also used his music to identify and stigmatize others. Mel Brooks underscored this point in *Blazing Saddles* when rowdy white cowboys ordered a gang of black railroad workers to sing a song. Startled when the laborers burst into a sophisticated rendition of Cole Porter's "I Get a Kick Out of You," the cowpokes countered with a version of what they expected African Americans to sing: "Camptown Races." Many an African American has been humiliated by "Old Black Joe." When utilized to glorify the Old South or to demean African Americans, Foster's songs can be as hateful as lawn jockeys. And they can outrage even when no hurt is intended. Although "My Old Kentucky Home, Good-Night!"

was inspired by an abolitionist novel and expresses deep sympathy for enslaved African Americans—a sympathy that Frederick Douglass and W. E. B. Du Bois saluted—two African Americans threatened to quit the Yale Glee Club if it sang the song (and another "plantation melody") at a 1996 concert celebrating Charles Ives. The group's president burned a copy of the song, a majority voted not to perform it, and the program was changed.[19]

Just as there are periodic attempts to ban *Huckleberry Finn* from public school libraries, Foster has been repeatedly blacklisted or whitewashed. That's one reason two 1970s recordings by mezzo-soprano Jan DeGaetani, baritone Leslie Guinn, and pianist Gilbert Kalish concentrated on Foster's genteel parlor ballads, and baritone Thomas Hampson consigned many of Foster's most familiar melodies—including "Oh! Susanna" and "Old Folks at Home"—to wordless, instrumental renditions on his 1992 collection. "I like those songs, and I defend them," said Mark Morris, who nonetheless steered clear of them when he choreographed *Somebody's Coming to See Me Tonight* to nine Foster tunes in 1995. "But it's complicated, because some people think *Huckleberry Finn* is horrifyingly racist, and I don't. What is better than 'Way down upon the Swanee River'? We all know it, and we're horrified to sing it."[20]

The survival of Foster's music attests as much to the transcendence of racism, however, as it does to its persistence. Historically, blackface music has proven to be not just a racist rip-off (though it surely has been that) and not only the sincerest form of flattery (it's been that, too), but also, in some instances, a genuine musical achievement and, in a few cases, even an expression of genius. Foster pioneered a path that has been followed by many, including Irving Berlin ("The King of Ragtime," and before that a singing waiter at Nigger Mike's Chinatown restaurant), Benny Goodman ("The King of Swing"), and, of course, Elvis (just "The King").

Stephen Foster was among the first white boys to do what white boys (and the occasional girl) have been doing ever since—mimicking black music, or what they think is black music and black style. Minstrelsy did not die with the nineteenth century. It has outlasted *Amos 'n' Andy* in the twentieth. Burnt cork is as up-to-the-minute as The New Kids on the Block, Vanilla Ice, or Ted Danson at the Friars Club.

Blackface represented to Foster, as it has to many generations since, a means of escape and a form of rebellion. This is, after all, one of the great ironies of blackface, from minstrel shows to rock 'n' roll: it represents a certain freedom to whites—freedom from bourgeois conventions and expectations—even though that illusion of freedom is largely the consequence of white oppression and exclusion.

Charles Correll and Freeman Gosden, the white creators of *Amos 'n' Andy,* met when they were working for the Joe Bren Company, which staged minstrel-show civic fundraisers for Kiwanis Clubs, Odd Fellows, and the like throughout the Midwest. According to a fascinating book by Melvin Patrick Ely,

> Their shows went over best . . . when they could get the mayor, a few lawyers, maybe a college professor into the company they put together in each town. . . . Gleeful newspaper accounts . . . show how thoroughly audiences enjoyed the once-a-year opportunity to see the local elite as blackface comics. One luminary in a North Carolina city "out-darkied any darkey you ever heard of, whether of flesh or fable." A doctor in West Virginia won applause "by turning himself loose without restraint". . . and proving that he "possesses, in a wonderful degree, the talent to assume the exaggerated and glorified characteristics of the shuffling, singing Senegambian."[21]

I think often of that doctor, like me, from West Virginia. What a savage irony: that aping a black man reinforced that physician's sense of racial superiority and social respectability while at the same time it relieved him for an evening from the pressures that superiority and respectability created!

Stephen Foster is at the heart of the tangled, tortuous interchange between whites and blacks that both dishonors America and yet distinguishes its culture worldwide. "The proof of a poet," wrote Whitman, "shall be sternly deferr'd till his country absorbs him as affectionately as he has absorb'd it."[22] Foster is so absorbed in the air that we breathe and in the airs that we hum, in our blood and in our assumptions, that we seldom if ever think of him. Yet an America without Foster is as unthinkable as an America without Whitman or Twain, without Louis Armstrong or George Gershwin, without rock 'n' roll, without racism—or without those instances of amazing grace when, if only for an instant, we transcend that racism.

Chapter One

AMERICAN EDEN

On July 4, 1826, smoke smudged the green, leafy heights of Coal Hill, the steep ridge overlooking Pittsburgh from the opposite, southern bank of the muddy Monongahela River. A seam of coal near the hill's summit had been burning for years, and try as they might, no one had been able to extinguish the fire. America's fiftieth birthday did not dispel the perennial pall over Pittsburgh. "Scarce half a century is gone by since Pittsburgh was an inconsiderable hamlet," Samuel Jones marveled in his guide to the city and its environs, when the "appalling yell of the savage" was "heard where this prosperous and populous city now attracts the attention of the stranger, as the bustling workshop of the west."[1]

Mike Fink, Fort Pitt's most famous native son, was dead and gone. The king of the keelboatmen was swiftly receding into legend as a half-horse, half-alligator pulp-fiction marksman who could drill a hole through a tin cup on a man's—or his own wife's—head and shoot the tail off a piglet, the scalp-lock off an Indian, or the heel off a flat-footed Negro. Yet it had been only three or four years before this Fourth of July that Fink, fleeing the onrush of civilization and the competition from steamboats, lit out like Huck Finn for the territories. On the Yellowstone River in Montana, perhaps while showing off his tin-cup trick once too often, Fink had killed a man and been gunned down in retaliation.[2]

The embattled outpost at the point where the Monongahela and Allegheny rivers meet to form the Ohio had burgeoned almost overnight into Pittsburgh, the "Birmingham of America," the "Emporium of the West," a leading manufacturer of iron, glass, steam engines, and steamboats that packed a population of more than 10,500 under its "sulphurous canopy." As early as 1819, a visitor had noted, coal dust was so ubiquitous that he "did not see a white man or woman in the place. The more you wash, the blacker you get. . . . Pittsburg in appearance suggests the idea of Moscow smoking and in ruins."[3]

Yet two miles east of Pittsburgh, up the Philadelphia–Greensburg Turnpike, the only whiffs of smoke came from the barbecue, muskets, and cannons saluting the fiftieth Fourth. William Barclay Foster was the host of an outdoor banquet at Foster's Grove, the woods behind his home in Lawrenceville, a suburb he had developed. Foster had bought 123 acres for $35,000 in 1814, laid out the lots and named his venture in real estate speculation in honor of Captain James Lawrence, the naval hero of the War of 1812 whose famous last words had been, "Don't give up the ship."[4]

Lawrenceville overlooked the Allegheny River and the spot where the young George Washington had given up the raft, capsizing and nearly drowning on an icy evening in December, 1753, as he and a companion returned from an unsuccessful mission to persuade the French to clear out of western Pennsylvania. Now, as his presidential successors, John Adams and Thomas Jefferson, lay dying, Washington's portrait adorned the head of the head table at Foster's Grove. (A likeness of General Lafayette, who had visited Pittsburgh the year before, graced the table's foot.) Pittsburgh's mayor, John M. Snowden, presided over the festive proceedings, and William Foster, a delegate to the Pennsylvania House of Representatives in Harrisburg, was the banquet's first vice president.

At the age of forty-six, Foster was a proud patriot. Although nominally still a Federalist, Foster, like the others at his picnic tables, now identified himself as a Democratic Republican.[5] An early and ardent supporter of Andrew Jackson, Foster had played a bit part in Old Hickory's Louisiana campaign during the War of 1812, as well as in the history of steamboat navigation. Appointed Deputy Commissioner of Purchases for the United States Army in the war's dying days, Foster had loaded the steamboat *Enterprize* with ammunition and other supplies and dispatched the vessel down the Ohio River to the Mississippi, thence to New Orleans. The stern-wheeler's cargo was deeply appreciated even though it arrived the day after Jackson's victory in the Battle of New Orleans. Returning home, the *Enterprize* became the first steamboat ever to make it all the way up the Mississippi and Ohio rivers to Pittsburgh and even beyond, up the Monongahela to Brownsville—a round-trip of well over 4,000 miles.[6]

After the celebrants at Foster's Grove were treated to a reading of the Declaration of Independence, a speech and "an excellent dinner . . . spread with much taste and elegance," they raised at least three dozen toasts. Since William Foster would not take the temperance pledge for another seven years, he probably drained his cup as deeply and repeatedly as his comrades. "Well, the Americans may have great reason to be proud of this day, and of the deeds of their forefathers," a British traveler observed of a Fourth of July celebration in New York City a decade later, "but why do they get so confoundedly drunk? Why, on this day of independence, should they become so *dependent* upon posts and rails for support?"[7]

William Foster hoisted his glass to toast

> *The independence of the United States*—Acquired by the blood and valor of our venerable progenitors. To us they bequeathed the dear bought inheritance; to our care and protection they consigned it; and the most sacred obligations are upon us to transmit the glorious purchase, unfettered by power, to our innocent and beloved offspring.[8]

His audience included six of his children, and that very day his wife, Eliza Clayland Foster, bore him another "innocent and beloved offspring."

"I remember so well," wrote Ann Eliza Foster Buchanan late in her life,

> how we children were seated at the table & saw & heard all that went on taken there for the purpose, as I now understand of keeping the house quiet for our dear Mother—I also have a distinct recollection of the anxiety expressed by those in attendance at the house, lest the cannons of the national Salute should deafen the little infant, not more than an hour or two old.[9]

The cannon fire came from a nearby arsenal, built on land Foster had sold to the U.S. government for $12,000. James Monroe had inspected the facility in 1817, and Ann Eliza could remember that notable event, too, when "Pa rode out with President Monroe" and later took a seat "in the midst of the uniforms . . . by which 'His Excellency' was surrounded."[10]

In the 1850s, Ann Eliza's mother wrote a lightly fictionalized account of her life that mixed romance with religiosity, perfume with piety. Pittsburgh became Duquesne, and the Fosters, the Grenvilles, but the White Cottage that had been the Fosters' Lawrenceville home was too cherished a memory to rechristen. On this Glorious Fourth of 1826, Eliza Foster was confined to what she later described lovingly as her "half cottage half chateau," with its "large windows daily polished with whiting and buckskin" and its "dark marble coloured steps, the full blown roses blooming on the green sward, the white graveled terrace gently sloping off into a broad turf."[11]

Here, in the lap of patriotism and apparent prosperity, in the bosom of suburban bliss, a safe stone's throw from a cradle of the American Industrial Revolution, in sheltered circumstances as close to heavenly as earth can provide, Stephen Foster was born at approximately noon on America's Day of Jubilee.

Less than an hour later, Jefferson was dead; by six that evening, Adams had joined him. Dropping the final curtain on the political and cultural era of the American Revolution, their deaths also ushered in a new age of Jacksonian democracy and popular culture in which Stephen Foster would play a defining role.

Resisting a relative's playful suggestion that they call him Jefferson Adams, the Fosters named their new child after the son of dear friends, Stephen Collins, who had recently died at the age of twelve. Thomas Collins, a graduate of Trinity College, Dublin, was one of Pittsburgh's foremost attorneys, and his wife, a childhood playmate of Mrs. Foster's on the Eastern Shore of Maryland, is said to have been "the first lady in town to ride in her own carriage."[12]

Stephen Collins Foster was baptized on April 22, 1827, in Pittsburgh's recently built Trinity Episcopal Church, an imposing, Gothic-looking pile that Samuel Jones praised as "by far the handsomest edifice in the city. The others are very ordinary and common place, being built more for cheapness than ornament."[13]

Stephen was the last child to survive infancy in a large, lively, and musical family. "Your father has been drawing a few tunes on the violin for your little brother and sister to dance, this evening," Eliza Clayland Foster had written five years earlier to her eldest daughter, Charlotte, while she was attending boarding school in Maryland. "[T]hey have not forgot the danceing tunes you used to play on the pianno; Henry whistles and Henrietta sings them yet. Duning begins to walk around a chair he has six teeth and can say *dont*." [14] Charlotte Susanna Foster had been born in 1809; Ann Eliza, who would later describe the day of Stephen's birth, in 1812; Henry Baldwin in 1816; Henrietta Angelica in 1818; Dunning McNair in 1821; and Morrison in 1823. (James Clayland Foster, born in 1829, would die the following year.)

The Foster children had a half brother in William Barclay Foster, Jr., an illegitimate child William Foster had probably fathered shortly before his marriage. The boy's mother, whose identity is unknown but who may have been Irish, deposited him at the Fosters' doorstep around 1815, when he was somewhere between seven and ten, and disappeared, possibly on a boat bound downriver. Whatever hurt or anger the startled Eliza Foster may have felt was overcome by her maternal instincts and by her grief at the recent loss of her first son, who had died in March 1815 at the age of ten months. The lad was given that infant's name, William Barclay Foster, Jr., and raised as if he were Eliza's child. [15]

"Brother William," as he was called, left home a few months before Stephen's birth to learn surveying by working on the Pennsylvania Canal. "The first official shovelful of earth" for this ambitious but ultimately unsuccessful attempt to compete with New York's Erie Canal was dug in Harrisburg the very day Stephen was born. [16]

By this time the Foster family had called America home for a century. Stephen Foster's great-grandfather, Alexander Foster, emigrated from Londonderry, Ireland, about 1725. After a brief sojourn in Freehold, New Jersey, he settled in Little Britain Township in Lancaster County, Pennsylvania, establishing a farm and family there. [17]

Alexander's oldest son, James, was Stephen's grandfather. Born in 1738, James married Ann Barclay, also of Lancaster County, in 1766 and crossed the Susquehanna River to the more mountainous clime of Berkeley County, Virginia (now West Virginia). Loyal to his new country as well as to his Scots-Irish roots, James enlisted at the outset of the Revolution in the Liberty Company of Londonderry Volunteers. He later served in the Tenth Pennsylvania Regiment, and family legend has it that, as a member of a Virginia regiment, he observed the surrender of Cornwallis at Yorktown.[18] Clearly his military service was not unfurloughed, for during the war he fathered his third son and fifth child, William Barclay Foster, born in Berkeley County on September 5, 1779.

William Barclay Foster, Stephen's father, was still a toddler when James moved his family farther west, across the Allegheny Mountains. Settling near Canonsburg, Pennsylvania, nineteen miles south of Pittsburgh, James became an elder in the Presbyterian church and supported the little log-cabin Presbyterian school, Canonsburg Academy, that young William attended. When the academy became Jefferson College (the first college west of the Alleghenies) in 1802, James Foster was a trustee. (In 1869, Jefferson would merge to become part of Washington and Jefferson College, in Washington, Pennsylvania.)

William Barclay Foster left home in April 1796 to seek his fortune in the big city—Pittsburgh, population 1,300.[19] Two years earlier, Major General "Mad Anthony" Wayne had devastated the Miami, the Shawnee, and warriors from other tribes in the Battle of Fallen Timbers, making the Ohio River Valley safe for whites and opening it to a flood of commerce and settlement. U.S. cavalry had swept through the streets of Pittsburgh, suppressing the Whiskey Rebellion and making it safe for townspeople to make money from that flood. Now that Indians were no longer even a remote threat, and the farmers who had protested the federal excise tax on liquor had been pacified, Pittsburgh could settle down to business. Among the city fathers dismantling Fort Pitt to build row houses with its bricks was Major Ebenezer Denny, a Revolutionary War hero who would become Pittsburgh's first mayor when it became big enough, in 1816, to require one.[20]

William Barclay Foster found work with Major Denny and Anthony Beelen's merchant firm, and adventurous work it was—although Foster may have added a few embellishments when he regaled his children with tales of his youth. Morrison Foster remembered his father's stories of flatboat expeditions to New Orleans:

Sometimes he returned by land . . . traveling with large parties strongly armed, for the Indians were hostile and dangerous. At other times he took ship and sailed to New York. On one of these voyages . . . he was . . . captured by pirates off the coast of Cuba, but was rescued by a Spanish man-of-war.[21]

Indians . . . pirates . . . it's surprising Foster didn't throw in Mike Fink for good measure! It would have been a good yarn, and it might even have been true, since they were plying the same rivers at the same time.

When Foster returned by way of New York and Philadelphia, he bought merchandise there and transported it in Conestoga wagons over the mountains to Pittsburgh. According to Morrison Foster, it was on one such return trip, in Philadelphia, that his parents met.

Nine years younger than William Barclay Foster, Eliza Clayland Tomlinson was born in Wilmington, Delaware, in 1788. Her mother's family, the Claylands, were wealthy slaveholders who had been proliferating and intermarrying somewhat incestuously on Maryland's Eastern Shore since the Reverend James Clayland arrived there from England around 1670.[22] By her first marriage, Eliza's mother, Elizabeth Clayland, had four daughters (three of whom wed other Claylands). After her first husband's death, Elizabeth married Joseph Tomlinson, son of a Delaware farmer, and died shortly after bearing their only child, Eliza. Tomlinson soon remarried and moved to Kentucky, leaving Eliza to be raised by Clayland relatives in Baltimore.

The teenaged Eliza was in Philadelphia visiting a Tomlinson aunt when William Foster first encountered her. Her father's sister, Sarah Tomlinson, had married Oliver Evans, America's answer to Britain's James Watt. The Columbian High-Pressure Steam Engine that Evans patented in 1804 was the prototype for the mobile engines that drove the steamboats on the Mississippi and Ohio, and for the stationary ones that powered Pittsburgh's industrial development. He charged gawkers twenty-five cents to watch his steam-driven amphibious dredge—the *Orukter Amphibolos*, as he christened it in Greek—circle Philadelphia's Centre Square before it proceeded to the wharfs. Eliza Clayland Foster would tell her children that "she saw him walk with great pride beside it as it moved out of his yard into the street and down into the river."[23]

When William Barclay Foster and Eliza Clayland Tomlinson wed on November 14, 1807, they were already en route to Pittsburgh. The Reverend David Denny, Ebenezer Denny's first cousin, married them in Chambersburg, Pennsylvania. Evidently Eliza charmed the local press, for *The Franklin Repository* described her as "amiable and sprightly."[24]

In her memoir, Eliza recalled how she

wended her way, a young and joyous bride, accompanied by her gallant groom, over a rough and mountainous road, to reside in what was then called the far west. Not having the present advantages of canal, or turnpike or railroad the journey was slow and monotonous and it was not until the fourteenth day after staging in an uncomfortable coach, that she hailed with delight the dingy town of Duquesne, her future home, where every joy and every sorrow of her heart since that bright period has been associated with the joys and sorrows of its people.[25]

Their first stop was the home of Ebenezer Denny. William Foster was now his partner, having replaced Anthony Beelen. Denny & Foster's ledger for 1807–1808 indicates that the firm sold everything from clover seed to "charmay" shawls.[26]

The young couple was welcomed warmly by the first families of Pittsburgh. In her memoir, Eliza Foster described a visit to the mansion of General John Wilkins, whose sons became the presidents of Pittsburgh's two banks. Here "the children of the elite" gathered to demonstrate, accompanied by harpsichord, the steps their French dancing instructor had taught them.[27]

"Why did this people hold the reins of custom in their hands and extend their influence to new comers[?]" Eliza asked. "Because they were a consolidated federal voice," she answered. The Dennys and Wilkinses and others "were one voice in state affairs and gave the same tone to every opinion. . . . Cheerfulness and gaiety seemed to be the order of the day. . . ."[28]

And why not? Business was booming. The Monongahela River provided access to the immense coal fields of southwestern Pennsylvania and Virginia, and this cheap fuel stoked Pittsburgh's iron and glass industries. The Ohio River, meanwhile, provided access to immense markets for those industries in the West and South. The clear flint glass that Benjamin Bakewell began producing in 1807 became world-famous. Pittsburgh's first iron foundry was established in 1806; Anthony Beelen followed shortly with the Eagle Foundry. In 1812, Eliza Foster's uncle, Oliver Evans, and his son George, having already opened a steam-driven flour mill in Pittsburgh, started making steam engines there, too.[29]

William Foster briefly owned a steam mill, according to an 1813 city directory. By then he, Eliza, and two daughters were living in a two-story brick house at the corner of Sixth Street and Cherry Alley.[30] About the time he built the White Cottage in Lawrenceville, he also became involved in the stagecoach business as a manager of the Pittsburgh and

Greensburgh Turnpike Company, whose coaches and wagons passed right by his new home's front door. The company's president, William Wilkins, was General Wilkins's son as well as founder of the Bank of Pittsburgh.[31] William Wilkins would go on to become a federal judge, a U.S. congressman and senator, ambassador to Russia, and secretary of war. No one in Pittsburgh would awe the up-and-coming Andrew Carnegie more than Wilkins, by then in his seventies, and Carnegie felt honored to be invited to Wilkins's mansion, Homewood, the most fashionable and aristocratic county seat in western Pennsylvania.[32]

The Fosters, in short, were friends, business associates, and political allies of Pittsburgh's highest circles. When William Foster was elected to the House of Representatives in Harrisburg, it was on the same Federalist ticket as Harmar Denny, Ebenezer's son. Paying calls in "the family barouche," Eliza was intensely sensitive to and impressed by social rank. A friend who had moved from Pittsburgh to Troy, New York, complained to Eliza in a letter that "there is no Mrs. *Foster* here, who will take me in their family, and tell me who is in the first society, and who in the second."[33]

William Foster was the grand seigneur of Lawrenceville, dispensing favors, Eliza would recall, to

> newcomers who daily came . . . to ask for assistance. Indeed some came to that place to settle without any money, expecting not only to get their lots from Mr. Grenville, but to be supported by him also without recompense. Some there are that by the blessing and favor of God are now living in affluence in the large city of Duquesne who at that time had reason to bless and pray for Wilford Grenville, whose liberal hand always stretched forth to help the needy, had saved them from poverty and want.[34]

When the legislature was in session in Harrisburg, Foster missed his home and family. "Kiss my Dear children," he ended one letter to Eliza. "I long to see you all very much; if I could fly, over the mountains and light down at the gate & return the next day I would soon be with you."[35]

The White Cottage was worth yearning for. According to Morrison Foster, it commanded a spacious view up and down the Allegheny River.[36] Morrison's daughter, Evelyn Foster Morneweck, described the house in loving detail, much of which she learned from her father and other relatives, since it was torn down decades before her birth.

The main building measured fifty feet across the front, and contained four rooms on one floor with a center hall. It was painted white and finished with green shutters. A two-story wing of three or more rooms stretched to the east. Rising through the center of the house were the two main chimneys, and large fireplaces were built into the inside corners of each of the four rooms of the main part of the homestead. . . . The Foster homestead also contained a basement "summer kitchen" and in the rear of the house were the usual bake oven, smokehouse, cow barns, horse stable, and hog-pens of a country place that was partly self-sustaining.[37]

Eliza Foster described in her memoir the optimism that pervaded early Pittsburgh, or at least her social set:

With business men there was none of that running to and fro with hollow cheeck and sunken eye, there were no failures, no broken down families. All were gradually rising, the lawyers, the physicians, the merchants, the mechanics. The lawyers have been in the Cabinet and in the senate, the physicians died rich, the merchants became large land holders, and the mechanics retired to their country residences.[38]

Eliza Foster's memoir is written, by and large, in the third person, and when it bursts into the first person, the effect can be startling and poignant. "When fancy lends her wings to bear my memory back," she suddenly interjects, "it seems as if in some sweet dream my happy buoyant steps had been within Eden's walls."[39]

Yes, the White Cottage in Lawrenceville long, long ago, when there were no failures, no broken-down families and all were gradually rising, *was* Eden, from which Eliza and the infant Stephen Foster were abruptly and irrevocably expelled. At the Fourth of July banquet when Stephen was born, one of the guests had toasted *"Our host*—May the society of friends and the smiles of plenty, never forsake the cheerful giver."[40] Talk is cheap, for William Foster and his family were swiftly and rudely forsaken.

Chapter Two

A FATHER'S FALL

liza Foster's memoir includes a story that seems amusing at first. Not only is the pre-Freudian phallic imagery innocently and uproariously overt, but the plot and the pathos appear to parody one of the most popular ballads of the nineteenth century, Henry Russell's "Woodman! Spare That Tree!" Russell, who has been called "the most important songwriter in the USA before Stephen Foster," was sort of the Elton John of his era: an Englishman who set other people's lyrics to music (George P. Morris wrote the words to "Woodman!") and sang histrionically to his own piano accompaniment.[1] He dressed more demurely than Elton John, to be sure, but he performed songs such as "The Maniac" and "The Ship on Fire" almost as melodramatically as the "Madman Across the Water" used to pound out "Burn Down the Mission."

"Woodman! Spare That Tree!" was published in 1837, after the events Eliza Foster described but long before she described them. Especially since Stephen Foster and his brother Morrison were in the audience when Russell performed in Pittsburgh in early 1843, their mother may have known full well that she was playing with a pop-culture cliché.[2] Still, the story ceases to be funny when one realizes how accurately it foreshadows the devastation of Eliza's life—and her family's.

"That chopping sounds very near the house," observed "Mrs. Grenville" as she finished her morning toilet. Her husband, putting on his bathrobe, assured her it was an echo. She took his word for it, but soon she was

> startled by the sound of a terrific crash. The first thought that struck her was that some one had shot her husband, for he leaped into the room and reeled to a seat exclaiming ["]That rascal has done the business.["]
>
> . . . Jack Devlin the woodman had cut down the great tree, the pride of all the country side. . . .
>
> Yes, there lay the splendid tree that had flourished for ages in his majesty, sheltering with its giant arms the polished and the rude, prostrated never to rise again, hewn down by the hand of a stupid clown. . . .
>
> "Stop that axe you stupid monster," roared Mr. Grenville, as he rushed to the terrace, ["]and never let me catch you on this ground again.["]
>
> ["]Didn't you tell me to cut the tree down[?"] said Jack in alarm.
>
> ["]Why no you fool, I told you that dead sycamore.["]

Mr. Grenville soon forgot his anger, but that evening "shadowy thoughts . . . gloomed" through his wife's imagination.

> The fate of the tree seemed to her ominous of some dark prospective, although there was nothing in her affairs to induce such fear. She entered her nursery, kissed all her children, and retired to her room, where falling upon her knees she prostrated herself before the throne of Omnipotence, saying, Lord, thy will be done; If these joys must pass away nourish me with grace to bear it.
>
> Her tears fell fast. Why, she knew not, for her cup of lifes joys was full to the brim. . . . [W]hy should a careless woodman cutting down a favorite tree cast such sombre shadows over her future path.[3]

After losing the stately tree that shaded the White Cottage, William Foster lost his left hand or, more precisely, the use of it. So it would seem from a letter his sixteen-year-old daughter, Ann Eliza, wrote him in 1828 while he was attending a legislative session in Harrisburg. ". . . [D]o dear father be careful," she implored, ". . . for you know from what a slight cause the loss of your left hand proceeded. . . . Oh, what a dreary time it was when you (our only earthly supporter) were stretched out on what all thought to be your bed of death." William's granddaughter, Evelyn Foster Morneweck, speculated that blood poisoning might have been to blame. Maybe it was a stroke or perhaps a fall. In any event, William was impaired.[4]

At about the same time, William Foster lost his home. When Stephen was born, he had already defaulted on his mortgage. In May 1826, the Bank of the United States foreclosed on all his Lawrenceville property south of the turnpike. This included the White Cottage, in which the Fosters continued to live as tenants until shortly after its sale in September 1827 to a Pittsburgh grocer.

The Foster family's finances were extremely precarious ever afterward, and its housing makeshift. Stephen Foster would compose so many songs about home in part because he seldom knew one for long. He was shunted from rentals to boarding houses to relatives, from Pittsburgh and Allegheny City (a suburb on the northern side of the Allegheny River that was annexed by Pittsburgh in 1907) to Youngstown and Coitsville, Ohio. The house he lived in the longest, in Allegheny City, was owned by his half brother, William Barclay Foster, Jr.

As Brother William graduated from axeman to rodman to levelman and then assistant engineer for the Pennsylvania Canal, he became a surrogate Father William, on whom the entire family depended for money and advice. "I was gratified to learn," Brother William wrote his parents in 1838, with regard to a grocery store his younger brother Henry had opened with a partner, "that the prospect for business is good . . . but I know so well Father's sanguine temperament on such matters that, I in my own mind make allowances. . . ."[5]

William Foster protested his son's skepticism: "I confess I am sometimes sanguine in my calculations of business, but in this case, you will agree that I have facts to justify my hopes. . . ."[6]

The store failed in a matter of months.

Hope sprung eternal in William Foster's breast, and holes just as frequently in his pockets. The financial troubles that dogged him most of his life began with that first round-trip by steamboat between Pittsburgh and New Orleans. Foster paid personally for a lot of the cannon balls he loaded on the *Enterprize*. The deputy commissioner of purchases did not wait for authorization and money to arrive from charred Washington, lest New Orleans fall in the meantime to the same British troops that had torched the capitol. But when Foster submitted his expenses at war's end, he was reimbursed for $21,308.08—$2,704.90 less than he claimed —and declared publicly to have defaulted on his debts. Foster sued, and eventually the United States Court at Pittsburgh ruled in his favor.

"The defendant," the judge charged the jury, "however this cause may eventuate, has established a character for zeal, promptitude, patriotism, and disinterestedness, which will not soon be forgotten, and has placed a laurel on his brow, which will not soon fade."[7] Nonetheless Foster was awarded only $1,107.89, and he spent the next quarter century trying to recover the remainder.

In 1818, the Pittsburgh and Greensburgh Turnpike Company went bankrupt, leaving William Foster liable for some of its debts. This resulted in a mare's nest of suits and countersuits that wasn't untangled until 1841. By this time Foster had spent so much time and money in Erie, Pennsylvania, where one of the company's directors had defaulted on a piece of property and Foster tried to claim some of the proceeds from its forced sale, that his settlement for $2,000 was probably a net loss.[8]

Having soured on turnpikes, William Foster became a big booster of canals. He told fellow legislators in Harrisburg that a canal would bind eastern and western Pennsylvania with "cords of commerce" and encourage immigration and the settling of the West:

> [O]pen your canal to lake Erie, sir, and you will see the hardy sons of oppression landing on your shores, they will ship on board a canal boat their rosy girls, and chubby boys, and will cheaply and safely wend their way towards your western regions, where they can have *land cheap* and liberty for nothing.[9]

After two terms, Foster traded his seat in the legislature for the promise of a position from the Board of Canal Commissioners. Ultimately he was rewarded with the post of Collector of Tolls on the unfinished Blairsville-Pittsburgh Canal. While awaiting its completion, Foster was asked by the Secretary of the Treasury to collaborate on a report on manufacturing, for use in revising the tariff. Treasury was impressed by the report, but Congress never appropriated the money to defray its authors' expenses.

When the canal was finally in operation, William Foster could scarcely contain his excitement and relief. Writing Brother William to borrow one hundred dollars in order to repay another debt, he underlined: "The Canal Commissioners have raised my salary from *30 to 60* Dollars a month!!!"[10] Yet a year later he quit, complaining, again to Brother William, that he could not scrape by because

> while I was handling money *it must be had,* no matter what it was to be replaced from; so that I was kept in eternal misery between Constables on

one hand, and the fear of involving my Bail's men on the other, and blasting my reputation for ever by being dismissed from service for using public money. . . . [11]

It was the *Enterprize* and the Treasury report all over again, although this time the bureaucrats with whom William Foster was at odds dawdled in Harrisburg, not Washington. Unable to get the public money he needed to do what must be done, and equally incapable of keeping that money separate from his personal funds, William Foster was forever spending what he didn't have. Overdrawing on future expectations was not the only tendency Stephen Foster would acquire from his father.

Difficulties in both his public and private ventures condemned William Foster to a vicious cycle of debt and litigation. He kited checks, grumbled about "jew brokers" and groused as he filed one suit after another that "you can't get a lawyer to stir an inch without stuffing him with money." In the letter to Brother William containing the latter complaint he also confessed that he had just returned from Youngstown to Pittsburgh partly to take advantage of "the benefits of the insolvency laws here"—apparently more lenient in Pennsylvania than in Ohio— should he be imprisoned for his debts, which amounted to "some five or six hundred dollars to different persons." In order to free himself from some of those obligations, he filed for bankruptcy a couple of years later, which must have caused him considerable embarrassment because he was Mayor of Allegheny City at the time.[12]

William Foster was so preoccupied with suing for money that was owed him that he neglected ever to earn any, condemning his family, at a time when so many others in Pittsburgh were "gradually rising," to inexorable downward mobility. Eliza Foster, for all her outward show of resignation, seethed with resentment. "Pa continues temperate as you left him," she wrote to Brother William,

whilest he is so I will not thwart his plans beleiving them to be wiser than my own indeed I am but a dependent being in every respect, being too timmid to contradict one so cute as your Father, for if I made a devided house and led of to somthing of my own invention he would be sure to overthrow it all, so that I will ever and annon train myself into the first great nesasary lesson of resegnation, and raise my thoughts morning and evening to Jehovah for my daily bread, and to forgive me my trespasses as I forgive those who trespass against me.[13]

William Foster's trespasses included not only improvidence but also, for a considerable period of time, intemperance. In Pittsburgh as throughout the West in the early nineteenth century, politics was spirited in more ways than one. In 1888, a Captain Hazlett recalled election day in Allegheny City in the 1820s, when

> voters had to walk the three miles at every election, and stayed there all day. They nearly all engaged in some kind of sport, such as raffling and shooting matches, throwing the big stone, running races, hop, step and jumps, playing cards and throwing high dice for a picayune. Then there were the politicians. . . . Whisky was the only drink at that time, and as it only cost three cents a gill a dollar would go a long way in buying drinks. . . . I can't say I ever saw any of the above party drunk. Some would have a pretty good load on, but could always navigate.[14]

Not long before Stephen Foster's birth, in January 1826, William wrote Eliza and tried to reassure her: ". . . I stretched a point and bot a pint of wine, the only one I have bot since I came to Harrisburgh. . . ." The American Society for the Promotion of Temperance was founded the very next month in Boston. The reform movement took its time, however, crossing the mountains to Pittsburgh, where in 1829 there was one liquor license for every 123 residents of Allegheny County. The Pittsburgh Temperance Society was not formed until April 1832. The following year, William Foster wrote to Brother William that he had joined it "and sign'd the constitution . . . since which I have touched not, nor handled the poisonous article, & trust I never will."[15]

In the interim William Foster seems to have inflicted considerable sorrow on his family. Years later, his daughter Henrietta would write her own son, admonishing him to abjure alcohol:

> When I recall the days of youth, and my own sweet mother, with her sad care worn face and troubled countenance on account of those we all loved so dearly, but who had allowed themselves to be dragged inch, by inch, into the vortex of intemperance, my eyes are filled with hot burning tears. . . . [16]

Henrietta's use of the plural "those" suggests a second weakness that William Foster bequeathed Stephen.

Chapter Three

DEATH AND
THE MAIDEN

The Foster family's fortunes had not yet fallen when a caller at the White Cottage asked Charlotte, the Fosters' eldest daughter, to "sing and play some of those favorite little airs of yours." "Sophy," as she was called in her mother's memoir, "walked modestly to the piano, and seating herself, sang, 'There's nothing true but heaven,' in a manner that touched the feelings and moved the hearts of all present."[1]

Charlotte Susanna Foster was "a prodigy," remarked another admiring visitor. Like many other daughters of Pittsburgh's elite, she was a pupil of Mrs. Brevost, who purportedly "had been educated in Paris and presented at the court of Louis 16th and Marie Antoinette," and who taught "French music and dancing in addition to the other branches." One recital by the émigré's students included a gavotte danced by two girls accompanied by a third girl on the piano and a fourth on the harp, and a "shawl dance" by four girls waving "white muslin scarfs filled with silver spangles."[2]

If this seems somewhat effete entertainment in what was still a rude town, it was not unusual. Anthony Philip Heinrich, the first significant composer of classical and orchestral works in the United States, offered Pittsburghers violin and piano lessons "at the Philadelphia rates" in

1817, the same year he conducted, in Lexington, Kentucky, the first Beethoven symphony heard in America. William Evens, a prominent figure on the local musical scene for more than thirty years, advertised lessons on nearly every instrument, from the hautboy to the viola. "Pitts-burghers probably enjoyed more good music than any other Westerners," one historian has observed.[3]

In 1821, Charlotte was sent away to St. Joseph's Academy, a convent school founded by Mother Elizabeth Seton near Emmitsburg, in western Maryland. It's unclear how long she stayed or how long her family could afford to keep her there. In her late teens, Charlotte was back in Pitts-burgh and restless to escape. The hard-pressed Fosters could no longer afford a piano for her to play, and helping care for her infant brother Stephen held little appeal. In May 1828, Charlotte set out on a steam-boat romantically named *Waverley*, after Sir Walter Scott's novels. She was chaperoned by Henry Baldwin, a prominent Pittsburgh attorney and family friend after whom her brother Henry Baldwin Foster had been named, and by Baldwin's wife. (In 1830, Andrew Jackson would appoint Baldwin to the Supreme Court.)

Her destination, Cincinnati, the "Queen City of the West," had only recently surpassed Pittsburgh in population—claiming 24,831 residents in 1830, compared to 22,433 in Pittsburgh and its suburbs—and sup-planted it as the commercial capital of the Ohio River Valley (though Pittsburgh retained its supremacy in manufacturing). It "is the most beautiful city in the western country," Charlotte wrote home, "to me who had been accustom'd to see houses look black it appear'd to have been all built in [a] week." She attended a dizzying round of parties, at which the chief entertainments were eating strawberries, promenading with one beau or another, singing and sometimes even dancing.[4]

Frances Trollope, who had arrived in Cincinnati a few months earlier on her ill-fated American sojourn, took a dim view of such soirées, perhaps partly because, as a "short dumpling" of an English matron pushing fifty,[5] she was relegated to the sidelines:

> The women invariably herd together at one part of the room, and the men at the other. . . . Sometimes a small attempt at music produces a partial reunion; a few of the most daring youths, animated by the consciousness of curled hair and smart waistcoats, approach the pianoforte, and begin to mutter a little to the half-grown pretty things, who are comparing with

one another "how many quarters' music they have had." . . . But the fate
of the more dignified personages . . . is extremely dismal. The gentlemen
spit, talk of elections and the price of produce, and spit again. The ladies
look at each other's dresses till they know every pin by heart. . . . [6]

But Anthony Trollope's mother was disdainful of almost everything in
America. Cincinnati, which she dismissed as a "triste little town" because it failed to patronize the preposterous Moorish-Egyptian-Gothic
bazaar she opened, was for Charlotte a fairy tale.[7]

From Cincinnati Charlotte ventured downriver to Louisville, Kentucky, where she stayed at the home of cousins, Joshua G. and Sally
Barclay, and their daughters, Kitty and Mary. Joshua Barclay was de-
scended from the uncle or great uncle of William Barclay Foster's by
now long-dead mother, Ann Barclay.[8] Not only did the Barclays have a
brand-new piano, but on the same street lived a schoolteacher whose
daughters played the harp and piano. Charlotte wrote her father in
unpunctuated excitement that the temptation to take harp lessons was
too great to resist:

> . . . [W]hat money I have will pay for it I would much rather do without
> some gegaw and make a little improvement of some kind while I am away
> . . . the Piano Mr. Barcklay has is a delightfull one so that between it and
> the Harp I almost live on musick I have only taken three or four lessons
> on the Harp and can play; Come rest in this bosom, Flow on thou shining
> river, and, I have loved thee, they say I learn very fast.[9]

Anticipating her parents' anxiety about the lower Ohio River Valley's
miasmal climate in the summer and fall—Louisville had been dubbed
the "Graveyard of the West" after an 1822 epidemic of "bilious fever,"
probably malaria, killed more than 120 people—Charlotte reassured
them that it was "not the sickly season yet." [10]

William Foster all but ordered Charlotte home. "Your Ma is not in
good health," he wrote, and "many people begin to complain of indispo-
sition since the commencement of warm weather." [11] Charlotte dallied.
"I should feel very solisetus about my Dear Mother," she replied, "if I did
not think it was a sickness she is troubled with evry two years." (Eliza
Foster was indeed, it turned out, pregnant with her last child, James
Clayland Foster, who would not survive infancy.) Then Charlotte whee-
dled:

... if only I had a Piano home would be the happyest place on earth to me could not Brother William assist you to get one Mr Valtz will trust you for a year and if in that time it cannot be paid for let him take it back, perhaps dear Father you will think it thoughtless in me to mention such a thing but you know my fondness for musick and will forgive me.[12]

Charlotte's wish was granted. No sooner did Brother William win a raise that summer to $3.50 a day, and a promotion to the rank of engineer on the Pennsylvania Canal, than he purchased a piano for the Fosters. Still, Charlotte tarried, visiting a plantation where "they kept [her] playing constantly and singing." Charlotte's renditions of "Go, My Love" and "Like the Gloom of Night Retiring" were especially popular. "I think a Kentucky farmers life is very happy," she wrote her mother, "those who are rich and have thier negros and overseer. . . . [I]t reminded me of the happy times I used to spend in the country at home."[13] The Fosters had had servants, not slaves, but one infers from this letter that one of the reasons Charlotte refused to come home was that she no longer had the White Cottage to come home to.

The headstrong Charlotte traveled farther south to Bardstown, Kentucky, where A. P. Heinrich, after losing his job at a Pittsburgh theater, had retreated and begun his composing career in a nearby log cabin. Charlotte visited a more palatial residence, Federal Hill, the summer home of the Rowan family, cousins more distant than the Louisville Barclays. "They claim me as a relation and treat me as such," wrote Charlotte, too flattered to dare trace the attenuated blood connection.[14] John Rowan, an attorney, had built Federal Hill on land his father-in-law had given him as a wedding present. With thirteen windows on its facade, thirteen-foot-high ceilings, thirteen steps on each flight of the central stairway, and thirteen spindles in the landing, the brick home was an homage to the original colonies and its name a tribute to the Federal Party—although John Rowan, like William Barclay Foster, had become a fervent Jacksonian Democrat.

John Rowan, fifty-five years old when Charlotte met him, was unlike her father in every other regard. Or, to be more exact, he was everything William Barclay Foster had failed to become. He was rich, owning extensive land holdings, a quarter interest in Louisville's bustling wharf and ferry, and, when he signed his will in 1840, at least eighteen slaves. He was famous. Shortly after killing a man in a duel provoked by an argument over which of them knew more Latin and Greek, Rowan was elected to the United States Congress. He later served briefly on the United States Court of Appeals and was "Judge" Rowan ever after. When Charlotte Foster was his guest, Rowan was a United States Senator. Six feet one-and-a-half inches tall, his gold-framed glasses with extensible stems often perched atop his full head of hair, he was an imposing yet inviting presence. "I never met a man so agreeable, to be a great man as Judge Rowan is," Charlotte wrote her father. "I sometimes listen to his conversation, until I am lost, and fear to draw my breath least I should loose a word, his family almost adore him he is one of the kindest husbands and Fathers. . . ."[15]

Charlotte wasn't about to come home. "Bardstown is said to be one the healthyest places in the world," she insisted, and tried to divert her father's attention by inquiring about her brother: "How is dear little Stephen I am uneasy about him I suppose it is the Summer complaint and teathing. . . ." (In an earlier letter William Foster had written that "the mesquetos" were "verry troublesome at our house" and that Stephen had been "very unwell" for a few days, but he had fully recovered.)[16]

Returning from Bardstown to Louisville, Charlotte confessed in a letter to her mother that one of Federal Hill's attractions had been a suitor. The Judge's middle son, Atkinson Hill Rowan, was "very clever and generaly considerd handsome," Charlotte acknowledged, but "I could not love him and would not do him or my self the injustice to make promises I was not inclined to perform."[17]

"I am too hard to pleas'e, when I consider I have niether wealth or beauty to attract," Charlotte wrote a couple of weeks later.

I know I should be more humble in my expecttations but let the con'se-quence be what it may I cannot help it, I suppose the end will be I shall be an Old maid left to take care of You and Pa in your Old days, but I deny the charge of my being a *Coquett*.[18]

Charlotte had attracted a second suitor, William Prather, in Louisville, and her mother had warned that maybe she *was* a bit of a coquette: "Mr. Baldwin told Mr. Foster the other day you were the Belle of Louisville now is the time to bring her home said he, as much as to say before her value is lesson'd." But it wasn't until November that Charlotte finally went back, once again on the *Waverley*, to Pittsburgh, where the family was living in a house on downtown Water Street.[19]

Charlotte didn't stay home for long. James Clayland Foster was born on February 3, 1829, and by the end of that month Ann Eliza Foster had departed for a visit to the Barclays in Louisville, followed shortly by her older sister. Ann Eliza paid a visit to Federal Hill and returned to Pittsburgh, while Charlotte lingered as she had the previous summer. Once again her parents were uneasy, especially as the Ohio's falling water level made traveling upstream more difficult (in addition to creating shallow, stagnant pools in which malaria-bearing mosquitoes could breed). Asked the whereabouts of his oldest sister, little Stevie Foster would reply, "Sister Charlotte down the ribber, 'tuck in the mud!"[20] William and Eliza Foster were so concerned about the dangers of "autumnal fever," as malaria was often called, that they ignored propriety and urged Charlotte to come home even if it were in the unchaperoned company of William Prather. But that romance seems to have cooled.

This time fever rather than flirtation kept Charlotte from home. She returned from a visit to Bardstown to find Joshua and Sally Barclay's oldest daughter stricken with "bilious fever." Then Sally Barclay fell ill, too, and Charlotte tended both until she took sick—sicker than either of her charges. The Fosters were summoned and Ann Eliza was dispatched, but before she arrived, on the morning of October 20, 1829, Charlotte died.

Atkinson Hill Rowan, his younger brother John, Jr., and two of their sisters had rushed to the Barclays and taken turns at Charlotte's bedside. The rejected suitor was faithful to the very end. Hill Rowan wrote Ann Eliza Foster an account of Charlotte's death that is worth quoting at length because of what it suggests, among other things, about the role music would play in the developing imagination of young Stephen Foster. Rowan speculated that a contributing factor to Charlotte's demise may have been "a deep melancholy" that "indicated its seeming existence *alone* in the wild, plaintive and touchingly tender songs which she always sang." An hour before dawn on the morning of her death, Charlotte burst into

> a song preserving with much melody & great accuracy, every note, but her voice was then so thickened that she did not articulate sufficiently plain for the words to be heard, or for the song to be recognized.

Rowan wrote that "never, never" had he "seen anyone die so easy":

no convulsions, not the writhing of a feature. The ravages of diseases were scarcely perceptible on her face, and her eyes closed, and her position in bed easy and kindly & gracefuly accommodating to the hovering spirit of slumber which seemed as tho shedding its shaddoway & stilling influences upon & around her; That death might steal away her breath alike uncon-[scious?] to her as to her friends, and so it did. For there she lay serene, placid & quiescent—all the innocence of her soul complexion'd out in a countenance which seemed chastened by the tranquillity of a sweet sleep. . . .

Hill Rowan mourned Charlotte's loss deeply, yet he urged Ann Eliza Foster not to grieve excessively but to "think only of her happy death."[21] His letter is a remarkable period piece that documents what cultural historian Ann Douglas has called "the domestication of death." It's living proof that the morbidity of an antebellum poet like Lydia Sigourney—who was apt, Douglas wrote, "to overlook the apparently trivial distinction between the living and the dead female," and whose lugubrious verses William Barclay Foster pasted into his scrapbook—was more than just a literary idiosyncrasy. Rowan's highly wrought account of Charlotte Foster's demise looks forward, too, to the deaths of Little Eva in *Uncle Tom's Cabin* and Emmeline Grangerford in *Huckleberry Finn*, whose surviving sketches and poems were so funereal Huck "reckoned, that with her disposition, she was having a better time in the graveyard."[22]

But this letter, pored over and preserved by the Foster family, has a personal as well as a period pertinence. "Is there a peculiar love given us for those that God wills to take from us," Harriet Beecher Stowe wrote after losing a son, one-and-a-half-year-old Charley, to cholera in 1848.

Is there not something brighter & better around them than around those who live—Why else in so many households is there a tradition of one brighter more beautiful more promising than all the rest, laid early low.[23]

For Stephen Foster and his family, Charlotte was that "something brighter & better." Stephen developed a "fondness for musick" that exceeded even Charlotte's, and his compositions were steeped in the "deep melancholy" of Charlotte's "wild, plaintive and touchingly tender

songs." Meanwhile, William Foster wrote in his scrapbook a poem entitled "Lament by Her father" that ended:

> Yet on as we journey o'er time's rapid wave,
>   Our hearts her blest image still keeping—
> Fond mem'ry sad vigil shall keep by the grave
>   Where her dear sainted relics are sleeping.

Charlotte's sleep was disturbed in 1852. Informed that the Louisville
cemetery in which she had been buried was to be built over with houses,
Dunning and Morrison Foster unearthed their sister's remains and
brought them to Pittsburgh, where she was reinterred in Allegheny Cemetery, not far from the White Cottage. Someone snipped a lock of Charlotte's strawberry blond hair, which is preserved to this day along with
one of Ann Eliza's dark blond, almost brunette tresses.

By this time Stephen Foster had metaphorically rifled Charlotte's grave
and brought her back to life in his first famous song:

> I had a dream de udder night, when ebry ting was still;
> I thought I saw Susanna dear, a coming down de hill. . . .

Susanna was Charlotte's middle name.

Charlotte's death, followed seven months later by little James Clayland
Foster's, drove their mother to despair and what today we would call a
nervous breakdown. In 1832 she described her collapse in a letter that
also paints the first picture we have of Stephen, now nearly six. After
describing to Brother William her "weak and tremulous state," she wrote
that

> although the vessels are all broken which I hew'd out to hold the sources
> of my earthly joys and all my gone by hopes are nothing but a dream, the
> song of joy, the delightfull cottage, and the sound of the deep tone'd
> instrument, still comes danceing on in the arrear of memory, with pain,
> and sorrow at thought of how it closed, with the departure from this
> transotary stage of her we love'd so dearly. . . .

In a postscript, she added:

> Stevan . . . has a drum and marches about after the old way with a feather
> in his hat, and a girdle about his waist whistling old lang syne. he often

asks why you dont come home, there still remains something perfectly original about him.[24]

Already Stephen was looking back to "auld acquaintance," and away to people far removed. In this case it was his big brother, just as earlier it had been Charlotte, "down the ribber, 'tuck in de mud!" With a feather in his hat, he was a Yankee Doodle Dandy like George M. Cohan (who claimed the Fourth of July, fifty-two years later, as his birthdate). But there was something wistful in his whistle and rum-tum-tum as they sought to fill the silence left by Charlotte's piano, that "deep-tone'd instrument," and the hole left by the home Stephen could remember scarcely, if at all.

Chapter Four

THE CRYING GAME

lthough Hill Rowan couldn't identify Charlotte Foster's swan song, it was probably copyrighted in London. Of the seven songs we know, from her letters and other accounts, that Charlotte performed, only one was composed by an American.

Oliver Shaw wrote the music for "There's Nothing True But Heaven," with which Charlotte entertained visitors to the White Cottage.[1] A sea captain's son born in Middleborough, Massachusetts, in 1779, Shaw was accidentally blinded in one eye as a child and in the other when he stared into the sun while taking a navigational reading aboard his father's ship. He took up music and eventually settled in Providence, Rhode Island, flourishing there as a church organist, music teacher, composer and publisher. He was the first American-born songwriter to enjoy widespread commercial success, and "There's Nothing True But Heaven," published in 1816, proved his most popular song.[2]

But Shaw did not pen the song's lyrics, which ghoulishly foreshadowed Charlotte's death: "And love, and hope, and beauty's bloom / Are blossoms gathered for the tomb." Those lines were written by Thomas Moore, a minor Romantic poet, Lord Byron's Dublin-born friend and biographer, who also furnished the lyrics for two other songs in Charlotte's repertory, "Come Rest in This Bosom" and "Flow On, Thou Shining River," both arranged by John Andrew Stevenson. Moore's other chief collaborator, Henry Rowley Bishop, wrote the words as well as the music for "Go My Love" and "Like the Gloom of Night Retiring," also performed by Charlotte—although he is far better known for having composed the music for "Home! Sweet Home!" James Hook, one of Bishop's predecessors as the musical director of the Vauxhall Gardens, where promenading Londoners were entertained by a chorus of nightingales as well as by a human orchestra, wrote "I Have Lov'd Thee, Dearly Lov'd Thee" (among roughly 2,500 other songs). And a disciple of Moore, Thomas Haynes Bayly, wrote "I'd Be a Butterfly."[3] (In addition to these songs, Charlotte also played an instrumental piece, "Swiss Waltz," composed by an Irishman, Peter K. Moran, before he emigrated to New York.)[4]

There is nothing unusual in Charlotte Foster's having sung so many songs connected, directly or indirectly, with Thomas Moore. Three of them made musicologist Charles Hamm's "Top 44" of the most popular songs in America from 1801 to 1825. Once, running into an old flame in Philadelphia, Edgar Allan Poe invited the woman home and implored her to sing "Come Rest in This Bosom"—a lyric, Poe declared, that was unsurpassed by Byron and embodied "the *all in all* of the divine passion of love." In 1830, an English visitor to New York was startled to hear a black woman singing "I'd Be a Butterfly" outside his window.[5]

Because it did not include "musical compositions" until 1831, U.S. copyright law encouraged Americans to ape English fashions in music. A reciprocal international copyright agreement did not become effective until 1891. Since American publishers could pirate English sheet music for free, why pay an American songwriter? Few songs by American composers were published before 1815, and their numbers didn't increase dramatically until the 1830s.[6]

Yet the pump was being primed for original, indigenous popular music in the United States, including Pittsburgh, where pianos were manufactured as early as 1813.[7] All that remained was to put sheet music in the parlor—a home delivery system that was expedited by innovations in transportation, communications, and printing. The canal, the steamboat, the railroad, the telegraph, the high-speed rotary steam press, the paper-cutting machine, color lithography, new ways to convert rags into paper —all these forces converged in Stephen Foster's childhood to revolutionize Jacksonian America and make popular culture in general, and pop music in particular, possible.[8]

Walt Whitman celebrated this revolution:

> See, in my poems, cities, solid, vast, inland, with paved streets, with iron
>   and stone edifices, ceaseless vehicles, and commerce,
> See, the many-cylinder'd steam printing-press—see, the electric telegraph
>   stretching across the continent. . . .

The revolution culminated, for Whitman, in "a word of the modern, the word En-Masse."[9]

The American mass audience, at least at the outset, was predominantly female. It was largely women, and especially young women not yet burdened with child-rearing, who had the leisure to cultivate a taste for popular music. William Foster pasted in his scrapbook an item from the *National Intelligencer,* signed "M.," that opined:

> . . . I would humbly submit to the young ladies of this precocious, intellectual, and highly accomplished generation, that all the sounds which are produceable from a piano are not Music. Oh! is it not a torture to "sit with sad civility" and listen to that disease, (excuse the bull,) called a popular song? Why, the thing is more contagious than the cholera. . . . Oh! Satan, what a sad blunderer you were to kill Job's daughters! why did you not teach them to play on the piano, and sing, "Come rest in this Bosom!" Your business would have been done at once, you silly fiend. Job could not have stood it—he would have cursed and died.

Some things—and some metaphors—never change. A century later, George Gershwin wrote that "the majority of the purchasers of popular music are little girls with little hands, who have not progressed very far in their study of the piano." Mitch Miller of "Sing Along with Mitch" fame, the head of Artists and Repertoire at Columbia Records in the early 1960s, dismissed rock 'n' roll: "It's not music, it's a disease."[10]

Popular songs were disseminated not only by sheet music but by songsters—collections of lyrics, for the most part without music, that were often published in pocket-sized volumes. The introduction to one songster, *The Singer's Own Book: A Well-Selected Collection of the Most Popular Sentimental, Amatory, Patriotic, Naval, and Comic Songs,* attests to the largely female audience for popular music by reassuring that "not a single line has found admission into this book, which can directly or indirectly offend the nicest modesty, or mantle the cheek of beauty with the faintest blush." *Grigg's Southern and Western Songster: Being a Choice Collection of the Most Fashionable Songs, Many of Which Are Original* shows how heavily Americans relied on the British Isles as late as 1835. Although it kicks off with "The Star-Spangled Banner" and promises "many of our 'native wood-notes wild,' " the contents are still primarily imports: songs by the Englishman Charles Dibdin, Thomas Moore, Robert Burns ("Auld Lang Syne") and Walter Scott ("Hail to the Chief," with its now long-forgotten Gaelic chorus, *"Roderigh Vich Alpine Dhu, ho! ieroe!"*). The American efforts in this anthology, such as "Laura's Grave—By a Gentleman of Kentucky" ("Of all the streams that gently flow / In murmurs to the sea, / The stream that winds by Laura's grave, / The sweetest seems to me"), do not leave one hankering for more. Indeed, for the most part they seem more insipid as well as more morbid than their models across the sea.[11]

Daniel Drake, a pioneering Cincinnati physician and friend of Harriet Beecher Stowe, complained that "our musical *soirées* are of feeble and limited interest, from a prevailing want of relish for melody, and the absence of a national ballad music." Walt Whitman blamed "a parcel of dandies and ennuyees, dapper little gentlemen from abroad, who flood us with their thin sentiment of parlors, parasols, piano-songs, tinkling rhymes, the five-hundredth importation."[12]

Thomas Moore was a dapper little gentleman, to be sure, but his rhymes did more than tinkle: They laid the foundation for much of American popular song. The new lyrics Moore set to traditional melodies from Ireland and elsewhere ("Flow On, Thou Shining River," for example, was set to a Portuguese air) were the most popular English-language songs, along with Stephen Foster's, of the nineteenth century. " 'Tis the Last Rose of Summer" may have been the first song ever to sell more than a million copies.[13] Although the *Irish Melodies,* the *National Airs* and *Sacred Songs,* all collaborations with John Stevenson or (later) Henry Bishop, are seldom sung anymore, their echoes are everywhere. Tara, Scarlett O'Hara's beloved plantation in *Gone With the Wind,* conjures up Moore's "The Harp That Once Through Tara's Halls." Moore's verbal facility and fecundity stocked a storehouse of lyric conventions and catch-phrases we are still drawing on, however unwittingly. The Five Satins' classic doo-wop ballad, "I'll Remember (In the Still of the Night)," inevitably evokes, a century and a half later, Moore's "Oft in the Stilly Night," the second verse of which begins, "When I remember all / The friends, so linked together. . . ." Stephen Stills's "Love the One You're With," also a hit for the Isley Brothers, unconsciously updates Moore's "Oh! 'Tis Sweet to Think": ". . . When we're far from the lips we love, / We have but to make love to the lips we are near!"[14] When Bessie Smith protested that her man had "a heart that's like a rock cast in the sea" in W. C. Handy's "St. Louis Blues," or country singer Randy Travis sings Hugh Prestwood's lines, "I feel like a stone you have picked up and thrown / To the hard rock bottom of your heart," there are ripples, ever so faint, of Moore's "I Wish I Was By That Dim Lake":

> Cold, cold, my heart must grow,
> Unchanged by either joy or woe,
> Like freezing founts, where all that's thrown,
> Within their current turns to stone.[15]

Stephen Foster would pay homage to Moore by publishing a song, "I Would Not Die in Spring Time," under the pseudonym Milton Moore. According to Morrison Foster, the Milton stood for John Milton.[16] The very phrase, "Paradise Lost," probably held a deep personal meaning for Foster. Likewise, the nostalgia Moore expressed for Ireland's past, for a "home" lost to history, devastated by the English and depleted by emigration, resonated with Foster's yearning for the lost home of his infancy.

Foster was profoundly influenced not only by Moore's lyrics, but also by the music Moore and other composers in the Anglo-Scots-Irish school contributed to Charlotte's repertory. One characteristic of many of these songs, derived from Irish and Scottish folk tunes, is an octave leap near the outset, so that the melody starts out with a running jump. Thus "I'd Be a Butterfly" darts from E to high E—"I'd be a Butterfly BORN in a bow'r"—in much the same way "Old Folks at Home" vaults from D to high D: "Way down upon de Swa-NEE ribber." Thomas Haynes Bayly's first hit made such an enduring impression on the young Foster that when he grew up he taught it to his nieces. The distinctive rhythmic pattern of "RIB-bbeerr," accenting the first syllable but snapping it off and prolonging the unstressed, second syllable, is another legacy of such tunes: the so-called Scottish snap.[17]

Charles Hamm has argued convincingly that Moore's nostalgia appealed to nineteenth-century Americans because whether they had crossed the Atlantic, the Alleghenies, or the Mississippi, they were an uprooted people, ever on the move. In making their new homes, they missed their old ones.[18] There is something else in Moore's music that makes it quintessentially American popular music: a sentimentalism that is slightly but discernibly disingenuous. No matter how insistently Moore twanged on "the harp that once through Tara's halls," etc., hymning "Old Erin's native Shamrock!," the truth is that he moved to London as a young man and became, in the words of one commentator, "an adopted Englishman, whose heart may have hankered after Ireland and who retained his beguiling Irish manners, but whose feet, for practical purposes, were firmly planted upon English soil." Moore "dearly loved a lord," according to Byron, who ought to have known, since he was one.[19]

An anonymous American critic commented on the artificiality of Moore's songs in 1856, noting that he

> seems to have taken his old airs to make melodies for Anglo-Saxondom, as others took the stones of the old castles to make elegant modern houses —thinking they put them to a very good use, too. His songs have too much refinement, and too little pathos and simple heartiness, to be popularly cherished among his countrymen.[20]

In other words, popular music posed problems from its very beginnings in America that concern it to this day: issues of sincerity, authenticity and kitsch.

George F. Root, who wrote some of the Civil War's greatest songs ("The Battle Cry of Freedom," "Tramp! Tramp! Tramp!") and published others (Henry Clay Work's "Marching Through Georgia"), expressed these misgivings in his autobiography when describing the spell Henry Russell had cast on him (as Russell did upon Foster as well). Russell's songs, Root wrote,

> were exceedingly pathetic, and always made people cry when he sang them. He looked so pitiful and so sympathetic—"he felt every word," as his listeners would think and say—and yet, when he retired to his dressing room, he was said to have been much amused at the grief of his weeping constituents, showing that he had not really the heart in his song that he appeared to have.[21]

Born in 1812 in Kent, Russell continued and extended the Anglo-Scots-Irish influence on American popular music while introducing strains from the Italian operas that were beginning to enjoy international popularity. Of Jewish descent, he joined a children's opera troupe and was dandled on the knee of King George IV. When his voice changed he traveled to Italy, where, according to his autobiography, he studied with the composers Rossini and Bellini, and upon his return to London he made his adult operatic debut under the direction of the ubiquitous Henry Bishop.[22] Soon he set sail for Canada but found a warmer reception in Rochester, New York, where he landed a job as organist and choirmaster of a Presbyterian church.

It was there, in 1836, that Russell heard a stemwinder by Henry Clay, the Kentucky senator and Whig leader, and was inspired by the "peculiarly musical tone" of Clay's oratory:

> I asked myself: Why, if Henry Clay could create such an impression by his distinct enunciation of every word, should it not be possible for me to make music the vehicle of grand thoughts and noble sentiments, to speak to the world through the power of poetry and song![23]

Drawing on verses by a variety of authors, including Burns and Dickens, Russell composed elaborate narratives melodramatizing disasters at sea, the downfalls of drunkards and gamblers and the evils of insane asylums, as well as simpler, sentimental ballads. The former sometimes amounted to mini-operas, crammed with instrumental interludes, theatrical shifts of tempo and nearly spoken recitatives, in addition to full-throated melodies. The ballads, such as "Woodman! Spare That Tree!," melded Moore and the Anglo-Scots-Irish tradition with the arias and rippling arpeggios of Rossini, Bellini, and Donizetti. These songs prefigured and influenced Foster's. "The Old Arm Chair," as Charles Hamm has pointed out, ends almost identically to (in addition to rhyming with) Foster's "Jeanie with the Light Brown Hair."[24]

Accompanying himself on piano, Russell crisscrossed the states from Maine to Louisiana. He earned most of his money on the road, which in those days was often corduroy, a bumpy ride over tree trunks or split logs. Performing his songs helped sell his sheet music, which in turn helped sell tickets to his concerts. It scarcely differs from how rock bands today tour to promote their CDs and make CDs to promote their tours.

According to John Hill Hewitt, the American songwriter best known for "All Quiet Along the Potomac To-Night," Russell was "remarkably fond of the prefix of *old*; a wag of a poet once sent him some words addressed to an 'Old Fine-tooth Comb.' " Russell, whose repertory included not only "The Old Arm Chair" but "My Old Wife," "Nature's Fine Old Gentleman," "The Old Night Lamp," "The Old Bell," "The Old Farm Gate," "The Old School House," "The Old Sexton," "The Old Water Mill," and "Old King Time," once asked Hewitt to write him a song about an "Old Family Clock." Not liking the results, he asked him to write a temperance song. Hewitt's lyric began: "The *old* lamp burned on the *old* oaken stool."[25]

Anything old possessed a certain charm in a nation where nearly everything was new. "An American 'always' means eighteen months," observed James Fenimore Cooper in his most cantankerous novel, *Home as Found*, "and . . . 'time immemorial' is only since the last general crisis in the money market!"[26] The charm of the antique was all the greater because it was valued so cheaply in a go-ahead, get-ahead country that spared little, and certainly not a tree, in pursuit of profit. Asked if he had ever treasured a tree or a house or an altar from his childhood, Aristabulus Bragg, a character in *Home as Found*, replied that "the pleasantest tree I can remember was one of my own, out of which sawyers made a thousand feet of clear stuff, to say nothing of middlings." Popular music allowed people to indulge at their leisure in a sentimentality they could seldom afford in workaday life. It may have been bad faith, but the belief endured. The nostalgia that characterized Moore's music continued in Russell's, and it would carry on and culminate in Foster's.

Russell didn't enthrall every American. Likening him to P. T. Barnum, George Templeton Strong, the assiduous New York diarist and concert-goer, called Russell's music "humbug."[27] The charge rolled off Russell's back. Strolling down London's Southampton Street one day, he fell in with Louis Jullien, the French composer and conductor who helped popularize the promenade concert, the precursor of today's "pops" concert. Jullien complained about the reception of his new opera, *Peter the Great*.

> "Vat you tink, ze singares and ze orchestra zey call me 'ombog.' "
> "No," [Russell] said.
> "Yes, it ees so, and vat you tink?"
> "I don't know, I'm sure."
> "Well, zey call you 'ombog,' too."
> "Oh, never mind what they call me, as long as they don't forget me."[28]

Chapter Five

OUT OF THE MOUTHS
OF BABES

When Stephen Foster, almost six, whistled "Auld Lang Syne" in 1832, he was marching to his own drum in a house his family had taken for the summer in Harmony, a village then some twenty-five miles north of Pittsburgh that had been founded by a Lutheran pietist sect called the Harmony Society. The Harmonists emigrated from Germany in 1804 and practiced communal living, celibacy, and a great deal of music. In 1831, their orchestra performed what may have been the first symphony composed west of the Alleghenies, William Cummings Peters's *Symphony in D*.[1]

Peters, who had emigrated from England with his parents as a child, arrived in Pittsburgh between 1825 and 1827. In addition to arranging and composing for the Harmonists, Peters gave the Foster girls music lessons and was a partner with John H. Mellor and W. D. Smith in a music store. It was at this establishment, according to his brother Morrison, that Stephen, at the age of seven, "accidentally took up a flageolet . . . and in a few minutes so mastered its stops and sounds that he played Hail Columbia in perfect time and accent." If Stephen was indeed seven when he displayed his precocity and patriotism (in those days, "Hail Columbia" rivaled "The Star-Spangled Banner" as America's unofficial anthem), Peters was probably not on the premises, because in 1832 he had moved to Louisville. But their paths would cross later when Peters, by then a successful music publisher in Cincinnati, brought out "Oh! Susanna" and several other early Foster songs.[2]

The recorderlike flageolet was not the first instrument young Stephen essayed. Morrison wrote that when Stephen was two, he would lay his sister Ann Eliza's guitar on the floor "and pick out harmonies from its strings. He called it his 'ittly pizani' (little piano)." Stephen Foster would eventually play a real piano, but it was when he graduated from the flageolet to the flute that he realized his greatest instrumental proficiency. His musicality developed largely by instinct and partly, perhaps, under the influence of his sisters. "He had but few teachers," Morrison wrote. Not only was musical instruction chiefly for females, but by the time Stephen was old enough to profit from lessons, his parents could ill afford them.[3]

Ann Eliza attended to Morrison and Stephen's education in Harmony when the weather became so warm that their mother took them out of school. She wrote their father, who had stayed behind with Dunning in Pittsburgh, to bring with him on his next visit, in addition to her parasol and pink calico wrapper, " 'Plutarch's Lives,' and the first two volumes, of 'Hume's History'—these I wish partly for the children." It sounds like tough sledding for a hot summer, even if Ann Eliza included among her pupils thirteen-year-old Henrietta (Henry was boarding at a nearby school for training in manual labor).[4]

Stephen was a less than diligent student. Morrison recalled Stephen's first collision with organized education:

> He was sent, along with the rest of us, to an infant school taught by Mrs. Harvey, an elderly lady, and her daughter, Mrs. Morgan. He was called up for his first lesson in the letters of the alphabet. He had not proceeded far in this mystery when his patience gave out, and with a yell like that of a Commanche Indian, he bounded bareheaded into the road, and never stopped running and yelling until he reached home, half a mile away.[5]

This was not the last time Stephen would drop out of school.

In the fall of 1832, the Fosters moved to the suburb of Allegheny City, where the population in 1830 was only 2,801 "freemen" and eight slaves. The coal smoke was thinner on the north bank of the Allegheny River, and a spacious commons preserved a rural air while congested Pittsburgh, a visitor noted, suffered from a "total want of public squares, and, indeed, of an agreeable promenade of any kind."[6]

William Foster had assumed his duties as Collector of Tolls on the Blairsville–Pittsburgh Canal, and at the beginning of 1833—perhaps fulfilling a New Year's resolution—he took the temperance pledge. In April, he gave away his oldest surviving daughter, Ann Eliza, to James Buchanan's sickly and impecunious youngest brother, the Rev. Edward Buchanan. James Buchanan was abroad at the time in St. Petersburg, where President Jackson, who felt a lifelong mistrust for his scheming fellow Democrat, had banished him as U.S. ambassador.[7]

Brother William, working on the canal in central Pennsylvania, was also unable to attend the ceremony, but without his generosity it might have been a threadbare affair. "Your very kind present of 50 dollars to Ann Eliza came in good time to enable her to complete her wardrobe comfortably," wrote the father of the bride, "and was most gratefully received, my means being so limited as to render it painful for her to ask me for anything." In the same letter, William Foster asked to borrow two hundred dollars and implored, as one last favor, "Could you get Henry or Dunning a situation as a rod bearer on the Canal? They must both of them go to business this Spring—I can't keep them together, they are both good boys."[8]

No sooner was Ann Eliza off to Meadville, Edward's first parish, in northwestern Pennsylvania, than Eliza Foster, with Henrietta and Stephen in tow, boarded the steamboat *Napoleon* and visited her half brothers in Augusta, Kentucky. Sons of Eliza Foster's father by his second marriage, after Eliza Foster's mother had died, Joseph Tomlinson, a Methodist minister, was the president of Augusta College and John Tomlinson a doctor. The Fosters stayed for three weeks with Joseph, whom Eliza found "a fine ameable gentlemanly little man." Not only did he own a piano that Henrietta played, but he paid their way farther down the Ohio to Cincinnati, where the Fosters stayed for another week, "handsomly treated free of cost" by old friends from Pittsburgh, the Cassillys. Reboarding the *Napoleon*, the Fosters traveled to Louisville and stayed with the Barclays. Surely the home where Charlotte had died brought back memories, but her mother expressed only her relief, once she was back in Allegheny City, that the "destroying Angle" of cholera had spared them.[9]

This was Stephen's first recorded trip on a steamboat, as well as his first visit to Cincinnati, where he would later live for several crucial years. It was also his first and possibly his last sojourn in Kentucky, which would claim one of his greatest compositions as its state song.

Stephen, Henrietta, and their mother returned home to find William Foster engrossed in politics and exasperated by his job. In March 1834, he resigned his canal post in personal and financial embarrassment. In May, he moved his family to a rented house on the northern bank of the Ohio River. In June, he became a candidate for sheriff on the Democratic ticket.

". . . The boys are going to school and I am doing Nothing," William Foster wrote Brother William. "Our election will be a Warm one, how it will terminate is quite uncertain. . . ." In conclusion he noted that "little Stephen's learning verry fast. Mr. Kelly says that he & Morrison are the most sensible children he ever saw in his life. . . ." [10]

Stephen and Morrison were attending Allegheny Academy, founded by Joseph Stockton, pastor of Allegheny's First Presbyterian Church. Rev. Stockton, according to Morrison, taught English and the classical languages as well as mathematics and was assisted by Mr. John Kelly from Dublin. Kelly "was a thorough disciplinarian," Morrison wrote. "While he was of genial disposition and out of school played ball and prisoner's base with the boys, and excelled in every manly athletic exercise, in school he required rigid attention to business." [11]

William Foster and the rest of the Democratic ticket were trounced by the Whigs and Anti-Masons, and by the end of 1834 the family had moved to "a three story Brick House about 100 yards north of the Allegheny Bridge, a verry pleasant place," William Foster wrote. "We are now very poor, but hope and good health keeps us up." [12]

Their "very pleasant place" notwithstanding, the Fosters began to spend considerable time in Youngstown, Ohio, where Brother William had moved upon securing a position as assistant engineer on the Pennsylvania and Ohio Canal. His next-door neighbor was Henry Wick, and it wasn't too long before Brother William fell in love with the farmer's consumptive daughter, Mary, while Henrietta fell for the farmer's only somewhat healthier son, Thomas. Over the next five years there was a great deal of bewildering back and forth between Youngstown and Allegheny, some sixty miles part, as various Fosters stayed with Brother William, with Henrietta and Thomas Wick after their marriage in 1836, or boarded at local homes.

William Foster's financial affairs were as unsettled as his family's housing. Bankrolled by Brother William, he opened a general store in Pittsburgh in partnership with a Mr. Hall. From the very outset, it was "a loosing business." In February 1836, he went to Washington to try to collect the money still owed him from the War of 1812—"all in vain." He filed a claim related to his Lawrenceville property and the arsenal, and another against William Wilkins, the former president of the bankrupt turnpike company, who had recently returned from Russia, where he had succeeded James Buchanan as ambassador. "I don't care one cent about him," William senior wrote Brother William, "he is a great rascal." In other attempts to recoup his turnpike losses, William Foster went to Erie to press a claim, unsuccessfully, and accepted sixty-eight dollars worth of sugar and coffee in partial payment of a judgment he won against one of his old partners (and his third son's namesake), Dunning McNair.[13]

Sugar and coffee were a better deal than "shinplasters," the paper notes that replaced hard currency when the banks suspended specie payments in the disastrous panic of 1837. "There has been several failures," Eliza Foster wrote Brother William:

> Pittsburg looks very dull as to business in Market Street, but yet one would not suppose business to be going down when they see the elegant coaches with silver trapings on the splendid Horses by which they are drawn, and to hear of ladies copeing for the hiest pric'd and most accomplish'd drivers; but for my part I am truly thankful that I have shoes to put on my feet without haveing earned them by the swet of my brow, and that my ancles are again strong enough to enable me to step my way on a pleasant Sunday down the Hill and over the bridge to Trinity Church. . . .

No longer was there a "family barouche" to convey Eliza Foster, but in the same letter she confessed to being "much better fixed than I expected to be by this time." Brother William was largely responsible for the fixing: The Fosters were back in Allegheny, installed in a house Brother William had bought on the East Common, at Gay Alley. William Foster fended off idleness by weeding their "beautifull little garden" daily, and Stephen, having "recovered from the whooping cough," was "going to school with Morison to Mr. Todd."[14]

Reverend Nathan Todd, Morrison would write, was "a learned professor, who gave much attention to instruction in Latin and Greek, as well as in the English branches." He told William Foster that Stephen "was the most perfect gentleman he ever had for a pupil."[15]

". . . You never saw boys cut up as Morison and Stephan did," Eliza Foster wrote Henrietta. "they had been at what they cald a cosmarama a sort of a shoe [show] and Steve had the figure complete to no small amusement of the little audience his brothers . . . and myself."[16]

"Cosmoramas" were miniature, dramatically lit scenes that one peered at through glass. They were a staple at New York City's American Museum long before P. T. Barnum purchased it and devoted an entire "Grand Saloon" to these popular panoptical peep shows.[17] Stephen Foster's delight in them marks his youthful discovery of what was then called "the show business." Indeed, he played a more active, front-and-center role as a youngster than he did as an adult, when he seldom performed publicly.

"When he was nine years old," Morrison wrote,

> a thespian company was formed, composed of boys of neighbor families, Robinsons, Cuddys, Kellys and Fosters. The theatre was fitted up in a carriage house. All were stockholders except Stephen. He was regarded as a star performer, and was guaranteed a certain sum weekly. It was a very small sum, but it was sufficient to mark his superiority over the rest of the company.

Stephen didn't sing "There's Nothing True But Heaven" or "Come Rest in This Bosom." He performed crude comic songs written in blackface dialect: "Zip Coon," "Long Tail Blue," "Coal Black Rose," and "Jim Crow." According to Morrison, his "performance of these was so inimitable and true to nature that . . . he was greeted with uproarious applause, and called back again and again every night the company gave an entertainment, which was three times a week." The boys cleared enough to spend their Saturday nights in the pit in downtown Pittsburgh, watching Junius Brutus Booth, Edwin Forrest, Mrs. Drake, and Mrs. Duff chew the scenery.[18]

It's not hard to envision young Stephen at the theater, spellbound by everything that offended Frances Trollope, who found Forrest's Hamlet so dreadful that she left before the fourth act. What appalled her about American audiences could easily have thrilled the impressionable young Stephen:

> Men came into the lower tier of boxes without their coats; and I have seen shirt sleeves tucked up to the shoulder; the spitting was incessant, and the

mixed smell of onions and whiskey was enough to. . . . The noises, too, were perpetual, and of the most unpleasant kind; the applause is expressed by cries and thumping with the feet, instead of clapping; and when a patriotic fit seized them, and *Yankee Doodle* was called for, every man seemed to think his reputation as a citizen depended on the noise he made.[19]

It takes a greater leap of imagination—although it is a leap that white boys, from ragtime's Joseph Lamb (a composer widely assumed to be black) to swing's Benny Goodman to rock 'n' roll's Elvis Presley to hip hop's Beastie Boys, have been making ever since—to picture little Stevie casting aside his Latin primer to sing:

> Jim Crow is courting a white gall,
>   And yaller folks call her Sue;
> I guess she back'd a nigger out,
>   And swung my long tail blue.[20]

Or:

> Lubly Rosa Sambo cum,
> Don't you hear de Banjo tum, tum, tum
> Oh Rose de coal black Rose,
> I wish I may be cortch'd if I don't lub Rose,
> Oh Rose de coal black Rose.[21]

It's a far cry from the precious "I'd be a Butterfly born in a bow'r, / Where Roses and Lillies and Violets meet." Yet it is here, at the intersection where these opposing voices and frames of reference—the genteel and the raunchy, the parlor and the alley—collide in jarring juxtaposition, that we hear for the very first time Stephen Foster's own voice, preserved in the earliest letter he wrote that survives. On January 14, 1837, ten-year-old Stephen wrote, from Youngstown to Allegheny:

My Dear father
    I wish you to send me a commic songster for you promised to. if I had my pensyl I could rule my paper. or if I had the money to by Black ink But if I had my whistle I would be so taken with it I do not think I would write atall. . . .
    I remane your loving son
    Stephen C. Foster[22]

Chapter Six

JUMPING JIM CROW

If William Foster complied with little Stephen's scrawl and gave his son a "commic songster" in 1837, it probably registered the early shocks of a seismic change in American popular culture and taste. Just as the *The Singer's Own Book* of 1832 had promised not to "offend the nicest modesty, or mantle the cheek of beauty with the faintest blush," *The Parlour Companion, or, Polite Song Book*, also published in Philadelphia only four years later, guaranteed that nothing between its covers would "tinge the cheek of modesty with the slightest blush, nor . . . offend the most fastidious ear." True to its word, *The Parlour Companion* commenced with nine songs adapted from Bellini's *La Sonnambula*. Evidently American ears were becoming considerably less fastidious, however, because this songster included "Long Tail Blue" and "Sich a Gitting Up Stairs." While one selection began decorously, "Hark, the convent bells are ringing," another kicked off rudely, "I am science nigger, my name is Jim Brown."[1]

If Stephen Foster had asked for a songster only a year or so earlier, what he wanted and what he might have gotten would have been altogether more genteel. But now the blackface revolution had begun, and its songs swept away not only young Stephen, but the world.

"In the four quarters of the globe," a British critic had sniffed a few years earlier, "who reads an American book? or goes to an American play? or looks at an American statue?"[2] It would be a while before American literature enjoyed an international audience, longer still before American theater and sculpture achieved global renown, but by 1836 the world was pricking up its ears to American popular music. It was in this year that the United States began trafficking in its most successful cultural export before the movies. Thomas Dartmouth "Daddy" Rice wheeled about and "jumped Jim Crow" in two English theaters nightly, bowling over Britain and creating such a stir with his grotesque gyrations —120 years before Elvis!—that the celebrated Shakespearean actor William Charles Macready cut short his London engagement. (It would not be the last time the unfortunate Macready was upstaged by an American. In 1849, Edwin Forrest's Anglophobic fans disrupted Macready's *Macbeth*, leading to the Astor Place riot that claimed the lives of twenty-two New Yorkers.)[3]

An earlier American-English contest, the War of 1812, inspired not only our national anthem but the first American song of note in black-face dialect. Indeed, the two songs were synchronized so closely that it's almost as if blackface were inseparable from our national identity. Micah Hawkins, the mentor and uncle of the famous genre painter William Sidney Mount, was a New York City musician, innkeeper, and grocer who installed a piano beneath his counter, where a shopkeeper today might conceal a weapon, and "played a running accompaniment" to his customers' requests for tobacco, pork, and cheese.[4] Hawkins wrote "Backside Albany" to commemorate the United States' victory in the Battle of Plattsburg, a September 1814 engagement on and off the shores of Lake Champlain that thwarted the British invasion of New York and New England. Only a couple of days later, the bombardment of Maryland's Fort McHenry moved Francis Scott Key to write "The Star-Spangled Banner." While Key's poem was set to an English song, John Stafford Smith's "Anachreontic Song (To Anachreon in Heaven)," Hawkins chose a traditional Irish melody that Thomas Moore also used, the ballad, "The Boyne Water."

Many African Americans fought in the War of 1812. From 10 to 20 percent of the American naval force at Plattsburg was black, so it was not inappropriate that Hawkins put his comic account into the mouth of a black man. But the dialect is so puerile—"Bow wow wow den de cannon gin't roar"—that it's unclear how much of the laugh is on the

British and how much on the African-American sailor. First performed in 1815, "Backside Albany" remained popular nationally well into the 1850s.[5]

In 1824, Hawkins tried his hand at this formula a second time. He adopted the voice of an African-American soldier in the Continental Army to mark the visit to the United States of General Lafayette—the same triumphant return that would take him to Pittsburgh. "Massa Georgee Washington and General La Fayette"—a song that was unashamed to pun, "He laugh-a-yet!"—was performed on the New York stage on several occasions.[6] At least one of these was during the short run of Hawkins's *The Saw-Mill: or A Yankee Trick,* the first "opera"—a musical comedy, actually—by an American-born composer on an American subject.[7]

The illustration adorning the original sheet music of "Massa Georgee Washington and General La Fayette," of the actor James Roberts in blackface and military uniform, exaggerates the jaunty figure's long nose and chin, so that he resembles a European nutcracker more than an American racial caricature. And Hawkins's two songs were isolated ditties. A few more ditties in blackface dialect followed, but it fell to George Washington Dixon to take blackface several crucial steps further.

In 1829 if not earlier, Dixon, a Virginian by birth, performed "Coal Black Rose" in New York City.[8] The song's very first lines announced the arrival of full-blown blackface: "Lubly Rosa, Sambo cum, / Don't you hear de Banjo, tum, tum, tum. . . ." A travesty of a troubadour, Sambo came a-courtin', serenading the beauteous Rosa (or Rose) and promising her "possum fat and hominey, and sometime rice, / Cow heel and sugar an ebery ting nice" as he warmed his shins by her fire. Sambo, the banjo, the phonetic spelling, and vagrant consonants became stocks-in-trade of the "Ethiopian delineators," as the blackface entertainers who followed Dixon were initially called. (There were Yankee delineators, too, and specialists in backwoods Kentuckian roles, in this era when America was sorting out and cementing some of its most durable regional and racial stereotypes.)[9]

Several people in addition to Dixon claimed authorship of "Rose," but Dixon made it famous and soon expanded the song into a playlet. Not until the 1850s and *Uncle Tom's Cabin* was an evening at the theater devoted to the performance of a single play; before then one might sit through a serious play, for instance, then an entr'acte or two and a farce finale. It was in the cracks between plays that blackface took root and flourished, like weeds between the boards. Blackface also thrived as a kind of clowning in the sawdust of the circus ring. It was at a benefit for a tightrope walker at New York's Bowery Theatre in 1829 that Dixon played Sambo in *Love in a Cloud*, widely considered the first blackface play.[10]

Dixon also popularized (again, the actual authorship is disputed) "Long Tail Blue" and "Zip Coon," songs that ridiculed the effrontery (as white folks considered it) of African Americans up North who emulated their urbane superiors. In the first of these songs, a would-be city slicker brags about his "long tail blue," a spiffy swallow-tailed coat. "Zip Coon" may not have been originally intended to put down as uppity such a dandified Negro. Apart from describing Zip, sarcastically, as "a larned skoler," most of the verses seem as down-home as "Turkey in the Straw," the rural reel that preserves (and may well have inspired) "Zip Coon's" melody. But a lithograph illustrating an early edition of the sheet music immortalized a blackface Beau Brummell, twirling a lorgnette on one extended finger, his other hand pulling aside his long-tail blue to expose watch fobs and a key that dangle from his waist like an extra cock and balls.[11]

In addition to its enduring incarnation as "Turkey in the Straw," "Zip Coon," or at least its nonsensical chorus—"O Zip a duden duden duden zip a duden day"—also survives in "Zip-A-Dee-Doo-Dah," from the soundtrack for *Song of the South*, Walt Disney's animated version of Joel Chandler Harris's "Uncle Remus" tales.[12] This is but one of many echoes of blackface in Disney. Mickey Mouse himself, who first appeared in the aptly titled *Steamboat Willie*, was a cartoon of a cartoon, his black skin, exaggerated facial features, white gloves, and big feet an updated Ethiopian delineation.[13]

The songs Dixon sang lasted longer than he did. An editor as well as an entertainer, he launched a scandal sheet whose insinuating articles allegedly helped drive a young actress to her death. He was caned, shot at, and jailed for libeling a preacher. When war broke out with Mexico, he returned briefly to the limelight with new lyrics to "Zip Coon" ("And spite of any rumors / We'll vanquish all the Montezumas"). After filibustering in Central America, Dixon died in a New Orleans charity ward in 1861.[14]

Daddy Rice's raggedy "Jim Crow" from down South was the complementary opposite of Dixon's northern dandy. A native New Yorker, Rice played minor roles in Manhattan theaters before joining a troupe that played principally in Cincinnati and Louisville. It was most likely in Louisville that Rice observed—or so he claimed—an African American singing to himself as he performed his lowly duties at a stable owned by a man named Crow. He may have been deformed, he may have been clumsy, or maybe his motions as he tended the horses looked odd only to a recent arrival from the East Coast. In any event, Rice was struck as much, if not more, by the black man's movements as by his melody. By most accounts Rice paid the stable hand a pittance for, in effect, appropriating his entire identity.[15]

When he interpolated "Jim Crow" into his role as a "Kentucky corn-field negro" in the play *The Rifle*, Rice's crazy, lopsided little dance, in which he executed a pixilated pirouette on the heel of one foot and landed on the toes of the other, hunching one shoulder while extending his other arm in a waggling "hi-de-ho" salute, won twenty encores. The chorus Rice sang did little more than describe his fancy footwork: "Weel about and turn about, / And do jis so; / Eb'ry time I weel about, I jump Jim Crow." The verses, meanwhile, were largely extemporized and often political. In Cincinnati, a prisoner sentenced to death is said to have provided Rice with a steady flow of squibs, and "Jim Crow" was published there by the Foster family's former music teacher, W. C. Peters.[16]

It wasn't long before Rice strutted his stuff in Pittsburgh. Although Stephen Foster, no more than five or six years old, was probably too young to have seen Rice then, he certainly heard his song. According to Stephen's friend, Robert Peebles Nevin, "Jim Crow" was

> on everybody's tongue. Clerks hummed it serving customers at shop count-ers, artisans thundered it at their toils to the time-beat of sledge and of tilt-hammer, boys whistled it on the streets, ladies warbled it in parlors, and house-maids repeated it to the clink of crockery in kitchens.[17]

Rice wended his way back to New York, where he first jumped Jim Crow in November 1832 and enjoyed a triumphant homecoming. By January 1833, Rice had expanded his entr'acte at the Bowery Theatre into an "Ethiopian Opera," *Long Island Juba, or, Love by the Bushel*. For two decades as he presented other farces, burlesqued Shakespeare and opera (*Lucia di Lammermoor* became *Lucy Did Lam a Moor*) and added more blackface songs to his repertory, Rice was celebrated as *"the negro, par excellence."* In his waning days he played matinees at Barnum's American Museum and Uncle Tom in at least one production of the wildly popular play based on Harriet Beecher Stowe's novel. By the time he died in 1860, however, he was nearly forgotten.[18]

Why did blackface take off so dramatically in the 1830s? What social and cultural forces boosted its ascent? For starters, blackface was clearly an expression of nationalism, of Andrew Jackson's America flexing its muscles and feeling its oats. "Backside Albany" had celebrated a victory in the War of 1812, and later blackface songs returned repeatedly to the "Second War of Independence," especially to the Battle of New Orleans, which inspired pop songs as late as 1959, when Johnny Horton's recording of "Battle of New Orleans" was a number one hit. One hundred and twenty-five years earlier, "Zip Coon" crowed: "I pose you heard ob de battle New Orleans, / Whar ole Gineral Jackson gib de British beans. . . ."[19]

It may appear paradoxical that patriotism and blackface would be so closely linked. Daddy Rice in burnt cork and rags would seem a source of national shame rather than pride. On the other hand, a shared feeling of superiority to blacks was one of the few things that united a nation of immigrants, many of them more recent arrivals than the African Americans they mocked. By the late 1830s, for example, more than half of Pittsburgh's population had been born abroad.[20] Blackface helped immigrants acculturate and assimilate by inculcating a common racism.

Furthermore, how humiliating to the British to be derided even by "darkies"—all the more so after Parliament emancipated the slaves in their Caribbean colonies in 1833. The next year, in a preview of the Astor Place riot, a New York mob stormed the Bowery Theatre to protest the appearance there of George Farren, a British actor rumored to have "insulted the American flag." The rioters drove Farren from the stage but were not assuaged until an American was brought on to sing "Zip Coon."[21] As late as 1841, American antipathy toward Great Britain, aggravated by disputes such as the border between Maine and Canada, was so great that, to William Foster, a third war seemed "inevitable."[22]

The Bowery Theatre riot had originated in an assault on the home of Lewis Tappan, a prominent abolitionist. Racial tensions rose in the 1830s. In 1831, as Daddy Rice was jumping Jim Crow in Ohio River

Valley venues, William Lloyd Garrison launched his crusading abolitionist paper, *The Liberator;* Nat Turner mounted his ill-fated slave rebellion;
and two African Americans arrived in Pittsburgh who would have considerable influence on race relations not only there but, less perceptibly,
throughout the country.

Lewis Woodson, born in Virginia in 1806, had been a slave until the
age of 19, when his father bought his freedom. As rector of the Bethel
African Methodist Episcopal Church, Woodson preached a gospel of
self-help and separatism to Pittsburgh's small African-American community, which numbered fewer than 500 in 1830 and 714 in 1840.[23]

One parishioner who fell under Woodson's spell was Martin R. Delany,
six years his junior and also a Virginian by birth. The son of a free mother
and a slave father who was eventually able to purchase his own freedom,
Delany also came to Pittsburgh in 1831, seeking a better education than
a black man could get in Chambersburg, Pennsylvania, where his mother
had fled after being threatened by Virginia authorities for daring to teach
her children to read. During his long and remarkable life, Delany would
publish and edit in Pittsburgh one of the first black newspapers in the
United States, become one of the first blacks admitted to Harvard Medical School, lead the first African-American expedition to Africa, become
the first black field major in the Union Army and have the distinction
of being probably the first American ever to wear a dashiki in public.
Most important, he may have been the first African American to articu-
late a fully developed black nationalist and Pan-African ideology. To this
day, Delany is cited as a forebear and influence by radical Pan-Africanists
like Kwame Toure (formerly the civil-rights leader Stokely Carmichael).
Naming one of his thirteen children Ethiopia and another one Rameses,
Delany believed that the ancient Egyptians were black Ethiopians from
whom Jews had "borrowed" monotheism, Christians had derived the
concept of the Trinity and Arabs had "stolen" their numerals. The black
race, he wrote, built "a great political fabric long before the whites,
imparting to them the first germs of civilization, and enlightening the
world by their wisdom." Delany was, in short, Afro-centric more than a
century before the term was coined.[24]

Although Delany would break off his one novel, *Blake,* with a threat
of racial apocalypse that anticipated the Nation of Islam—"Woe be unto
those devils of whites, I say!"—he was generally respected in Pittsburgh,
where the African-American population was too small to endanger the

status quo. When Delany applied to medical school, seventeen white doctors wrote letters of recommendation. "Perhaps there is less prejudice than in most places," observed an abolitionist visiting Pittsburgh. "At any rate the white people are too much engrossed in their own business. . . ."[25]

Compared to New York, Philadelphia or Cincinnati, Pittsburgh was seldom ravaged by anti-abolitionist or racist mobs, and when rioting did occur—in 1834 and 1839, for example—the authorities usually came to the defense of blacks. In the second instance, Delany helped the town fathers enlist a police force of black as well as white citizens that quickly reimposed peace.[26]

Still, Pittsburgh was not insulated from the country's increasing racial anxiety. Although Pennsylvania had been the first state to legislate an end to slavery in 1780, it amended its constitution in 1838 to deny African Americans the vote. Allegheny County's representatives to the constitutional convention opposed this amendment, but William Foster was delighted by its passage. Deprived of the 1,500 black votes that had helped elect him governor on the Anti-Masonic ticket, Joseph Ritner didn't have a prayer of reelection. Ever the devoted Democrat, William Foster bid a gloating good-bye to "antimasonry, abolitionism and all other abominations."[27]

Early blackface was in large measure a racist reaction to (and release from) rising racial tensions, but it was not invariably hostile to " 'bobalishun," as Ethiopian delineators frequently lampooned it. When P. T. Barnum, for instance, first went on the road with a blackface act, his fiddler was thrown in jail in Camden, South Carolina, for urging a black barber to run away. (Barnum lost not only his fiddler but also his blackface singer and dancer in Camden, and had to black up and perform "Zip Coon" and other songs in his place. One evening Barnum, still in makeup, became embroiled in an argument with a man who drew a gun, swearing, "You black scoundrel! How dare you use such language to a white man!" Barnum quickly rolled up his sleeve and replied, "I am as white as you are, sir." According to Barnum's autobiography, the man "dropped his pistol in positive fright and begged my pardon.")[28]

One version of "Jim Crow" poked fun at the political wrangling between John Calhoun and "ole Hickory" over tariffs, nullification, and states' rights and then turned suddenly, startlingly, serious:

> Should dey get to fighting,
>   Perhaps de blacks will rise,
> For deir wish for freedom,
>   Is shining in deir eyes.
>
> An if de blacks should get free,
>   I guess dey'll fee some bigger,
> An I shall concider it,
>   A bold stroke for de niggar.
>
> I'm for freedom,
>   An for Union altogether,
> Aldough I'm a black man,
>   De white is calld my broder.[29]

The message here is mixed if not outright oxymoronic. The dialect is derisive, but the sentiment suggests that blackface could appeal to feelings among whites not just of superiority, but of sympathy, too.

Blackface was born and nurtured in the Northeast and the Ohio River Valley. Residents of the most rapidly industrializing regions of America, the creators and consumers of blackface knew little if anything about plantations, but they were beginning to learn from firsthand experience about factories. They'd never met a "massa," but more and more of them had a boss. If they couldn't be whipped, they could be broken on the wheel of the economic cycle. Their families could not be divided and sold, but the panic of 1837 devastated households. It certainly scattered the Fosters. It was during the 1830s and 1840s that the terms "white slavery" and "slavery of wages" entered American discourse.[30] Blackface expressed an urban nostalgia for an agricultural economy, for a preindustrial, pastoral state of affairs, at the same time that it drew parallels between bondage on the Southern farm and in the Northern factory.

Blackface was unquestionably more reactionary than revolutionary. But it was more than an expression, however direct or displaced, of racial anxiety, economic insecurity, and class resentment. It was also a rejection of the femininity, the foreignness, and the effete affectations of parlor ballads. One of Thomas Haynes Bayly's last hit songs, in the 1830s, was "Long, Long Ago," which began:

> Tell me the tales that to me were so dear,
> Long long ago, long long ago:

Sing me the songs I delighted to hear,
Long long ago, long long ago:
Now you are come my grief is remov'd,
Let me forget that so long you have rov'd
Let me believe that you love as you lov'd,
Long long ago, long long ago.[31]

Meanwhile, Daddy Rice was singing:

O I was born down ole Varginee, Long time ago.
O I was born down ole Varginee, Long time ago.
O Massa die an make me free, Long time ago.
O Massa die an lef me free, Long time ago.

O I ax Massa ware he gwoin,—Long time ago.
He hab a Gun an Dog to show im,—Long time ago.

He say he gwoin to kill a Niggar,—Long time ago.
He aim he Gun, he pull de triggar,—Long time ago.

He shoot de Niggar trough de libber,—Long time ago.
Vich make de Niggar kick an quiver,—Long time ago.[32]

The vapidity of Bayly's "Long, Long Ago" is worlds—and an ocean—removed from the vulgarity and violence of "Long Time Ago." More than simply a revolt against decorum, blackface was also a veil and a vehicle for discussion of sex and violence, money and class—all the dirty stuff of life that many white Americans preferred to sweep under the parlor rug. Behind a mask of burnt cork, they felt freer to speak their minds and express their urges; they could even, as in "Long Time Ago," get away with murder.

It was the fakery of blackface, as preposterous as opera, that made this freedom possible; its very disingenuousness paradoxically encouraged honesty. Blackface reveled in the fraudulence that disturbed George F. Root in Henry Russell. Gleefully flouting the proprieties of sincerity and sentimentality, blackface delighted unabashedly in its irony and even its humbug. That's what made it "pop" and P. T. Barnum one of its patron saints and purveyors.

Blackface even landed Barnum in a Pittsburgh jail for a brief time in 1841. He had gone on the road with a troupe that included a Yankee delineator and a young Irish blackface dancer, dubbed "Master John Diamond," who "could twist his feet and legs, while dancing, into more fantastic forms," one theater manager marveled, "than I ever witnessed before or since in any human being."[33] Diamond eventually absconded, as did the Yankee delineator. When Barnum pulled into Pittsburgh with the straggling remains of his company, a blackface dancer advertised as Master Diamond was playing in town. An indignant Barnum charged that he was not the "real" John Diamond—as if anyone performing in blackface under an assumed name could be the genuine article. Suits and countersuits ensued, and Barnum ended up spending the better part of a day in a cell. Upon his release, Barnum sued the counterfeit Diamond's presenter for false advertising and sent *him* to jail for a few hours.[34]

Three years later, the "real" John Diamond—a mean drunk who sometimes performed balancing a brandy snifter on his head—was bested in a series of cutting contests in New York City by William Henry Lane, an authentic African-American dancer from Long Island who won fame performing as "Juba."[35] Strutting his stuff in Almack's, a dive in the infamous slum of Five Points, Juba astounded a visiting Charles Dickens:

> Single shuffle, double shuffle, cut and cross-cut; snapping his fingers, rolling his eyes, turning in his knees, presenting the backs of his legs in front, spinning about on his toes and heels . . . ; dancing with two left legs, two right legs, two wooden legs, two wire legs, two spring legs—all sorts of legs and no legs—what is this to him?

Juba concluded his act, according to Dickens, "with the chuckle of a million of counterfeit Jim Crows."[36] As if he were performing in some postmodern hall of mirrors, Juba was renowned for "correct Imitation Dances of all the principal Ethiopian Dancers in the United States," which he capped with "an imitation of himself."[37]

How much did Daddy Rice, "*the negro,* par excellence," and other Ethiopian delineators draw upon real blacks and their music? To answer this question, it's necessary first to dispense with some preconceived notions of what African-American music was like in the nineteenth century. The grossest of these stereotypes is exemplified by the surprise expressed by that British traveler upon hearing a black woman sing "I'd Be a Butterfly."

African-American music has never been monolithic or immune to white influence. Frederick Douglass played Handel, Haydn, and Mozart on the violin.[38] In 1837, only a year after Daddy Rice ventured to England, a black Philadelphian's five-man brass band helped celebrate

Queen Victoria's coronation. Frank Johnson was probably the first American (though he may have been born in Martinique) of *any* color to take a musical ensemble abroad. His repertory included Bellini and Mozart, and he dedicated his "Victoria Galop" to the new Queen, for whom he is reputed to have given a command performance (and to have been rewarded by her with a silver bugle). In London, Johnson was impressed by the promenade concerts originated by Philippe Musard. On his return to America, fifteen years before Louis Jullien brought his "Monster Concert for the Masses" to America and nearly fifty years before the Boston Symphony Orchestra offered light musical fare and refreshments to summertime audiences, Johnson introduced Philadelphians to the "pops" concert. At a typical Grand Soirée Musicale, Johnson's orchestra would play everything from Strauss waltzes to "Woodman! Spare That Tree!," concluding with Johnson's own performance, on the keyed bugle, of variations on "The Star-Spangled Banner" and "Yankee Doodle."[39]

Some have discerned in Johnson's music the antecedents of ragtime and even jazz.[40] As early as 1819 a visitor to Philadelphia remarked on Johnson's "remarkable taste in distorting a sentimental, simple, and beautiful song, into a reel, jig, or country-dance"—as if he were "ragging" the classics or swinging a pop song a century later.[41] Even if he was a funky Arthur Fiedler, Johnson, for decades the favorite bandleader of Philadelphia high society, hardly conforms to any preconceived notions of black musicians. This may be why he was derided in the blackface song "Jim Brown," if it is indeed a caricature of Johnson who brags:

> I am science nigger, my name is Jim Brown,
> De one dat plays de music up and down de town;
> Tho' to de common niggers I would not deign my hand,
> Be kase I'm de leader ob de fam'd brass band.[42]

Stephen Foster would cross paths with Johnson later, in the 1840s, but Pittsburgh had its own, lesser equivalent of Johnson, whom Foster may well have heard as a boy. John Julius (born Julien Bennoit), a Louisiana Creole and, like Johnson, a veteran of the War of 1812, managed a concert hall in Pittsburgh "attended by the first people of the city," and led a band of violinists that advertised "New Cotillions, from France."[43]

It's difficult to separate black from white music in America because from the very outset there was musical as well as sexual "amalgamation" —as miscegenation was generally called before the Civil War. When a trio consisting of a drummer, a fat black fiddler, and a "red-faced" trumpeter struck up "Cooney in de Holler" at Dickens's Place—as Almack's was renamed after the novelist's account of his visit to Five Points made the joint famous—the music was as racially mixed as the audience and the "yellow-boys" fathered by Pete Williams, the club's "coal-black" proprietor. According to Davy Crockett (or, more likely, a Whig ghostwriter for the coonskin conservative), the fiddling and dancing and drinking at Five Points mixed "Black and white, white and black, all hug-em-snug together."[44]

This makes it harder still to generalize about the relation of blackface music to black music. Nonetheless, that relationship seems to have been rather tenuous in early blackface and in the songs with which Stephen Foster and his friends amused neighbors in the Allegheny carriage house.

Micah Hawkins, for instance, had ample opportunity to observe African-American song and dance. Anthony Clapp, a slave belonging to the Hawkins family, was a noted fiddler, and Micah engraved on Toney's tombstone a paean to his playing. On holidays, slaves, mostly from Long Island, would flock to lower Manhattan, where Hawkins kept shop. According to one account, after dancing "a jig or break-down," the blacks would pass the hat among their white spectators. Some enterprising performers went further and danced on a five- or six-foot-long wooden board. This, of course, is exactly what "break dancers" did in the early 1980s, lugging cardboard pads about the boroughs of New York at the outset of hip hop's popularity. Except, instead of dancing to the beat of a boom box, one of these early-nineteenth-century entertainers would keep time by clapping his hands, slapping his thighs and stomping his heels—patting juba as it was called.[45]

Some whites knew and practiced this style of dance and percussive accompaniment. Mark Twain described in *Life on the Mississippi* (and also in *Huckleberry Finn*) a raft of drunken boatmen who "turned themselves loose on a regular old-fashioned keel-boat break-down" while one played "an old fiddle" and "another patted juba."[46] Although no one in George Caleb Bingham's famous painting, *The Jolly Flatboatmen,* is patting juba (instead a youth flicks his wrist against a pan, an impromptu tambourine), a white man is dancing a breakdown on the roof of the fore cabin, which serves as a resonant wooden stage.

Yet when Hawkins devised the music for "Backside Albany," he shut his ears to what was going on outside his window and adapted an Irish ballad.

The songs George Washington Dixon performed can be traced to Scottish and Irish tunes. Rice's "Jim Crow" may have been born in a Louisville stable, but its ancestry dates back to Irish folk music and the English stage. Indeed, it could be argued that blackface borrowed more brazenly from African-American dance—that stablehand's gyrations, Juba's spectacular "heelology"—than from African-American music.[47]

Morrison Foster wrote that Stephen's youthful imitations of white performers imitating blacks were "true to nature," but what nature, or whose? Pittsburgh's black population was minuscule when Foster was a child, and the only African Americans mentioned in the Foster family's copious correspondence are a few servants—whom the Fosters could seldom afford.

When they lived in the White Cottage, their household included Olivia Pise, whom Eliza Foster fondly recalled in her memoir as "Dinah." Morrison Foster, who never forgot her "handsome" looks or the exotic gold hoop earrings she wore, wrote that "Lieve" was "a mulatto bound-girl," the "illegitimate daughter of a West Indian Frenchman" who had taught dancing locally. According to Morrison, she used to take Stephen to "a church of shouting colored people," whose "singing and boisterous devotions" made a lasting impression on him. But Stephen would have been little more than an infant at the time, since Olivia Pise left the Fosters' employ when they lost the White Cottage. Moreover, the decorum of African-American religious services varied widely, so it's unsafe to assume that congregants at Lewis Woodson's Bethel African Methodist Episcopal Church or any other black church in Pittsburgh during this period necessarily "shouted."[48]

In 1834, a family friend gave Eliza Foster "a present of an excellent coloured girl." Another bound or indentured servant, she had "upward of three years to serve," wrote the unemployed William Foster, "so much saved for girls hire." This was also a time of considerable coming and going for the financially strapped Fosters, however, as they shuttled between Pittsburgh and Youngstown, and it's unclear how long this servant remained with them. In 1842, an African American named Catharine Russell kept house for the Fosters in Allegheny City, but she was not a live-in.[49]

So when Stephen Foster performed "Zip Coon" and "Jim Crow," he had little notion or knowledge of what he was singing about. That's not unusual. The blackest thing about much early blackface music may have been the burnt cork, and frequently it disguised none other than Davy Crockett. In one version of "Zip Coon," Zip succeeds Andrew Jackson and offers Davy the vice-presidency: "Zip shall be President, Crocket shall be vice, / And de dey two togedder, will hab de tings nice."[50] Crockett played the fiddle and relished blackface. He took in a show in Philadelphia and opined (or a Whig propagandist opined for him) that the performer who jumped Jim Crow, who may well have been Daddy Rice, "makes as good a nigger as if he was clean black, except the bandy-legs." Crockett even had a songster named after him. *Crockett's Free-and-Easy Song Book* included "Coal Black Rose," "Jim Crow," and "Backside Albany," and went through many editions.[51]

The Walt Disney–inspired Davy Crockett boom that swept America in 1954 and 1955 was a whimper compared to the bang Crockett made in 1834 and 1835. He became even more famous after his death at the Alamo in 1836. Paperback almanacs celebrating his exploits proliferated and helped resurrect Mike Fink, dead more than a decade but reborn as Crockett's sidekick. Sometimes the two even merged in myth, so that Crockett became a keelboatman, too. (Never mind that Crockett was so incompetent a riverman in real life that he nearly drowned when he tried to float two rafts down the Mississippi.)[52]

Early blackface music owed as much to the backwoods and rivers of the Midwest as it did to the plantations of the South or to the urban North. The rugged individualism of the frontier was reflected in the swaggering self-assertion of the emerging urban proletariat. The so-called b'hoys of New York City, and Mose, their firefighting hero whose stage exploits the b'hoys applauded in Bowery theaters, wore precariously tilted top hats rather than coonskin caps; they pomaded their side curls with soap instead of bear grease. ("The b'hoys shouting round me there," ran one ditty sung to the tune of "Zip Coon," "Yes, you fellers *wid de twist in de hair!*") Yet at least one contemporary chronicler of New York's mean streets likened the b'hoy to the backwoodsman and Mose to Davy Crockett.[53]

Blackface, in other words, was at once urbane and nostalgic for a frontier that was rapidly passing, *au courant* yet as autumnal as the craze for Crockett and Fink. As the United States became more urban and industrialized, blackface diverted and consoled white Americans with the imaginary primitivism not just of black Americans, but of their own pioneering predecessors.

Chapter Seven

"I PREFER
NOT TO"

Stephen Foster enjoyed a glimpse of the fading frontier a few miles southeast of Youngstown, where his uncle, John Struthers, Jr. lived in what was then Coitsville and today is Struthers, Ohio.[1] Foster spent several stretches of time between 1837 and 1840 on the farm of the octogenarian Struthers (born in 1759), who had married William Foster's sister, raised a family and, in 1819, buried the woman who, had she lived longer, would have been Stephen Foster's aunt. Some of Stephen's visits were family vacations; at other times the Fosters, having rented the Allegheny house, had no place else to go and stayed in Poland, Ohio, on the opposite bank of the Mahoning River from Coitsville, or cut their expenses by wearing their old clothes at the farmstead. Uncle Struthers's was a convenient place to deposit the youngest child of a family in flux.

It seemed to make little difference to Stephen why he was at his uncle's; he simply loved being there. A teenaged Indian scout and spy during the Revolution and one of the original settlers of the Northwest Territories (his son Ebenezer was said to be the first white boy born in the Western Reserve), Struthers was a Natty Bumppo–like character who, like Cooper's Leatherstocking, had outlived his era. "[O]ne of nature's noblemen," according to an obituary that may have been written by his brother-in-law William Foster, Struthers took a liking to Stephen and predicted that he would become "a very great man" as he was "possess'd of Superior talents for one of his age." The old man entertained his nephew with tales of tomahawks, scalpings, and Indian ambushes. Now he raised his rifle only to take potshots at possums and coons, and Stephen must have tagged along on these nocturnal hunting expeditions and learned how to shoot, because his older brother Morrison bought him a gun.[2]

"Stephen enjoys himself finely at Uncle Struthers," wrote his sister Henrietta, recently married to Thomas Wick and living in Youngstown:

> he never appears to have the least inclination to leave there and don't seem to feel at all lonely Uncle just lets him do as he pleases with the horses and cattle which makes him the greatest man on the ground.[3]

Once Struthers missed Stephen and searched high and low before discovering him "sitting up to his neck in a pile of chaff, watching the movements of the chickens and other barnyard animals—'just thinking,' as he briefly explained."[4]

Just hiding is more likely, for the world beyond the barnyard seemed to offer few possibilities. For a while in 1839, three Foster brothers, Henry, Morrison, and Stephen, boarded at a Mr. Reno's in Youngstown. The panic of 1837 had cost Henry his job as a warehouse clerk and given him a bad case of piles—"again."[5] The store he had borrowed $1,500 to start up in Warren, Pennsylvania, went bust within months. Now Henry was deeply in debt and desperate for work. Morrison, like Stephen, was attending public—that is to say, "free"—school. Though he was only sixteen, Morrison's school days were numbered, and a college education was out of the economic question. His father arranged a job for Morrison in Pittsburgh, where William Foster would shortly flee from Youngstown, partly to take advantage of Pennsylvania's bankruptcy laws. At least Dunning Foster, born between Henrietta and Morrison, had escaped to a life on the Ohio River, working as clerk on a steamboat and then going partners in a keelboat.

Sickness clouded the horizon, too. Mary Wick had died of consumption only a couple of months after her marriage to Brother William. Now the health as well as the grocery business of Mary's brother Thomas, Henrietta's husband, was failing. The opium he took "constantly" to ease his pain made Wick so irritable that William Foster confessed to Brother William that he "wanted to take a small piece out of one of his ears. (This between ourselves)." William Foster feared that his son-in-law was "not to be with us long," and he was right: Thomas Wick died in May 1842, leaving Henrietta with little money and three children.[6]

William Foster, who complained of an unspecified "afflicting *disease*," wasn't getting any younger. At the age of sixty-one, he was living with Eliza in a boarding house in Youngstown and still seeking "a permanent Situation.—Where we may 'totter doon the Hill together' in peace and quietness,—'and Sleep together at the foot' and be forgotten by all the world except our dear children." His quotation from Robert Burns's ballad, "John Anderson My Jo," may have been more accurate than his characterization of his wife as "quite composed and resign'd to her destiny."[7]

Young Stephen was even more dependent than his parents on Brother William's generosity. "As to Stephen I leave every thing; regarding the future for him to your own judgement," Eliza Foster wrote Brother William in 1840. ". . . [Y]ou are not only his brother but his Father; and I trust all his feellings will assend to you as his patron."[8]

In March 1839, Brother William was appointed principal engineer on the northern branch of the Pennsylvania Canal and moved to Towanda, in the northeastern part of the state near the New York border. "He has been an excellent son to his father and mother throughout their reverse of fortune," reported one of his letters of recommendation to the Pennsylvania Canal Commission. The distant tone of this letter from Washington suggests that its author, James Buchanan, didn't know his younger brother's in-laws very well.[9]

After Brother William had settled in, the widower proposed that Stephen come join him in Towanda and attend school there. Not only was this "an excellent chance for the dear little fellow to get education," as William Foster acknowledged, but it was probably Stephen's only chance.[10] The family leapt at it. Shortly after Christmas, on January 14, 1840, Brother William and thirteen-year-old Stephen set out from Youngstown in a two-horse open sleigh.

Their first stop was Pittsburgh, where Morrison was apprenticed (there had even been some talk of his becoming legally indentured) to his cousin, Cadwallader Evans, who sold and operated steam engines. Now, for the first time, Eliza Foster had no children at home. "[T]ell me little particulars about Stephen," she wrote Morrison from Youngstown, "while with you, did he get a clarionette. and did you see him when he started. was he well wrapt up."[11]

In Harrisburg, Stephen visited the house of representatives, met the governor, and attended a concert by the "Tyrolese Minstrèls," the Rainer Family. The Trapp Family Singers of their day, these "good natured goat milkers and cow-boys," in the opinion of one skeptical Pittsburgher, laid on their Alpine act with a trowel. "[V]ive! la humbug!" Charles Scully noted in his diary. The four Rainers, two men and two women, were indeed related, however, and from the Tyrol. They wore traditional costumes and sang Tyrolese folk songs in four-part harmony. Among their popular numbers was a comic song whose chorus consisted of sneezes; it's unclear whether they sneezed in harmony, too.[12]

The Rainers toured America extensively from 1839 to 1843 and left an impression that lingers faintly to this day. They inspired a raft of American "family" singers, such as the Hutchinsons, the Alleghenians, and the Orpheans, who were united by their four-part harmonies if not always by blood. Many of these groups made considerable show of their rural roots, often in the mountains—substituting the Alleghenies or another range for the Alps. In their self-conscious celebration of rustic virtue and the sweet simplicity of their music—which was usually composed rather than traditional and performed for a fee at concerts rather than on communal occasions—these family singers anticipated and set the pattern for the factitious folk music that flourished in the 1950s and 1960s. The Hutchinson Family, who sang political protest songs and were even blacklisted, briefly, in Philadelphia, were kissing cousins of the Weavers, whose "If I Had a Hammer" updated the Hutchinsons' "If I Were a Voice" a century later.[13]

The Rainers were also instrumental in the evolution of blackface music from individual Ethiopian delineators to full-fledged minstrel bands. The first blackface groups, the Virginia Minstrels and Christy's Minstrels, billed themselves as minstrels to jump on the bandwagon of the Rainers' popularity. (They weren't alone: Henry Russell composed and performed "The Minstrel of the Tyrol.") G. W. Dixon and Daddy Rice never called themselves minstrels, at least not until much later. Their songs—which they sang solo, after all—did not feature the four-part harmonies that, thanks to the Rainers and the American family groups that followed them, characterize the choruses of many later blackface songs. The Ethiopian Serenaders even advertised a song, "The Guinea Maid," as sung "a la Rainers."[14]

But this is getting ahead of Stephen Foster's sleigh ride to Towanda, where he lived for the next year and a half. Actually, he spent some of this time in Athens, seventeen miles farther up the Susquehanna River, since he attended both Towanda and Athens Academies.

The 1841 catalogue of Athens Academy listed Stephen Foster among its 200 students (seventy of whom were girls).[15] The private school, founded in 1814, had evidently been shuttered for a while, because an August 1840 handbill announced that it had reopened its "commodious building" with John G. Marvin as principal, his brother Edwin as assistant and a Miss Stevens as music teacher. If Athens Academy had indeed suspended classes before August 1840, it's likely that Stephen, arriving in Towanda in January of that year, attended school there first, in a five-year-old, two-story brick building on what townspeople dubbed "Science Hill."[16]

Athens Academy was a somewhat grander as well as older edifice, with four white pillars out front and a bell tower on top. Stephen boarded in Athens with a Mr. Herrick, the son of one of the academy's trustees. A letter he wrote Brother William in November 1840 indicates he was miserable:

> I have no place to study in the evenings as the little ones at Mr. Herricks keep such a crying and talking that it's impossible to read. There is a good fire place in my room and if you just say the word I will have a fire in it at nights and learn something. . . . I must stop writing as I am very cold.[17]

In a subsequent letter written from Towanda to Brother William, who was presumably traveling, Stephen pleaded not to be forced to return to "Athens that lonesome place," and warned Brother William not to pay the inhospitable Herrick "for fire in my room as I have not had any since you paid him last."[18]

There is no indication that Stephen took music lessons from Miss Stevens (these were offered for an extra charge), but he did study philosophy, grammar, and arithmetic, and he asked Brother William's permission to add Latin or bookkeeping to his courses. Sixty-five years later, one of Stephen's Athens schoolmates, Raymond M. Welles, recalled him as a "studious" sort who "kept much to his room and did not join the boys in their sports. I do not remember that he spent any time in society." Welles described him as "rather delicate in health, mainly, I think, because of lack of physical exercise."[19]

This description does not entirely jibe with that of a schoolmate at Towanda Academy, William Wallace Kingsbury, who recollected that Foster, far from retiring indoors, loved to take outdoor "excursions without leave," wading barefoot and "rambling by shady streams or gathering wild strawberries in the meadows and pastures." It shocked Kingsbury that Foster, "who wore a fine quality of hose," would blithely toss them away when soiled "by perspiration or muddy water."[20]

Perhaps it was easier to play hooky in Towanda than in Athens, but Kingsbury's recollection is in keeping with Stephen's comportment at Uncle Struthers's and with Morrison Foster's story of Stephen's flight with a Comanche whoop from his first lesson in the ABCs. Where both accounts agree is that Stephen was shy and unsociable, withdrawing either to his room or to the woods.

Athens Academy offered four terms a year, each followed by two weeks' vacation. Presumably it was on one of these breaks that Stephen begged Brother William to be allowed to stay in Towanda, proposing to room with a painter, Mr. Kettle, and take his meals at Brother William's. He may have been all the more eager to stay in Towanda because his brother Henry was now there, working for Brother William as a rod-bearer—the very job that had launched Brother William's career fifteen years earlier.[21] No more hooky, Stephen swore:

> . . . I promise not to be seen out of doors between the hours of nine & twelve A.M. and one & four P.M. Which hours I will attribute to study, such as you please to put me into. I will also promise not to pay any attention to my music until after eight Oclock in the evening. . . .[22]

Stephen Foster was already studying music, but he feared that his family would consider it a diversion from more serious studies. Stephen is said to have played "a good deal" on the "clarionet" in Towanda— possibly the "clarionette" his mother had inquired about in her letter to Morrison.[23] W. W. Kingsbury, his Towanda Academy schoolmate, recalled his flute-playing fondly. But it was in Athens that Stephen made his debut as a composer at the age of fourteen. It wasn't with a blackface ditty, the trashy kind of song he'd sung a few years previously. "The Tioga

Waltz," an instrumental scored for three or four flutes, was far more decorous. Since the composition survives today only in an arrangement based on a melody Morrison Foster whistled to a musician friend in the 1890s, it's hazardous to say anything about "The Tioga Waltz" musically other than that it was indeed in 3/4 time, which two or three flutes marked doggedly while a lone flute capered in the higher register.[24]

Stephen played the lead flute in "The Tioga Waltz" in April 1841, at Athens's Presbyterian church, where the academy held an exhibition or commencement exercise. It was a dressy occasion and Stephen wore pumps, which he had borrowed money to buy. According to Morrison, who was not there, the performance "was rewarded with much applause and an encore."[25] "The Tioga Waltz" may have been named in honor of Frances Welles, a seventeen-year-old cousin of R. M. Welles and a fellow student at Athens Academy, who was married that same month just south of Athens on her family's 400-acre estate, Tioga Point Farm.[26] Stephen need not have had so specific an allusion in mind, however, since Tioga was an old but still familiar name for the Chemung River, which flows into the Susquehanna at Athens, and Athens itself had been Tioga Point until the Greek Revival inspired a change of names.

A few months after the Athens concert, in July 1841, just after turning fifteen, Stephen was in Canonsburg, at the school his father had attended and his grandfather had served as a trustee (Brother William may have been a student there, too). He stuck it out at Jefferson College a little longer than he had at nursery school. A week after his father dropped him off, Stephen Foster dropped out.

William Foster had conveyed his son to Canonsburg from Pittsburgh. The elder Fosters had returned there from Youngstown and were boarding with a widowed Mrs. Paul. Sometime during the summer, Brother William and Stephen came to visit, perhaps to celebrate Stephen's birthday. Possibly because he wanted to be nearer his parents—or they wanted him nearer to them—he enrolled in Jefferson College, less than twenty miles away. His father paid Stephen's tuition in advance but left him with little cash. Within four days, Stephen was complaining—as college kids do to this day—that he was short of funds.

He wrote Brother William that he couldn't join a literary society because it cost two or three dollars. Laundry was $1.25 a week. "I have to keep myself very clean here," said the boy who had thought nothing of soiling and discarding excellent hose. He also needed "another coat or two especially for summer." Stephen pleaded for money, forgetting in his agitation whatever spelling and grammar he had picked up at Athens Academy:

> . . . [A]s Pa has not much more than the means of getting along I thought I would write you this letter that you might considder the matter. . . . and if you see fit to send me a little of the bino. once in a while I will insure you their is no inducements here to make me spend any money unnecesarily.[27]

A few days later, another student was going into Pittsburgh. Stephen went with him and never came back. He had left three schools in eighteen months.

It was five weeks before Stephen summoned up the courage and composure to write Brother William again. Full of excuses and false cheer, he tried to make light of his embarrassment:

> I hope that you will pardon me for writing you so extensively on the money subject. But at the same time I will let you know that a boy comes out mighty thin in Canonsburg without some in his pocket.

Because he'd gone to Jefferson in the middle of a term, he explained, he couldn't get into the classes he wanted and "became more disgusted with the place as long as I stayed in it." Besides, he'd gotten a headache, dizzy spells and a nosebleed. He felt so faint he could scarcely get out of bed. And when he accompanied Sam Montgomery to Pittsburgh, it was because "he asked me to."[28]

Eliza Foster had already written to Brother William that

> Stephen will not stay at Cannansburg he says he has lost conseat of himself because he was once in his life a great fool. and that was when he did not go back with brother William. he begs me to ask you to say that he must board with Ma and go to day skool.

Stephen was a Mama's boy, and Ma was delighted to have him back by her side: "[I]ndeed if I am in Alleganey town I shall be almost too lonely without one child with me."[29]

Mrs. Paul had moved across town, and the Fosters could not afford the board in the posher Pittsburgh neighborhood. So Stephen helped them move into the house Brother William owned in Allegheny and moved in with them. He studied mathematics with a teacher in Pittsburgh, Mr. Moody, but mostly he hung around the house.

William Foster was more exasperated than Eliza by their son's fecklessness. To Brother William he wrote:

> I regret extremely that Stephen has not been able to appreciate properly your exertions on his behalf by availing himself of the advantage of a College education; which will cause him much regret before he arrives at my age. . . .

And yet, William added, sounding somewhat mystified:

> he does not appear to have any evil propensities to indulge; he seeks no associates; and his leisure hours are all devoted to musick, for which he possesses a strange talent.[30]

Morrison was now working as a clerk and messenger for Pollard McCormick, the proprietor of a cotton factory in Allegheny City that manufactured yarn, twine, and batting. He ran errands on a little pony and was delighted that his duties didn't include lighting lamps, sweeping up the warehouse, or anything else that might dirty his clothes. Dunning was off on the river somewhere. Henry's only hope of rising above rod-bearer was that his father might secure him a clerkship in Washington— if William Foster didn't take the job for himself. When William Foster wasn't out of town in vain pursuit of a lawsuit or on some trivial business errand, he was off making a spectacle of himself at a temperance convention, admitting, sometimes before thousands of people, that he was a "reform'd drunkard," and urging his auditors to sign the teetotal pledge.[31]

How was Stephen going to earn a living or at least contribute to the family's mite? There was talk of the navy ("Now a midshipman is just what I fancy," he wrote Brother William) and later of West Point, but it was idle. No, Stephen took a look at the pathetic strivings of his family, at their shabby-genteel attempts to keep up appearances; at the futility and fatuousness of his father's blustering, slap-on-the-back optimism; at the resentment and envy that ate away at his mother while she bit her tongue; at the self-denial of Brother William's dour devotion to his onward-and-upward career; at the reduced circumstances of his other siblings and their even punier aspirations—and he recoiled. "Mitty is as steady in his office as an old man," William Foster wrote to Brother William about Morrison, who had just turned sixteen. Was old age something to emulate in your teens? Asked to pitch in and put his shoulder to the greasy wheel, to be a man and an American and go ahead and get ahead, Stephen Foster mustered all his indignation and indolence and took the flute from his lips and the words right out of the mouth of America's archetypal slacker—"Bartleby the Scrivener." And he did so more than a decade before Herman Melville wrote those words down: " 'I prefer not to,' he replied in a flutelike tone."[32]

Chapter Eight

O TEMPERANCE, O MORES!

The house into which Stephen helped move his parents in Allegheny City was a haven, the grassy commons it faced, a bucolic retreat. To an out-of-towner, Pittsburgh seemed hellish. Coal stoked every household hearth as well as local industry. The "hissing of steam, the clanking of chains, the jarring and grinding of wheels and other machinery, and the glow of melted glass and iron, and burning coal beneath" assaulted a visitor's senses:

> The surface of the houses and streets are so discolored as to defy the cleansing power of water. . . . The very soot partakes of the bituminous nature of the coal, and falling—color excepted—like snow-flakes, fastens on the face and neck, with a tenacity which nothing but the united agency of soap, hot water, and the towel can overcome.[1]

It would take a couple more years for the unrest of industrial workers to rise to the surface, but African-American anger was already roiling the Three Rivers. A month after Stephen Foster dropped out of college, black Pennsylvanians held a convention in Pittsburgh. At the top of their agenda was restoring black suffrage. Two years earlier, Martin Delany had been awarded a prize by the Young Men's Moral Reform Society of Pittsburgh for inscribing the Lord's Prayer on a piece of paper no bigger than a sixpence. Now Delany was operating on a much larger scale. One hundred and twenty-five years before the Congress of Racial Equality and the Student Non-Violent Coordinating Committee purged whites from their ranks in the name of black power, Delany organized an unprecedented gathering to which no whites, not even outspoken abolitionists, were invited.[2]

The first presidential election in which black Pennsylvanians—the largest African-American population north of the Mason-Dixon Line— were barred from voting marked a new low in American politics. Slogans, songs, and gimmicks prevailed over discussion of policies in William Henry Harrison's 1840 campaign against Martin Van Buren. Hyping Harrison's dubious victory over the Shawnee thirty years earlier and plugging his vice-presidential running mate, parading Whigs bawled "Tippecanoe and Tyler, Too"—a ditty that Henry Russell, with characteristic grandiosity, claimed to have composed.[3]

The campaign that gave us "O.K."—for Old Kinderhook, Van Buren's home outside Albany—was a victory not just for Whiggery but for popular culture. The same innovations in transportation, communications, and printing that made hit songs possible enabled political parties to drown out discourse with campaign jingles, burying debate beneath a blizzard of buttons, badges, and paraphernalia.

William Foster was swept up in the popular frenzy for Harrison, although he insisted he remained true to the principles of Jacksonian Democracy. When Harrison carried Pennsylvania by the micro-thin margin of 343 votes, Foster was quick to claim credit. Since the Whigs carried Allegheny County in every presidential election from 1836 through 1852, Foster was flattering himself, but he was desperate for a job and pinned his hopes on the promise of Walter Forward, a Whig attorney in Pittsburgh whom Harrison appointed controller of the treasury. A protégé of Henry Baldwin, Henry Foster's namesake and now a Supreme Court justice, Forward was probably acting as much out of pity and friendship as to return a political favor when he offered William Foster a clerkship in the Treasury Department. (The founding president of the Pittsburgh Temperance Society, Forward may also have wanted to help out a fellow crusader against alcohol.) ". . . [H]e says he wants me at Washington, as a companion, *and political, adviser!!,*" William Foster wrote to Brother William. "So, our prospects begin to brighten a little."

He was kept on tenterhooks, however, as President Harrison's death after only a month in office and Forward's promotion by John Tyler from controller to secretary of the treasury delayed Foster's appointment.[4]

Not until November 1841, was William Foster officially tendered a post, for a salary of one thousand dollars "or more." By the time he arrived in Washington—"Completely high and dry in money matters," he had to borrow fifty dollars from Brother William—he was no longer sure he wanted the job. Since it was purely a patronage position (if any fruit of the Jacksonian spoils system could be called pure), one Foster was as good as another. So William summoned Henry from Brother William's side in Towanda to fill in for him.[5]

During these months of vacillation, William Foster was asked to stand as an independent candidate for mayor of Allegheny. He did so and won by 135 votes. Deciding to stay in Allegheny, William Foster let Henry keep the clerkship, and instead of Mr. Foster going to Washington, Mrs. Foster did, visiting her children and then childhood friends and relations in Maryland. Just before or after she departed in the spring of 1842, William Foster filed for bankruptcy protection.[6]

A nineteenth-century historian of Allegheny City could not "recall to memory any special event that marked" William Foster's two year-long terms as mayor. He must have been doing something right, however, because the second time around he trounced a heavily favored Democrat and two other candidates in a walkaway that left everyone "astonished" as the "big bell" of Allegheny City rang "like mad."[7]

The Mayor wrote Brother William that his

> office affords me about business enough to keep me from despairing; but is painful in many respects, to witness as I must do the awful depravity of por human nature; in many cases of female intoxication and prostitution is truly lamentable.

Stephen, he continued, "is a very good boy, but I cannot get him to stick a school, he reads a good deal and writes some in the office with me."[8]

One of the few events to punctuate this period of near paralysis on Stephen's part—an adolescent identity crisis in a household that could ill afford such unremunerative inertia—was the arrival of Charles Dickens. The first tour of America by "Boz," the famous author of *The Pickwick Papers,* was such a triumph that it was even commemorated in blackface:

Dey fed ole massa Boz so tall
His trowzaloons dey grow too small;
In Boston I couldnt get any pickins
Caze all de victuals went to de Dickens.[9]

The novelist spent three days in Pittsburgh, later observing, "It certainly has a great quantity of smoke hanging about it." At the Exchange Hotel—which he pronounced "excellent"—Dickens was mobbed. "A great crowd they were . . . and a very queer one," he wrote in a letter. Morrison Foster called on Dickens on March 30; William and Stephen scheduled a visit the following day, and the teenager who would become the nineteenth century's most popular songwriter in the English language met the century's most popular English-language novelist.[10]

Meanwhile, Eliza Foster was enjoying her travels. Escorted to Washington by Brother William, she was "handsomely received" by President Tyler. Justice Baldwin called at the boarding house where she was staying as did Senator James Buchanan. She felt like one of "the Elite," and even more so when she visited "the elegant mansions along the extensive Eastern shore of Maryland, the land of my ancestors whose bodies are moulder'd with the dust of their fields, and whose tombs compose the portico's of their palaces." One plantation, where she stayed for three weeks, was presided over by a widowed Mrs. Skinner, a Clayland on her mother's side. It adjoined the plantation of the Lloyd family that originally owned (and possibly fathered) Frederick Douglass. "The Skinners, the Peakers, the Tilgmans, the Lockermans, and the Gipsons, are in the same boat," Douglass wrote; "being slaveholding neighbors, they may have strengthened each other in their iron rule." Whereas Dickens, like many other English travelers, was revolted by slavery, Eliza Foster was impressed and envious that her distant kinswoman "owned two hundred and fifty negroes."[11]

She had a "great time" with another old friend, "making out the Cronicles of the Clayland family."[12] Fantasizing about an English castle to which an unknown American Clayland was the long-lost heir, she developed a new sense of entitlement—and resentment. She wrote to Brother William that when she returned to Allegheny City, she was resolved

to make people walk the chaulk and take some pains to make me happy. I have passed a long life studying the comfort of others. I will try to let them see that I must be considered. . . .[13]

This bitterness seeped into her correspondence frequently, not only between but in the lines of her pinched penmanship. In dramatic contrast to William Foster's bold strokes, Eliza wrote in a dry, diminutive hand, scratchy on the nib and stingy with the ink. After Henrietta's opium-addled husband died, Eliza wrote, of her own daughter:

> When she gets to be as old as I am all such flattering fixtures in her imagination will be shorn of its dazling tints; and the shadows in the landscape of life will become browner and browner, untill they are put on with so heavy a brush as to become almost black. She will find that no design of a woman can ever be put in practice without money or influence; that all her care and watching and labour has only been spent for the bennefit of others; that if she were to give her body to be burn'd it would not produce one martyr in her cause, such is the force of all powerful selfishness. . . .[14]

In August 1842, Eliza and Stephen Foster went to Youngstown to help out Henrietta, and Stephen, with nothing better to do, stayed there all fall. He went to school with a Mrs. Rockwell, and his father sent him a dollar for "Powder and Shot," which he presumably discharged at Uncle Struthers's.[15]

The temperance movement commanded more of William Foster's energies than the mayoralty. Perhaps it was the rise of the Washingtonian movement that inspired him, or possibly a relapse on his part caused him to renew his devotion to the cause. Probably it was both. The wary relief in Eliza Foster's 1841 letters to Brother William suggests there had been some backsliding since William Foster went on the wagon in 1833. "Pa continues temperate as you left him whilest he is so I will not thwart his plans," Eliza wrote in August. In September she reassured Brother William, "your father is so steady and managing that I am quite releived from uneasiness . . . my confidence in him being entirely reinstated."[16]

Within three years of its founding in 1840 in a Baltimore tavern, the Washingtonian movement claimed millions of followers. In July 1841, 3,600 people signed the teetotal pledge in Pittsburgh and Allegheny City alone, and weeks later purportedly just two of them had failed to stick to it.[17] The previous generation of crusaders had preached temperance from the pulpit, extolling sobriety on the basis of religious conviction rather than personal experience. The Washingtonians replaced "Thou shalt

not" with "We shall overcome," and the sermon with the self-help meeting—a precursor of Alcoholics Anonymous, except this was mass rather
than group therapy. A Washingtonian might confess his addiction before
a crowd of thousands, and everyone knew his last as well as first name. "I
have been a drunkard!" began one Washingtonian who then stopped
short, overcome by memory and emotion. Only after his audience
clapped and encouraged him did he resume his story, which inspired his
listeners to stand up, as if at a religious revival, and testify:

> [O]ne after another rose, and spoke the innermost truth out of their heart's
> or their life's experience. One voice out of many exclaimed, "Is there,
> then, hope even for me?" "Yes! yes!" cried another; "come brother, come
> and sign! We will stand by you!" [18]

William Foster spoke at three such temperance conventions in a single
day in 1841, on a program with five other speakers, all "acknowledging
ourselves reform'd drunkards." At one meeting more than three hundred
people signed the pledge. "The shout of Washingtonians is heard on
every gale," sang the Hutchinson Family, who were as dedicated to temperance as they were to abolition; "they're chanting now the victory o'er
cider, beer and ale." [19]

The temperance and abolition crusades attracted some of the same
foot soldiers and field marshals to the ranks of reform. In addition to
editing *The Liberator*, William Lloyd Garrison, the son of a drunken
shoemaker who deserted his family, was active in the temperance movement. Martin Delany was the recording secretary of The Temperance
Society of the People of Color of the City of Pittsburgh. [20] Anxieties
about race and about temperance converged and combusted when Frank
Johnson's band of ten black men performed a benefit for sobriety at
Allegheny City's Washington Ark on May 16, 1843.

Johnson had played on April 28 and 29 in Cincinnati, arriving there
on the same steamboat as Morrison Foster, who was purchasing cotton
for Pollard McCormick. A newspaper ad for Johnson's "Grand Soirée
Musicale" promised Cincinnatians an extraordinarily mixed bag of a
program. The String Band would perform the overture to Rossini's *Semi-
ramide*, and the Brass Band would play "The Postillion of Lonjuineau's
Song"—"with Bells and Whip accompaniment." In addition to the inevitable "Woodman! Spare That Tree!," Moore's "The Last Rose of Sum-

mer," and selections from Bellini's *Norma,* the ensemble would perform an original waltz composed by Johnson and, "By request, Johnson's celebrated 'Voice Quadrilles,' with the laughing choruses." As if this weren't enough, the band would also play Franz Kotzwara's blunderbuss, "The Battle of Prague."[21]

Presumably Johnson offered a similar program in Pittsburgh. The first of his four concerts at Philo Hall "was largely and fashionably attended and the audience seemed perfectly delighted." This came as no surprise. Not only had Johnson been society bandleader of *le tout* Philadelphia for a quarter century—"leader of the band at all balls, public and private; sole arbiter of all serenades, acceptable and not acceptable; inventor-general of cotillions"—but during the summer he entertained at wealthy white watering holes such as Saratoga and White Sulphur Springs. He'd even performed at a Princeton commencement.[22]

But trouble broke out when Johnson surrendered Philo Hall to the Rainer Family and crossed the river to play a benefit performance at the Washington Ark, Allegheny City's capacious new temperance hall, which its supporters—Mayor Foster among them—had not yet entirely paid for. A notorious gang of local rowdies called the "Rats"—Pittsburgh diarist Charles Scully called them "a disgrace to that reputable quadruped vermin"—surrounded the hall and raised a ruckus. They didn't disrupt the concert with their racket, but they drew blood with a shower of eggs and deadlier missiles when Johnson and his men tried to escape afterward. Mayor Foster exhorted the mob to disperse, but in vain. When he courageously escorted some of the musicians, on foot, toward Pittsburgh, the prestige of his office provided little protection. As they neared the bridge they were set upon, and a stone gashed one musician's forehead. Another band member, riding in a carriage conveying the rest of the musicians, was also hit, along with the carriage's driver. The injuries weren't severe, but the day after the attack pools of blood stained the pavement.

Four youths were arrested, and Mayor Foster's office was jam-packed when he set bail at two hundred dollars for each of them. Two skipped town before trial, and the other two were eventually acquitted. Either for want of evidence or because the jury would not convict whites of assaulting blacks, the defendants got off with a slap on the wrist—they had to pay court costs.[23]

Johnson and his band did not let the "Rats" run them out of town, however. A couple of days later they performed in Pittsburgh at a charity ball managed by a young lawyer, Richard Cowan. They kicked things off with "a series of cotillions which for gayety, good feeling & spirit have never been equalled here," according to Cowan's best friend, Charles Scully, who danced with at least ten young ladies and didn't get home until daylight.[24]

When Johnson died the following year, a Philadelphia paper eulogized him as "one of the most celebrated personages" in the city. He had just presented, with several prominent white singers, the first integrated concerts in American history. Yet the man who had performed for Lafayette, an American president (Van Buren), and reputedly a British queen was, at the height of his national renown, stoned in Allegheny City.[25]

And where was Stephen? After his return from his sister Henrietta's home in Youngstown in December 1842, the record of his life is nearly blank until the copyrighting of his first song, "Open Thy Lattice Love," almost two years later. Morrison Foster wrote that he studied German and French with Captain Jean Herbst, a Belgian.[26] He continued studying music—or at least fooling around with it. Stephen went with Morrison to a Henry Russell concert in early 1843, and it's hard to believe he didn't hear Frank Johnson when he came to town a few months later— if not at the Ark, surely at one of his Pittsburgh performances.

While Stephen was schooling himself in the genteel tradition of the parlor ballad—which "Open Thy Lattice Love" would epitomize—he was doubtless also listening to the rawer, racier (in every sense of the word) music of blackface, which had made a quantum leap in popularity. Just two months before Frank Johnson, a "splendid looking, bright, aristocratic and well dressed" black man purveying light, semi-classical "pops" music, was assaulted, the Virginia Minstrels were applauded at the first evening-length "Ethiopian Concert," at Boston's Masonic Temple. Daniel Decatur Emmett, Billy Whitlock, Dick Pelham, and Frank Brower —four white men in burnt cork and crazy calico costumes—played the fiddle, banjo, tambourine, and bones, sang, danced, told jokes, and acted out skits. They ended with a parody of Henry Russell, whose "Fine Old English Gentleman" Emmett turned into "The Fine Old Colored Gentleman"—a gin-sucking, banjo-toting "nigger" named (what else?) Sambo.[27] The minstrel show, which would dominate American popular entertainment for fifty years and influences it to this day, was born.

Chapter Nine

"GENUINE
NEGRO FUN"

When Max Maretzek, the Bohemian-born conductor and impresario who did more than anyone else to popularize Italian opera in the United States, took over New York City's Astor Place Opera House, he was disconcerted to hear the company's tailors "singing nigger-songs" while the chorus whose costumes they were sewing rehearsed its parts. Blackface and classical music may have seemed at odds, but economic adversity made strange bedfellows in the early 1840s, when hard times left many New York musicians of every ilk unemployed. In self-defense they banded together and organized, within months of each other, the Philharmonic Symphony Society of New York and the first minstrel band.[1]

One day in the winter of 1842–43, Dan Emmett was sitting idly in the Bowery—at the North American Hotel at 30 Bowery, by his account; at a boarding house at 37 Catherine Street, by others. Born in 1815 in Mount Vernon, Ohio—a small country town that retained, like John Struthers's farm, a frontier flavor—Emmett had worked as a printer in Cincinnati during the winter months and performed in the summers as a drummer, banjo player, and blackface singer in traveling circuses. With him this day in New York were two other veterans of the sawdust circuit. Frank Brower, a dancer who had occasionally toured with Emmett, is also said to have been the first blackface bones player, clattering sawn lengths of horse ribs like outsized castanets. Billy Whitlock played the banjo and had danced with John Diamond under P. T. Barnum's management and at Barnum's American Museum. Rounding out the foursome was Dick Pelham, a blackface dancer on the New York stage.[2]

Their impromptu jam session—with Emmett on fiddle, Whitlock on banjo, Brower on bones, and Pelham on tambourine—created a "horrible noise," Emmett recalled delightedly years later, and established the instrumental lineup of the minstrel band. After a few performances at New York theaters and circuses, when the Virginia Minstrels presented a whole evening's entertainment in Boston on March 7 and 8, 1843, they cut the pattern for the minstrel show. Ethiopian delineation had evolved from isolated, entr'acte solo performances into full-blown minstrelsy.

The minstrel band became the basic unit of American pop music through most of its permutations, the forerunner of the jazz band, the bluegrass band, and the rock band. The banjo shared the melody with the fiddle— like the clarinet and cornet in early jazz—while the bones chattered and the tambourine, which had a larger drumhead and fewer rattles than today's version, thumped and jingled a beat that is still heard 'round the world.[3]

"Our study of the great romantic composers has trained us in the method of the *legato*," George Gershwin observed nearly a century later,

whereas our popular music asks for *staccato* effects, for almost a stencilled style. The rhythms of American music are more or less brittle; they should be made to snap, and at times to cackle. The more sharply the music is played, the more effective it sounds.[4]

Snap, cackle: pop. Gershwin's formulation is the Rice Krispies recipe.

There was no way the banjo—a gourd with four strings when slaves brought it with them from Africa—could play a *legato* line. Even after it acquired a fifth gut string, the instrument retained its percussive twang and was still considered by one white commentator "of all instruments the best adapted to the lowest class of slaves." The banjo would also prove best adapted to low-class, brawny popular music, without any aspirations to high, "sissified" art. "I like Gottschalk well enough," Mark Twain wrote.

He probably gets as much out of the piano as there is in it. But the frozen fact is, that all that he *does* get out of it is "tum, tum." . . . The piano may do for love-sick girls who lace themselves to skeletons, and lunch on chalk, pickles, and slate pencils. But give me the banjo. . . . When you want *genuine* music—music that will come right home to you like a bad quarter, suffuse your system like strychnine whisky, . . . ramify your whole constitution like the measles, and break out on your hide like the pin-feather pimples on a picked goose,—when you want all this, just smash your piano, and invoke the glory-beaming banjo![5]

The minstrel show, mixing music, dance, and comedy, was a progenitor of vaudeville, the revue, and, through these, of musical comedy. The walk-around with which the minstrel show soon concluded became the cakewalk that in turn gave ragtime its syncopated strut. And the stump speech or sermon full of mispronunciations and malapropisms, which was part of the act from the very beginning—in Boston, Billy Whitlock delivered "A Negro Lecture on Locomotives"—cropped up everywhere. In the 1850s, the *Pequod*'s black cook, Fleece, admonished the "woracious" sharks to mind their manners in a stump sermon in *Moby-Dick*. In the 1950s, Tim Moore's Kingfish followed a similar script when he warned a fellow Mystic Knight of the Sea, "There was a proxy vote in dere, and you just got peroxided into dah job" in television's *Amos 'n' Andy*.[6]

None of these individual elements—musical, terpsichorean, or theatrical—originated with the Virginia Minstrels, but they were the first to put them all together. Thanks to them, "the bones and banjo struck up an alliance and attracted attention in a 'break-down' and the 'Essence of Old Virginny,' " as a critic recalled twenty years later.

> . . . The insoluble conundrum and the indigestible jest were borrowed from the circus, and the process of reducing the youth of the country to the level of gibbering idiots was duly organized and entered upon.[7]

Unfortunately, no sooner had the Virginia Minstrels gotten their act together and taken it on the road than they fell out during a tour of England, performing for the last time together on July 14, 1843. By then they had already inspired, among many others, the Kentucky Minstrels, the Ethiopian Serenaders, the Congo Melodists, the African Minstrels, and an especially flagrant counterfeit that advertised itself as "Christy's Original band of Virginia Minstrels."[8]

Christy's Minstrels got their start in a Buffalo tavern that provided entertainment and Monongahela whiskey to the boatmen who plied the Great Lakes and the Erie Canal. Edwin Pearce Christy, a Philadelphia-born former traveling shoe salesman and circus performer, led a blackface trio there that specialized in what impressed a visiting English actor as "genuine negro fun." Christy had the business acumen and his costar, "George Christy" (George N. Harrington, son of the tavern's barmaid, and Edwin's stepson), had the theatrical talent to capitalize on the Virginia Minstrels' success and institutionalize their innovations.[9]

Christy's Minstrels played the South and West (including Pittsburgh and Cincinnati) for four years, perfecting their act and adding various performers to it. By the time they made their New York City debut in 1846, settling into Mechanics' Hall the following year for an unprecedented decade-long run on Broadway, the minstrel show's structure was becoming formalized. The "end men," who flanked the other performers and played tambourine and bones (and who were sometimes called that: Tambo and Bones), functioned not only as the ensemble's rhythm section but as its principal comedians. George Christy was a celebrated end man, excelling on the bones and also in drag as minstrelsy added "wench" roles to its repertory of derision. The first part of an evening's entertainment became a miscellany of songs, not all of them ostensibly inspired by or illustrative of black life. E. P. Christy, for instance, was only a passable banjo player, but acclaimed for his "sweet voice" and its way with a ballad. This segment was followed by an "olio," a series of individual virtuoso and novelty acts that often included a stump speech, and the finale featured the entire company in a playlet or a large-scale recreation of an African-American frolic down home on the plantation.[10]

Christy's Minstrels also sang four-part harmonies that a New York reviewer praised "as some of the sweetest chords to which the human ear ever listened." The Virginia Minstrels had sung individually or in unison, but not in harmony. After all, the African Americans they claimed to be imitating generally favored solo and unison song in call-and-response patterns that did not approximate conventional Western harmonies. But Christy's and other minstrel groups emulated the Rainers and Hutchinsons, and in so doing they helped revolutionize the pop song. The harmonized chorus is so integral to popular songs of the past 150 years, from "Jingle Bells" to "I Want to Hold Your Hand," that it's hard to imagine them otherwise. But early blackface songs, since they were sung by solo delineators, had no such choruses, just refrains. This was also true of most of Charlotte Foster's ballads, since these, too, were generally popularized on stage and played in the parlor by a single performer. Minstrel groups multiplied the possibilities for harmonized choruses, which gradually crossed over to parlor balladry as well, narrowing the gap between the two genres.[11]

In the meantime, the teariness of parlor songs began gradually to seep into the minstrel show, particularly its first part. Mark Twain noted this shift from "rudely comic" to "sentimental" songs. It is dramatized by the differences between two "wenches" named Lucy apostrophized in extremely popular minstrel numbers.[12]

Billy Whitlock composed the tune of "Miss Lucy Long," which was a staple in the repertory of the Virginia Minstrels and the early Christy's Minstrels.[13] Although the singer asks Lucy Long to marry him (and is turned down, for the time being), he couches his admiration for her in crude caricature:

> Miss Lucy, she is handsome,
>   And Miss Lucy, she is tall;
> To see her dance Cachucha,
>   Is death to Niggers all. . . .
>
> Oh! Miss Lucy's teeth is grinning,
>   Just like an ear ob corn. . . .

The singer also warns that if Lucy ever does consent to wed and becomes a "scolding wife," he'll "tote her down to Georgia, / And trade her off for corn." So much for romance.[14]

(The cachucha, incidentally, was a Spanish classical dance made famous by Fanny Elssler, the daughter of Haydn's valet, whose sensational tours of America in 1840 to 1842 paved the way for Jenny Lind's a decade later. That a sensuous stylization of a Spanish dance, which made a Viennese ballerina the toast of Paris and then the States, could pop up in a song ostensibly about an African-American woman performed by blackfaced white Americans, Frank Brower's bones rattling like Elssler's castanets, illustrates how new modes of communication and transportation were creating a new, international, carnival culture.)[15]

James Sanford, a blackface singer and dancer, published "Miss Lucy Neale" only two years later, in 1844. Like "Miss Lucy Long," the song is in 2/4 time, the key of G and marked *allegretto*. Both compositions have a five-measure introduction, a verse and refrain of seventeen measures and a concluding instrumental "dance" of eight and a half measures. Although the songs share the identical framework and the women are the same color, Sanford's Lucy is an object of affection rather than ridicule:

> Miss Lucy she was handsome,
> From de head down to de heel,
> And all de niggas fell in love,
> Wid my pretty Lucy Neale....

This Miss Lucy accepts the singer's marriage proposal, but the lovers are torn apart when their master sells him down the river "Because he thought I'd steal." When he receives the announcement of her death, the singer grieves sincerely: "And oh! poor Lucy Neale, / If I had her in my arms, / How glad 'twould make me feel." [16]

It would be gratifying to attribute the sentimentality of "Miss Lucy Neal" (as it was more frequently spelled) and a bevy of similar songs to an upwelling of popular opposition to slavery and sympathy for its victims. But cultural critic Ann Douglas's skeptical definition of sentimentality as "the political sense obfuscated or gone rancid," the handmaiden of "failed political consciousness," is a healthy reminder not to make too much of this. [17] Commercial calculation probably played as great a role as politics in softening the minstrel shows E. P. Christy and other impresarios produced.

E. P. Christy was above all else a businessman. He proudly publicized his yearly receipts, and he was able to retire on his profits at the age of thirty-nine after George Christy defected to a rival company. (Eight years later, however, in a fit of despondency during the Civil War, E. P. Christy jumped out a second-story window to his death.) Like Barnum, Christy recognized the importance of titillating while never offending. In order to appeal to the broadest possible audience, to women and families as well as to young men, he smoothed the rough edges of the Virginia Minstrels' raucous act and toned down the raunchy repertory. He was Dick Clark, if you will, to Dan Emmett's Alan Freed. Christy advertised that his minstrels' "chaste performances [had been] patronized by the elite and fashion in all the principal cities of the Union." Barnum, who

bragged that his museum was "nice & genteel & . . . patronized by the
best class of society," would have approved heartily. And Christy's claim
—unlike his boasts that he had preceded the Virginia Minstrels and
written both "Miss Lucy Long" and "Miss Lucy Neal"—was more than
mere hype. Years later a New Yorker recalled that Christy's Minstrels
were "well patronized by 'good families' and 'nice people,' who were glad
to go for a hearty laugh and an hour's enjoyment of the pretty music."[18]

Did this mean that blackface had become bleached, that the minstrels'
music was even more remote from African-American music than the
songs of the Ethiopian delineators? The relationship of blackface entertainment to black culture was a source of anxiety even to minstrelsy's
admirers. That's why the British actor who encountered E. P. Christy in
Buffalo insisted in consecutive paragraphs that "the fun of these three
nigger minstrels" was "so genuine" and that "the staple of E. P. Christy's
entertainment was fun—mind, genuine negro fun." Twain professed his
affection for the banjo's "*genuine* music" and "the real nigger show—the
genuine nigger show," and yet protested elsewhere that the "so-called
'negro minstrels' simply mis-represent the thing. I do not think they ever
saw a plantation or saw a slave sing."[19]

Many minstrels tried to reassure the public of the authenticity of their
performances. The Virginia Minstrels claimed to reproduce "the songs,
refrains, and ditties as sung by the southern slaves at all their merry
meetings such as the gathering in of the cotton and sugar crops, corn
huskings, slave weddings, and junketings." E. P. Christy sounded almost
like an anthropologist when he (or a ghostwriter) described how carefully
he had studied the slaves he had supervised in a New Orleans ropewalk
and their holiday antics in the Crescent City's Congo Square. He was
the "most truthful" of delineators, and his troupe possessed "sufficient
science and practical skill . . . to harmonize and score systematically the
original NEGRO SOLOS, quartettes, chorus and concerted pieces."[20]

The Virginia Minstrels were managed by a close friend of George
Washington Dixon. Daddy Rice was only seven years older than Dan
Emmett and appeared on the same bill as Christy's Minstrels in 1848.
Generational distinctions, therefore, are difficult to draw. Yet it does
seem that many minstrels in the 1840s were better acquainted with
African-American music than the delineators of the 1830s had been.
Rice was a northern newcomer to the Ohio River Valley when he first
jumped Jim Crow, while travels with the circus had taken Emmett and

Frank Brower (born in Baltimore) to Kentucky, Virginia, and South Carolina. Billy Whitlock had also toured the South, where it was reported he would "quietly steal off to some negro hut to hear the darkeys sing and see them dance, taking with him a jug of whiskey to make them all the merrier." Joel Walker Sweeney, a virtuoso blackface banjo player said to have given lessons to Whitlock, claimed he received his own lessons from a Virginia slave.[21]

White minstrelsy's renditions of black music were as cartoonish as the knock-off of "Got My Mojo Working" that every white blues band banged out in the 1960s. Yet just as the blues revival that swept American college campuses stirred in some students an interest in the genuine article, minstrelsy contributed to an appreciation, at least among a select few, of authentic African-American music. Micah Hawkins's nephew, William Sidney Mount, for instance, had an extensive collection of sheet music that included "Miss Lucy Long," and he had to remind himself in his diary, "I must fiddle less and paint more." When his ne'er-do-well brother Robert, then a dancing teacher in Georgia, sent him a sketch of a reel to "saw away on," he included the advice, "If you wish to give it the Negro-touch, you must raise the bass string one note."[22]

It may seem absurd to detect "the Negro-touch" in a semicircle of white men in calico rags and burnt cork, their painted lips leering like gashed watermelons as they laughed at their own racist jokes. But minstrelsy became increasingly complicated as it drew on and distorted black music—and even more complex as African Americans in turn took up minstrel tunes and remade them their own. Like the whirling tiger stripes in the politically incorrect children's story, *Little Black Sambo*, black and white began to blur.[23]

Shelley Fisher Fishkin, a professor of American studies at the University of Texas, made the *New York Times* when she rediscovered a sketch Mark Twain had contributed to the *Times* in 1874 that recorded his conversation with a voluble black boy. According to Fishkin's subsequent book, *Was Huck Black? Mark Twain and African-American Voices*, "Sociable Jimmy," as the lad was dubbed, reconnected the novelist to the black speech he had heard as a child, inspired the narrative voice of *Huckleberry Finn* and helped Twain "open American literature to the multicultural polyphony that is its birthright and special strength."[24]

This "multicultural polyphony" had already appeared in American music. Twain knew this full well and even dropped a hint of his awareness in the "Sociable Jimmy" article that *Was Huck Black?* overlooked. After the boy entertains Twain with his free-associating chatter, the sketch bids him good-bye with a stage direction: "[Exit, whistling 'Listen to the Mockingbird.']"[25]

"Listen to the Mocking Bird," whose refrain is still faintly familiar today, was one of Abraham Lincoln's favorite songs. The tune was composed by Richard Milburn, an African-American street musician who whistled it as he played the guitar. It caught the ear of Septimus Winner, a white songwriter, music-store proprietor, and publisher in Philadelphia, who issued the song in 1854. He listed Milburn by name as composer but concealed his own role, attributing the words and arrangement to the pseudonymous "Alice Hawthorne."[26]

"Listen to the Mocking Bird" in particular and American popular music in general are, like *Huckleberry Finn,* "[b]lack and white, white and black, all hug-em-snug together." ("Multicultural polyphony" would have been too hifalutin a phrase for Davy Crockett's ghostwriter to slip into a description of the goings-on at Five Points.) There comes a point as one tries to unravel the racial intricacies of minstrelsy when, without denying or excusing its racist insults and injustices, it seems most accurate to say, as Alain Locke, herald of the Harlem Renaissance, described jazz, another mongrel music, in 1936: "It is now part Negro, part American, part modern. . . ."[27]

Chapter Ten

PIGEON WING
AND MOONBEAMS

s the teenaged Stephen Foster groped for an identity, trying to imagine some kind of life he might lead that involved the only thing for which he'd ever displayed any aptitude or enthusiasm—music—he must have considered the alternatives. Any career in music was by definition disreputable in a society that venerated the Protestant work ethic, the virtues of practicality and profitability. Music was for women and children; men outgrew it. As anything other than a hobby, music was not just ungentlemanly, it was unmanly. Still, even within the world of music there were degrees and distinctions of unrespectability. During this indecisive period in Stephen's life, he became acquainted with two men, Henry Kleber and Dan Rice, whose contrasting careers illustrated the opportunities and the pitfalls popular culture presented. Although Stephen Foster ultimately declined to follow in either man's footsteps, both of them influenced his decision to strike out on an unprecedented path of his own.

Henry Kleber emigrated in 1832 from the German state of Darmstadt to Pittsburgh, where his father had settled a couple of years earlier. Soon he was teaching music at an exclusive girls' academy run by a Mr. Lacy. When a student eloped, however, the scandal closed the school and Kleber lost his job. Kleber was too gifted a tenor and musician to be out of work for long, though. He performed in concerts as early as 1836, and in 1839 he published a song, "Early Love Can Never Die," the first of scores of compositions. He was a church organist and led the choir. He formed the Troubadours, a male vocal quartet that included his brother Augustus, and a brass band to which, like Frank Johnson, he later added strings. He was an active member and accompanist of the Pittsburgh Philharmonic Society, a forerunner of the Pittsburgh Symphony.[1]

Kleber also gave music lessons and conducted informal *soirées musicales* at which he, pupils, and guests performed and sometimes danced. Robert McKnight, a young and wealthy Princeton-educated lawyer, described in his diary a rehearsal for one such *soirée* at the Allegheny City home of Thomas Irwin, a Foster family friend and U.S. District Court judge. A Mr. Foster—probably Morrison but possibly Stephen—was there when a Mrs. Butler tripped over an ottoman and splattered a saucer of preserves over everyone.[2]

In 1846, Kleber opened a music store to compete with John Mellor, the former partner of W. C. Peters and proprietor of the store where a toddling Stephen Foster is supposed to have tootled "Hail Columbia." Business thrived, enabling Kleber to move in 1850 to bigger quarters that he advertised as the "Sign of the Golden Harp."[3] Kleber secured the franchise to sell Steinway pianos and wrangled with Mellor over the exclusive rights to sell Chickerings. The Pittsburgh agent for the New York City firm of Firth, Pond, which would become the principal publisher of Stephen Foster's music, Kleber was also an impresario who produced concerts locally, playing host to, among others, Louis Moreau Gottschalk (a Chickering artist).

Kleber was, in sum, a Jack of all genteel trades. But he was also a tough customer: short, fiery, and irascible. Stung by a bad review in 1850, Kleber borrowed a cowhide whip from his brother Augustus and thrashed his detractor, who fled into his house and cried "Murder!" out the window. Both brothers were apprehended and released on bail. The following day, Augustus Kleber chased the critic into a dry goods store and whipped him in front of several terrified lady customers. Each brother was fined one hundred dollars, plus court costs.[4]

Kleber cut a prominent figure in Pittsburgh, although he was little known elsewhere. According to Morrison Foster, he taught Stephen Foster.[5] Familiar with the classical and religious repertories, fluent in parlor ballads and polite dances, Kleber epitomized the genteel tradition and exploited it to the fullest with entrepreneurial energy. He was welcome in all but the haughtiest homes and lived in a nice one himself, near the Fosters in Allegheny City.

The other man who influenced the young Stephen Foster contrasted dramatically with Kleber. A clown, trick-rider, and sometime blackface singer, Dan Rice was the kind of man ministers warned their congregations about. Harriet Beecher Stowe's brother, Henry Ward Beecher, could easily have had Dan Rice in mind when he inveighed against the "whole race of men, whose camp is the Theatre, the Circus, the Turf, or the Gaming-table . . . a race whose instinct is destruction, who live to corrupt, and live off of the corruption which they make."[6]

Born Daniel McLaren in New York City in 1823, he ran away from his stepfather's home at the age of thirteen, and within a year or so landed in the Pittsburgh area, where he worked as a stable boy and learned his way around horses. About 1840 he seems to have entered "the show business," enjoying his first success with an exceptionally intelligent pig named Sybil or, in one account, Lord Byron. Responding to the scarcely audible click of Rice's fingernails, the creature could curtsy, tell time, and spell words, nudging the proper letters with its snout.[7]

After the pig and he parted ways, Rice performed strongman and trick-riding routines, played Barnum's American Museum in New York, married a Pittsburgh girl, and made and lost several fortunes as America's most famous circus performer. One of his costumes, which wrapped him in red, white, and blue stripes, was purported to have inspired the caricature by Thomas Nast that to this day is our image of Uncle Sam.

Rice became friends with Morrison and Stephen Foster in the early 1840s. "We are doing a Big Business," Rice wrote Morrison from Harrisburg in 1843. He was earning twenty-five dollars a week. "I am clowning and also my nigero singing and danceing is drawing good houses."[8]

It should not be surprising that Rice's bag of tricks included blackface, for such acts were "indispensable to every circus," according to one theatrical historian, and Rice was working in the same milieu that spawned the Virginia Minstrels and many other blackface performers. Daniel McLaren may have chosen his stage name in emulation of Daddy Rice, and he appeared as an "Ethiopian Serenader" with Dan Emmett in 1845 and 1846. After all, what were Jim Crow and Sambo *but* circus clowns, in blackface rather than the whiteface traditionally associated with funnymen? Minstrels, circus performers, and actors alike traveled from town to town, without a parlor, much less the responsibility of a fixed home or conventional family, to call their own. Their fly-by-night existence was inherently illicit; their now-you-see-'em, now-you-don't appearances provided transitory thrills. They were like the Duke and the Dauphin in *Huckleberry Finn*, in which Dan Rice may make a guest appearance as the ostensibly drunken backwoodsman who staggers into the circus ring, clumsily mounts a horse and, instead of breaking his neck, astounds the credulous crowd by performing fabulous equestrian feats. (Rice's burlesques of the Bard may also have inspired Capet and Bilgewater's travesties of Shakespeare.)[9]

Stephen Foster oscillated between the alternatives Kleber and Rice embodied. Emulating either man as an entertainer was not at issue. Despite his childhood turns in the Allegheny carriage house, Foster, once past puberty, was too shy and retiring to perform publicly. "It was difficult to get him to go into society at all," Morrison wrote, echoing the recollections of his classmates at Towanda and Athens academies. Morrison continued:

> He had a great aversion to [society's] shams and glitter, and preferred the realities of his home and the quiet of his study. When he was eighteen years old, a lady who was an old friend of the family, gave a large party, and invited us all, and added, "tell Stephen to bring his flute with him." That settled it so far as he was concerned. He would not go a step. He said, "tell Mrs. — I will send my flute if she desires it." This dislike to being classed as a mere performer characterized him during his whole life. . . .[10]

What pulled Foster in two directions were the gravitational tugs of the very different musical worlds Kleber and Rice inhabited. If he were to become a songwriter, should he hearken to the genteel muse or heed the siren call of blackface? Eventually, in his greatest songs, Foster's own voice would subsume and synthesize both strains of music—and, as we have seen, E. P. Christy would nudge minstrelsy in that direction—but at the outset Foster zigzagged.

The first song Stephen Foster published, "Open Thy Lattice Love," was very much in the parlor ballad tradition. It was copyrighted by the Philadelphia publisher George Willig (who had been Frank Johnson's first publisher, too), on December 7, 1844, when Foster was eighteen.[11]

How Foster got to Willig or Willig to Foster is unknown, and so is how much, if anything, Foster was paid. Perhaps it was a vanity publication. In any event, the relationship cannot have been close: the sheet music credits *L. C. Foster.* It was an inauspicious but altogether appropriate debut for a songwriter whose most popular composition would be published under another man's name and would come to be considered nearly anonymous folk music while his own name was all but forgotten.

"Open Thy Lattice Love" sets to music lines by George P. Morris printed in the October 14, 1843, edition of *The New Mirror,* a weekly Morris coedited. Morris's fertile pen had provided lyrics for popular songs for well over a decade, and in some circles he was already becoming a bit passé. The very month "Open Thy Lattice Love" was published, a Cincinnati critic dismissed one of Morris's lyrics as "mush and milk effusion."[12] But what better exercise for a beginning songwriter than to set to music verses by the man who had written "Woodman! Spare That Tree!"

Morris's poem is a pallid serenade, inviting a young lady to open her window and her arms, and sail away with the singer on the moonlit waves of love, "whose shell for a shallop will cut the bright spray." It must have taken stronger words than these to woo away the young woman from Mr. Lacy's boarding school. The artificiality of the lyric admits no urgency. Rafts, canoes, pirogues, arks, barges, bateaux, skiffs, broadhorns, flatboats, and keelboats, not to mention steamboats, plied Pittsburgh's waters, but a "shallop"?[13]

Serenading, on the other hand, was a popular pastime, and Kleber frequently helped organize such outings. The year before Foster published "Open Thy Lattice," Charles Scully, the young man who had danced all night at Frank Johnson's charity ball, arranged with Kleber an expedition to Judge Wilkins's country estate. He met "Messrs the Serenaders" at 10:30 in the evening and headed out by carriage to Homewood, where at 11:30 they "discoursed most exquisite music." Scully didn't get to bed until four in the morning, and two weeks later he went serenading once again with "H Kleber & Co."[14]

Foster dedicated "Open Thy Lattice Love" to Susan Pentland, a next-door neighbor in Allegheny who was all of thirteen years old. Foster was beginning to creep out of his unsociable shell and to consort with a group he dubbed, in a poem dated May 6, 1845, "The Five 'Nice Young Men.'" Presumably they minded their manners, but you never know: a couple of years earlier, when an indignant mob attacked the Crow's Nest, a brothel in Pittsburgh's "Virgin Alley" that was a hothouse of interracial sex, out the back door with the whores and the madam flew what one newspaper described as "a few 'nice young men' . . . The besieged thus effected a retreat with flying *colors*."[15]

The "Nice Young Men" in Stephen Foster's poem were Charles P. Shiras, Charles Rahm, Andrew L. Robinson, Robert P. McDowell, and J. Harvey Davis. If the verses seem sophomoric, remember that Foster was a sophomore's age: nineteen.

> First, there's Charley the elder, the Sunday-school teacher,
>   Who laughs with a groan,
>   In an unearthly tone,
>   Without moving a bone
>   Or a feature
>
> Then Charley the younger, the Illinois "screecher,"
>   Who never gets mad,
>   But always seems glad
>   While others are sad;
>   Though his face is so long that it wouldn't look bad
>   On a methodist preacher.[16]

And so on.

In his memoir, Morrison Foster recalled somewhat differently the young men with whom Stephen began to share his interest in music in 1845. He omitted both Charleys and added J. Cust Blair and himself. But the roll call of the group matters less than the role it played as an audience and chorus for Stephen Foster's first blackface compositions and his own "beautiful though not robustious baritone." Morrison says that the men met twice a week in the Foster home to sing songs in harmony under Stephen's leadership:

> At that time negro melodies were very popular. After we had sung over and over again all the songs then in favor, he proposed that he would try and make some for us himself.

His first attempt, Morrison says, was "Lou'siana Belle," and a week later he came up with "Uncle Ned."[17] Especially since "Lou'siana Belle" was the first of Foster's blackface songs actually to be published, a couple of years later, there's little reason to doubt this was indeed Foster's first original attempt at "nigero singing," Dan Rice–style.

"Lou'siana Belle" dances to the 2/4 beat of the spanking new polka, which had taken nearly a decade to wend its way from Prague to Paris and beyond, arriving in the United States in 1844. Today it's difficult to imagine this oom-pah rhythm as an inducement to debauchery, but it appalled George Templeton Strong, the New York City diarist, when he first heard it in 1845. "It's a kind of insane Tartar jig," he harrumphed, "performed to disagreeable music of an uncivilized character. . . ."[18] Since no one, in the popular white imagination, was more uncivilized than Negroes, the polka was quickly appropriated by blackface composers and performers, even though its unsyncopated beat bore little relation to actual African-American rhythms.

While only a twentieth-century Freudian would interpret "Open Thy Lattice Love" as an invitation to spread one's legs,[19] the carnality of "Lou'siana Belle" was unmistakable even way back when:

> Lousiana's de same old state,
> Whar Massa us'd to dwell;
> He had a lubly cullud gal.
> 'Twas the Lousiana Belle.

The chorus implores:

> Oh! Belle don't you tell,
> Don't tell Massa, don't you Belle,
> Oh! Belle, de Lou'siana Belle,
> I's gwine to marry you
> Lou'siana Belle.

It's impossible to parse fully the sexual and racial politics of these lines. On the one hand, the blackface voice allowed Stephen Foster a license he could not have enjoyed as a nice (white) young man—a license that was racist insofar as he probably would not have dared address a white woman with such free-and-easy familiarity. On the other hand, the lyric implicitly criticizes a white master's presumption of owning a black mistress. A manuscript version of the song in Foster's hand explicitly criticizes slavery in terms reminiscent of "Lucy Neal": "My masa took my lub one day, / He put her up to sell, / I thought I'd pine my life away, / For de Lousiana belle."[20]

Just what were the young men thinking as they sang the chorus in four-part harmony at the Fosters' house? I don't think they—and this includes Stephen Foster—were thinking much at all, which is one reason "Lou'siana Belle" enjoyed little success when it was published in 1847. Like college kids who hired the Temptations and other black groups to perform at campus concerts in the 1960s while their fraternities still excluded blacks, like Republican political consultant and attack dog Lee Atwater, who played rhythm-and-blues guitar in the 1970s and 1980s while race-baiting Democratic candidates, Stephen Foster and his friends sang blackface because it was popular, because it was "cool," and because it offered a freedom that white middle-class culture couldn't furnish. But they seldom wondered what it meant or implied.

"Lou'siana Belle" bears out this thoughtlessness by stringing together, with little concern for continuity or development, catch-phrases from earlier blackface songs. The second verse introduces the "pigeon wing," a dance step originally popular among plantation slaves. (In the 1930s, a descendant of these slaves described the dance as "flippin' yo' arms an' legs roun' an' holdin' ya neck stiff like a bird do.")[21]

The third verse of "Lou'siana Belle" invokes "Dandy Jim ob Caroline," a farcical role Daddy Rice created after his return from England in 1836. The song, "Dandy Jim from Caroline," became so successful that its melody was adapted to a Whig campaign song and an abolitionist anthem. "Dandy Jim" proved exceptionally long-lived, making a comeback as the hero of LaVern Baker's 1957 rhythm-and-blues hit, "Jim Dandy." In a sense, Stephen Foster was doing exactly what Larry Williams, the valet for R&B singer Lloyd Price, would do more than a century later. In 1958, Williams stitched together names and phrases from recent R&B hits to fashion a hit of his own, "Short Fat Fannie." Amid the crazy quilt of "Long Tall Sally," "Tutti Frutti," "Blueberry Hill," "Blue Suede Shoes," and "Heartbreak Hotel," Williams featured prominently, in the chorus, LaVern Baker's "Jim Dandy."[22]

"Uncle Ned"—or "Old Uncle Ned" as it is also known—was a more consequential composition:

> Dere was an old Nigga, dey call'd him Uncle Ned
> He's dead long ago, long ago!

He had no wool on de top ob his head
De place whar de wool ought to grow.
Den lay down de shubble and de hoe
Hang up de fiddle and de bow
No more hard work for poor old Ned
He's gone whar de good Niggas go.

Like "Lou'siana Belle," "Uncle Ned" echoed earlier songs. There's more than a hint of Bayly's "Long, Long Ago" and of Henry Russell in its nostalgia, and the song draws specifically from Dan Emmett's parody of Russell, "The Fine Old Colored Gentleman." "The wool all dropt off from his head," Emmett wrote of the aging Sambo, and when

> . . . his teeth dropt out,
> it made no odds to him,
> He eat as many taters
> and he drank as many gin.[23]

Another possible inspiration was "Old Joe," published in 1844 by Emmett's fellow Virginia Minstrel, Frank Brower. After Old Joe "got done work an flung down de hoe," he strummed on "de ole banjo" and died of drink.[24]

But Foster's "Old Ned" is softened, sentimentalized. Emmett was spinning a tall tale and retailing racism. Uncle Ned's demise is more domesticated, an indoors instead of a backwoods affair:

> . . . Massa take it mighty bad,
> De tears run down like de rain;
> Old missus turn pale, and she gets berry sad
> Cayse she nebber see Old Ned again.

Even Frederick Douglass gave "Uncle Ned" his stamp of approval. "It would seem almost absurd to say it," he told the Rochester (New York) Ladies' Anti-Slavery Society in 1855,

considering the use that has been made of them, that we have allies in the Ethiopian songs. . . . "Lucy Neal," "Old Kentucky Home," and "Uncle Ned," can make the heart sad as well as merry, and can call forth a tear as well as a smile. They awaken the sympathies for the slave, in which anti-slavery principles take root and flourish.[25]

Martin Delany, on the other hand, was contemptuous and stood the song on its head in his novel, *Blake*. Delany's parody, which declines to mimic the degrading dialect of blackface, is a summons to insurrection. This time, it's massa who has died:

> He will no more tramp on the neck of the slave,
> For he's gone where the slaveholders go!
> Hang up the shovel and the hoe—o—o—o!
> I don't care whether I work or no!
> Old master's gone to the slaveholders rest—
> He's gone where they all ought to go! [26]

Sometimes it's a thin line between mourning and murder. One modern analyst of blackface and Foster has speculated that the appalling frequency with which black people die in Foster's songs—Uncle Ned is only the first of many victims—expressed a frustrated wish that African Americans simply disappear. This, after all, was the fervent desire of the colonization societies that campaigned to send blacks back to Africa. Abraham Lincoln sympathized with this movement, and so did many abolitionists, including Harriet Beecher Stowe. ("The truth is, dear madam," Frederick Douglass rejoined, "we are *here*, & here we are likely to remain.") [27]

Like most white Americans before the Civil War, Stephen Foster disapproved of abolitionists, but that does not mean he defended slavery. His pusillanimity was typically Pennsylvanian, if you credit John Updike's characterization of his native state's "mild misty doughy middleness, between immoderate norths and souths." Stephen was too preoccupied with his music to be engaged politically, as well as too rejecting of his father—where had politics ever gotten *him?* To the extent that he was political at all, Stephen was a so-called doughface Democrat like his in-law James Buchanan, supporting the Union above all and any compromises necessary to preserve it. Doubtless from this perspective the ideal preservative, and the surest solution to the nation's racial problem, would have been the elimination—by extinction, expulsion or magic— of the black race. Unquestionably, such wishful thinking translated into tolerating if not toadying to slavery—what Harriet Beecher Stowe belittled as "bearing everything in silence & stroking & saying 'pussy pussy' —so as to allay all prejudice & avoid all agitation." [28]

Yet it is undeniable that already, in what was probably only his second try at a blackface song, Stephen Foster was portraying African Americans more compassionately than most of his blackface predecessors. The moderate tempo, marked *andantino* when first published in 1848, is respectful. The way the first line of each verse crawls up the scale in halting, chromatic half-steps, only to fall abruptly at the end, reflects the hard labor of Uncle Ned's life and the finality of his death. The chorus's solo line for bass voice ("Den lay down de shubble and de hoe"), followed by four-part harmony ("Hang up de fiddle and de bow"), parallels the call-and-response of actual African-American music.

But "Old Uncle Ned" is as fantastical in its own fashion as "Open Thy Lattice Love" and its "shell for a shallop." As Morrison Foster would point out, when Stephen wrote that Uncle Ned's "fingers were long like de cane in de brake," he "had never seen a canebrake, nor even been below the mouth of the Ohio river."[29] Both the plantation and the moonlit sea were flights of fancy from grimy Pittsburgh and the grim future the Fosters faced there.

Chapter Eleven

PITTSBURGH
IN RUINS

*P*ittsburgh was grimier than ever after a horrendous fire swept through it on April 10, 1845. Like the great Chicago fire of 1871, it was blamed on an Irishwoman—in this case a laundress who had kindled a fire to heat her wash water—and it was almost as devastating, destroying roughly a third of the city and two-thirds of its wealth as it raged uncontrollably from noon until after dark. Only two lives but more than a thousand buildings were lost, leaving twelve thousand people homeless and an estimated $9 million in damages. A local artist, William Coventry Wall, painted two views of the still-smoking ruins in which Pittsburgh looks like Hamburg or Dresden after the Allies' incendiary bombings in World War II.[1]

According to one of their contemporaries, Morrison and Stephen Foster helped fight the flames, and Morrison saved the books from his employer's Pittsburgh warehouse before the building and thousands of pounds of cotton went up in smoke. Because it was just across the river in Allegheny City, Pollard McCormick's Hope Cotton Factory, where the cotton stored in Pittsburgh was converted to yarn and batting, was spared.[2]

The local disaster was a national news story, and accounts in the Pittsburgh papers were widely reprinted. One report that thus gained greater circulation, headlined "PITTSBURGH IN RUINS!!!," was Martin Delany's in the *Mystery*, the weekly news sheet he launched in 1843 and edited for nearly five years. For much of this time it was the only African-American newspaper in the United States. Despite its defiant Afro-centrism—the paper's initial motto was "And Moses was Learned in All the Wisdom of the Egyptians"—the *Mystery* and its editor were highly regarded by many whites, and Pittsburgh's mayor appointed Delany to the city's relief committee after the fire.[3]

Stephen Foster took a menial job in one of McCormick's warehouses. On September 15, the very day he wrote his sister Ann Eliza about his employment, an estimated five thousand working women—factory girls, their families, and friends—gathered in Allegheny City to strike for a ten-hour day in the cotton mills. They failed to dent the mill owners' united front, however, and within a few months returned to grueling twelve-hour shifts.[4]

Stephen Foster was coming of age smack-dab in the middle of the Industrial Revolution, amid the pitched class conflicts it engendered. And the precariousness of his own family's finances threatened to plunge Stephen, at any moment, into the belly of the beast. After his second year-long term as mayor of Allegheny City, William Foster, now sixty-five, found meager employment. An 1844 directory listed him as "weigh master, Chislett's row."[5]

Brother William had remarried in 1842, taking as his second wife a young widow named Elizabeth Smith Burnett. He became one of Pennsylvania's three canal commissioners in 1843, but failed to win reelection in 1846, when a Whig landslide swept the state. Recognizing that railways would soon render canals obsolete, he signed on as an associate engineer under J. Edgar Thomson with the Pennsylvania Railroad Company, which had recently received a state charter to connect Philadelphia to Pittsburgh by rail. He hitched his wagon to a star in Thomson, who would become a great railroad executive, a remarkable innovator in capital finance and a mentor to Andrew Carnegie. But as Brother William supervised the cutting and blasting of a rail-bed from Harrisburg to Hollidaysburg, his future was not yet assured.[6]

Morrison Foster was assuming greater responsibilities for Pollard McCormick and making longer business trips while Dunning Foster, on the other hand, left the river for the docks. He formed a partnership in Cincinnati with Archibald Irwin, Jr., whose father had moved from

Pittsburgh to Cincinnati in the 1820s. Located at 4 Cassilly's Row—the Cassillys had been Eliza Foster's hosts when she visited Cincinnati with Henrietta and Stephen in 1833—Irwin & Foster was a commission merchant firm that arranged the shipment of cotton and other goods, juggling timetables and rates to broker the best deal.[7]

In the meantime, Henry Foster's clerkship in the Treasury Department was leading nowhere. He thought about leaving his post to Stephen as his father had left it to him. Stephen toyed with the idea and also with the notion of attending West Point. Concerned about his youngest brother's lack of prospects, Henry tried unsuccessfully to wangle him an appointment to the military academy. Stephen was probably no more serious about the army than he had been about the navy five years earlier. "Tell Steve not to be discouraged," Henry wrote Morrison, "& try & get at some employment as soon as possible." But there is no evidence Henry's failure disappointed Stephen.[8]

The declaration of war against Mexico in May doubtless added to the family's anxiety about its future. Dunning and Morrison enlisted, although only Dunning was called to active duty. The patriotic fervor was hard to resist. When news of General Zachary Taylor's first victories reached Cincinnati, twelve thousand people thronged the riverfront to cheer old "Rough and Ready." In Pittsburgh, factory girls flirted with the volunteers, and the choir sang "Gird on Your Armor" at a church service bidding them farewell. As steamboats carried the troops down the Ohio and then the Mississippi, they were huzzahed by crowds on the riverbanks while ladies waved their handkerchiefs from windows and rooftops.[9] None of these blandishments rekindled Stephen's interest in a military career, however. The prospect of combat apparently squelched it forever.

A career in music was infinitely more appealing but scarcely more imaginable. Ann Eliza Buchanan asked Stephen to compose some organ music, presumably for her husband's new church in Paradise, Pennsylvania, where James Buchanan soon bought them a home. Writing "amidst the bustle of the Hope warehouse," Stephen Foster declined, protesting that "as I have no knowledge of that instrument I have thought it advisable not to explore my ignorance."[10]

In April 1846, Stephen and his friend Charles Shiras, "the Sunday-school teacher, who laughs with a groan," attended a concert by William Dempster, a Scottish composer and singer whose sentimental ballads, one critic observed, went "to the heart, if not by way of the head." In addition to songs by Henry Russell and others, Dempster performed his own "popular cantata," *The May Queen*, set to verses by Tennyson. The piece's three parts represented, according to one review, "the gradual decay of a young and beautiful Girl, from the bloom of health to a premature grave." *The May Queen* may or may not have reminded Stephen Foster of the death of his sister Charlotte, but it certainly brought tears to his eyes. According to Morrison, they often "could be seen on his cheeks" when he played or sang Dempster's song suite. It inspired not only Stephen but Charles Shiras to compose additional stanzas of their own.[11]

Foster and Shiras were not the only ones moved by *The May Queen*. The Hutchinsons added it to their repertory at about the same time they introduced their version of "There's a Good Time Coming," a Henry Russell song that Stephen Foster adapted, too. Charles Mackay, a Scottish poet and historian, wrote "There's a Good Time Coming" as well as the words to many other Russell songs. (Over several bottles of wine he once confessed to Nathaniel Hawthorne that he found it "excruciating" to hear them sung.) Mackay's "good time" was the near future to which good liberals, secure in their belief in the perfectibility of man and the onward-and-upward progress of society, looked forward with confidence. Russell, for all his affection for everything old, shared that faith in an egalitarian tomorrow, when the "pen shall supersede the sword, / And right, not might, shall be the lord"; when "Worth, not birth, shall rule mankind."[12]

The Hutchinsons had recently returned from a voyage to England during which they entertained Frederick Douglass, denied a first-class cabin because of his color, on Cunard's "rude forecastle deck." To them, "the good time" meant emancipation and, most likely, prohibition. Once, when they were performing in New York City, Henry Clay, a spirited drinker, offered the Hutchinsons wine. The teetotalers refused and launched into "There's a Good Time Coming."[13]

But Mackay's words meant little to Stephen Foster. He was too apolitical by temperament to care that one day "Shameful rivalries of creed / Shall not make the martyr bleed," yet not so antiwar on principle that he could agree that "Cannon balls may aid the truth, / But thought's a weapon stronger"—especially when two of his brothers were gung-ho to march into Mexico. To Foster, the developing songwriter, "There's a Good Time Coming" offered instead an exercise and a challenge: to compete with Russell and possibly with the Hutchinsons, too. (Foster may not have known their setting, which was published the same year as his.) Lyrics be damned. Foster indicated as much by punctuating them with piano passages pretentiously marked "Ritournelle Boiteuse" and "en boiteux"—*boiteux* meaning halting, lame, or limping. The song's initial direction is "Pia e scherzando"—playful or joking. While the Hutchinsons' "Good Time" is a straightforward activist anthem, Foster's version seems to mock the march of progress, or at least interrupts its advance, with florid filigree.[14]

Foster's "There's a Good Time Coming" was published in Cincinnati in October 1846 by W. C. Peters, and dedicated to Mary Keller, the daughter of family friends of the Fosters. When she died shortly thereafter, Foster composed a lovely ballad entitled "Where Is Thy Spirit Mary?" Rendering in elaborate calligraphic curlicues and flourishes the title, his own name, and a dedication, "to the memory of Mary Keller," he presented the song, which wasn't published until 1895, to Mary's sister, Rachel.

Stephen Foster was not the only young man who fell under the Keller sisters' spell. They bewitched Charles Scully when he accompanied them back to Pittsburgh from a "fete champetre" at Judge Wilkins's Homewood. In his diary, he recorded that they had

> excellent taste in music & sang duetts the whole way in. Some were exquisite; we had a bright moon & fields & gardens shone out beautifully; which heightened the effect of the Music; 'twas so good that "methought" the orange lily & the poppy lifted up their drooping heads to peer at our sweet minstrels, the "morning glory" opened up to listen to these well according voices, to which also the young & springing corn did not turn a "deaf ear"; affectation aside it was *very* good.

The Keller sisters were so enchanting that Scully had to eat oily sardines to dispel their charm.[15]

How did "There's a Good Time Coming" get to Peters? Years later the publisher told a Cincinnati journalist that Foster's music had been brought to his attention by a Mr. Blancnagiel of Louisville, where Peters had a second music store. Blancnagiel, according to Peters, had heard Foster "at some musical soiree in Pittsburgh." Foster's early songs circulated haphazardly. He sang them among friends; he gave manuscript copies to some of them and to a few performers as well. Any one of these could have brought "Good Time" to Peters. Maybe it was Dunning Foster, newly established in Cincinnati; Peters's music store was just six blocks from Irwin & Foster. In any event, it had not yet occurred to Stephen Foster that he could make money from his music.[16]

Which is why, sometime at the close of 1846 or the very beginning of 1847, he moved to Cincinnati, took a room at the boarding house run by Mrs. Jane Griffin, and reported to work as a bookkeeper for Irwin & Foster. He was a twenty-year-old college dropout (having lasted less than a week at Jefferson College) whose only job had been briefly pushing a broom or toting bales at a warehouse. He was a drag on a family struggling to keep financially afloat. It was time to earn a living and unlikely that anyone would offer him higher wages than his own brother. The path of least resistance led 470 miles downstream.

Chapter Twelve

HOG HEAVEN

*W*hen Charles Dickens unpacked his bags in Cincinnati after arriving there from Pittsburgh, he looked out his hotel window and saw in the street a "black man talking (confidentially) to a pig." Cincinnati, wrote another English traveler,

> is in fact what its nickname, "Porkopolis," implies—the Empire City of Pigs, as well as of the West; but it is fortunate that they condescendingly allow human beings to share that truly magnificent location with them.[1]

Slaughtering an average of 375,000 porkers a year, Cincinnati was "Hog Butcher for the World" long before Carl Sandburg apostrophized Chicago. By the time Stephen Foster arrived, the city had diversified. It was "the great whisky mart of the world," and rivaled Pittsburgh in shipbuilding and iron and engine manufacturing. Its population more than doubled in the 1840s, to 115,435—almost twice the size of Pittsburgh, including Allegheny City—and nearly as many workers toiled in its shops and factories as in Pittsburgh, Louisville, St. Louis, and Chicago combined. Its thriving clothing industry was run mostly by German Jews who had graduated from the rag trade to readymade. Dan Emmett's very first blackface song, "Bill Crowder," written while he was working as a printer in Cincinnati in the late 1830s, recounted a brawl with "a Jew sellin close by de poun." There were more Jews (3,346 in 1850), more African Americans (3,237), more Germans (over 30,000), more of just about *everything* in Cincinnati than Stephen Foster had encountered in Pittsburgh.[2]

There was also more turbulence, for racial tensions were more acute. African Americans had never enjoyed the right to vote in Ohio. The state's constitution made sure of that. "Prejudice against the negro attains its rankest luxuriance not in the rice-swamps of Georgia, nor the sugar fields of Louisiana," noted one abolitionist, "but upon the prairies of Ohio." While theaters in Pittsburgh reserved segregated seating for black patrons, one Cincinnati establishment reportedly advertised, "Niggers and dogs not admitted." In contrast to Pittsburgh, white riots often occurred in Cincinnati with the acquiescence, and sometimes the complicity, of city officials.[3]

Race wasn't the only reason residents rioted. When the banks didn't open one morning in 1842, a mob sacked them and fought the militia to a bloody draw. A year after Foster arrived, Cincinnatians stormed the jail in an attempt to lynch two men accused of rape; although the accusation turned out to be false, the bullets that claimed eleven rioters' lives were all too real.[4]

The city was also more beautiful than Pittsburgh. Pigs and Mrs. Trollope's by now antique aspersions notwithstanding, other English visitors found it a comely metropolis-in-the-making. Dickens was charmed by Cincinnati's "clean houses of red and white, its well-paved roads, and footways of bright tile."[5]

Still, East Front Street, where the firm of Irwin & Foster was initially located (in 1849 it would move a couple of blocks away from the river, to 22 Broadway, between Front and Second Streets), was anything but well paved. It ran alongside the river from the Public Landing to the eastern edge of town and was heavily rutted by regular traffic and irregular floods. Contributing to commerce but not to comfort, railroad tracks ran along part of the street, making it even bumpier. The Cincinnati *Daily Enquirer* complained that the city was neglecting this "street of mountain and morass" and charged there was "scarcely a worse strip of road in any of the back settlements, and certainly none where as many teamsters are mired and broken."[6]

In the summer of 1848, the daguerreotype studio of Charles Fontayne and W. S. Porter fashioned a remarkable panorama of the Cincinnati riverfront, consisting of eight sequential daguerreotypes taken from Newport, Kentucky, on the opposite bank of the Ohio. The onion dome of Mrs. Trollope's abandoned bazaar peeps over the horizon. In the foreground, nearly as far as the waterfront stretches, are docked seventeen steamboats—striking testimony to Cincinnati's commercial prosperity. Painted signs on the storefront facades advertise tarpaulins, tin, copper and sheet iron, ship chandlery and boat stores, lard oil and commission merchants like Irwin & Foster on Cassilly's Row—a long block of four-story buildings with intermittent awnings shading their entrances.[7]

When Stephen Foster looked out the front windows of Irwin & Foster, he could see the steamboats his firm represented: packets like the *Messenger* and the *Monongahela* that steamed to Pittsburgh and boats bound downriver to St. Louis, Memphis, and New Orleans. He conscientiously accounted for every bill of lading—his ledgers, his brother Morrison would write, were "models of neatness and accuracy." Perhaps Brother William had acceded to his request years earlier that he be allowed to study bookkeeping at Athens Academy. But if his mind and eye wandered past the twin stacks and side-wheels of the steamers, across the river he saw Kentucky, a slave state.[8]

The Ohio River was the major thoroughfare for America's expansion westward. Walt Whitman paid tribute to its centrality when he predicted that eventually "the dominion-heart of America will be far inland, toward the West," and "the main social, political, spine-character of the States will probably run along the Ohio, Missouri, and Mississippi rivers."[9]

In addition to bridging East and West, the Ohio River both united and divided North and South. How great that division could be is dramatized in a painting by Robert Scott Duncanson, one of America's first noteworthy black painters. Early in his career, Duncanson had a studio on Cincinnati's Fourth Street, and one of his first patrons, Charles Avery, a wealthy businessman, Methodist minister, and ardent abolitionist, lived close by the Fosters in Allegheny City and also encouraged Martin Delany. Duncanson's *View of Cincinnati from Covington, Kentucky*, painted around 1850, shows the same bustling riverfront Fontayne and Porter's daguerreotypes depicted a couple of years earlier. That's not surprising, since Duncanson was working from an anonymous daguerreotype published the same year, 1848. But the painting takes significant liberties

with this daguerreotype, in which all of the figures in the foreground—
that is to say, in Kentucky—are white. Duncanson turned a white man,
leaning on a rifle and apparently directing two children, into a black
man with a scythe who seems to be waiting on them. The woman
hanging wash on the line by a rustic cabin is changed from white to
black. This, Duncanson seems to be saying, is the difference between
Kentucky and Ohio. On one side of the river is rural poverty, slavery and
the past; on the other side is urban enterprise, freedom and the future.[10]

Cincinnati was a major hub on the Underground Railroad for fugitives
crossing the Ohio River from Kentucky or traveling upriver from points
farther south. Long before she dramatized the inner workings and hair's-
breadth escapes of this clandestine network in *Uncle Tom's Cabin*, Harriet
Beecher Stowe acquired some experience of it firsthand. Several months
after the Stowes hired a black serving woman, they learned that a man
from Kentucky was looking for her, claiming that she was his escaped
slave. To insure the woman's freedom, Harriet's husband and brother,
Calvin Stowe and Henry Ward Beecher, armed themselves and escorted
her by back roads to a stop on the Underground Railroad and safety
farther north.[11]

Ironically, many slave owners visited Cincinnati to enjoy its relative
racial freedom. Planters would leave their wives behind and take their
concubines to Ohio, sometimes installing their mixed-race families in
the Dumas House or another black hotel. Some sent their illegitimate
offspring to Cincinnati to be educated at Gilmore High School, a private
academy for blacks founded by an English clergyman. Out-of-towners
were not the only ones who crossed racial lines. Cincinnati was a hotbed
of amalgamation, judging from the 1850 census, which classified 60 percent of the city's African-American population as mulatto. The only
other American cities in which persons of mixed race outnumbered
those categorized as black were deep Southern ports like New Orleans.
Light-skinned African Americans like Robert Duncanson, great-
grandson of a Virginia planter, felt at home in Cincinnati, and the city
was so identified with what had not yet been named miscegenation that
a sailors' song, "Shallo Brown," forswore darker women for "a bright
mulatto, she's from Cincinnati." Yet even as the city ignored racial restrictions, it sought to enforce them: As late as New Year's Eve 1861,
Ohio passed a law "to prevent the amalgamation of the white and colored
races." The frequent flouting of taboos seems to have aggravated rather

than eased racial antagonism in Cincinnati. Amalgamation was more of an abstraction in Pittsburgh, where it was relatively easy to be an abolitionist (if not for the Fosters, for many of their friends and neighbors) because slavery was far away and African Americans were comparatively few.[12]

Stephen Foster had more opportunities to hear genuine black music in Cincinnati, both because of the greater number of African Americans there and because his new job brought him farther down the river and closer to its edge. Roughly 20 percent of the Cincinnatians in the "colored" section of a city directory from the 1840s were listed as "following the river" or working as steamboat stewards or cooks. Whether they toiled on the deck, in the galley, or down below in the engine room, blacks working on steamboats and sailing vessels enjoyed more mobility than most African Americans. Along with cotton and passengers and gossip, they conveyed music from town to town, and the first fellow blacks to hear that music were often stevedores like the ones on the docks within earshot of Irwin & Foster.[13]

In 1850, a Swedish traveler, Fredrika Bremer, went below-decks on a steamboat on the Ohio River and listened to the singing of the black men, stripped to the waist in the lurid heat, who stoked the boilers:

> ... the negro up aloft on the pile of fire-wood began immediately an improvised song in stanzas, and at the close of each the negroes down below joined in vigorous chorus. It was a fantastic and grand sight to see these energetic athletes lit up by the wildly flashing flames ... while they, amid their equally fantastic song, keeping time most exquisitely, hurled one piece of fire-wood after another into the yawning fiery gulf.[14]

Three years later, Frederick Law Olmsted, who would afterward win fame as the designer of New York's Central Park, described his departure from New Orleans aboard the *St. Charles*. The steamboat's forecastle was piled high with freight, on top of which stood a dozen black boathands who "began to sing, waving hats and handkerchiefs, and shirts lashed to poles, towards the people who stood on the sterns of the steam-boats at the levee." According to Olmsted's notebook, their song went:

> Ye see dem boat way dah ahead.
> Chorus.—Oahoiohieu.

De San Charles is arter 'em, dey mus go behine.
　Cho.—Oahoiohieu.
So stir up dah, my livelies, stir her up;
　(pointing to the furnaces).
　Cho.—Oahoiohieu.
Dey's burnin' not'n but fat and rosum.
　Cho.—Oahoiohieu.
Oh, we is gwine up de Red River, oh!
　Cho.—Oahoiohieu.[15]

Stephen Foster heard and absorbed songs such as this on East Front Street, and he would echo them in his own music. Martin Delany, no friend of Foster or of blackface, confirmed the authenticity of Foster's sources and his fidelity to them when, in *Blake*, he painted a scene much like the one Olmsted had depicted. Delany described the enslaved boatmen on the New Orleans levee as "men of sorrow" who, "reconciling themselves to a lifelong misery," were "seemingly contented by soothing their sorrows with songs and sentiments of apparently cheerful but in reality wailing lamentations." The first song they sang, led by one "poor fellow in pitiful tones," began:

　　Way down upon the Mobile river,
　　　Close to Mobile bay;
　　There's where my thoughts is running ever,
　　　All through the livelong day. . . .[16]

The tune, of course, is that of Foster's "Old Folks at Home," and the lyrics, too transparently and unironically imitative to be a parody, are almost Foster's, too.

Delany's and Foster's paths nearly crossed several times. Perhaps they did in a Pittsburgh dentist's office, where, Charles Scully noted in his diary, "Mr. Martin Delaney (a black nig) agt. of Dr. Fundenburg inserted a plug in one of my front teeth in apparently a very skillful manner."[17]

Not long after Foster left for Cincinnati, in August 1847, William Lloyd Garrison and Frederick Douglass came to Pittsburgh, barnstorming for the abolitionist cause. Among the men who greeted them was Delany, whom Garrison described in a letter to his wife as "black as jet, and a fine fellow of great energy and spirit." Delany accompanied Garrison to

New Brighton, Pennsylvania, where Foster's good friend Charles Shiras joined Garrison for a hike in the hills outside town.

Garrison and Douglass inspired Shiras to start up a newspaper and Delany to abandon his. The Nice Young Man launched the *Albatross,* a crusading abolitionist journal. It was short-lived, closing down after only three months, but Shiras's zeal was longer-lasting. In 1852 he would publish a volume of antislavery and anticapitalist verse, *The Redemption of Labor.* Delany, in the meantime, was so captivated by Douglass and his plans for an African-American abolitionist organ that he dropped the *Mystery* and hit the road to drum up subscribers for *The North Star.* When the paper first saw print in December 1847, its masthead listed Delany as coeditor with Douglass.[18]

Delany's travels took him all over Ohio. In the small town of Marseilles, his lecture was disrupted by a man who denounced it as "a *darkey* burlesque." Delany and a companion fled to their hotel, where they were besieged by a mob that reinforced the minstrel-show metaphor by making a racket with a tambourine, fiddle, jaw-bone, castanets, and other instruments. When they made their escape at daybreak, their horse and buggy were pelted with stones.[19]

When Delany gave several lectures in Cincinnati in May 1848, the *Daily Enquirer* initially welcomed the "ebony gentleman" as a "second Daniel come to judgment." Three days later, however, the newspaper shifted 180 degrees and deplored Delany's appeal to "the morbid appetites of negro loving and country hating *patriots.*" How could white men "set calmly and approvingly by, and hear their race and country maligned by even a *'colored gentleman'* "?[20]

What instigated this outrage was as much (if not more) Delany's vehement opposition to the Mexican War as his opposition to slavery. If by any chance Stephen Foster was in the audience at one of Delany's lectures, he probably shared the *Enquirer*'s disgust, because his brother Dunning had not yet returned from military service, and Stephen himself commemorated America's victory with his first published instrumental work, "Santa Anna's Retreat from Buena Vista," a sprightly quickstep for piano "as performed by the military bands."

It's more likely that Stephen Foster went to the circus than to one of the churches where Delany held forth. A circus was nearly always in town and, in April 1848, just before P. T. Barnum arrived with General Tom Thumb in tow, the circus in Cincinnati headlined Dan Rice. He had recently appeared in an "Original Burlesque, entitled the Battle of Buena Vista, or Dan Rice in Mexico," and Zachary Taylor himself had taken in a performance.[21]

"Santa Anna's Retreat from Buena Vista" joined the crowded ranks of "General Taylor's Encampment Quickstep," "The Rio Grande Quick March," "The Mexican Volunteer's Quickstep," and the "Rough and Ready Polka." Foster's own publisher, William Peters, composed the "Matamoros Grand March" and "Santa Anna's March to which is added a Popular Melody composed on the Battle Field of Buena Vista by an American Officer." There was even an entire *Rough and Ready Songster*.

The Mexican War was declared, waged, and won to musical accompaniment. When New Yorkers celebrated the declaration of war at a mass meeting, they sang a new "national anthem" composed by none other than George Pope Morris. On the eve of the Battle of Buena Vista, Santa Anna's band serenaded the American volunteers as well as the Mexican troops. As Winfield Scott's army landed at Vera Cruz, regimental bands aboard the troop ships played "Yankee Doodle" and "Hail Columbia." When the soldiers emerged from the surf and waved Old Glory on the beach, the offshore orchestra saluted with "The Star-Spangled Banner." In the camps, men danced breakdowns, did the pigeon wing, and blacked up to perform minstrel songs.[22]

The United States was exploding with patriotism and, at the same time, seething with racial tension. Americans were thrown together, and exposed to each other, as never before by improved transportation and communication and the Mexican War (as well as, a year later, by the California gold rush). Yet they were divided more deeply and dangerously than ever before by race and competing economic imperatives. East and West, North and South, black and white converged and collided in Cincinnati. It was at this crucial juncture that Stephen Foster wrote a new national anthem that has lasted far longer than Morris's and far longer than the bookkeeper on East Front Street could ever have dreamed.

Chapter Thirteen

ICE CREAM AND THE
ANNIHILATION OF
TIME AND SPACE

*O*n March 1847, there began to appear in *The Pittsburgh Daily Gazette and Advertiser,* amid news "By Magnetic Telegraph" of the Mexican War, an advertisement for the imminent opening of a new, improved Eagle Ice Cream Saloon. "A large amount of money has been expended," the proprietor, a Mr. Andrews, promised, "in order to make the Saloon the most attractive and pleasant place of resort in the western country, for the approaching season." [1]

In August 1847, Andrews advertised "Musical Entertainment Extraordinary!" plus a dish of ice cream for just twenty-five cents. The program, which changed every evening, featured "the highly gifted vocalists, Mrs. Sharpe and Miss Clara Bruce, from the Metropolitan Concerts," under the musical direction of "Mr. Kneass, whose versatile talent has rendered him a favorite wherever known." [2]

Nelson Kneass, who was Mrs. Sharpe's husband and Miss Bruce's brother-in-law (the ladies were sisters), was a musical magpie. He had made his stage debut at the age of five, in *Richard III* in Philadelphia, and by the time he turned eleven he was performing in New York. A jack of all theatrical trades, he acted, he played piano and banjo, he sang opera straight and burlesqued it in blackface. [3]

In 1846 Kneass went west, performing in Pittsburgh and Cincinnati with the Sable Harmonists. He became an on-again, off-again member of this all-male minstrel group, which specialized in opera parodies. As musical director at the Eagle Ice Cream Saloon, he hired some of the Harmonists and then engaged family and friends from New York, including the tenor George Holman and Holman's wife, Harriet Phillips. The Kneass Opera Troupe, as they called themselves when they performed in Cincinnati subsequently, was considerably tonier than a minstrel group like Christy's or the Sable Harmonists. Like Kneass, Holman and his wife had sung legitimate opera. Three members of the closely knit group were women; Kneass accompanied them on piano rather than banjo, and it's unclear how much, if any, of their repertory was performed in blackface. Their Pittsburgh programs were a hodgepodge of opera, operatic burlesques, and "Ethiopian Refranes and Extravaganzas."[4]

Soon the Eagle Saloon was "crowded with fashionable audiences," according to *The Pittsburgh Daily Gazette*. "To make the entertainment more interesting," the *Gazette* announced, Mr. Andrews, "the enterprising proprietor" (and regular advertiser), was offering "a premium for the best melody, to be set to music by Mr. Kneass." A silver cup would be awarded to the author of the best "original words of an Ethiopian Melody or Extravaganzas," the winner to be determined "by the spontaneous voice of the audience" at a "Trial Concert" on Monday evening, September 6. All entries were due by noon on Friday, the third, so the company would have time to rehearse them over the weekend. Learning of the competition, Morrison Foster quickly sent word to Stephen in Cincinnati, obtained a copy of a new song, "Away Down Souf" (or "South"), and submitted it.[5]

"We understand that there are about fifteen competitors," the Pittsburgh *Daily Morning Post* reported on the morning of the concert, "all of whom have sent in excellent songs. A great number of trashy concerns have been thrown out. We anticipate some exquisite fun this evening. . . . Come on, and let all who are good looking and can afford it, bring ladies." By evening the field had been narrowed to ten, and the Eagle Saloon, packed with an "immense crowd," was turning people away at the door. A "more respectable audience never assembled in Pittsburgh," according to the *Post*, but its "spontaneous voice" was rather raucous. "[T]here was some confusion in arriving at the determination," the *Gazette* reported, "each competitor having his friends to applaud and opponents to hiss."[6]

Stephen Foster's friends were outnumbered or outshouted, because the winner was not "Way Down Souf," which Kneass sang, but "Wake Up Jake," written as well as performed by the company's own George Holman, who accepted the prize remarking, "Ladies and Gentlemen: With your approval, I believe I take the cup, and hope I could take many such without taking a cup too much."[7]

Foster's supporters were convinced that the fix was in, that the contest had been rigged to favor Holman. Morrison Foster dismissed "Wake Up Jake" as "a vulgar plagiarism without any poetry or music in it," but the truth is, it's a worthy song and was better calculated to amuse a hometown crowd than the entry by Pittsburgh's native (though absent) son. Its verses flattered Pittsburgh while making literary and topical allusions to Milton, Byron, "Zachey" Taylor and the Mexican War, ending with Jake's brag to Santa Anna, "yah-yah! I'm one of de b'hoys, / dat come from de Iron City." The song was more than a passing fancy, for it reappeared in a songster eight years later as "Wake Up Mose," tipping its hat to the Bowery's favorite volunteer fireman.[8]

Foster, on the other hand, ignored the Iron City as he would throughout his songwriting career. "Away Down Souf" is a flight into fantasy, to a cartographically confused Southland "Whar de corntop blossom and de canebrake grow; / Den come along to Cuba, and we'll dance de polka-juba." The tall-tale exaggeration of the second verse ("My lub she hab a very large mouf, / One corner in de norf, tudder corner in de souf; / It am so long, it reach so far / Trabble all around it on a railroad car") as well as the simplicity verging on monotony of the melody seem retrograde, as if Foster were imitating early blackface ditties instead of making the idiom his own.

"Away Down Souf" was an also-ran, but that did not deter Kneass and/or someone else in the troupe from trying to copyright it. The very next day while Morrison Foster was registering the song at the United States District Court, he encountered one or more company members—Morrison's own accounts differ—attempting the same thing. Since the federal judge at the time was the Foster family's friend and Allegheny neighbor Thomas Irwin, the matter was swiftly settled in Stephen Foster's favor. Attributed to the appropriate authors, both "Away Down Souf" and "Wake Up Jake" were published the following year by W. C. Peters as "Songs of the Sable Harmonists."[9]

Having failed to filch "Away Down Souf," Kneass soon composed a far more successful song of his own, "Ben Bolt," that would give even "Oh! Susanna" a run for its money. Svengali taught the mesmerized Trilby to warble Kneass's song in George Du Maurier's 1894 novel, *Trilby,* and Vivien Leigh sang "Ben Bolt" amid the Foster tunes quoted in *Gone With the Wind.* Thus Kneass dogged Foster for nearly a century.[10]

Kneass and his company performed other Foster songs at the Eagle Ice Cream Saloon. Clara Bruce sang "What Must a Fairy's Dream Be?," a sticky-sweet ballad Foster dedicated to Judge Irwin's daughter, Mary, that echoed a song from the 1820s composed by Peter K. Moran, whose "Swiss Waltz" Charlotte had played.[11]

On Saturday, September 11, 1847, the Eagle Saloon advertised in the *Daily Commercial Journal* a "GRAND GALA CONCERT!" for that very evening. "VICE PRESIDENT DALLAS AN INVITED GUEST!!" blared the ad in the *Post.* George M. Dallas was indeed in town, staying at the St. Charles Hotel and jockeying for position with his fellow Pennsylvanian, Secretary of State Buchanan, in the race for the Democratic nomination to succeed James Polk as president. (Buchanan won their state delegation's support, but Lewis Cass carried the convention and lost the election to Zachary Taylor.) If the Vice President declined the invitation, he missed the performance of "Wake Up Jake," "Away Down Souf," and other songs, along with "Susanna—A new song, never before given to the public."[12]

It's uncertain whether Stephen Foster composed "Oh! Susanna" before leaving Pittsburgh, to be sung by the "Five 'Nice Young Men,'" or after he had settled in Cincinnati.[13] But September 11, 1847, is a firm date for the birth of pop music as we still recognize it today. No popular song is more deeply rooted in American consciousness than "Oh! Susanna." Everyone knows it, and yet, the more closely one considers it, the clearer it becomes that we scarcely know it at all.

Starting with the lyrics:

> I come from Alabama
> With my Banjo on my knee
> I'se gwine to Lou'siana
> My true lub for to see.
> It rain'd all night de day I left,
> De wedder it was dry;
> The sun so hot I froze to def
> Susanna, dont you cry.

Oh! Susanna, do not cry for me;
I come from Alabama,
Wid my Banjo on my knee.

I jump'd aboard the telegraph
And trabbled down de ribber,
De lectrick fluid magnified,
And kill'd five hundred Nigga.
De bulgine bust and de hoss ran off,
I really thought I'd die;
I shut my eyes to hold my bref
Susanna dont you cry.

Oh! Susanna, do not cry for me....

I had a dream de udder night,
When ebry ting was still;
I thought I saw Susanna dear,
A coming down de hill,
De buckwheat cake was in her mouf,
De tear was in her eye,
I says, I'se coming from de souf,
Susanna dont you cry.

Oh! Susanna, do not cry for me....

I soon will be in New Orleans,
And den I'll look all around,
And when I find Susanna,
I'll fall upon the ground.
But if I do not find her,
Dis darkie'll surely die,
And when I'm dead and buried,
Susanna, don't you cry.

Oh! Susanna, do not cry for me....[14]

Many of these words and phrases had a familiar ring for the audience at Andrews's ice cream parlor. "Jim Along Josey," for instance, had been in the minstrel repertory for a decade. The dedicated follower of fashion who sings that song "comes from Lucianna" (Louisiana) and can't wait to put on his new pair of "tight-knee'd trousaloon" and strut "up and down Broadway wid my Susanna / And de white folks will take me to

be Santa Anna." The next verse dimly prefigures the dream in "Oh!
Susanna":

> My sister Rose de oder night did dream,
> Dat she was floating up and down de stream,
> And when she woke she began to cry,
> And de white cat picked out de black cat's eye.[15]

"Ole Tare River" was published in 1840 and anticipated not only "Oh!
Susanna" but also "Old Folks at Home":

> Way down in North Carolina
> On de banks of Ole Tare River,
> I go from dar to Alabama
> For to see my ole Aunt Hannah. . . .

> Now Miss Dinah I'm going to leave you
> And when I'm gone dont let it grieve you
> First to de window den to de door
> Looking for to see de banjo.[16]

A song published in 1846 praised "my brack ey'd Susianna. / She's brack
dat's a fac. . . ."[17]

Can the lyrics of "Oh! Susanna" be traced to black as well as blackface
sources? A compilation of songs sung by "contraband" and freed slaves
during the Civil War included one said to be typical "of the strange
barbaric songs that one hears upon the Western steamboats." "I'm gwine
to Alabamy, Oh . . . ," it began, "For to see my mammy, Ah. . . ." But by
then African Americans had been singing "Oh! Susanna" for so long
that it was sometimes mistaken for a black folksong. Indeed, the same
anthology included a spiritual that echoes "Oh! Susanna" in its verse
and "Camptown Races" in its chorus. If the words to "Oh! Susanna" had
African-American antecedents, the song's universal popularity trampled
their traces.[18]

The musical sources of "Oh! Susanna" run the gamut. You can hear a
premonition of its melody in "Mary Blane," published a year earlier by
Billy Whitlock, one of the original Virginia Minstrels. But scholars have
noted affinities far beyond blackface, ranging from the balladry of

Dempster's *May Queen* to the foursquare "Missionary Hymn" by Lowell Mason ("From Greenland's icy mountains . . .").[19]

Like "Lou'siana Belle" it's a polka, and like "Away Down Souf" it's in the key of G, but "Oh! Susanna" is a bounding leap forward to a uniquely and profoundly American anthem. Its very title suggests its anthemic aspirations by echoing the Hebrew and English *Hosanna*.[20]

The banjo on the singer's knee makes him a parody of a European troubadour and, at the same time, an archetypal African American—a racial hybrid like "de Polka pigeon wing" and blackface in general. This is the first of Foster's songs to mention the instrument, which there's little evidence he ever played himself. On the back of some music he wrote in the early 1850s is a detailed pencil drawing of a five-string banjo that indicates each string's tuning, and some fingerings are jotted down, too—suggesting Foster was unfamiliar with the instrument and wanted to figure it out for arranging purposes.[21]

The comic contradictions that conclude the first verse of "Oh! Susanna" have beguiled nearly every commentator into praising and, at the same time, affectionately dismissing the song as Uncle Tomfoolery, as "a glorious bit of nonsense," "irresponsible fun," and "nonsensical, prattling lines."[22] But "Oh! Susanna" is far more ambitious and unsettling than that, as the second verse begins to make clear.

The telegraph aboard which the singer jumps could have been either of two brand-new steamboats, *Telegraph No. 1* and *No. 2*. These packets plied between Louisville and Pittsburgh and were familiar sights from the windows of Irwin & Foster. They were fast: *Telegraph No. 2* made it from Cincinnati to Louisville in record time (six hours and twenty-six minutes, for an average of twenty-nine miles an hour) and competed in two famous races against the *Brilliant*, a Pittsburgh boat. It lost the first race but won the second, setting a record time and upstream speed (an average of twelve miles per hour) from Cincinnati to Pittsburgh.[23]

In 1849, ice and low water forced President-elect Taylor to disembark from *Telegraph No. 2*. "Rough and Ready" had to trudge through the snow to Moundsville, where he caught a sleigh to his inauguration. Sowing seeds of insurrection wherever he traveled, Martin Delany's fictional hero, Henry Blake, also took the *Telegraph No. 2*, from Cincinnati to Louisville.[24]

The next line of "Oh! Susanna" transforms the steamboat into its namesake, the telegraph, a newer and even more startling technological advance. The Mexican War was the first conflict to be reported by telegraph in American newspapers, which covered the progress of telegraph lines as assiduously as they did the arrivals and departures of steamboats. The day "Oh! Susanna" made its debut, the *Daily Morning Post* reported that "Pittsburgh will be in communication with Louisville on the 20th ult. . . . We shall be glad to hear occasionally from the Falls City." "The wires on the O'Reilly line between Louisville and Nashville have been stretched," announced the March 3, 1848, Cincinnati *Daily Enquirer*, "and the new instruments made to work it. That line will use the new inventions by Zook and Barnes."

New instruments! New inventions! The march of progress is a breathless race, and in the blink of an eye (during which—oops!—"five hundred Nigga" disappear) "Oh! Susanna" transforms the telegraph into a train. A "bulgine" is the steam engine of a locomotive, saluted by Walt Whitman as "Type of the modern—emblem of motion and power— pulse of the continent" and by Andrew Carnegie as America incarnate: "The old nations of the earth creep on at a snail's pace; the Republic thunders past with the rush of the express." Whitman exhorted the train "[f]or once [to] come serve the Muse and merge in verse." But Foster's bulgine balks, exploding and scaring off a horse that might have fetched more at auction than one of those "Nigga." No wonder the singer, dizzied by the madcap machinations and metamorphoses of technological progress, shuts his eyes, holds his breath and hopes he'll survive. ". . . [F]or steel and iron," Dickens observed in his account of America in *Martin Chuzzlewit*, "are of infinitely greater account, in this commonwealth, than flesh and blood."[25]

Steamboats made Dickens nervous. Their high-pressure boilers were indubitably dangerous. When the *Moselle* exploded in 1838, at least 150 passengers died within sight of Cincinnati's Public Landing. In 1843, Charles Scully boarded the wreck of the *Cutter*, which had exploded the previous day just after leaving a Pittsburgh wharf. The casualties included the engineer, whose body was hurled some thirty feet, ripping through a partition. "How truly furious must have been the current of the electrical steam," marveled Scully, conflating steam and electrical power just as "Oh! Susanna" would four years later in "de lectrick fluid."[26]

Even for steamboats, the number of explosions, fires, and collisions that occurred from 1847, when "Oh! Susanna" received its public premiere, through 1852 was extraordinary. Noting that explosions were "most awfully and fearfully frequent," Martin Delany wrote in the *North Star* that a "person, now-a-days, taking passage upon a Western steamboat, might be viewed in the light of a child thrown upon the Ganges— a victim to the element." One twelve-month period saw 695 people killed, and seven major disasters struck in the eight months before Congress finally passed legislation regulating steamboats in August 1852.[27]

Although steamboats were at the peak of their commercial importance when Foster wrote "Oh! Susanna," their days were already numbered by the locomotive—the faster, more dependable, and eventually cheaper mode of transportation into which Foster's "telegraph" finally turns. In the spring of 1853, Pittsburgh and Cincinnati would be linked by rail, and four years later there would no longer be regular steam packet service between the two cities.[28]

When the young Louis Moreau Gottschalk arrived in France to further his musical education, the head of the Paris Conservatory's piano department turned him down flat. "America is only a land of steam engines," Pierre Zimmerman declared, dismissing the prodigy from New Orleans without so much as an audition.[29] Ever since Eliza Clayland watched her uncle Oliver Evans's *Orukter Amphibolos* chug around Philadelphia, the Foster family had witnessed and participated in the development of America's steam technology and transportation system. The transformations in the second verse of "Oh! Susanna" are no swifter or more disruptive than the ones Stephen Foster experienced in his life. His father had been beggared in succession by a steamboat (the *Enterprize*), a coach company (the Pittsburgh and Greensburgh Turnpike Company), and the Main Line Canal. His half-brother, William, had begun his career as a canal surveyor and was now working for the railroad that would literally put the canal out to pasture, after acquiring it in 1857, by letting nature reclaim stretches of the waterway.

The steamboat, the train, and the telegraph: This technological trinity presided over Stephen Foster's life on Cincinnati's East Front Street, where the steamboats docked, the train tracks led, and Stephen followed the reports by wire of the war in which his brother Dunning was serving. In an essay entitled "Cincinnati—Its Destiny," a local booster named S. H. Goodin pondered "the great disturbing forces, which have come into use within the past ten years, the railroad and the telegraph":

These are the first great results which strike us—the almost entire annihilation of space by the one, and of time by the other.[30]

(In a similar vein, James Gordon Bennett, the shrewd editor of the New York *Herald*, remarked that the telegraph "totally annihilated what there was left of space.")[31]

The second verse of "Oh! Susanna" dramatizes the American dream and nightmare that Goodin and others described. Not only does it chronicle the conquest of time and space, it also unriddles, retroactively, the conundrums of the first verse: the confusions of day and night, wet and dry, hot and cold that ensue when time and space are collapsed.

Of course the second verse of "Oh! Susanna" is also racist—appallingly so. In *Blake*, Delany took sardonic satisfaction in transforming the song's refrain into a rallying cry and prayer for runaway slaves:

> O, righteous Father
> Wilt thou not pity me;
> And aid me on to Canada
> Where fugitives are free?[32]

Delany mocked "Oh! Susanna" because it made a mockery of African Americans, and it first did so publicly less than a month after Frederick Douglass and William Lloyd Garrison visited Pittsburgh and electrified Delany and Charles Shiras. Only white men enjoyed the free-and-easy mobility of Foster's blackface singer, "come from Alabama," "gwine to Lou'siana," who "trabbled down de ribber" and is "coming from de souf." An issue of the Pittsburgh *Post* urging readers to turn out for the silver cup competition at Andrews's ice cream parlor also contained this item:

> John H. Winston, a negro about nineteen years of age, who left his home in this city some time last spring, and went as a fireman on one of our steamboats, is now in the jail of Henderson county, Kentucky, committed because of the absence of a certificate of freedom. He will soon be sold unless the jail fees be paid. His mother, brothers and sisters reside here, but they are quite poor.[33]

One of Charles Scully's chores as an attorney was to provide steamboat captains with the proper papers for their black hands. "What an odious spectacle does not this present in civilization," he commented in his diary.[34]

Yet the casual slaughter of "five hundred Nigga" also betrays a recognition, which runs through the nostalgia of much minstrel music, that agrarian life and the plantation economy are threatened by progress, that slaves and their owners alike are in danger of becoming roadkill on the macadam of a rapidly industrializing America. (The very day he clambered through the wreckage of the *Cutter,* Charles Scully attended a meeting to discuss a "McAdamized Road" its promoters argued was crucial for Pittsburgh's economic development.)[35]

Contemplating the train tracks that defiled Walden Pond, Thoreau expressed similar misgivings about "modern improvements" that were only "an improved means to an unimproved end." Thoreau's mind, like Foster's, hopped immediately from the train to the telegraph: "We are in great haste to construct a magnetic telegraph from Maine to Texas; but Maine and Texas, it may be, have nothing important to communicate." Thoreau—who, like Foster, played the flute, claiming to have charmed perch to Walden Pond's surface on warm summer evenings—warned of trouble down the line:

> . . . though a crowd rushes to the depot, and the conductor shouts "All aboard!" when the smoke is blown away and the vapor condensed, it will be perceived that a few are riding, but the rest are run over,— and it will be called, and will be, "A melancholy accident." [36]

The mishap in "Oh! Susanna" may be more mirthful (for white folks) than melancholy, but the anxiety Foster expressed was common to the culture and made the song's first two verses a broadly American anthem. "Great improvements of the age!" snorts the narrator of Herman Melville's short story, "Cock-A-Doodle-Doo!," after describing a steamboat explosion on the Ohio River and a head-on collision of trains. "What! to call the facilitation of death and murder an improvement!" [37]

The third verse of "Oh! Susanna" sounds a more personal note. The sudden hush of "when ebry ting was still" signals a shift to more intimate revelations as "Susanna dear," who bears the middle name of Foster's beloved Charlotte, comes "down de hill"—as young Stephen and the rest of his family did when expelled from the White Cottage perched above Pittsburgh. "Oh! Susanna" isn't written in confessional code, but it does harbor deep psychological resonances, hints of the losses that traumatized the infant Foster. He may have been nearly as unconscious of these as listeners have been for a century and a half. But *unconscious of* does not mean *insensitive to,* and one of the reasons we respond so deeply to the song, I suspect, is that we apprehend, however vaguely, a real cry beneath the burnt cork.

Thus "Oh! Susanna," at once jaunty and forlorn, pines for the past even as it hurtles into the future—not a bad description of how many Americans must have felt as they returned from the Mexican War and rushed to California, where gold was discovered just months after "Oh! Susanna" made its debut. Irwin & Foster advertised boats bound for Independence, Missouri, the jumping-off point for the overland route to California, and both Dunning and Morrison Foster felt a twinge of gold fever themselves. "If I had nothing to bind me to home," Dunning wrote, "and could leave without creating a pang in the breast of any person I should leave behind me, I would start immediately. . . ."[38]

Thousands of other Americans braved that pang and heard in "Oh! Susanna" their own mixed feelings of homesickness and hope. Often improvising lyrics of their own, they sang it on their way to El Dorado:

> Oh California!
> Thou land of glittering dreams,
> Where the yellow dust and diamonds, boys,
> Are found in all thy streams.[39]

And they sang it when they got there:

> Oh! Susanna,
>   Go to Hell for all of me;
> We're all a livin' dead
>   In Californ-ee![40]

"The spirit of the music is always encouraging," observed one visitor to the mining camps and towns that sprang up overnight, "even its most doleful passages have a grotesque touch of cheerfulness—a mingling of sincere pathos and whimsical consolation. . . ."[41]

Stephen Foster lost in his childhood the home and loved one(s) the forty-niners forsook as adult adventurers. In California there convened what Walt Whitman would call (in an entirely different context) "interminable swarms of alert, turbulent, good-natured, independent citizens, mechanics, clerks, young persons." Such a "mass of men, so fresh and free, so loving and so proud," struck Whitman with awe, and with dejection and amazement, that among our geniuses and talented writers or speakers, few or none have yet really spoken to this people, created a single image-making work for them, or absorb'd the central spirit and the idiosyncrasies which are theirs—and which, thus, in highest ranges, so far remain entirely uncelebrated, unexpress'd.[42]

Whitman was seeking in the "highest ranges" what Foster had already achieved in the foothills of popular culture: "a single image-making work" of an era, and of America.

Chapter Fourteen

WHISTLED ON
THE WIND

Oh! Susanna" was not an overnight success. When the Kneass troupe promoted its next concert, two days later, it promised reprises of "Old Iron City" and "Way Down Souf," but "Oh! Susanna" went unmentioned. Nor was it advertised for the following evening, when the singers shared the Eagle Saloon's stage (if they could fit on it) with, direct from Barnum's museum, the Fat Boys—eleven-year-old Charles Stuart, who weighed 275 pounds, and nine-year-old Alexander Stuart, a bonny 223—who performed feats of mesmerism and clairvoyance garbed in ample kilts.[1]

Yet it wasn't long before the song swept the concert halls of New York as well as the mining camps of California. On November 30, 1848, Henri Herz, the Austrian-born Parisian piano virtuoso, staged a grandiose "Musical Solemnity" at Manhattan's Tabernacle theater. Leavening the operatic arias and overtures, he introduced a new composition, his own "Impromptu Burlesque for solo piano on two minstrel tunes": "Oh! Susanna" and Charles White's "Carry Me Back to Old Virginny" (or "De Floating Scow"), sometimes confused with James Bland's much later and better-known song with the same title.[2] Ethiopian entertainers frequently burlesqued classical music; that a classical musician—and a professor, to boot, at the conservatory that had spurned Gottschalk—would burlesque minstrelsy shows how intimately and inextricably music was mixed up before the centrifugal forces of economics and class separated high from low culture in the latter half of the nineteenth century.[3]

Perhaps Herz had heard Christy's Minstrels sing "Oh! Susanna" in a nearby New York theater. Or maybe he had encountered it in Cincinnati, where he performed several concerts in July 1847. Stephen Foster's songs, an unnamed "old friend" recalled years later, "seemed to travel like the wind from city to city, and one had hardly heard them in Pittsburgh when they were being whistled on the streets of New York or Cincinnati." Foster's early music moved in mysterious, roundabout ways, and Foster himself played a passive, elusive role in its circulation.[4]

Stephen Foster was not in the audience at the Eagle Ice Cream Saloon when his songs were introduced there. He was in Cincinnati, and it was Morrison Foster who took the initiative. Evidently thinking they were of little value, at least monetarily, Stephen Foster handed out copies of his songs as casually as if he were still sharing them with the Five Nice Young Men. W. C. Peters published "Lou'siana Belle" and "What Must a Fairy's Dream Be?" in October 1847, shortly after the Eagle Saloon concerts, and "Uncle Ned," "Santa Anna's Retreat," "Oh! Susanna," and "Stay Summer Breath," a parlor ballad, the following year, but Peters's title to these compositions was hardly free and clear.

In 1849, Stephen Foster wrote almost apologetically to William E. Millet, a New York publisher who had issued presumably unauthorized editions of "Oh! Susanna" and "Uncle Ned":

> I gave manuscript copies of each of the songs "Lou'siana Belle"—"Uncle Ned"—& "Oh, Susanna" to several persons before I gave them to Mr. Peters for publication, but in neither instance with any permission nor *restriction* in regard to publishing them, unless contained in a letter to Mr. Roark accompanying the m.s. of "Uncle Ned"—although of this I am doubtful. . . .[5]

William Roark was a member of the Sable Harmonists, the minstrel group that sometimes included Kneass. While Kneass was occupied with his own troupe in Pittsburgh, the Harmonists played Cincinnati in August and early September 1847 and then Pittsburgh on September 15. Meanwhile, on August 20–23, the Christy Minstrels appeared in Cincinnati, where they might easily have heard Roark and the other Harmonists. Connect the dots of all these dates and it's tempting to speculate that Roark was the point man for much of Stephen Foster's early music, passing it along by performance or in manuscript to Kneass and Christy's Minstrels, with or without the composer's complicity. One way or another, at least sixteen different publishers came out with thirty different arrangements of "Oh! Susanna" between 1848 and 1850, and Foster may not have made a single penny from them.[6]

Foster's diffidence may have been due partly to embarrassment, a genteel reluctance to acknowledge these blackface ditties as his own. "Open Thy Lattice Love" had proudly borne Foster's name (though the wrong first initial); so had "There's a Good Time Coming." But rather than crediting any author, "Lou'siana Belle" was published simply as "Written for and Sung by Joseph Murphy of the Sable Harmonists." W. C. Peters's first editions of "Uncle Ned," "Away Down Souf," and "Oh! Susanna" ("as sung by Mr. Tichnor of the Sable Harmonists") included Foster's name, but only on the inside of the sheet music. The title page described them (and George Holman's "Wake Up Jake") as "Songs of the Sable Harmonists." Song plugging wasn't born at the turn of the next century with Tin Pan Alley: It was to Foster's advantage to associate his music with popular performers. Foster wasn't bashful, however, about advertising his authorship of parlor ballads and piano pieces.

According to his friend Robert Nevin, Foster "did not look for remuneration," and for "Uncle Ned" he "received none." Morrison Foster wrote that his brother also gave "Oh! Susanna" to Peters for free, and that the publisher made $10,000 from the song.[7]

Stephen Foster was ripped off, to be sure, but only in retrospect, for Peters's business practices were no worse than those of other publishers in that era—or in the early days of rock 'n' roll, for that matter, when once again a new kind of miscegenational music arose outside the mainstream of cultural commerce. Foster had been prodigal with his manuscripts, making it easy for pirates to publish them and impossible for Peters to exercise first or exclusive rights. It had not yet become standard for composers to receive royalties, either; more often they sold their work outright.

That's why John Hill Hewitt, the composer of one of the most popular songs of the 1820s, "The Minstrel's Return'd from the War," as well as of the 1860s, "All Quiet Along the Potomac Tonight," threatened to abandon songwriting: "For the simple reason that it does not pay the author";

Hewitt wrote, "the publisher pockets all, and gets rich on the brains of the poor fool who is chasing that *ignis fatuus*, reputation."[8]

"There was no such thing as a royalty in those days, and when a song was sold it was sold outright," recalled Henry Russell, who peddled his work for an average of ten shillings a song and "Woodman! Spare That Tree!" for two dollars. "Had it not been that I sang the songs myself, and so in a certain measure conduced to their popularity, the payment for their composition would have meant simple starvation."[9]

"Oh! Susanna" and "Uncle Ned" became national and then international hits, but because they brought him little celebrity and even less money, it dawned only gradually on Foster that songwriting might earn him a living. He recognized that such a living might be as disreputable as it was dicey. George Root, so envious of Foster's success that he sought to emulate it by writing "Hazel Dell" and other songs, nonetheless published them under the pseudonym G. Friedrich Wurzel, *Wurzel* being German for "root." "It wasn't reputable. . . ," Root later wrote. "Indeed, any line of music, as a business, was in those days looked down upon. . . ."[10]

But Root did not devote himself to songwriting full-time. No one did, because no one had ever dreamed he could make a go of it—not Root, an influential music educator and later a music publisher, nor Russell, who made his money on the road. Gottschalk toured, too, and supplemented his income by promoting Chickering pianos. So Stephen Foster hung fire, either dallying or deliberating, but writing music all the while.

Dunning Foster returned from Mexico weakened by tuberculosis. No sooner had he rallied and recovered some strength than Morrison was stricken with malaria in May 1848 while buying cotton in New Orleans. It was not a salubrious time. For now, as if malaria, yellow fever, typhoid, and dysentery weren't enough to withstand, a great wave of cholera, the second to strike America, swept up the Mississippi and Ohio rivers. As surely as AIDS is a jet-age epidemic, cholera was a scourge of the steam age, hopping the sidewheelers and riding the newly laid rails.

Seven thousand, five hundred people would die in Cincinnati alone, many within hours of the first appearance of the dehydrating symptoms of diarrhea, vomiting, and cramps. The Hutchinson Family celebrated the Christmas of 1848 in Cincinnati, but left shortly thereafter for fear of the disease, whose advance up the river was monitored as anxiously as the flood tide's rush downriver in spring. "It is not yet in Cincinnati,"

Dunning Foster wrote to Morrison in Pittsburgh on December 29, "but is *hourly expected.*" [11]

Two weeks later, however, Dunning wrote again, dismissing cholera as "all a *bugbear*" and urging Stephen, who was visiting in Pittsburgh, to return to Irwin & Foster. When he was back on the job, Stephen wrote Morrison reassuringly: "Tell Ma she need not trouble herself about the health of Cincinnati as our weather here is very healthy the cholera not having made it appearance." [12]

One reason Dunning and Stephen sounded so nonchalant may have been that they were having too good a time to entertain thoughts of leaving Cincinnati. "I have entered considerably into the fashionable world again and may now be put down as one of the beaux (not b'hoys) of Cincinnati," Dunning wrote. "We have a party almost every night." One of these was a masquerade at the home of Mrs. Ann Marshall. (Dunning, the veteran, dressed as a Mexican soldier.) Ann Marshall was a daughter of the Cassillys who had attended St. Joseph's Academy in Maryland with Charlotte Foster. Stephen Foster dedicated "Stay Summer Breath" to *her* daughter, Sophie B. Marshall, a gifted amateur soprano. [13]

Stephen Foster was not as outgoing as his older brother and employer, but he, too, appeared on Cincinnati's social and musical scene. When the soprano Elisa Biscaccianti performed three concerts in April 1849, Stephen called on her and her husband, the cellist and ostensible aristocrat, Count Alessandro Biscaccianti. Granddaughter of the early American composer, conductor and publisher James Hewitt, and niece of the songwriter John Hill Hewitt, Elisa Biscaccianti was the first American-born opera singer of consequence. But not, according to some contemporary reviews, of merit. One described her voice as "utterly ruined," and another criticized her "harsh croak." Eventually Count Biscaccianti abandoned her, taking with him, so the Hewitts charged, a precious Amati cello that had been a family heirloom. The ex-countess was reduced to drink and to performing in dance halls. Except for the harsh reviews, however, all this was in the future when Stephen Foster pronounced himself "as much delighted by her conversation and agreeable manners as I was subsequently by her singing at her concerts." [14]

Cincinnati was a frequent stop on the itinerary of touring classical performers. Foster had the opportunity to hear a number of artists (though there's no record of his attendance). There was, for example, the English soprano Anna Bishop, who had scandalously abandoned her husband and three children to live and tour with a fat harpist, Robert Nicholas-Charles Bochsa, who was wanted for forgery in France. (Ironically, the husband she deserted was Sir Henry Rowley Bishop, the composer of "Home! Sweet Home!," as well as of several songs Charlotte Foster had sung. The defiant adulteress often performed "Home! Sweet Home!" as an encore.) When Henri Herz came to town in 1847, he capped his four concerts with a performance of the *William Tell* overture played by sixteen local pianists on eight pianos. W. C. Peters tried to get a local symphony orchestra off the ground, but it expired after three concerts, one of which prompted a critic to complain that "there was a little too much *catgut*, which might profitably have made more room, for something more sonorous." Cincinnati, in sum, offered Foster ample exposure to classical music as well as to minstrelsy.[15]

Cholera struck Cincinnati in full force in June 1849, when, as luck would have it, two weddings took Dunning and Stephen to Pittsburgh. Andrew Robinson, who had put on minstrel theatricals with Morrison and Stephen as children, and who had sung "Lou'siana Belle" and "Uncle Ned" as one of the Five Nice Young Men, married Susan Pentland, to whom Stephen had dedicated "Open Thy Lattice Love." A week later, Andrew's sister Anne married J. Cust Blair. Morrison Foster had been a rival for Anne's affections, and Blair was one of his closest friends, a charter member of the Knights of the Square Table, a convivial crew that succeeded the Five Nice Young Men after Stephen moved to Cincinnati.

In July, while the body count mounted in Cincinnati and Harriet Beecher Stowe watched helplessly as her one-and-a-half-year-old son Charley writhed in his death agony, Stephen Foster visited his remarried sister, now Henrietta Foster Wick Thornton, in her new home in Warren, Ohio, a few miles northwest of Youngstown.

The suffering Stephen Foster had left behind may still have been much on his mind. Sometime that spring or summer he came across a poem in the May 12, 1849, *Home Journal*, a weekly that the duo of G. P. Morris and N. P. Willis edited after *The New Mirror* changed ownership. The unattributed lines were written by the Irish poet Denis MacCarthy.[16] Entitled "Summer Longings," the poem began, "Ah! My heart is weary waiting, / Waiting for the May." In successive verses the poet's heart was "sick with longing," "sore with sighing" and "pained with throbbing" as the arrival of spring and summer seemed interminably delayed. It was a heartsickness that Harriet Beecher Stowe would have recognized. That very March, unaware of the tragedy the summer would bring, she wrote to her sister-in-law:

> It is all shoreless tideless hopeless unmitigated mud here—mud without hope or end . . . & still the weather is cross & sour & doleful & every one is sleepy and has the head ache my own poor self among the number—I now long for spring—this betwixst & betweenity I dont admire.[17]

What makes MacCarthy's poem particularly doleful is that when summer finally comes in the fifth and final verse, it, too, is "dark and dreary / Life still ebbs away." It becomes clear, in an ironic (if maudlin) turn, that man is always weary, always waiting, always suspended, no matter what season of the year, in "this betwixst and betweenity." Foster's setting of "Summer Longings" is more eloquent than MacCarthy's verses deserve, partly because it was composed in full awareness that, in this summer of 1849 in particular, morbid thoughts were not a conventional conceit but a natural response to the devastation cholera was wreaking. "Summer Longings" is a simple but substantial piece of music, in which the piano punctuates and plays off the vocal line by descending, step by halting step, down the treble clef in a dying fall of dignified pathos.

Foster dedicated "Summer Longings" to Samuel P. Thompson, a clerk who roomed with Foster at Mrs. Griffin's boarding house in Cincinnati.[18] Although it never won a popular following, it was the first song of real distinction Foster didn't write in blackface dialect. It was also the last Foster song published by Peters, who brought it out in November 1849. (The following February, he published a piece for piano, the "Soirée Polka.")

Peters shifted his base of operations from Cincinnati to Baltimore in 1849. It doesn't seem to have been distance, however, but the desire for a better deal (or *any* deal) that led Foster to look elsewhere. Finally he seemed to have realized that "Oh! Susanna" and "Uncle Ned" (though none of his parlor ballads) were making money for everyone but him. So he struck bargains with one of the firms that had already profited from pirated editions of his music, F. D. Benteen of Baltimore, and with another publishing house that would play a major role in the rest of his career, Firth, Pond & Co. of New York.

John Firth had been born in England and apprenticed to a musical instrument maker in Albany, where he met William Hall. Together they formed a music publishing company, later joined by Sylvanus Pond from Milford, Massachusetts, that became one of the most successful in the country. Headquartered in the house George Washington had rented when the Congress of the Confederation met in New York City, Firth & Hall published "Woodman! Spare That Tree!" and many other popular songs, as well as sacred hymns and classical compositions. When Hall departed in 1847, the firm became Firth, Pond.

Foster was in touch with Firth, Pond by the spring of 1849, because in the same letter to Morrison in which he described his meeting with Mme. Biscaccianti, he asked his brother:

> In writing to Gil Smith please say that I am very much grieved at having been the cause of so much trouble and humiliation to him on account of a miserable song, and tell him if he has not already burned the copyright (as I certainly should have done) he may give it to Mess Firth & Pond any time that he may be in the neighborhood of No. 1 Franklin Square. If they will give him 10$ 5$ or even 1$ for it, let him make a donation of the amt to the Orphans Asylum or any other charitable or praiseworthy institution. Mess. F. & P have written me for the song.[19]

Gilead A. Smith, the brother of Brother William's second wife, lived in New York. Evidently he had been charged with delivering to Firth, Pond the copyright for a song that Morrison Foster later indicated was "Nelly Was a Lady." That title had been copyrighted in Pittsburgh on December 5, 1848, presumably by Morrison, who had copyrighted "Away Down Souf," too. Once again, it was just in the nick of time. On February 6, 1849, Firth, Pond copyrighted (but apparently did not publish) "Toll the Bell for Lovely Nell, or My Dark Virginia Bride, a favorite Ethiopian Song & chorus by Chas. White." This title was the chorus of "Nelly Was a Lady." Either Foster had sent a copy of the song to Charles White, a New York minstrel leader and author of "Carry Me Back to Old Virginny," or White had obtained or heard it elsewhere. In any event, Stephen and/or Morrison Foster contacted Firth, Pond and sent them the song, which the publishing firm copyrighted in New York on July 18, 1849, properly crediting Stephen Foster as its composer.[20]

On September 12, Firth, Pond sent to Stephen Foster in Cincinnati a letter that was obviously part of an ongoing correspondence:

> Your favor of 8th inst. is received and we hasten to reply. We will accept the proposition therein made, viz. to allow you two cents upon every

copy of your future publications issued by our house, after the expenses of publication are paid, of course it is always our interest to push them as widely as possible. From your acquaintance with the proprietors or managers of the different bands of "minstrels," & from your known reputation, you can undoubtedly arrange with them to sing them & thus introduce them to the public in that way, but in order to secure the copyright exclusively for our house, it is safe to hand such persons printed copies only, of the pieces, for if manuscript copies are issued particularly by the author, the market will be flooded in a short time.

It is also advisable to compose only such pieces as are likely both in the sentiment & melody to take the public taste. Numerous instances can be cited of composers whose reputation has greatly depreciated, from the fact of their music becoming too popular, & as a consequence they write too much & too fast, & in a short time others supercede them.

As soon as "Brother Gum" makes his appearance he shall be joined to pretty "Nelly," & your interest in the two favorites duly forwarded to your address, say 50 copies of each.

We remain in the hope of hearing from you very soon.[21]

This letter is intriguing for what it tells us about Foster: that he'd acquired a "known reputation," that he was assumed to be plugged into the minstrel circuit, that he still needed to be reminded of the very basics of copyright protection. It's equally fascinating for what it reveals about popular music. Then, as now, it was crucial that well-known artists perform a song in order to popularize it. Then, as now, it was imperative to give people what they want. But then, as now, the mass audience's insatiable demand for novelty quickly burned out those who strove to satisfy it, and then it was on to the next Big Thing.

Considering that sheet music generally sold for twenty-five cents, the two cents that Foster negotiated wasn't bad, amounting to a royalty of 8 percent. The one hundred free copies of "Nelly Was a Lady" and "My Brodder Gum," however, were worth only twenty-five dollars—and Morrison Foster claimed that "Nelly" alone made Firth, Pond "several thousand dollars."[22] In addition to those two songs, Firth, Pond published "Dolcy Jones" in 1849. All three were in blackface dialect—note that the firm's letter expressed interest only in minstrel material, not in Foster's parlor ballads.

"My Brodder Gum" and "Dolcy Jones" are not especially inspired—as if Foster were already disregarding the admonition not to "write too much & too fast." Unlike Foster's earlier songs, which he may have composed for friends like the Five Nice Young Men or their successors, the Knights of the Square Table, these two seem to have been written specifically for performance by minstrel groups. Each song begins by acknowledging an audience ("My Brodder Gum": "White folks I'll sing for you"; "Dolcy Jones": "Oh! ladies don't you wonder"), and emphasizes a minstrel instrument: the banjo in "My Brodder Gum," the bones in "Dolcy Jones." Underscoring their cookie-cutter character, both songs end each verse with a theatrically syncopated, rhythmically irregular rollick down the scale from high D. "Dolcy Jones" throws in for good measure a comic stutter: "Oh! dadda, D' D' Dolcy Jones!" "My Brodder Gum" trots out the stereotype of the shuffling lazybones with "Nuffin' else to do" but sing and "Spend my time a pickin on de banjo." The song's superficial and demeaning treatment of African Americans stands in dramatic contrast to the dignity accorded Nelly, "my dark Virginny bride."

"Nelly Was a Lady" is marked *adagio*, slower than any of Foster's previous songs in blackface. Even "Uncle Ned" was a faster-paced *andantino*. Whereas Ned was a slave, toiling in the fields, the singer who mourns Nell works on a steamboat, toting the cottonwood that fuels the engines (like the black boiler-stokers whose "fantastic song" enthralled Fredrika Bremer). It's possible that he's free (or as free as a black man could be on the Mississippi River before the Civil War), and his late bride, the chorus keeps reminding us, "was a lady." A lady? Minstrelsy's treatment of African-American women had come a considerable way, but Lucy Neal was just as much a "gal" as Lucy Long. To elevate a black (not even a "yaller") woman to such genteel status was unprecedented in blackface.

The language is remarkably elevated, too, the dialect notwithstanding. The fifth verse brazenly appropriates the funereal decorum of the parlor ballad:

> Close by de margin ob de water,
> Whar de lone weeping willow grows,
> Dar lib'd Virginny's lubly daughter;
> Dar she in death may find repose.

Only the dialect distinguishes the rhetoric here from George P. Morris's poetry for the parlor. And yet so strong was the aversion to blackface (and African Americans) in some refined circles that one J. A. Turner saw fit to improve upon Foster's lyrics:

> Jessie was a fair one,
>   Last May she died;
> Shed a tear for Jessie dear,
>   My bright, my gentle bride.[23]

"Nelly Was a Lady" was a milestone in Stephen Foster's development, a sign of progress in his songwriting and in his racial attitudes as well. By merging the minstrel ditty with the parlor ballad, he not only overcame and resolved some of his own musical ambivalence and conflict—the push-pull between respectability and rebellion, the bourgeois and the bawdy—he also reconciled black and white, rescuing blackface from the overt racism that had characterized it from the outset. The following year, William Sidney Mount was asked by a dealer in lithography "to paint him a Negro courtship. Rather genteel."[24] He might as well have illustrated "Nelly Was a Lady," which endowed African-American love with a dignity it had seldom enjoyed in white culture.

In only two or three years, with "Uncle Ned," "Oh! Susanna," and now "Nelly Was a Lady" to his credit, Stephen Foster had become a major American songwriter. His next challenge was to make a living at it—and to conduct a genteel courtship of his own.

Chapter Fifteen

JENNIE WITH THE
LIGHT BROWN HAIR

Early in 1850, Irwin & Foster lost its bookkeeper. By February 23, Stephen Foster was back in Pittsburgh. Doubtless his contracts with Firth, Pond and F. D. Benteen gave him the confidence to quit his day job. Probably another reason he returned home is that at last he had a home to return to. After moving briefly to Youngstown, Ohio, in 1847, William and Eliza Foster resided in a succession of hotels and boarding houses in Pittsburgh and Allegheny City. Since their bank account was nearly as empty as their nest, it made little sense to maintain a home.

But then the family expanded and so, slightly, did its income. William Foster set up office in Pittsburgh as a soldiers' claim agent. On behalf of veterans of the Mexican War or their survivors, he filed applications for back pay, pensions, and land warrants. Apparently not all of these claims were legitimate, because William Foster marked more than one entry in his account book "rascal."[1]

In a daguerreotype of William and Eliza Foster that was probably made between 1847 and 1851, William seems rather dejected and enfeebled. His right hand is tucked into his waistcoat Napoleonically, but his arm appears limp. The air and the power seem to have been let out of his sagging frame. It's Eliza, her sharp eyes fixing the daguerreotyper's gaze, who is in control. The focal point of the image is her hand on William's shoulder, which seems to be gripping him firmly.[2]

While William had found a job, his son Henry had lost one, swept out of the Treasury Department with other Democratic appointees by the new Whig administration of Zachary Taylor. Henry, who had wed Mary Burgess, from Pittsburgh, in 1847, and fathered a little girl, also named Mary, had little choice but to return home.

In April 1850, Stephen Foster, Henry's family, their parents and two servant girls moved into a brick house on Allegheny's East Common. (Morrison Foster visited the household and at times managed its accounts, but he was frequently on the road and maintained bachelor's quarters elsewhere.) Like the house next door in which the Fosters had lived a decade earlier, this one was owned by Brother William.

If determining to become a songwriter was a bold step forward for Stephen Foster, he was taking a couple of steps backward by returning to Allegheny and the family fold, not to mention by resuming a dependency on his eldest brother. In March he borrowed $100 from Brother William. Five years later he had yet to repay the loan, which Stephen, ever the scrupulous bookkeeper, noted had accrued $33.50 in interest.[3]

Stephen Foster's apron-string attachment to his family, the youngest child's reluctance if not outright refusal to separate, had long been evident in his life and would soon become obvious in his music: "Old Folks at *Home*," "My Old Kentucky *Home*." But Foster may also have returned to Pittsburgh on account of Jane Denny McDowell.

Jane McDowell was a daughter of Andrew N. McDowell, a Pittsburgh physician who had tutored Martin Delany in medicine. That a prominent white doctor, whose uncle had been president of St. John's College in Annapolis, Maryland, and provost of the University of Pennsylvania, would take under his wing a young African American was remarkable. Perhaps it owed to the fact that McDowell was born, reared, and had begun his medical practice in Chambersburg, Pennsylvania, where Delany had grown up, too.[4]

Dr. McDowell's wife, Jane Denny Porter, was from Pittsburgh, where the McDowells, who had married in Lewistown, Pennsylvania, in 1826, eventually settled and raised half a dozen daughters. Even before their arrival they were known, at least slightly, by the Foster family. An 1826 letter to Charlotte Foster refers to "your old acquaintance Mrs. MacDowell and the Doct. a very pleasant gentlemanly man," who were living in

Meadville, Pennsylvania, at the time. Dr. McDowell died the year before Stephen Foster returned from Cincinnati to Pittsburgh, and his widow lived on First Street with her unmarried offspring, including her second oldest daughter and namesake, Jane Denny McDowell.[5]

Jane (born December 10, 1829) was part of the Fosters' social set. She seems to have been on the circle's periphery, however. The first mention of her in Foster family correspondence occurs in the January 1849 letter to Morrison in which Dunning boasted of being "one of the beaux (not b'hoys) of Cincinnati":

> I am sorry that Jane McDowell is not with some of the young ladies that go into society, as I fear she will not have as favourable an impression of our people as she would have were she to see more of them. Mr. Stewart's family is not generally visited by people that would interest her much; however, she appears to enjoy herself very well and does not complain in any way. She is by the way a very sensible and interesting young lady.[6]

Stephen Foster was in Pittsburgh when Dunning wrote this, so he may not have seen Jane McDowell while she was visiting Cincinnati. Another letter to Morrison, from his friend Mary Anderson, gossiped that "Jane McDowell is engaged to some chap near New Lisbon" (most likely New Lisbon, Ohio, but possibly the New Jersey town of the same name). This letter was dated November 23, 1849, not long before Stephen Foster left Cincinnati for good.[7] Clearly, Stephen and Jane knew each other, but it is possible they did not strike up a romance until after Foster returned to Pittsburgh, that his attraction to her was not a motive for the move, but an unexpected consequence.

Jane McDowell may have participated in the musical evenings the Fosters and their friends organized, but she wasn't the life of the soirée, a talented singer or pianist like Sophie Marshall or the Keller sisters or Susan Pentland Robinson, to whom Stephen Foster showed and dedicated songs. Indeed, there's little evidence that she was in any way musical.

Yet she was the first and the last woman with whom Stephen Foster is known to have ever been romantically involved. According to their granddaughter, Jessie Welsh Rose, Stephen often told Jane it was with her hair that he had fallen in love first. It was auburn, with red in it as there had been in his dead sister's, and hair—be it "woolly" or "Saxon," "braided" or "waving," "golden," "dark glossy," or, most famously, "light brown"—figures prominently, even obsessively, in Foster's lyrics, appearing in at least sixteen of his songs. "Jeanie with the Light Brown Hair" was, in the original manuscript, "Jennie"—an elision of Jane Denny.[8]

Presumably Stephen Foster was attracted to more than Jane McDowell's hair. Maybe, given the riskiness of the career he was undertaking, he sought the reassurance and stability of a marriage and family. Songwriting can be a solitary affair, and Foster may have been as eager for companionship as sex. Possibly, given the unmanliness of his "profession" in the eyes of many Pittsburghers, he wanted to prove his mettle by taking a wife. Probably, he simply fell in love.

It's equally unclear what Jane saw in Stephen. Another suitor, the attorney Richard Cowan, might have proved a bigger catch. A good friend of Stephen and Morrison Foster, and best friends with Charles Scully, Cowan was somewhat musical himself. He often passed the evening playing flute duets with Scully, and he had managed Frank Johnson's charity ball. According, once again, to Stephen and Jane's granddaughter, Cowan was

> wealthy, handsome, and distinguished in appearance. Mr. Foster suffered somewhat from the contrast, as he was small in stature, and although his features were regular and pleasing, he was not of the type which women call handsome.

What did Stephen Foster look like as a young man? No likenesses are known to exist before the late 1850s, when for a while Foster sported a tuft of hair in the furrow between his lower lip and strong chin, but he may have been clean-shaven earlier just as he would be later. Morrison Foster wrote that he was "slender," not over five-foot-seven, and, concurring with Jessie Welsh Rose, twice in three sentences described his features as "regular." He had straight dark hair ("nearly black") and dark eyes. Robert Nevin said that "his shoulders were marked by a droop—the result of a habit of walking with his eyes fixed upon the ground a pace or two in advance of his feet."[9]

Diffident and distracted, "Steve," as his friends called him, did not cut a prepossessing figure. But his determination overcame Cowan's considerable appeal. Jessie Welsh Rose wrote that when both men were admitted to the McDowell parlor one evening, Stephen

> promptly turned his back upon the pair, took up a book and read the evening through (Grandma always delighted to tell this story).
>
> At 10:30, calling hours were over in those good old days, and Richard, punctilious in all things, arose, wrapping his military broadcloth cape about him elegantly, he [sic] bid the forbidding back of Stephen a low, sweeping, "Good evening, sir." No answer from Stephen. Jane accompanied Richard to the door, feeling in her heart that a crisis of some kind was impending. She often laughingly said that when she came back into the parlor that night, she scarcely knew where her sympathies lay, whether they had departed with Richard, or were present with Stephen. At any rate, she had small time for speculation—Steve had arisen, was standing by the table, pale and stern as she came in.
>
> "And now, Miss Jane, I want your answer. Is it yes, or is it no?" And Grandma, 19 in years, unused to quick decisions, made one then. . . .[10]

The abruptness of Foster's proposal and Jane McDowell's acceptance corresponds to the brusqueness of their wedding, on July 22, 1850, in the same Trinity Episcopal Church in which Stephen had been baptized. He informed his sister, Ann Eliza Buchanan, of his "small wedding" less than a week in advance.[11] According to the bridesmaid, Jane's sister Agnes, both the bride and the groom

> were pretty much frightened. Steve quite pale. They each had to repeat some part of the ceremony after [Rev. Theodore B.] Lyman, which made it, I think rather embarrassing. Jane repeated her part in a different kind of a voice altogether from her usual tone of voice. It was owing to her strain.

A gang of "callithumpians" added another discordant note that evening. In the European tradition of the charivari—or "shivaree," as it was sometimes Americanized—a group of raucous, pot-and-pan-thumping young rowdies serenaded the McDowell residence with the "most horrible music" and, when denied food or drink, threatened to return with an even more noisome "sheet-iron band."[12]

On the inside back cover of the musical sketchbook he started keeping in June 1851, Stephen Foster penciled a column of figures:

9
31
30
31
30
31
31
28
31
<u>18</u>
270

Nine days remained in the month of July when Stephen and Jane wed on the 22d. On April 18, 1851, just shy of nine months later, their only child, Marion, was born. There's something vaguely disquieting about this tabulation. Did Foster want to reassure himself that their child was conceived legitimately, or that she was his? The numbers suggest that Marion was conceived on her parents' wedding night and leave a lingering, creepy suspicion that they might never have had sex again.

The year 1850 was not an auspicious time to get married in Pittsburgh under any circumstances. The depression that had flattened the iron industry in late 1848 had yet to lift, and the city was reeling politically as well as economically.[13]

On January 7, just as Stephen Foster was returning from Cincinnati, Pittsburgh elected a new mayor, Joseph Barker, from the county jail. The rabble-rouser had been clapped there for fomenting a riot against Catholics. If there was one thing Barker hated as much as popery, it was the temperance movement. Hard-drinking, working-class resentment of moral reformers and "immoral" immigrants alike swept Barker into office for a tumultuous one-year term—as long as the prison sentence his election interrupted. Barker was a "know-nothing" ahead of his time, because it was not until 1854 that the nativist Know-Nothing Party made electoral inroads in Pennsylvania and elsewhere.[14]

The same month Barker was elected, 1,500 iron workers struck after manufacturers slashed their wages. When the owners imported replacement workers, the strikers' wives went on a rampage, assaulting the scabs and destroying a few furnaces. Workers railed against the "capitalistic aristocrats" who "lolled on sofas and lounges in their princely mansions."[15]

"Let us our outer garments cast aside," Stephen Foster's friend Charles Shiras exhorted readers in an interminable poem entitled "The Redemption of Labor," "And mingle with the workmen." "Dimes and dollars! dollars and dimes! / An empty pocket's the worst of crimes!" he wrote in "The Popular Credo":

> If a man is down, give him the thrust—
> Trample the beggar into the dust!
> Presumptuous poverty's quite appalling,
> Knock him over! kick him for falling!
> If a man is up, oh! lift him higher—
> Your soul's for sale, and he's a buyer! [16]

Shiras lived with his mother on Hemlock Street, a few blocks north of the Fosters. Both families' fortunes had fallen considerably since William Foster had founded Lawrenceville and the Shirases had built the first brewery west of the Alleghenies. Still, their relative gentility insulated Charley and Steve somewhat from the asperities of the Iron City. It may not have been prudent, but at least it was possible for Foster to kick over bookkeeping for songwriting and for Shiras to give up beer for a literary career.[17] But life was considerably harsher on Rebecca Street, several blocks closer to the river, where a family of four immigrants from Dunfermline, Scotland huddled in two second-story rooms.

William Carnegie, an unemployed weaver, had fled the Industrial Revolution in Great Britain, where steam-powered looms had replaced hand-driven ones, only to collide with it head-long in Allegheny City, where he arrived with his wife and two sons—covered with mosquito bites—in the summer of 1848. William was a loser in what his elder son Andrew would later call "the struggle . . . for elbow room in the western world." While he wove cheap tablecloths on a rented hand loom and peddled them door to door, his wife Margaret toiled late into the night, stitching shoe leather for a cobbler.[18]

Andrew, thirteen when the Carnegies came to America, received an early education in what he termed "the bracing school of poverty—the only school capable of producing the supremely great, the genius." By 1850 he had graduated from a bobbin factory floor to a telegraph office and was studying bookkeeping at night. Dipping spools in vats of oil had nauseated him, but delivering telegrams to the movers and shakers of

Pittsburgh, getting his foot in their office doors, was a thrill. "I felt that my foot was upon the ladder and that I was bound to climb." [19]

Carnegie's autobiography includes echoes of "Oh! Susanna's" tragi-comedy of industrialization. At the bobbin factory he tended a small steam engine and fired its boiler, which he was always fearful would explode. In 1852, he was in the telegraph office during a thunderstorm when lightning struck the telegraph key and knocked him off his stool. "Lectrick fluid" nearly short-circuited his career.[20]

Andrew Carnegie had a vision and a cunning that Stephen Foster and his brothers lacked. In his steely dedication to work and advancement, however, as well as in his choices of businesses, Carnegie resembled Brother William, whose colleague he soon became at the Pennsylvania Railroad, and Morrison Foster, "steady in his office as an old man." [21]

In 1891, Carnegie would return to Pittsburgh with President Benjamin Harrison to open the library he had presented to Allegheny City. To the president, Carnegie wrote in his autobiography, Pittsburgh's "flaming coke ovens and dense pillars of smoke and fire" seemed like "H––l with the lid off." He was almost as amazed when Carnegie introduced him to the department managers at his steel works. They were mere boys! "But do you notice what kind of boys they are?" Carnegie asked. "Yes," Harrison answered, "hustlers, every one of them." [22]

Stephen Foster refused to be a hustler, to follow the manly path to maturity that Brother William, Morrison, and Andrew Carnegie pursued. His brothers were "practical business men," Morrison later wrote, while Stephen's ambition and aptitude lay elsewhere.[23] His decision, on the strength of the success of "Oh! Susanna," to become a full-time song-writer, to marry and support a family, was a bold leap of faith and imagination. It was also even more foolhardy and ill-fated than Herman Melville's decision to wed and start a family after his first two books, *Typee* and *Omoo*, became bestsellers. After all, to write novels was a recognized, though seldom remunerative, profession. But a full-time songwriter? Like so many of Foster's lyrics, this flew in the face of reality.

Chapter Sixteen

GWINE TO WRITE
ALL NIGHT

*I*f Foster's choice of career was naive, he set about pursuing it in a very businesslike fashion. He worked behind locked doors in a back room on the top floor of the house on East Common, where the family was now joined by Jane. Stephen's inner sanctum was furnished with a chair, a lounge, a table, a music-rack, and a piano, and thick carpeting for soundproofing. Even his honeymoon mixed business with pleasure as he visited Firth, Pond in New York City and Benteen in Baltimore. Foster was so eager to see his publishers that he wrote his sister Ann Eliza Buchanan in eastern Pennsylvania that he could not spare the time to pay her a call en route. It was the first time in his life he had ever been East.[1]

Foster published sixteen original works (including instrumental pieces for piano) in 1850, and just as many in 1851, turning out one song after another as if they were so many bobbins. Even more remarkable than this industrial efficiency, however, was how distinctive and memorable so many of these songs were.

Most of the pieces he published during the first third of 1850 were minstrel songs, some of them doubtless written in full or in part before he had left Cincinnati. Benteen brought out the majority of them and began to identify them as "plantation melodies," as if "Ethiopian" were too old-fashioned and narrow a term to do justice to Foster's freshness and variety. At first the Baltimore publisher ignored a deal that Firth, Pond and E. P. Christy seem to have worked out in New York to promote Christy's Minstrels. The cover of Benteen's "Oh! Lemuel! Go Down to de Cotton Field" hyped Campbell's Minstrels as well as Christy's, and "Dolly Day" and "De Camptown Races" (originally entitled "Gwine to Run All Night") added a third "as sung by" band, the New Orleans Serenaders.

On February 23, 1850, Stephen Foster wrote apologetically to Christy, enclosing copies of "Camptown Races" and "Dolly Day" and indicating that he had "ordered" Benteen

> to have a new title page cut bearing the name of your band alone . . . as I wish to unite with you in every effort to encourage a taste for this style of music so cried down by opera mongers. I hope to be in New York in the Spring when I will probably have an opportunity to gratify the desire which I have to hear your band.[2]

Foster's wedding delayed his trip to New York until late summer, when he apparently did not hear Christy's Minstrels perform. Nor, remarkably, does he seem to have attended any of the band's previous performances in Cincinnati or Pittsburgh. Almost as surprising is that, after declaring his fealty to blackface, Foster published just one more Ethiopian song and then stopped abruptly. "No more are heard the pleasing notes / Of 'Coming through the Rye,' " an anonymous poem complained, "But turn you where you may, you'll hear / 'Susanna, don't you cry.' " The doggerel concluded with a curse upon "the list of *nigger*—pshaw!—I mean / Of *fashionable* songs." At Pittsburgh's Wilkins Hall, the Swiss Bell Ringers were performing an Ethiopian medley, including "Oh! Susanna," on forty-seven—count 'em—forty-seven bells. Henry Kleber's new music store at 301 Third Street was advertising ten of "Stephen C. Foster's latest songs" (in addition to "My Mother, I Obey," music by Henry Kleber and words by Charles Shiras).[3] Even as Foster's blackface songs were enjoying unprecedented and pervasive popularity, he turned his attention to parlor ballads and didn't publish another blackface song for eight months. Those published before this hiatus, however, include some of Foster's best.

The ejaculatory title of "Oh! Lemuel! Go Down to de Cotton Field," published by Benteen on January 7, 1850, obviously invokes "Oh! Susanna." The last measures of each verse galumph up the scale, as if this were a potato-sack race up a staircase—"Oh! Lem! Lem! Lem! Lemuel I say!"—and then theatrically dive a full octave to "Go down to de cotton field, and bring de boys away."

Lemuel is a "woolly headed boy" whom the singer is inviting to a ball, not to participate as a guest so much as to provide musical accompaniment, for Lemuel is a one-man minstrel band who "makes de fiddle hum," "de banjo tum," and "rattles on de old jaw bone, / And beats upon de drum." But if Lemuel wants to dance, the singer warns, "just dance outside de door; / Becayse your feet so berry large / Dey'll cover all de floor."

The racist rationale for Lemuel's exclusion from the dance floor harks back to Mike Fink, who justified sharpshooting a Negro in the foot because "the fellow's long heel prevented him from wearing a genteel boot."[4] On the other hand, it's not altogether fanciful to draw a more poignant parallel to William Sidney Mount's paintings, *Dance of the Haymakers* (1845) and *The Power of Music* (1847), in both of which a black figure stands in the right foreground, outside a barn in which white folks fiddle and dance. The latter of the two paintings is especially striking because the African American is the focus of pictorial attention, and both pictures seem to recognize—indeed, to dramatize—the unacknowledged contribution of blacks to white music making.

Foster may well have known *Dance of the Haymakers*, for it was widely circulated in 1849 as a lithograph, entitled *Music Is Contagious*.[5] Popular music in general and blackface music in particular were frequently described as "catchy" diseases. A month after "Oh! Lemuel" was published, a critic hailed Daddy Rice as the man "who first set in vogue the negro rage and mania which seized upon all the world in both its hemispheres like the infection of the cholera. . . ."[6]

The second verse of "Oh! Lemuel!" catalogues the women who will be at the ball: Juliana Snow, "cane-brake Kitty" and Nelly Bly. The last of these was celebrated in a song of her own that Firth, Pond published a month later. According to Rachel Keller Woods—to whose sister Foster had dedicated "There's a Good Time Coming" and in whose memory he composed "Where Is Thy Spirit Mary?"—Nelly Bly was a black servant girl in the Woods family. Her name struck Stephen Foster's fancy when he and several friends, including Richard Cowan, were serenading the Woodses and Bly "poked her head out of the cellar door to listen."[7]

Nelly was a name already on Foster's mind, since he had written "Nelly

Was a Lady." But while that song mourned a marriage torn asunder by death, this song seems eagerly to anticipate the joys of a marriage—or at least housekeeping—yet to come. The song's first verse invites Nelly to "bring de broom along"—quite possibly an allusion to the African-American wedding custom of "jumping the broom." It's tempting to read this song semiautobiographically and to imagine Foster looking forward to his own marriage, but in any event "Nelly Bly" is a sweet, domestic idyll, and apart from the blackface dialect, there's not a hint of conde-scension toward the object of the singer's affection, with her "heart warm as cup ob tea, / And bigger dan de sweet potato down in Tennessee."

"Nelly Bly's" "dulcem melody" has a merry, nursery-rhyme charm (in-deed, its repeated series of three scampering notes inverts the melody of "Three Blind Mice"). Ten years after its publication, the Hutchinsons adapted it as a campaign song for Abraham Lincoln: "Hi! Lincoln, Ho! Lincoln! An honest man for me: / I'll sing for you—I'll shout for you, the People's nominee."[8] A quarter century after that, the song provided Elizabeth Cochrane, a young reporter at the Pittsburgh *Dispatch*, with a byline, Nellie Bly, that would become internationally famous.

February 1850 was an active month for Foster. Not only did Firth, Pond publish "Nelly Bly," but Benteen copyrighted three other blackface songs.[9] "Dolly Day" attests to Foster's growing celebrity. At the height of the Beatles' fame, John Lennon reminded listeners of his earlier hit songs in "Glass Onion": "I told you about strawberry fields . . . I told you about the walrus and me. . . ."[10] In an identical spirit, Foster wrote 108 years earlier:

> I've told you 'bout de banjo,
>   De fiddle and de bow,
> Likewise about de cottonfield,
>   De shubble and de hoe;   ["Uncle Ned"]
> I've sung about de bulgine
>   Dat blew de folks away,   ["Oh! Susanna"]
> And now I'll sing a little song
>   About my Dolly Day.

"Angelina Baker" is to this day a popular country fiddler's tune, some-times called "Angeline the Baker," while its lyrics sound like a trial run for the following year's "Old Folks at Home." "Way down on de old plantation / Dah's where I was born," it begins. "I used to beat de whole creation / Hoein' in de corn."

"Gwine to Run All Night," of course, is the best known of the bunch. There had been horse racing in Pittsburgh on the Fourth of July when Foster was born, and the first novel written and set in Pittsburgh, Hugh Henry Brackenridge's *Modern Chivalry*, opens at the races, where the betting and swearing and jostling and "hurry-scurry" are so heated that the quixotic hero, Captain John Farrago, is thrown from his horse and bruises his head.[11] The novelist's son, Henry Marie Brackenridge, recalled that Pittsburgh's races were "an affair of all-engrossing interest, and every business and pursuit was neglected during their continuance." Not only was there racing, but there were

> booths as at a fair, where everything was said, and done, and sold, and eaten or drunk—where every fifteen or twenty minutes there was a rush to some part, to witness a *fisticuff*—where dogs barked and bit, and horses trod on men's toes, and booths fell down on people's heads![12]

It's hardly surprising that the singer of "Camptown Races" had his "hat caved in"!

What was popular was not necessarily reputable, however. Racing was ostensibly illegal in Pennsylvania, and the Camptown ladies' "doo-dah!" may well have been a hooker's come-on. After all, if the races really ran all night, they were literally ladies of the evening. The back-and-forth in Foster's verses between the solo voice ("De Camptown ladies sing dis song") and unison chorus ("Doo-dah! doo-dah!") is also a distinct echo of the call-and-response found in African-American songs. When Morrison Foster sang "Camptown Races" to his children decades later, incidentally, he pronounced the "dah!" in "doo-dah!" like the *da* in *dash*, rather than the *da* in *dark* we usually sing today.[13]

Was there a real Camptown? Residents of Camptown, New Jersey, just outside Newark, had considered adopting a more dignified name as early as 1840. The notoriety of Foster's ditty may have provided an additional incentive, because in 1852 the township settled on Irvington, after Washington Irving. Local boosters in Camptown (originally Campton), Pennsylvania, have been more eager to embrace the identification, citing a five-mile race that used to be run over an unpaved road between Camptown and Wyalusing. Camptown is fourteen miles from Towanda, where Stephen Foster briefly lived and studied.[14]

It's far more likely, however, that Camptown was a generic term for a temporary settlement, an African-American community, or both. Years

The White Cottage, circa 1828. (Courtesy of Richard K. Foster)

The old folks at home: Eliza C. Foster and William B. Foster, circa 1847–1851. (Courtesy of the Foster Hall Collection, Center for American Music, University of Pittsburgh Library System)

*"Brother William": William B. Foster, Jr.
(Courtesy of the Foster Hall Collection,
Center for American Music, University of
Pittsburgh Library System)*

*Dunning McNair Foster—"one of the beaux
(not b'hoys) of Cincinnati"—in an 1840 portrait by Pittsburgh artist William Cogswell.
(Courtesy of Sarah E. Foster)*

*Henry Russell. (Courtesy of
the Performing Arts Research
Center, New York Public
Library at Lincoln Center)*

Stephen's surviving siblings, left to right: Henry Foster, Ann Eliza Foster Buchanan, Morrison Foster, and Henrietta Foster Wick Thornton, circa 1864. (Courtesy of the Foster Hall Collection, Center for American Music, University of Pittsburgh Library System)

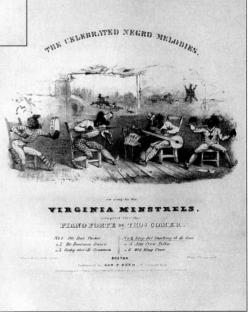

Blackface's greatest hits: sheet-music cover illustrations of G. W. Dixon's "Zip Coon," Thomas Dartmouth "Daddy" Rice's "Jim Crow," and the Virginia Minstrels' melodies. (Courtesy of the Foster Hall Collection, Center for American Music, University of Pittsburgh Library System)

Dan Rice: "I am clowning and also my nigero singing and danceing
is drawing good houses." (Courtesy of the Performing Arts
Research Center, New York Public Library at Lincoln Center)

Henry Kleber, who offered Foster "the post of first anvil player in the 'Anvil Chorus' from a new opera." (Courtesy of the Foster Hall Collection, Center for American Music, University of Pittsburgh Library System)

Martin Delany: "Woe be unto those devils of whites, I say!" (Courtesy of the Schomburg Center for Research in Black Culture, New York Public Library)

Frank Johnson, "sole arbiter of all serenades" and "inventor-general of cotillions." (Courtesy of the Harvard Theatre Collection)

FRANK JOHNSON.

Published at the Arch St. Gallery of the Daguerreotype, Philadelphia

Out of the ashes: William Coventry Wall's Pittsburgh After the Fire from Boyd's Hill, *circa 1845, above, and a view of the city in 1849, with Allegheny City at left, below. (Courtesy of the Carnegie Museum of Art and the Historical Society of Western Pennsylvania, respectively)*

Stephen Foster worked under the white awning between and beyond the steamboats Embassy (center) and Car of Commerce (right) shown in this 1848 daguerreotype of Cincinnati's Public Landing by Charles Fontayne and W. S. Porter. (Courtesy of the Public Library of Cincinnati and Hamilton County)

Nelson Kneass, whose "versatile talent . . . rendered him a favorite wherever known." (Courtesy of the Performing Arts Research Center, New York Public Library at Lincoln Center)

The "catching, melodic itch of the times": William Sidney Mount's 1849 lithograph, Music Is Contagious. (Courtesy of the Museums at Stony Brook)

Marion Foster, her father's "pet." (Courtesy of the Foster Hall Collection, Center for American Music, University of Pittsburgh Library System)

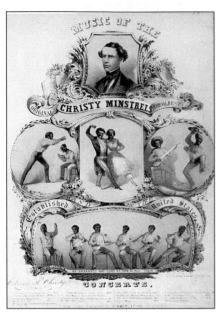

Left, E. P. Christy and his Minstrels: "I wish to unite with you," Foster wrote, "in every effort to encourage a taste for this style of music." Below, "What is a good name of two syllables for a Southern river?": "Swanee" supplants "Pedee" in Foster's sketchbook. (Courtesy of the Foster Hall Collection, Center for American Music, University of Pittsburgh Library System)

Louis Moreau Gottschalk, the first American "Signor Pound-the-keys." (Courtesy of the Performing Arts Research Center, New York Public Library at Lincoln Center)

The original title page of "Old Folks at Home": "I find I cannot write at all," Foster wrote Christy, "unless I . . . get credit for what I write." (Courtesy of the Foster Hall Collection, Center for American Music, University of Pittsburgh Library System)

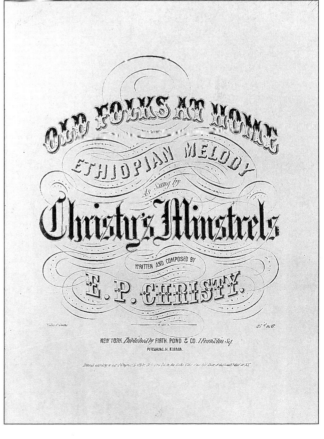

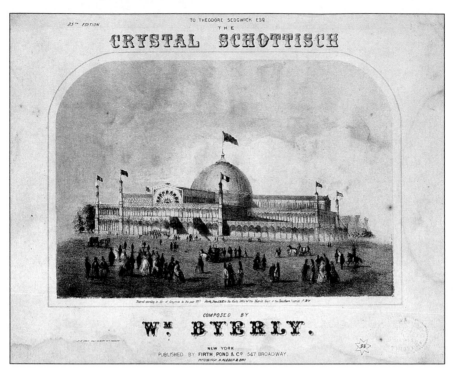

*America's first World's
Fair, in New York's
Crystal Palace, inspired
a schottische by
"William Byerly," prob-
ably a pseudonymous
Foster. (Courtesy of the
Foster Hall Collection,
Center for American
Music, University of
Pittsburgh Library
System)*

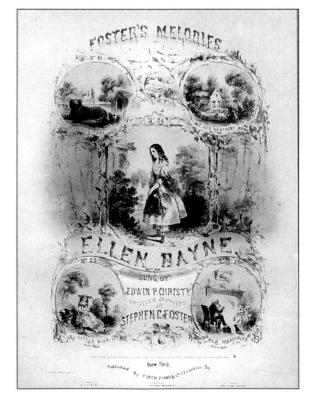

*The ornate lithograph
illustrating "Ellen
Bayne" promoted Foster
to a genteel audience.
(Courtesy of the Foster
Hall Collection, Center
for American Music,
University of Pittsburgh
Library System)*

A lay and a lied: Foster's manuscript of "Sadly
to Mine Heart Appealing." (Courtesy of the Foster Hall Collection, Center for
American Music, University of Pittsburgh Library System)

These two likenesses of Stephen Foster were probably made in 1859–1860. (Courtesy of the Foster Hall Collection, Center for American Music, University of Pittsburgh Library System)

41.   41.

Receipts On Music   **Receipts On Music — Continued.**

			9062 75
Old Folks at home	1647 46	Ring the banjo	35 24
My Old Kentucky home good night	1372 06	Village Maiden	36 08
Old Dog Tray	1080 25	Crystal Schottisch	44 06
Massa's in de Cold ground	906 76	Old Folks Quadrille	30 92
Ellen Bayne	642 34	Farewell Old Cottage	30 58
Nelly Bly	564 37	Wilt thou be gone love	22 20
Farewell my Lilly dear	551 12	My hopes have departed forever	25 04
Willie we have missed you	497 77	Gentle Annie	34 08
Oh boys carry me 'long	394 70	Dolcy Jones	21 46
Hard Times come again no more	283 84	Annie my own love	19 12
Maggie by my side	278 01	Lily Ray	18 08
Jeanie with the light brown hair	217 80	Voice of by gone days	17 54
Eulalie	203 04	Holiday Schottisch	17 37
Willie my brave	91 15	Jeannot Sing tonight	16 98
Old memories	62 52	Hour for thee and me	14 30
Some folks	59 91	Mary loves the flowers	8 98
Come where my love lies dreaming	59 88	Once I loved thee Mary dear	8 00
Little Ella	50 72	Social Orchestra	150 00
Come with thy sweet voice again	54 33	For Arranging, &c.	60 00
Way down in Cairo	44 72	From F. P. & Co. for bal. of Claim	1872 28
	9062 75		11550 06

Two pages from Foster's account book tote up his paltry profits through 1857, concluding with the sale of all his rights to publisher Firth, Pond. (Courtesy of the Foster Hall Collection, Center for American Music, University of Pittsburgh Library System)

Onward and upward: Andrew Carnegie in 1861. (Courtesy of the Carnegie Library of Pittsburgh)

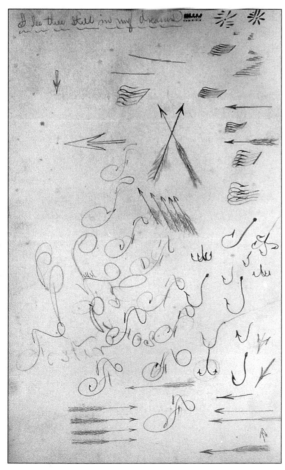

Doodles from Foster's sketchbook bristle with barbed anger. (Courtesy of the Foster Hall Collection, Center for American Music, University of Pittsburgh Library System)

Foster (left) and George Cooper, "the left wing of the song factory." (Courtesy of the Foster Hall Collection, Center for American Music, University of Pittsburgh Library System)

It takes one to know one: David Gilmour Blythe's down-at-the-heels Art versus Law. *(Courtesy of the Brooklyn Museum)*

"Dear friends and gentle hearts": Foster's purse and last scrap of words. (Courtesy of the Foster Hall Collection, Center for American Music, University of Pittsburgh Library System)

before Foster's song, John Diamond, the blackface dancer who left P. T. Barnum's road show in the lurch in 1841, used to perform, in addition to the Ole Virginny Breakdown, the Smoke House Dance and the Five Mile Out of Town Dance, "the Negro Camptown Hornpipe." And William Sidney Mount mailed a "Camptown Hornpipe"—popular in the eighteenth and nineteenth centuries and influential in the development of tap dancing, a hornpipe was an elaborate solo dance step and the tune to which it was performed—to his fiddling brother.[15]

Another song from the 1850s that is still alive and kicking today may owe a debt to "Camptown Races." In 1857, James Pierpont, J. P. Morgan's uncle, came out with "The One Horse Open Sleigh," which we now know as "Jingle Bells." "Just get a bob tailed bay" may not be the only echo of Foster in the Yuletide standard. In Foster's "My Brodder Gum," the singer "went one berry fine day, / To ride in a one horse sleigh." "Jingle Bells" may be even more deeply indebted to blackface. An 1854 Christy's Minstrels songster contains, in addition to "De Camptown Races," a song dubbed "The Darkey Sleighing Party" with the chorus: "Jingle, jingle, jingle, jingle, jingle, clear the way."[16]

The only blackface song Foster published during the rest of 1850 was "Way Down in Ca-i-ro," brought out by Firth, Pond on April 17, and it didn't mention Christy's Minstrels on the title page. Instead, on the inside, it read, "Written and Composed for James F. Taunt of the Empire Minstrels." Formed, like the Christy Minstrels, in Buffalo, the Empire Minstrels played extensively in Cincinnati and Pittsburgh in 1849 and 1850. The extremely popular group included John Diamond and "Cool" White (born John Hedges), a "Shakespearean Negro jester" who wrote (or at least claimed credit for) "Lubly Fan Will You Cum Out To Night?," the song that became Christy's Minstrels' "Bowery Gals" and in turn the Ethiopian Serenaders' still familiar "Buffalo Gals."[17]

After visiting Pittsburgh and Cincinnati, Charles Dickens, continuing down the Ohio River, had stopped at Cairo, Illinois, which he described as "a hotbed of disease, an ugly sepulchre, a grave uncheered by any gleam of promise." Fifty years later, the town's reputation had scarcely improved. The young W. C. Handy overheard work crews in his Alabama hometown singing, "Eh-oh, eh-oh, Ah wouldn't live in Cairo." "What was wrong with Cairo?" he wondered. "Was it too far up North to be considered down South, or was it too far down South to be considered up North?" Whatever the reason, Foster's chorus runs, " 'Way down in Ca-i-ro dis nigga's guine to die."[18]

The junction of the Ohio and Mississippi rivers, where slave and free states abut, would be a beacon of freedom for Huckleberry Finn and Jim —albeit a beacon they would inadvertently pass by in the night. Twain set his novel, however, in the 1840s of his childhood. In 1850, passage of the Fugitive Slave Law made Cairo and all the free states on the northern bank of the Ohio more perilous for runaway slaves and even free blacks. The year's great political debate and compromise over the future and extension of slavery exacerbated racial tensions. There's a flare of rebellion in one verse of "Way Down in Ca-i-ro" when the singer threatens to take Massa's "bran' new coat" and "wear it to de ball." Earlier, in "Angelina Baker," Foster acknowledged, however obliquely, the controversy when he veered from tall-tale humor to political commentary:

> Angelina am so tall
> She nebber see de ground,
> She hab to take a wellumscope
> To look down on de town—
> Angelina likes de boys
> As far as she can see dem,
> She used to run old Massa round
> To ax him for to free dem.

The more volatile political and racial environment may have made Foster feel uneasy about how blackface would be construed, and not just by "opera mongers." For the time being, he set the genre aside, and he never took it up again with the same regularity or concentration. In less than four years he had published thirteen songs in blackface dialect. In the remaining fourteen years of his life he would publish only nine more.

Congress enacted the Fugitive Slave Law on September 18, 1850, ten days after Stephen and Jane Foster returned from their honeymoon and settled into the Foster family house on East Common. On September 30, one of the largest throngs Allegheny City had ever seen assembled to protest the new law in what amounted to nearly a municipal mutiny by whites and blacks alike. The mayor vowed "that his arms might become palsied before they aided in the recapture of any fugitive slave." Another speaker linked racial injustice to labor unrest by coming out "not only for the freedom of the black slaves, but for the freedom of the white slaves in the Northern workshops."[19]

Martin Delany upped the ante from civil disobedience to violent self-defense when he told the crowd that his home was his castle. If anyone opened its door in search of a slave, even if he were waving the Declaration of Independence

as his banner, and the constitution of his country upon his breast as his shield,—if he crosses the threshold of my door, and I do not lay him a lifeless corpse at my feet, I hope the grave may refuse my body a resting-place, and Heaven my spirit a home. O, no! he cannot enter that house and we both live.[20]

The following month, Charles Shiras inveighed against the slave catchers in "The Bloodhound's Song":

> In the dingy streets of the City of Smoke
> They'll hear the bloodhound's bay;
> From factory, foundry, mill and shop,
> We'll drag our bleeding prey;
> And the stalwart smith shall his hammer drop,
> As the slave to him shall cling,
> For he will not dare to lift his arm
> When the bloodhound is his king![21]

But the City of Smoke did dare to resist. When a slave owner came to town and insisted that a Pittsburgh resident was his escaped property, the mayor and several other prominent citizens swore they'd known the man for years, and his accuser was jailed for perjury.[22]

Pittsburgh and Allegheny City also supported Delany, sending him off with recommendations from nineteen local white physicians to Harvard Medical School. When students protested Delany's admission (as well as that of two other African Americans and a white woman), Dean Oliver Wendell Holmes proved less of an autocrat at the medical school than he was at the breakfast table. He caved in, and the black students were kicked out at the end of the first semester (the female candidate had withdrawn her application).[23]

Convinced that white America would never overcome its prejudice and that blacks could enjoy freedom and respect only in a separate nation of their own, Delany embarked on a lecture tour. While Delany addressed "the comparative anatomy and physiology of the white and the Negro," Foster lay off the blackface.[24]

Chapter Seventeen

THE RAVEN AND
THE NIGHTINGALE

N ot once in his entire career did Stephen Foster write a
song, be it blackface or parlor ballad, that alluded to
Pittsburgh. He was in deep denial, if not outright defiance, of the economic, political, racial and even environmental realities of the city where
he passed most of his life. The floral patterns of "Mary Loves the Flowers," "Ah! May the Red Rose Live Alway!" and other parlor ballads he
published during 1850 and 1851 were rooted in another reality, however:
contemporary sentimental culture. In the best-selling American novel of
1850, Susan Warner's *The Wide, Wide World*, someone asks the young
heroine, "Do you love flowers, Ellen?" To which she replies demurely, "I
love them dearly, Miss Alice."[1]

In the late 1840s, a Pittsburgh music teacher, S. L. Bingham, introduced "Grand Floral Concerts": choral performances by schoolchildren
arrayed amid large displays of flowers. The program for one such concert
on May Day 1851, held in the Allegheny temperance hall where Frank
Johnson's band had played its ill-starred benefit, included "Song of Flora
and Her Attendants," "The Flower Girl," and "Moonlight Music, Love
and Flowers." *Flora's Festival*, a likeminded but more grandiose "juvenile
cantata," was staged several times in New York City, with as many as a
thousand children in the cast. It inspired George Root's first secular, or

"people's," cantata, *The Flower Queen, or The Coronation of the Rose*, as well as, perhaps, the "floral festival" in the second verse of Foster's "Ah! May the Red Rose Live Alway!"[2]

This ballad is more deeply rooted still in the Anglo-Scots-Irish tradition of popular song, its very title reminiscent of Thomas Moore's "The Last Rose of Summer." Foster's melody is simpler than Moore's, but eloquent from the vocal line's very first note: a sighing high D that is held with a fermata as if for dear life, a stay against the onrush and onslaught of time.

"Mary Loves the Flowers" asks, "The lily and the morning glory, / Can they, can they die?" And "Ah! May the Red Rose Live Alway!" reiterates, "Why should the beautiful ever weep? / Why should the beautiful die?," with the question marks that are typical of Foster's early parlor ballads. Foster's blackface songs bristle with exclamation points: "Oh! Susanna," "Oh! Lemuel!," "Doo-dah! doo-dah!" Their animation contrasts dramatically with the passivity of the questions Foster's parlor ballads from the same period pose: "Molly Do You Love Me?," "Tell me, have you ever met her / Met the spirit of my song?"

The exclamation point is bold and assertive, inherently masculine and typographically phallic. Foster's blackface songs were meant to be sung chiefly by men in groups, be they the Nice Young Men, Knights of the Square Table, or Christy's Minstrels. The curvaceous question mark, on the other hand, is unmistakably feminine. The parlor ballads were designed to be sung by one voice, frequently a woman's, even if the sentiments were ostensibly a man's.[3]

Foster's sexual dimorphism was partly a function of the marketplace. Most sheet music was purchased, played and sung by women. In an era when it was widely considered unladylike to appear on the stage (much less to go on the road), most public performers, apart from a handful of divas and kid sisters in singing family groups, were men. It was these men's performances that popularized songs so that women would purchase the music. (Just as in the 1950s, men—boys, mostly—sang rock 'n' roll but women—girls, really—bought the 45s and cached them in pink plastic carrying cases with appliquéd poodles.)[4]

More than the marketplace, American culture and even its domestic architecture in the middle of the nineteenth century created the great divide between most of Foster's early blackface and sentimental songs. It was during this period that the front parlor became institutionalized, a feature of every forward-looking home, while the dirty work and muddy boots of life were banished to the rear of the house. Parlors were "placid havens of economic inutility," in the words of cultural historian Richard L. Bushman, proof that a family "had a front to their lives as to their houses, where the rough ways of work and family intimacy were concealed, and that they could appear as polished beings capable of grace, dignity and propriety." Thus "the middle-class dwelling under parlor influence [became] a house divided against itself." [5]

Men and women work in Foster's blackface songs: cooking or sweeping up a storm, hoeing the cornfield, toting the cottonwood. They toil not just because they're slaves or poor, but also because it's the human condition. Nobody works for a living in Foster's parlor ballads, which for the most part are oblivious not only to the menial aspects of life, but to its moral dimensions as well. The antecedents of "Ah! May the Red Rose Live Alway!" usually drew some conclusion or consolation from the perdurability of virtue. Edmund Waller's "Go Lovely Rose!" was a seventeenth-century Cavalier poem, but even when recast as a nineteenth-century song or "Canzonet," it did not deny that "virtue lives, when beauty dies." [6] In Foster, however, there is no virtue, only innocence.

"Ah! May the Red Rose Live Alway!" treats death metaphorically. "The Voice of By Gone Days" is the first of his published parlor ballads explicitly about a dead young woman or girl. ("Where Is Thy Spirit Mary?" was private and personal, a gift to Mary Keller's family.) The "early love" who has joined the angels' "bless'd and happy train" goes unnamed here, but Lily Ray, Eulalie, two Annies, Belle Blair, Cora Dean, Ella, Eva, Lena, Linda, Lizzie, Virginia Belle, and many anonymous others will follow her to the grave.

"The Voice of By Gone Days" is as Italianate as "Ah! May the Red Rose Live Alway!" is Anglo-Irish, its melody echoing Donizetti rather than Moore, but otherwise the songs are in perfect, obsessive accord. [7] For here and in a third 1850 song, "Lily Ray," one of Foster's most persistent themes crystallizes—if *crystallize* isn't too hard-edged a word to describe Foster's liquid dreams of love and death, his dewy tears and vaporous sighs.

Not every parlor song Foster wrote during this period was lachrymose. "Molly Do You Love Me?" is a playful song of courtship that he composed as he was wooing Jane. But Foster shared the funereal fixation of his era, in which Lydia Sigourney, "death's shrillest devotee," according to cultural historian Carl Bode, "was collecting a full seventy of her poems—every one about death—in *The Weeping Willow* at the same time that Edgar Allan Poe was arguing in 'The Philosophy of Composition' that 'the death . . . of a beautiful woman is, unquestionably, the most poetical topic in the world.' " Mark Twain satirized this morbid mindset in *Huckleberry Finn's* Emmeline Grangerford, who crayoned pictures with captions like "And Art Thou Gone Yes Thou Art Gone Alas." It would be trite and reductive to chalk it all up to Charlotte, but Foster brought to such bathos a personal intensity as well as a melodic artistry that enabled his songs to survive while "Laura's Grave—*By a Gentleman of Kentucky*" is—alas!—forgotten.[8]

In 1851 Foster published "Eulalie," another mournful song, this time with words by Henry Sylvester Cornwell, a Connecticut physician and poet who often published in *The Home Journal*. Yesterday's euphony—" 'Neath the yew-tree, Eulalie!"—sounds hilarious today, but the song was commended by one reviewer as "probably the most correct and refined melody Mr. Foster has ever written," and it was the first of Foster's parlor ballads to become a modest commercial success, earning $203.04 in royalties.[9]

Cornwell once confessed he was subject to "Poe spasms," and Poe, too, wrote a poem entitled "Eulalie." Foster often recited Poe's poetry at length "with thrilling effect," and he had a fondness for women's names that ululate like Poe's Eulalie and Ulalume; he liked Lula so much he used it twice.[10]

The affinity between Foster and Poe extends further. Reprinted at least ten times within a month of its appearance in Morris and Willis's *New York Mirror*, recited, parodied and pirated across the nation (across the Atlantic, as well), "The Raven" was a smash hit in 1845 like "Oh! Susanna" three years later. The extraordinary success of both depended on the advances in mass communication and transportation (and lack of copyright protection) that made popular culture possible and triumphant. And it was Poe, after all, who termed melancholy "the most legitimate of all the poetical tones."[11]

Such stuff as Foster's dreams were made on usually turned into nightmares, however, in Poe's poems and tales. Death, in Foster's songs, is usually a kind of release for black men ("No more hard work for poor Uncle Ned") and a state of repose for white women (as "My Hopes Have Departed Forever" expresses it: ". . . morning will shine through the willows, / And find me forever at rest"). Death is anything but easeful for Poe's corpses, who have a ghastly habit of kicking out the jambs of their crypts. Yet both artists shared a kindred tendency toward abstraction and vagueness. Foster's women, for instance, are usually outlines, "forms" (the word appears in no fewer than twenty-two of his songs) that enable the singer and listener to fill in the blank with their own memories.

By now Foster usually wrote his own words as well as music—and these are unquestionably his most memorable songs—but he still occasionally set other writers' verses. In 1851 and 1852 he turned not only to Cornwell but to Metta Victoria Fuller, James Gates Percival, and Charles G. Eastman. Fuller, the "Singing Sybil," began at the tender age of fourteen to publish poetry in *The Home Journal*, where "The Spirit of My Song" struck Foster's fancy. Percival was a Connecticut polymath and poet whose "The Winds of the Winter Are Over" provided the basis for Foster's "My Hopes Have Departed Forever." This grim lyric, which ends with a jilted lover's implied suicide, is uncharacteristic of Foster but typical of the gloomy Percival, whose other poems include "Despondency," "Consumption," and "The Suicide's Grave." Firth, Pond published this song as "Written and Composed by A LADY," but the words appear in Foster's sketchbook. Possibly he recalled them from childhood —when his guitar-playing sister Henrietta wrote to Brother William that she had learned "a beautiful new song since I last saw you, My hopes have departed forever"—and rearranged an old tune.[12]

There's definitely a personal ring to Foster's setting of Eastman's "Sweetly She Sleeps, My Alice Fair," which Benteen copyrighted on March 18, 1851, along with "Mother, Thou'rt Faithful to Me," four days before Firth, Pond registered "Farewell! Old Cottage." Foster wrote the words to these other two songs, and together they form a domestic triptych: the first songs Foster ever wrote about a mother, a daughter, and home.

This sudden familial concern coincided with events in the Foster household. In the early spring, a stroke left William Foster, now seventy-one, bedridden and severely impaired. His war-claims account book peters out with entries in his sons' handwriting; Stephen, Morrison, and Henry all lent a hand. But even as one generation lingered at death's door, another one arrived at East Common. On April 18, Marion Foster was born and named after Jane's older sister.

Marion's impending birth must have drawn Stephen Foster to Eastman's poem, which, changing Eastman's anonymous "maiden" to a "child" named Alice, he adapted into a lovely, anticipatory lullaby. "Mother, Thou'rt Faithful to Me," to be sung *Con espressione*, was a tribute to Eliza Foster:

> Mother, dear mother, amid the strife
> Thy spirit hath borne in the battle of life,
> Mid envy, ambition, deceit, and pride,
> Thou'st ever fondly clung to my side.
> Time's running sands have furrowed thy brow,—
> Care hath bedimmed thy cheek's native glow;
> But, warm in affection of sacred hue,
> Mother, mother, thou'rt faithful and true.

"Farewell! Old Cottage," which Foster dedicated to Rachel Woods, the surviving Keller sister, seems on first hearing like yet another exercise in a familiar genre, an echo of Henry Russell's nostalgia. Indeed, Russell himself wrote a song entitled "My Old Cottage Home," and "The Cot Where We Were Born" was a staple of the Hutchinsons' concerts.[13] But there is a note not just of nostalgia but of personal grievance in Stephen Foster's

> Farewell! old cottage,
> You and I must part;
> I leave your faithful shelter
> With a poor breaking heart.
> The stranger, in his might,
> Hath cast our lot in twain;
> The term of our delight
> Must close in parting pain.

It's almost as if the stranger were the bank that foreclosed on the Fosters' White Cottage.

"A LADY" was not the only pseudonym under which Foster published in the early 1850s. Songs poured from his pen so prodigally that he didn't feel the need to acknowledge the paternity of them all. He ascribed the lyrics (though not the music) for "Once I Loved Thee Mary Dear" to

Wm. Cullen Crookshank, conflating the American poet William Cullen Bryant and Dickens's British illustrator, George Cruikshank.

In a more elaborate game of hide-and-seek, he published "I Would Not Die in Spring Time" in 1850 under the pseudonym of Milton Moore and followed it up in 1851 with "I Would Not Die in Summer Time," published under his own name and advertised as "An answer to the New and Beautiful Song I Would Not Die in Spring Time." Complicating matters further, two Philadelphia publishers brought out different versions of another "answer" song, "I Would Not Die in Winter," with lyrics by William H. Cunnington. Then John Hill Hewitt got the last word in edgewise with a parody, "I Would Not Die at All."[14] Pop music was playing the game of Can-you-top-this? long before the "answer" songs of rock ("Eve of Destruction"? No, it's the "Dawn of Correction") and rap (U.T.F.O.'s "Roxanne, Roxanne" riposted by Roxanne Shante's "Roxanne's Revenge").

Foster also tried his hand at duets, dedicating the first, "Turn Not Away!," to his friend Robert Nevin and the second, "Wilt Thou Be Gone, Love?," to Morrison's fiancée, Julia Murray. (Soon Miss Murray *was* gone as the engagement was broken off and she married the son of a prominent abolitionist and mentor of Martin Delany, Dr. F. Julius LeMoyne.)[15] "Turn Not Away!" is a rather stiff exercise almost entirely in parallel thirds, but "Wilt Thou Be Gone, Love?" is an elaborate, nearly operatic setting of Act III, scene v in *Romeo and Juliet*.

Operatic? Yes, a year after decrying opera mongers to Christy, Foster was becoming a bit of a buff himself, even translating the lyrics to a Meyerbeer aria. His increasing attraction to classical music may have owed partly to his growing friendship with Henry Kleber. In 1850 Foster dedicated a piano piece, "Village Bells Polka," to Kleber, and the following year Kleber returned the favor, dedicating his own "Spirit Polka" to Foster.

Foster's interest in opera may also have been stimulated by the excitement attending P. T. Barnum's visit to Pittsburgh on September 25, 1851, almost exactly a decade after he'd briefly been jailed there. This time, however, he wasn't limping into town with half a blackface act. He was arriving in triumph aboard the steamboat *Messenger No. 2* as the escort of a diminutive Swedish soprano named Johanna Maria Lind.

Barnum promoted "Jenny" Lind with all the hoopla he'd lavished on General Tom Thumb. (According to a newspaper item that was doubtless planted by Barnum if not made up out of whole cloth, when the midget met Lind in New Orleans, he offered as a keepsake his jeweled watch, which she graciously declined because it was too small for her wrist.)[16] The entire country was whipped into a pop frenzy, "Lindomania," which a Cincinnati journalist defined as "a certain species of enthusiasm and of nervous mania which is seen but once or twice in a lifetime." Once or twice in a century is more like it, since apart from the hullabaloo over Fanny Elssler in the early 1840s, the closest equivalent to the Jenny Lind craze is the "Beatlemania" of the 1960s. Merchandisers had a field day. "We had Jenny Lind gloves, Jenny Lind bonnets, Jenny Lind riding hats, Jenny Lind shawls, mantillas, robes, chairs, sofas, pianos—in fact, every thing was Jenny Lind," Barnum boasted. He forgot Jenny Lind hair gloss, Jenny Lind pens, Jenny Lind chewing tobacco, and Jenny Lind canes. Chambermaids even sold hairs from her hairbrush.[17]

Stephen and Jane Foster may still have been honeymooning in New York when thirty thousand people thronged Canal Street to greet "The Swedish Nightingale" on Sunday morning, September 1, 1850. Perhaps they milled about in the crowd that besieged the Irving House that evening, or stayed up until midnight to hear the serenade of American anthems that two hundred members of New York's Musical Fund Society performed beneath Lind's hotel window. Among the visitors Lind received in the following weeks were the Hutchinsons, who sang for her "The Cot Where We Were Born" and a new song, "Welcome to Jenny Lind," which became a staple of their concerts.[18]

Stephen and Jane Foster returned to Allegheny City before Lind's first concert at Castle Garden, the pleasure dome on a dot of an island off the Battery that N. P. Willis called "the amputated great toe of Broadway."[19] They were not among the five thousand fans who heard Lind, a little wobbly at first, sing *"Casta diva"* (Chaste goddess) from Bellini's *Norma*, Americans' favorite Italian opera. "Be weather clear, or damp, or stormy," one wag rhymed, "They're always playing, 'Hear Me, Normy.'"[20] Lind· was indeed a chaste diva, a pristine Protestant and unsullied Aryan (despite her illegitimate birth) whose popularity would plummet when she wed Otto Goldschmidt, who was not only a dull pianist and mal-adroit manager but a Jew. (Walt Whitman was one of the few who had never been impressed by Lind's holier-than-thou act. Reviewing one of her performances at Castle Garden, he wrote, "Her cheeks were well rouged, and her walk bad. The expression of her face is a sort of moral milk and honey.")[21]

Henry Kleber heard Lind perform in New York and came back with praise for her singing and, not coincidentally, copies of her songs for sale. (The same visit may have inspired him to compose "The Opera Schottisch," which Firth, Pond illustrated with an engraving of Max Maretzek conducting at Castle Garden.) Nevertheless, it was Kleber's rival, John Mellor, with whom Barnum confirmed that Lind would play two evenings in Pittsburgh, and it was Mellor who provided her suite at the Monongahela House and the stage at the Masonic Hall with Chickering pianos.[22]

A large crowd was at the dock when Lind arrived in Pittsburgh at nine in the morning on April 25, 1851. A member of Lind's party wrote that "a pale and sickly-looking sun peered through the grimy atmosphere, having very much the appearance of a yellow wafer floating in a bowl of dirty milk." Barnum got off the boat and into a carriage with a young woman whom the throng mistook for Lind. It was probably a deliberate ruse, the same sort of ploy the Beatles frequently used, and the diversion enabled Lind and a companion to disembark unmolested.[23]

Not everyone, of course, could afford the tickets that were auctioned off that morning, and the hall was surrounded with onlookers in the evening. Nearby buildings sagged with the weight of the people atop them—some of whom had paid money for their ringside, rooftop seats. The Masonic Hall was "beautifully decorated," according to one newspaper account, but construction had not yet been completed. One thing that seems to have been unfinished were the windows and their curtains, permitting people to peer in and dimly hear the concert.

As she sang, "a ruffian crowd" pelted Lind's dressing room window with pebbles. Afterward they besieged the hall in their eagerness to see her, and a terrified Lind was held captive until midnight, when a drayman conducted her down the back stairs and through a hole in a fence to Virgin Alley and back to her hotel.

Lind and Barnum may have been overreacting when they canceled the second concert and left the next morning in a huff. What happened in Pittsburgh was child's play compared to Cincinnati, where a mob had hurled brickbats and exchanged potshots with the police. Lind may have skipped town because her harried schedule had left her at the end of her rope—and at the end of her relationship with Barnum. In June, she canceled their contract while she was booked into a Philadelphia theater that was normally a circus and the reek of horse manure forced her to perform with a perfumed handkerchief pressed to her face. Finally she had tired of performing in Barnum's menagerie, although she had made a fortune doing so. When Barnum approached Gottschalk a couple of years later, offering him twenty thousand dollars and all expenses paid for a year's concertizing, the pianist's father nixed the deal, insisting that Barnum was "only a showman of beasts."[24]

There's no proof that Stephen Foster heard Lind at Masonic Hall, although the young Andrew Carnegie attended and thought her "the strangest woman I ever heard of." If only, he wrote, "she could . . . sing some Scotch songs if she could give us 'Auld Lang Syne' I would have been better pleased than with all the others put together." (His response was no more parochial than that of Emily Dickinson, who saw Lind in Northampton, Massachusetts, and wrote that her singing was no doubt "very fine," but apart from a few of her "curious trills," she'd "rather have a Yankee.")[25]

Foster soon turned his hand, however, to translating an aria popularized by one of the first of many divas who would rush to America to cash in on the Jenny Lind craze. The Irish soprano Catherine Hayes had taken up where Lind had left off as a Meyerbeer protégée, starring in the London premiere of the composer's *Le Prophète*. That opera's second-act aria, *"Ah, mon fils,"* became Hayes's signature tune and may well have appealed to Foster because it's a paean to apron strings: it praises (mistakenly, as the plot turns out) a young man's sacrifice of the woman he loves to save his sainted mother's life.

Dubbed "The Swan of Erin," Hayes arrived in New York in September 1851 and performed two concerts in Pittsburgh in the spring of 1852. At the first of these she sang *"Ah, mon fils,"* and one reviewer declared her "immeasurably above" Lind, with greater "feeling, and . . . purity of voice in the lower notes." Hayes achieved her greatest acclaim when she reached California, where she became the gold rush's golden girl and drove poor Elisa Biscaccianti to drink and South America. Two tours of California enabled Hayes to return to England and retire for life.[26]

An advertisement for one of Hayes's concerts at Pittsburgh's Masonic Hall (by now the windows had presumably been completed) advised that "Programmes, containing the words of the Songs in French, Italian and English, may be obtained in the Hall on the night of performance. Price 15 cents." The translation of *"Ah! mon fils"* may well have been Foster's, for Firth, Pond published sheet music for twenty-one songs in Hayes's repertory, and Foster furnished the anonymous translation, "Ah! My Child!"[27]

Foster received credit on its title page for a second translation that was published about this time. "In the Eye Abides the Heart" renders into English *"In den Augen liegt das Herz,"* Franz Abt's setting of a poem by Franz von Kobell. It's curious that Foster is listed as the translator while the musical arrangement is attributed to H.K.—Henry Kleber, whose command of his native tongue must have been superior to Foster's smattering of German. A reversal of roles would seem a more likely collaboration. Although Abt is all but forgotten today, this friend of Mendelssohn and Schumann, a choirmaster who published more than three thousand works, was for Foster a congenial composer. Abt's "When the Swallows Fly Homeward" was a popular parlor ballad in America during the 1850s, and his simple melodies, a critic has written, "are easily mistaken for genuine folksong." So, one might add, are Foster's.[28]

There was one problem with Foster's attempts to branch out beyond blackface: He was going broke. He spent much of 1850 and 1851 trying to diversify his songwriter's portfolio, but his own account book documents how unrewarding his investments were. In that ledger Foster tallied, in 1857, what each of his songs had earned in royalties thus far. In seven years, "Ah! May the Red Rose Live Alway!" had made only $8.12, "The Spirit of My Song" a mere $5.00. "Nelly Bly," in blackface dialect, had earned him $564.37—more than twice as much as "Eulalie" and $161.96 more than all eight original parlor ballads Firth, Pond published in 1851 and 1852. Foster's account book lists nineteen songs written in standard English during these two years. The average return in royalties was less than $31.00 a song. The average return for blackface songs published during the same period was more than ten times that: $319.44.

In 1956, Elvis Presley told a reporter he didn't know how long rock 'n' roll would last. "When it's gone, I'll switch to something else," he said. "I like to sing ballads the way Eddie Fisher does and the way Perry Como does. But the way I'm singing now is what makes the money. Would you change if you was me?"[29]

With not only a wife but a daughter now to support, Foster had to write the kind of songs that made money. It was time to get down to business, and business meant blackface.

Chapter Eighteen

FROM BLACKS
TO FOLKS

On June 12, 1851, Stephen Foster wrote to E. P. Christy in New York and proposed a deal:

I have just received a letter from Mess. Firth, Pond & Co. stating that they have copy-righted a new song of mine ("Oh! boys, carry me 'long") but will not be able to issue it for some little time yet, owing to other engagements. This will give me time to send you the m.s. and allow you the privilege of singing it for at least two weeks, and probably a month before it is issued, or before any other band gets it (unless they catch it up from you). If you will send me $10 immediately for this privilege I pledge myself, as a gentleman of the old school, to give you the m.s. I have written to F. P. & Co. not to publish till they hear from me again. This song is certain to become popular, as I have taken great pains with it. If you accept my proposition I will make it a point to notify you hereafter when I have a new song and send you the m.s. on the same terms, reserving to suit myself in all cases the exclusive privilege of publishing. Thus it will become notorious that your band brings out all the new songs. You can state in the papers that the song was composed expressly for you. I make this proposition because I am sure of the song's popularity.[1]

Foster may have been "a gentleman of the old school," but he was learning new tricks in a business that was still in its infancy. He had come up with a way to plug a song and turn an extra ten dollars in the process. He was hustling.

Nine days later he inscribed with the date a leather-bound sketchbook in which he worked on the lyrics for many of the songs he composed during the next ten years. The following month he rented an office—no doubt because Marion and her nurse made it more difficult to work in the house on East Common. (He was not able to separate professional from family responsibilities entirely: His sketchbook contains penciled remedies for tonsillitis and fever.)

Foster published two blackface songs in 1851 before he wrote Christy, and neither mentioned his minstrels. Copyrighted by Benteen on January 6, "Melinda May" was his first blackface song in the nearly nine months since "Way Down in Ca-i-ro" (which had also snubbed Christy). It was advertised "as Sung by the Celebrated New Orleans Serenaders," but apart from some mangled consonants and the chorus's mention of working "in de field," nothing identifies "Melinda May" as an Ethiopian melody. Only the dialect differentiates the song from a parlor ballad pitching woo. Foster seemed confused and halfhearted, fumbling for a way to infuse blackface with some class, but unable to figure out the formula.

"Ring, Ring de Banjo!," copyrighted by Firth, Pond in April, also omitted Christy's Minstrels from its title page. No one is mentioned save the author, as if Foster (or his publisher) hoped he were now famous enough to sell a blackface song on the strength of his own name alone. The lyrics try to invoke the spirit of Foster's first hit ("Den come again Susanna") even as they acknowledge the artificiality of such an attempt ("By de gaslight ob de moon"). "Ring, ring de banjo! / I like dat good old song," goes the refrain, "Come again my true lub, / Oh! wha you been so long." But the incoherence of the third and fourth verses makes it clear that you can't go home again, that the ambiguities of blackface can no longer be ignored or dismissed with a once-over-lightly. In the third verse the singer is freed by his master, but he returns to "massa's door" and vows to "lub him all de harder / [He'll] go away no more."

Here's what happens in the fourth verse:

> Early in de morning
> Ob a lubly summer day,
> My massa send me warning
> He'd like to hear me play.

On de banjo tapping,
   I come wid dulcem strain;
Massa fall a napping—
   He'll nebber wake again.

The singer returns to his beloved "massa"; then he kills him. If the banjo isn't the actual murder weapon with which he bludgeons his sleeping master, at the very least it's an accessory to the crime, its "dulcem strain" lulling Massa until he lets down his guard.

If Foster were a more deliberate and didactic writer, one might argue that the fourth verse of "Ring, Ring de Banjo!" is a self-conscious critique of minstrelsy, a warning that blackface mirth masks real black hostility. But Foster seldom worked out his lyrics so rationally. He followed his feelings without analyzing them deeply, and this song reflects the internal contradictions of minstrelsy without registering much awareness of them.

Neither "Ring, Ring de Banjo!" nor "Melinda May" was very successful, so Foster took "great pains" with "Oh! Boys, Carry Me 'Long" and special care to mend fences with Christy. Receiving his ten dollars, Foster quickly mailed his new composition to Christy, with instructions how to perform it. "I am not certain that you use a piano in your band," Foster wrote, suggesting once again that despite many opportunities, he had, incredibly, never seen the Christy Minstrels perform.[2] Although Nelson Kneass often played the piano in a minstrel setting, Christy's band rarely if ever featured a pianist. In fact, there's no hard evidence that Christy and Foster ever even met.

"If you have a tenor voice in the company," Foster continued, "that can sing up to 'g' with ease (which is very probable) it will be better to sing the song in the key of 'g.' Thus you will not carry the bass voice so low." He was trying to cover for his unfamiliarity with Christy's Minstrels by assuming an air of professionalism. Indeed, "Oh! Boys, Carry Me 'Long" can easily be transposed to G from the key of F in which it is written.

But Foster was on shaky ground. A half century later the leader of a Pittsburgh minstrel company recalled that "Foster's ear was correct as to melody, but he sometimes made amusing mistakes in trying to produce harmonies. On one occasion I heard him singing a song in one key and playing it on the piano in another." Foster was probably not doing this on purpose—unlike George Ives, who would "stretch [the] ears and strengthen [the] musical minds" of Charles Ives and other pupils by asking them to sing a Stephen Foster tune like "Old Folks at Home" in one key while accompanying it in another.[3]

Still, Foster lectured Christy:

> I hope you will preserve the harmony in the chorus just as I have written it, and practise the song well before you bring it out. It's especially necessary that the person who sings the verses should know all the words perfectly, as the least hesitation in the singing will damn any song—but this you know as well as myself. Remember it should be sung in a pathetic, not a comic style.

Foster's fastidiousness here is at once that of an artist and a naif, neither reconciled to the rough handling his creation will inevitably receive in the free-and-easy world of pop performance. The same fussy and futile pride caused Scott Joplin to caution students that his rags were "destroyed by careless or imperfect rendering, and very often good players lose the effect entirely by playing too fast. They are harmonized with the supposition that each note will be played as it is written."[4]

The irony is that, for all Foster's pedantic precautions, "Oh! Boys, Carry Me 'Long" is not a distinguished song. Essentially it's "Uncle Ned" rewritten in the first person, describing an elderly slave's death of old age and overwork and his gratitude that death will at last release him from servitude. "Oh! Boys, Carry Me 'Long" sharpens the earlier song's implicit criticism of slavery, however, by exulting, "I's guine to roam / In a happy home / Where all de niggas am free." (It is also the last song Foster ever published using the word "nigga" or "nigger.") The song ends on a fatuous note as the singer, ostensibly being borne to the burying ground, insists, "Massa, dont you cry." When Uncle Ned died, Massa took it "mighty bad," but at least the poor slave didn't jump out of his grave to urge him to dry his eyes. Foster's admonition that "Oh! Boys, Carry Me 'Long" "be sung in a pathetic, not a comic style" may be admirable. It attests, after all, to his refusal to reduce African Americans to mere laughingstocks. Yet it's hard to imagine the song being performed with a straight face. "The sentiment is absurd, untruthful and ridiculous," scoffed Jacob Little, a Quaker correspondent of the New York weekly, *The Musical World and Times*.[5]

Its absurdity didn't prevent "Oh! Boys, Carry Me 'Long" from attracting an audience, earning $394.70 in royalties over the next six years. Ironically, by the time Foster and Christy struck their bargain, Firth,

Pond had already engraved the song's title page, which makes no mention of Christy's Minstrels. Once again, Foster apologized, and he promised to place the band's name "on future songs, and will cheerfully do anything else in my humble way to advance your interest."[6] Soon Foster advanced Christy's interest and hurt his own by allowing Christy's name to appear, alone, on the title page of one of his most famous songs, "Old Folks at Home."

It was at his "own solicitation," Foster later acknowledged, that Christy was credited as the composer of "Old Folks at Home." What Foster solicited, no doubt, was a fee on top of the $10 for first performance rights that Christy had paid for "Oh! Boys, Carry Me 'Long." Although Morrison Foster claimed that he himself drew up a contract stipulating that Christy pay five hundred dollars for that privilege, another account quotes Stephen saying that he had sold it for only fifteen dollars.[7] Foster received royalties from "Old Folks" from the very outset, but not recognition as its author.

While the financial details of the publication of "Old Folks at Home" are uncertain, the drama of its composition is well documented in Foster's sketchbook. After finishing the translation of *"Ah, mon fils,"* he wrote down a line:

Way down upon de old plantation

Apart from the substitution of "upon" for "on," it was the first line of "Angelina Baker," the song he'd written a year and a half earlier in which the singer "used to beat de whole creation / Hoein' in de corn." Then Foster wrote a quatrain:

Way down upon de *Pedee* ribber
Far far away
Dare's where my heart is turning ebber
Dere's wha my brudders play

Maybe he was thinking of "Ole Tare River," which he had already echoed in "Oh! Susanna." But the Pee Dee, a river and region in South Carolina that had been Francis "Swamp Fox" Marion's stomping ground during the Revolutionary War, had already been used in a blackface song. "Ole Pee Dee," published in 1844, was the song that had described Dickens's first visit to America ("In Boston I couldnt get any pickins / Caze all de victuals went to de Dickens").[8] Evidently Foster wanted a more original geographical reference, because after he wrote a variation on his first verse—

> Way down upon de Pedee ribber
> Far far away
> Dere's where my heart is turning ebber
> Dere's where de old blacks stay

—he scratched out "Pedee" and inserted "Swanee."

Morrison Foster wrote that one day Stephen burst into his office and asked, "What is a good name of two syllables for a Southern river?" After Stephen rejected his brother's suggestions of Yazoo and Pee Dee, they consulted an atlas. Morrison's account is not entirely corroborated by the sketchbook, but he may have been correct about the atlas, for northern Florida's Suwannee River was hardly a famous waterway.[9]

That's not the only change between verses: "my brudders play" has become "old blacks stay." What might have been a reference, albeit in blackface dialect, to Foster's own brothers, including the one with the atlas in his office, has been distanced and racialized. Or has it? The "b" and the "c" in "blacks" are oddly drawn, almost as if they were an "f" and an "l": "flalks." It's as if Foster's pencil were teetering on the brink between blackface and a deeper identification with African Americans, an identification at once more personal and more universal. He had tried, in earlier songs, to cross the great divide between blackface and parlor ballad, black and white, them and us. Now he was inching closer than ever before. The next stanza almost bridges the gap, but not quite:

> All up and down de whole creation
> Sadly I roam
> Still longing for de old plantation
> And for de old flks at home.

"[F]lks" is not a misprint—it's as if Foster still couldn't quite spell out his intentions, not even to himself.

Foster then fills five pages with "Willie My Brave," in which a maiden mourns a dear, drowned sailor, and another four pages with campaign doggerel, set to the tune of "Camptown Races," for the Bigler brothers, William and John, who were the Democratic candidates for governor of Pennsylvania and California, respectively. The chorus goes "I'll bet my money on the Bigler boys / For the Whigs have had their reign," and Foster bet right. Both men won.

When Foster finally returns to "Old Folks," he's not yet in the clear. He introduces "my kind old mudder," which rhymes with "brudder." But a discordant note follows:

> Long time ago I left my fadder
> > Why tell me why
> Oh take me to my kind old mudder
> > Dere let me lib and die.

Unlike "mudder" and "brudder," which survive in the published version of the song, "fadder" doesn't make the final cut. Not just because it doesn't rhyme with "mudder" or with "sadder" (which Foster also tries), but also because Foster's feelings about his father are more conflicted.

Foster also encounters a little more difficulty with "folks." The first time he writes it, the "o" looks suspiciously like an "a." Four lines later, "folks" is boldly legible and the song is all but complete. Finally, blackface and first person, "de old plantation" and the White Cottage, have merged:

> All round de little farm I wandered
> > When I was young
> Den many happy days I squandered
> > Many de songs I sung.

It's ironic that Foster wrote this song of weary estrangement and exile while still a young man in the bosom of his family. Far from roaming "All up and down de whole creation," he'd stuck closer to home than any of his siblings. Not even marriage and fatherhood had driven him from the nest. He wasn't "far from de old folks at home"—he was living with them on East Common. He was anticipating a separation he had seldom experienced, imagining (guiltily, no doubt) the imminent deaths of his parents with a premature burst of nostalgia.

It's amazing how elementary the melody is: only six phrases, all but one of which begin with two identical measures. The octave leap that dramatizes the distance between the singer and home, the gulf between mother and child, repeats and repeats like a scratched record. Anybody could sing it, and everybody did.

While Christy's Minstrels were belting it out at Mechanics' Hall, the actress Emily Mestayer was singing it at Barnum's nearby museum in what had been euphemistically christened "The Moral Lecture Room." If prudes needed still more assistance in overcoming their scruples against attending the theater, the play entitled *The Old Folks at Home* was advertised as a *"moral* [emphasis added] domestic drama." Miss Mestayer, an actress whose "vast protuberance of bosom" made a lifelong but not notably moral impression in other roles on the young Henry James, starred as a "betrayed wanderer who, robed in black, was returning to the house whence a father's curse had followed her." According to one account, "The song was not only the feature of that drama, but it was absolutely the rage everywhere, having no rival unless it was 'Ben Bolt'. . . . [E]very band, some borrowed from as far as Nyack, was playing 'Old Folks at Home' in the streets of New York." [10]

Slaves sang it in Georgia, and so did New York City's Short Boys. In 1852 the notorious street gang besieged Henrietta Sontag, the cigar-smoking soprano whom Beethoven had chosen to perform in the premiere of his Ninth Symphony, in the Union Place Hotel. They demanded that she favor them with a song, and when the diva hesitated, they broke into "Old Folks at Home." [11]

One reviewer called the "homely tune" a "catching, melodic *itch* of the times" (there's that association of pop music with disease again), and nearly everyone scratched, be they Irish or German immigrants feeling homesick for the old country, frontiersmen or forty-niners pining for the folks they had left behind in the East or African Americans forcibly separated from their birthplaces and families. [12] "Old Folks at Home" was all things to all people. As late as the 1930s, the *Negro Year Book* claimed that the song had been composed by an African American—"a slave woman from the banks of the beautiful Suwanee River" who had been "sold into North Alabama" and yearned for her lost home. Her lament made its way up the Ohio River, where Foster heard it sung by the slaves of friends and was so taken by it that he hopped a steamboat to Florence, Alabama, sought out the singer and bought the song from her, thus receiving "credit for it being his own." [13]

For every claim there was a disclaimer. Jacob Little, the Quaker who had ridiculed "Oh! Boys, Carry Me 'Long," was equally scornful of "Friend Christy's" "Old Folks at Home," which he had no reason to suspect was actually another Foster song. "Our negro melodies," Little wrote, "(like our negro minstrels) are black things whitewashed, or white things blackwashed. They are imitations—counterfeits—not nature." [14]

The one person who couldn't claim credit for "Old Folks" was its composer. On May 25, 1852, Foster wrote this tortured letter to Christy:

As I once intimated to you, I had the intention of omitting my name on my Ethiopian songs, owing to the prejudice against them by some, which might injure my reputation as a writer of another style of music, but I find that by my efforts I have done a great deal to build up a taste for the Ethiopian songs among refined people by making the words suitable to their taste, instead of the trashy and really offensive words which belong to some songs of that order. Therefore I have concluded to reinstate my name on my songs and to pursue the Ethiopian business without fear or shame and lend all my energies to making the business live, at the same time that I will wish to establish my name as the best Ethiopian song-writer. But I am not encouraged in undertaking this so long as "Old folks at home" stares me in the face with another's name on it. As it was at my own solicitation that you allowed your name to be placed on the song, I hope that the above reasons will be sufficient explanation for my desire to place my own name on it as author and composer, while at the same time I wish to leave the name of your band on the title page. This is a little matter of pride in myself which it will certainly be to your interest to encourage. On the receipt of your free consent to this proposition, I will if you wish, willingly refund you the money which you paid me . . . and I promise in addition to write you an opening chorus in my best style, free of charge, and in any other way in my power to advance your interests hereafter. I find I cannot write at all unless I write for the public approbation and get credit for what I write. As we may probably have a good deal of business with each other in our lives, it is best to proceed on a sure basis of confidence and good understanding, therefore I hope you will appreciate an author's feelings in the case and deal with me with your usual fairness. Please answer immediately.
Very respectfully yours,
Stephen C. Foster [15]

Christy turned a deaf ear to Foster's abject plea. The man who had brazenly claimed to have composed "Lucy Long" and "Lucy Neal" could not be shamed into relinquishing "Old Folks at Home." A deal was a deal, and another man's name stared Foster in the face as long as he lived. Not until the original copyright ran out in 1879 did Foster's name replace Christy's on "Old Folks at Home."

Chapter Nineteen

POSSUM FAT
AND FLOWRETS

*O*f at first you succeed, try and try again. Stephen Foster embraced what has always been pop music's motto by following up "Old Folks at Home" with two blackface songs that were nearly carbon copies of it. For good measure, the chorus of "Farewell My Lilly Dear" ends with "Don't weep for me," an echo of "Don't you cry for me" in "Oh! Susanna." According to its title page, this "Plantation Melody as sung by Christy's Minstrels" was "written & composed by S.C.F." These were hardly household initials, and Christy may have paid Foster an extra five dollars on top of the ten dollars for first performance rights, as he had for "Old Folks at Home," to keep Foster's full name off—and Christy's on—the sheet music.

"Farewell My Lilly Dear" was copyrighted on December 13, 1851. Foster didn't publish another song for nearly seven months, and then it was an even closer facsimile of "Old Folks." "Massa's in de Cold Ground" (only later, after the Civil War, was a second "Cold" added to the title) is in the same key as "Old Folks"—D major—and in the same 4/4 time. It makes the identical octave leap from D to high D in its opening measures—"Round de meadows am a RING-ing"—and it, too, consists of six phrases, of which all but the fifth (the first line of the chorus) are nearly the same.

The title may have been suggested by the Thomas Moore ballad, "When Cold in the Ground," but the scenario was probably inspired by Foster's own "Uncle Ned" and "Oh! Boys, Carry Me 'Long."[1] "Massa's in de Cold Ground" is the flip side; here it's the slave owner, rather than a slave, who has died of old age and the slaves, rather than the massa and his missus, who are crying their eyes out.

Such racial naiveté and racist delusion are easy to denounce and tempting to travesty. Martin Delany mocked "Massa's in de Cold Ground" as well as "Uncle Ned" in *Blake* when a rebellious slave sings at the top of his lungs, "Old master's gone to the slaveholders rest— / He's gone where they all ought to go!"[2] But "Massa's in de Cold Ground" has a staying power that cannot be denied, and it derives, at least in part, from Foster's deep and ambivalent involvement in the song. This plantation fantasy is a personal fantasy, too—although one that was embedded in reality.

Massa is unmistakably Father, William Barclay Foster, dying not in the Big House but in the modest one on the East Common: " 'Twas hard to hear old massa calling, / Cayse he was so weak and old." Foster's lyrics are both parricidal and anticipatory, a compound of guilt and grief. A slip in Foster's sketchbook reveals how conflicted his feelings were. He initially wrote, "Massa made de darkeys love him / Cayse he was a scold." Although the seeming contradiction may have rung true psychologically, it made little sense dramatically. Foster crossed out "was a" and substituted "nebber."

"Massa's in de Cold Ground" was the first of only four songs that Foster published in 1852. The fall-off in productivity was precipitous. Perhaps, given his prolific output during the two previous years, Foster was simply exhausted. Or, given the success of "Old Folks at Home," for which he was receiving all of the royalties if none of the credit, maybe he could afford to relax. But he was also still struggling to reconcile commercial appeal with social respectability, confronting a crisis of language—of diction and dialect—that he did not resolve until year's end. Foster nearly eliminated the racy (and racist) idiom of blackface in "Farewell My Lilly Dear," changing words like "lebe" and "nebber," which he had originally written in his sketchbook, to "leave" and "never" in the published version. "Massa's in de Cold Ground," on the other hand, reverted to dialect.

Two songs that Foster worked on in his sketchbook during this period show the extremes between which he vacillated, and perhaps it was because they were extremes that he never published either song. One was a perfumed parlor ballad beginning, "While the flowrets gently Tremble." The other was a rush of verses under the heading, "going INDIAN," that sprawls over five pages. In these Foster did indeed seem to "go native" with a verbal violence and a blunt, almost jungle-drum rhythm unlike anything else he ever wrote. The song is heavily peppered with the words "nigga," "nigger" and "nig." Some of the verses are parallel on the page, as if part of a back-and-forth minstrel exchange between a Tambo and Bones:

Massa hab　　　　　　　Wooly head
A woolly dog　　　　　　Where's your wife
Ketch a weasel　　　　　gone to town
In a log　　　　　　　　Bet my life
Bite him in　　　　　　Dah she goes
De marrow bone　　　　Down de lane
Better leabe　　　　　　Through de mud
De dog alone　　　　　　In de rain
　　　　　　　　　　　Better run
See de mouse　　　　　Help her out
See de rat　　　　　　Habbent time
Drink de milk　　　　　Got de gout
Feed de cat
What you want
　Possum fat
Want de tail
Tell me dat
　Keep de tail
　For yourself
　Hung it on
　de upper shef. . . .

Nigga drunk
Draw your knife
　Nebber drunk
　In all my life

Smell your breff
Hear you fall

> See your shadow
> On de wall
> Cut your lip
> bung your eye
> Tell you nigga
> Dat's a lie

The lyrics hark back to the brutality of early blackface songs like "Long Time Ago" ("He shoot de Niggar trough de libber . . . / Vich make de Niggar kick an quiver") and also look forward to the razor-toting stereotypes of "coon songs" at the end of the nineteenth century. Possum fat and flowrets—Foster's songwriting, like his culture, was nearly schizophrenic at times.

Another song underwent a total personality change before it saw publication in 1852. Foster started out writing:

> Roll on ye breakers
> O'er de troubled tide
> Fair wedder all de day
> Wid Fanny by my side.

The maritime imagery metamorphosed into the Mississippi as Foster invited Fanny to "down de ribber glide":

> Down in de sunny souf
> Upon de sandy plain
> Dah's wha I used to lib
> I'm going back again. . . .

Eventually Foster changed Fanny to Maggie, the blackface dialect to unidiomatic English, and the mise-en-scène back to the sea, publishing "Maggie By My Side" as a jaunty nautical ballad.

The meandering course of "Maggie By My Side," as well as Foster's reduced productivity during 1852, may have owed in part to his own trip down the Mississippi River. During this month-long vacation he presumably had little time to compose.

On February 20, 1852, Stephen and Jane embarked on the *James Millingar*, a steamboat owned and operated by Dunning Foster, who had left the commission merchant business not long after Stephen and purchased the 285-ton sidewheeler.[3] Not only was his brother the captain, but several of Stephen's good friends were fellow passengers bound for Mardi Gras. The party included Susan and Andrew Robinson, Richard Cowan (Jane McDowell's former suitor), and Jesse Lightner (Morrison Foster's future wife). In Cincinnati they were joined by three more friends.

It was the first and last time in his life that Stephen Foster traveled farther south than Kentucky, following at long last in the wake of his father and brothers, and he had already composed most of his plantation melodies. Just as he had written about separation from family and the death of his father before either occurred, he had written about the South before he ever saw it. Lounging on the deck in the moonlight, the vacationers sang "Old Folks at Home"—with its chorus, "Oh! darkeys how my heart grows weary"—while slaves burned brush and cotton stalks on the plantations they passed in the night. Perhaps some of the slaves, like Delany's "men of sorrow," the black boatmen in *Blake*, sang the same song right back at them.[4]

Jessie Lightner, like Susan Pentland Robinson, was an excellent singer, and together they entertained the rest of the party with Foster's Shakespearean duet, "Wilt Thou Be Gone, Love?" Their performance, and lines published by Edgar Allan Poe four years earlier—"Save only thee and me. (Oh, Heaven!—oh, God! / How my heart beats in coupling those two words! / Save only thee and me.)"—may have inspired Foster to write another duet. Firth, Pond issued "The Hour for Thee and Me" a few months after his return to Pittsburgh.[5]

Shakespeare and Poe were probably just as real—and as unreal—to the travelers as Foster's blackface songs. No account of their pleasure trip mentions anything that occurred off-board the *James Millingar*—as if the tourists viewed everything from the safety and distance of the deck, through the dark lenses of literary and minstrel conventions.

Long afterward, Susan Robinson recalled a bizarre shipboard incident. Stephen Foster was a heavy smoker, she told a reporter, and he chewed tobacco, too. (Stephen Foster, spitting tobacco juice as he wrote "What Must a Fairy's Dream Be?" and "Sweetly She Sleeps, My Alice Fair"? That and cigar smoke suggest another source of the dew drops and vapors that fog his songs.) Overcome by nicotine, Foster swooned in his stateroom, his throat so inflamed and swollen he could scarcely breathe. An Irish nurse accompanying the Robinsons rushed in and revived Foster by applying piping-hot potatoes to his mouth and throat.[6]

Dunning Foster piloted the party homeward as far as Cincinnati. Morrison Foster met the Pittsburghers there and together they took the *Allegheny*, Captain Charles W. Batchelor's brand-new boat, the rest of the way home, arriving on March 21. (In May, the *Allegheny* would break the *Telegraph No. 2*'s record time from Louisville to Cincinnati, making it in just ten hours and five minutes.)[7]

It was during this trip, either coming or going, that Foster is widely reputed to have visited Federal Hill in Bardstown, Kentucky. There are two reasons for dating a visit to this time. The first is opportunity. It is possible that the *James Millingar* docked at Louisville and that Foster, alone or with other members of the party, dashed forty-odd miles down the Louisville turnpike to Bardstown. The second is timing, because Foster published "My Old Kentucky Home, Good-Night!," legendarily inspired by this visit, the following January.

The second presumption is wrong, for "My Old Kentucky Home," Foster's sketchbook clearly documents, was not the Rowan manse but Uncle Tom's cabin in Harriet Beecher Stowe's novel, which was published the day before Foster's return to Pittsburgh. And the first reason is unnecessary, since Foster might almost as easily have traveled to Bardstown during the years he lived in Cincinnati.

There is, of course, a third and much more pressing argument in favor of Foster's visit to Bardstown: its importance to Kentucky. "My Old Kentucky Home" is sung on national television every Derby Day. (The lyrics have been altered, of course, since "the darkies are gay" is now doubly offensive.) The state's official song is key to its identity, both to outsiders and among Kentuckians themselves. (Floridians, on the other hand, whose state song is "Old Folks at Home," seldom seem to mind that Foster never dipped his toe in the Suwannee.) Bardstown is a heavily promoted tourist destination and deservedly so, since it's a charming town of historical and architectural interest. But its popularity depends on Federal Hill, My Old Kentucky Home State Park, and the identification with Foster, which is celebrated in an outdoor musical, *The Stephen Foster Story*. Even Federal Hill's semiofficial historical handbook, however, after describing Stephen Foster as John Rowan, Jr.'s "most important guest," concedes in a footnote that his visit is surrounded by "some controversy" and "has not actually been verified."[8]

The strongest evidence in favor of such a visit did not appear until forty-eight years later, when the unveiling of the first public monument to Foster, Giuseppe Moretti's sculpture in Pittsburgh's Highland Park, attracted national publicity. In 1900, a newspaper article that included an interview with Susan Pentland Robinson described the excursion to New Orleans and reported that the "stately old southern mansion" near "Beardstown" [sic] was "visited by Foster on this trip." This statement is not attributed to Robinson, nor is she quoted. The same year, Morrison Foster indicated in pencil on a letter of inquiry that he had received about Stephen, "He was not a protege of Judge Rowan, but only an occasional visitor at Federal Hill." Morrison did not date one of those visits to 1852, however, and four years earlier his biography of his brother had not mentioned *any* visits by Stephen to Bardstown, even though it described the trip to New Orleans that Morrison had joined at its tail end.[9]

Unfortunately, the person who could readily have confirmed these belated memories, John Rowan, Jr.'s widow, Rebecca Carnes Rowan, died in 1897. It may not be entirely coincidental that the legend of Foster's visit to Federal Hill burst into full flower after the death of the woman who would have been Stephen's hostess in 1852. Her daughter, "Madge" Rowan Frost, who was born in 1853, loved to play "the Southern grand dame." The Foster legend probably enhanced that role, and also the value of Federal Hill, which she sold to the state for $65,000 in 1922.[10]

Most of the other evidence placing Foster at Federal Hill is hearsay, handed down from generation to generation, and much of it doesn't hold up to scrutiny, especially with regard to the 1852 date. Rebecca Rowan, for instance, is reported to have told people that Foster composed "My Old Kentucky Home" in "the bright summer weather" at Federal Hill, but his excursion down South occurred in February and March. The widow of the songwriter Will S. Hays wrote that her husband had met him when Foster's coach stopped in Louisville and Foster asked directions. Maybe so, but not in 1852, since she also recounted that the coach's other occupant was Henry Clay. When the Great Compromiser died in Washington's National Hotel on June 29, 1852, he hadn't laid eyes on Kentucky since November, 1851.[11]

It's entirely possible that Stephen Foster visited Bardstown sometime in his life and impossible to prove that he never set foot in Federal Hill. But the burden of proof falls on Bardstown's boosters, and all the facts point to *Uncle Tom's Cabin* rather than Federal Hill as the inspiration of "My Old Kentucky Home."

Chapter Twenty

A SHOCK OF RECOGNITION

Stephen Foster probably didn't read *Uncle Tom's Cabin* as it was originally serialized in the *National Era*. It was an abolitionist magazine, and Foster was one of those "Doughfaces, Crawlers [and] Lice of Humanity" whom Walt Whitman anathematized for supporting compromise with the South on the slavery issue.[1] "If South Carolina makes a fuss, / Hurrah! Hurrah! / Oh, why should *we* be in the muss?" Foster had written in his campaign song supporting William Bigler, the Democratic candidate for governor of Pennsylvania. The song called William F. Johnston "an ass," and the chief reason Bigler was able to turn the Whig governor "out to grass" was Johnston's vehement opposition to slavery and the Fugitive Slave Act.

Few Pennsylvanians were sympathetic to slavery. The Underground Railroad was first named so in southeastern Pennsylvania, where fugitive slaves found many friends. But the Christiana Riot in September 1851—in which African Americans in Lancaster County shot and clubbed to death a Maryland man trying to reclaim an escaped slave—spooked many Pennsylvanians and riveted national attention on their governor's race. With Bigler's election, James Buchanan heaved a sigh of relief. It had done more, he wrote, "to restore peace & harmony between the Slave and the non-slave-holding States & to preserve the Union, than any event which has occurred since the commencement of the unfortunate agitation."[2]

Johnston carried Pittsburgh, however, and so, shortly, did *Uncle Tom's Cabin*. Published in book form on March 20, 1852, by May 1 it was said to have sold twenty thousand copies in Pittsburgh alone. Maybe Charles Shiras pressed Foster to read it, but he could hardly have avoided the book or the craze it created anyway. With souvenir candlesticks, handkerchiefs, wallpaper, dolls, toys, and board games—in one of which players competed to reunite slave families—*Cabin* fervor rivaled the Lindomania of a couple of years earlier. "We are all abolitionists . . . ," an excited Andrew Carnegie wrote in 1855. *"Uncle Tom's Cabin* is lauded to the skies, read in every parlor, taught in some Sunday Schools & played in our theatres."[3]

Foster may well have resisted the novel at first. Not only were its politics distasteful, but in addition to slavery Stowe also repeatedly condemned minstrelsy, still Foster's sole claim to fame. In the very first chapter, Mr. Shelby, the feckless Kentucky planter, calls Eliza's son Harry, whom she will spirit to freedom across the ice floes of the Ohio, "Jim Crow." He tosses the child some raisins, puts him through the contortionist paces of a darky dance routine for the amusement of a slave dealer, and throws him in as a package deal with Uncle Tom.[4] Reviewers also used the book as an occasion to rebuke blackface. "The slang of 'Ethiopian Serenaders' for once gives place to thoughts and language racy of the soil," the *New York Daily Times* observed, "and we need not say how refreshing it is to be separated for a season from the conventional Sambo of the modern stage."[5]

And yet, if Foster read *Uncle Tom's Cabin*, he had to have recognized, if not a kindred spirit, at least a common experience. Moving to Brunswick, Maine, Stowe had left Cincinnati in April 1850, only a few months after Foster. She, too, was writing about a South she had never seen, and she was encouraging whites to identify with blacks, playing on familial emotions—"If it were *your* Harry, mother, or your Willie, that were going to be torn from you by a brutal trader . . ."—in much the same way Foster had in songs like "Nelly Was a Lady" and "Old Folks at Home."[6]

Foster could not have missed the similarity of angelic Eva, doomed daughter of the New Orleans aristocrat, St. Clare, to his own dear dead Charlotte. Into her histrionic evocation of Eva's death from consumption Stowe poured all her grief for the still recent loss of her own son, her *"summer child"* Charley. Her rapt description of Eva at death's threshold

—"On the face of the child . . . there was no ghastly imprint,—only a high and almost sublime expression,—the overshadowing presence of spiritual natures, the dawning of immortal life"—condensed Hill Rowan's rhapsodic account of Charlotte's "happy death." "Has there ever been a child like Eva? Yes, there have been," Stowe wrote, and Stephen Foster could only have nodded in agreement as she continued,

> but their names are always on gravestones and their sweet smiles, their heavenly eyes, their singular words and ways, are among the buried treasures of yearning hearts. In how many families do you hear the legend that all the goodness and graces of the living are nothing to the peculiar charms of one who *is not!* [7]

"Come, aunty, shear the sheep!" cries Eva, asking that her tresses be cut and distributed to friends and attendants at her deathbed. On September 10, 1852, with the memory of *Uncle Tom's Cabin* probably fresh in his mind (although it cannot be proven exactly when or even if Foster actually read the book), Stephen and Henry Foster met Dunning and Morrison at the wharf. Dunning and Morrison Foster were returning from Louisville with Charlotte's remains. It was then, before they reburied her in Pittsburgh's Allegheny Cemetery, that someone snipped and saved a lock of Charlotte's hair. [8]

The first draft in Foster's sketchbook of the song that would become "My Old Kentucky Home, Good-Night!" is entitled "Poor Uncle Tom, good night." The verses are almost exactly as they would appear in the published version but written in dialect, every "th" a "d," and each verse ends, "Den poor uncle Tom good night." That thought became a chorus that was ultimately discarded:

> Oh good night, good night, good night
> Poor uncle Tom
> Grieve not for your old Kentucky home
> Your bound for a better land
> Old Uncle Tom

The "better land," of course, is not down the river, where Uncle Tom has been sold, but the heaven where "de good Niggas go" ("Uncle Ned") and "all de niggas am free" ("Oh! Boys, Carry Me 'Long").

Foster was still too much the doughface, however, to come right out and condemn slavery for breaking up the old Kentucky home. He wasn't about to jeopardize sales of his song by offending Southerners, one of whom mailed anonymously to Stowe a severed black ear. For the slave-driving Mr. Haley, Foster substituted an abstract "Hard Times" that "comes a knocking at the door." There was precedent for this in the novel. One of the slaves who buries Tom says, "Hard times here, Mas'r!" But by shifting the emphasis from slavery to economics, Foster also shifted the focus away from the novel to his own experience, extending the autobiographical strain of past songs like "Farewell! Old Cottage."[9]

Before the Bank of the United States foreclosed, Stephen Foster and his siblings had rolled on the floor of White Cottage as gaily as "de young folks roll on the little cabin floor" in the slave quarters of the song. Although she believed that slavery was not as harsh in Kentucky as it was farther South, Stowe did not idealize the border state. "Heaven is better than Kintuck," Uncle Tom says before expiring.[10] But heaven, for Foster, wasn't way up there, it was way back when. The paradisiacal home of his childhood and his holidays at Uncle Struthers's Ohio farm, where he hunted "for the possum and the coon," blurred with "de old Kentucky home" (it was not yet, in the first draft, "my old Kentucky home"), so that a song originating in outrage over slavery became, ironically, a former slave state's celebratory anthem.

Had Stephen Foster published "Poor Uncle Tom Good Night" as it exists in his sketchbook, it might easily have been lost in the shuffle of the dozens of other songs the novel and subsequent stage versions inspired. John Greenleaf Whittier, the Quaker bard of abolition, tried his hand at "Little Eva," and Henry Russell weighed in with three songs, plus a piano instrumental, "Uncle Tom's Cabin Quadrilles." At a musical soirée at Pittsburgh's Washington Hall, the Misses Tomer, assisted by half of the Pittsburgh Quartette, performed "The Uncle Tom's Cabin Song," a new piece "composed on the highly popular work of that name," in addition to singing Stephen Foster's duet, "Turn Not Away!" *Uncle Tom's Cabin* inspired painters as well as composers and playwrights: Robert Scott Duncanson painted *Uncle Tom and Little Eva,* in which the white child teaches the black slave to read the Bible and points heavenward. The *Cincinnati Daily Commercial* dismissed the canvas as "an Uncle Tom-itude."[11]

But Foster made three imaginative leaps before publication that are not recorded, unfortunately, in his sketchbook. He dropped the blackface dialect almost entirely (though not the word "darkey," which was far less insulting then than "nigger"). By writing a plantation ballad in nearly standard English, Foster overcame the blackface/parlor ballad, possum fat/flowrets dichotomy that had long bedeviled him. Second, he eliminated the references to Uncle Tom, freeing the song from the novel, its politics, and its period, and thereby evoking nearly timeless and universal emotions about losing one's family, home, and childhood. When "[t]he day goes by like a shadow o'er the heart," it touches almost everyone's. And last but by no means least, Foster scrapped the original chorus and replaced it with:

> Weep no more, my lady,
> Oh! weep no more today!
> We will sing one song
> For the old Kentucky Home,
> For the old Kentucky Home, far away.

Where did this chorus come from? Its immediate sources were *Uncle Tom's Cabin*—"All had faded from his sky,—moon and star; all had passed by him, as the trees and banks were now passing, to return no more. Kentucky home, with wife and children, and indulgent owners . . ."[12]—and Foster's own unfinished "While the flowrets gently tremble," which included the words, "Weep no more." But the chorus concentrated in its few lines a long literary and cultural history, and virtually Foster's whole career.

Poe once purported to explain how he had come up with his famous refrain, "Quoth the raven, 'Nevermore.'" In order for a refrain "to have force," he wrote, it

> must be sonorous and susceptible of protracted emphasis, admitting no doubt: and these considerations inevitably led me to the long *o* as the most sonorous vowel, in connection with *r* as the most producible consonant.[13]

Poe was parodying ratiocination, of course, with a humbuggery worthy of Barnum, but still he was on to something. He was by no means the first poet to recognize the pathos and potency of "no more." Thomas Moore's "The Harp That Once Through Tara's Halls" includes the lines:

> . . . And hearts, that once beat high for praise,
> Now feel that pulse no more!
>
> No more to chiefs and ladies bright
> The harp of Tara swells. . . .[14]

The phrase appeared repeatedly in parlor ballads—an 1835 songster included "Mary's Dream," with the chorus, "Mary, weep no more for me"—and even in their titles: "No More," by a Young Lady of Georgia (1836); "Maiden Weep No More," a "sweet little song" that Emily Dickinson learned to play in 1845; Laura A. Hewitt's "Oh! Must We Part to Meet No More?" (1851); and "Broken Hearted Weep No More," music by Isaac B. Woodbury (1852).[15]

But it was Poe who made "no more" a poetic obsession and mantra:

> I reach'd my home—my home no more—
> For all had flown who made it so.
>
> ("Tamerlane," ll.213–14)

> They use that moon no more
> For the same end as before. . . .
>
> ("Fairy-Land," ll.35–36)

> And, Guy de Vere, hast *thou* no tear?—weep now or
> never more!
>
> ("Lenore," l.3)

> For, alas! alas! with me
> The light of Life is o'er!
> No more—no more—no more—
>
> ("To One in Paradise," ll.14–16)

> How many visions of a maiden that is
> No more—no more upon thy verdant slopes!
> *No more!* alas, that magical sad sound
> Transforming all! Thy charms shall please *no*
> *more,*—
> Thy memory *no more!*
>
> ("Sonnet—To Zante," ll.7–11)

> A hideous throng rush out forever,
> And laugh—but smile no more.
>
> ("The Haunted Palace," ll.47–48)

... his name's "No more."
He is the corporate Silence: dread him not!

("Sonnet—Silence," ll.9–10) [16]

Poe's only rival in the monomania of "no more" was Foster:

No more hard work for poor old Ned. . . .

("Uncle Ned")

We'll work no more today.

("Oh! Lemuel!")

For winter, gloomy winter
Then reigns o'er us no more.

("I Would Not Die in Spring Time")

I'll go away no more.

("Ring, Ring de Banjo!")

Der's no more trouble for me.

("Oh! Boys, Carry Me 'Long")

There's joy for my bosom no more.

("My Hopes Have Departed Forever")

After "My Old Kentucky Home," Foster would write:

While her gentle fingers will cull them no more.

("Jeanie with the Light Brown Hair")

Hard Times, come again no more.

("Hard Times Come Again No More")

Shall we never more behold thee . . . ?

("Gentle Annie")

Never more will come those happy, happy hours. . . .

("Our Bright, Bright Summer Days Are Gone")

Why have my lov'd ones gone,
Gone to return no more . . . ?

("Why Have My Loved Ones Gone?")

We will hear no more her winning melody. . . .

("Little Belle Blair")

To Foster, however, "no more" echoed more than Thomas Moore's nostalgia and Poe's inconsolable woe. In addition to this backward-looking tradition, Foster drew upon the phrase's quite different resonance in African-American music, where it expressed a forward-facing yearning for liberation, be it in Canada or heaven. "No more," in this second sense, denotes a hopeful break with the past rather than a doleful enslavement to it. It's the theme of several spirituals, such as "No More Rain Fall For Wet You" ("No more sun shine for burn you").[17] One of its most eloquent expressions is "No More Auction Block," which has endured in the twentieth-century repertories of Paul Robeson, Odetta, and Bob Dylan (who credited it as the inspiration of his own "Blowin' in the Wind"). "No more auction block for me," the song begins, "No more; no more." Foster fused hoping and moping, black and white in "Weep no more," an integration suggested by his line, "We will sing one song. . . ."[18]

Who is the mystery lady in the chorus of "My Old Kentucky Home"? If we take the song literally as a musical rendition of *Uncle Tom's Cabin*, "my lady" is Mrs. Shelby, Uncle Tom's mistress in the Big House, or possibly Aunt Chloe, Uncle Tom's wife in their cabin. (If Nelly, that "dark, Virginny bride," was a lady, surely Chloe could be one, too.) But Foster, as we have seen, rid his song of explicit references to the novel, and this female figure, unmentioned in the verses, appears in the chorus from out of nowhere, an apparition like Susanna in "Oh! Susanna" 's dream. I like to think of her as the ghost of Charlotte Foster, whose visit to a Kentucky plantation reminded her "of the happy times [she] used to spend in the country at home."[19]

The Hutchinson Family shared Harriet Beecher Stowe's moral abhorrence of slavery, but not her religious aversion to theater. Asa Hutchinson sought permission to adapt *Uncle Tom's Cabin* for the stage and was refused. "The world is not yet good enough for it to succeed," Stowe wrote. She was spectacularly wrong, and because copyright protection did not extend from the printed page to the stage until 1856, she was powerless to prevent *Uncle Tom's Cabin* from becoming, in various versions from which she derived no profit, the most popular American play of the nineteenth century. The association of several of Foster's songs with the play(s) won his music still greater renown.[20]

Uncle Tom's Cabin hit the boards as early as August 1852, in an adaptation by Charles Western Taylor that played fast and loose with the novel: Instead of dying at the end, Taylor's Uncle Tom wins his freedom and lives happily ever after. Stowe would have been even more dismayed by another entertainment on the same bill at New York's National Theatre, starring the creator of the "Jim Crow" act that her book had repeatedly disparaged. In Daddy Rice's burlesque *Othello*, Desdemona, when asked for her handkerchief, answered the Moor: "Blow yah nose on yah sleeve, nigger, and git on wid de show!"[21]

This *Uncle Tom's Cabin* closed quickly, but many more followed, one headlining Rice himself as Uncle Tom and another featuring Nelson Kneass in the wench role of Aunt Chloe (and his daughter as Eva). In 1853 alone, at least four versions were presented in New York City. One, at Barnum's American Museum, starred Emily Mestayer, who had helped make "Old Folks at Home" a hit at the same venue.[22] The most successful and revolutionary adaptation, written by George L. Aiken and starring George C. Howard, Howard's wife, and their five-year-old daughter, opened on July 18, 1853, at the National Theatre, where Taylor's version had failed eleven months earlier.

Aiken's *Uncle Tom* was America's first evening-length play, the first ever to be presented without entr'actes. Recognizing that it was on to something good and eager to attract a more distinguished and diverse audience to its seedy Bowery neighborhood, the National Theatre's management banned prostitutes and admitted African Americans to "a neat and comfortable parquette" (albeit segregated, with a separate entrance) near the pit, where they could watch white actors in burnt cork play black roles. In another innovation, the theater offered matinees, so women and children could attend in the safety of daylight. People came in droves, and the production ran for a record-breaking 325 performances.[23]

Fliers and advertisements during this remarkable run gave top musical billing to four songs by George Howard, but they also promoted "Old Folks at Home," credited to E. P. Christy, Esq. Act V, scene iii of the Aiken adaptation opens "to the symphony of 'Old Folks at Home' " in "A Rude Chamber" on Simon Legree's plantation, where Uncle Tom holds in his hand a paper containing a lock of Eva's hair. Tom kisses the curl, sings "Old Folks at Home" and is interrupted by Legree: "Shut up, you black cuss! Did you think I wanted any of your infernal howling?"[24]

American theater in the nineteenth century was an improvisatory affair, so not only "My Old Kentucky Home" but other Foster songs, old and new, were swiftly and easily interpolated in various productions of

Uncle Tom's Cabin. The itinerant "Tom shows" that plied the backroads and railway spurs of small-town America well into the twentieth century —as late as 1902, an estimated sixteen traveling companies were presenting the play—amounted to an extraordinarily effective though unremunerative distribution system for Foster's music.[25] Foster didn't earn a cent from this traffic any more than Stowe did, but he achieved total market penetration—indeed, *saturation*—long before radio.

When Pittsburgh saw its first performance of *Uncle Tom's Cabin*, on November 17, 1853, in a version based on the Aiken script, the musical numbers included "Old Folks at Home," "My Old Kentucky Home," and "Massa's in de Cold Ground."[26] The composer, however, the local boy made good, was nowhere to be seen. He was living in New York and had left not just the old folks but the young folks—his wife and daughter— back in Pennsylvania.

Chapter Twenty-one

WHITE MEN'S MUSIC

*O*n the spring of 1853, Jane Foster left Stephen and Stephen left Pittsburgh. "Tell him to come out and stay a while with me," Stephen's sister, Henrietta, wrote from Warren. But Ohio wasn't nearly as enticing as New York City, where his music had won renown up and down Broadway.[1] The music publishing industry—*all* publishing, for that matter—was becoming increasingly concentrated in New York, and it made sense to go where the money was.

"The Village Maiden," a song Foster wrote in 1853 (but did not publish until two years later), describes a happy wedding that in three short verses declines into a funeral. Foster doodled in his sketchbook as he worked on the song, writing his last name several times and embellishing the "F" with cursive curlicues that elongated the bottom of the letter into a listing half-note. He also inscribed "Pittsburgh Pa" and "Pitts." It was as if he were not only brooding over the deterioration of his own marriage, but also identifying with the fate of the maiden who languished and died in provincial obscurity.

While Stephen Foster moved to the big city, Jane Foster departed to the small town of Lewistown, Pennsylvania, where her widowed mother had moved a year or two earlier. With so many daughters but no sons to help support her, Mrs. McDowell could stretch her widow's mite further there, in the mountainous middle of the state. Jane McDowell may also have had sentimental reasons for returning to the town where she had wed and the Presbyterian minister who had married her still preached. Now Jane Foster followed, with Marion in tow.[2]

"How sorry I feel for dear Stephy," Henrietta wrote, though she said she was "not at all surprised" that Stephen and Jane had parted: "I last winter felt convinced she would either have to change her course of conduct or a separation would be inevitable." Some lines in this letter were later effaced by Henrietta or Morrison to conceal either the identity of person(s) or the nature of their (mis)conduct.[3]

Had Jane done something to endanger her marriage? "Course of conduct" could mean anything, from ill temper to adultery. A year and a half later, after Stephen and Jane had reconciled, split up a second time, and reunited yet again, one of their nephews would write, ". . . to tell the truth, I never found out what the nature of her sin was."[4] We won't, either, but whatever the young couple's differences were, their living conditions probably exacerbated them. Sharing a rented house with a preoccupied songwriter was bad enough, but sharing it with his paralyzed father, possessive mother, and sundry siblings may have made Jane climb the walls.

When Stephen Foster wrote a song, his wife didn't sing it in manuscript—Susan Pentland Robinson or Rachel Keller Woods or Jesse Lightner (soon to become Mrs. Morrison Foster) did. "If Mrs. Foster was a musician, I never knew it," an acquaintance during the 1860s recalled.[5] By another account, Jane "did not care for music and hoped that Stephen would give up song-writing. . . ." She "nagged Stephen constantly so that he became increasingly moody."[6] But their incompatibility was more than musical; it may have been sexual as well. Maybe it was just coincidence that they had only one child, born nine months after their wedding, but it's striking how infrequently sexual sparks fly in Stephen's letters and music. If Jane wasn't his "type," no one else seemed to be, either. Most of the females in his songs are distant, dreaming, dead, or under the age of legal consent. Although Poe eroticized corpses and children with a whiff of the perverse, Foster deodorized them with sentimentality.

Foster's lack of ardor need not be construed as evidence of repressed homosexuality. A gay Stephen Foster may make fictional sense—for example, in Peter Quinn's historical novel, *Banished Children of Eve*—

but it is not corroborated by the historical record.[7] One can't prove that Foster wasn't a repressed homosexual any more than one can prove he never visited Bardstown. Still, rather than labeling him hetero- or homosexual—labels that did not exist in that era for behaviors that did not exist in quite the same forms we recognize today—it's more helpful to consider Foster as a- or presexual, or as simply not very highly sexed. Arrested by traumatic events in his childhood—the expulsion from the White Cottage and the death of his sister Charlotte—he may never have fully developed an active adult sexuality.

Music was on Foster's mind more often than sex or even companionship. His friend Robert Nevin wrote that he was so preoccupied that he would nod distractedly at acquaintances, and spoke with "a broken style" and "certain hesitancy."[8] His daughter recalled that even though she was "his pet," she

> could not quite understand his sudden change from my gay, almost child-like companion of the street to the thoughtful, preoccupied, almost stern, man in the study. He could not bear the slightest noise or interruption in his work.[9]

Music was in some ways an escape from adulthood and the manly responsibilities, economic as well as erotic, adulthood usually entails. So was drink. When alcohol began to interfere with Foster's marriage is unclear. Whether the relationship began to fray because he was drinking, or he drank because it was beginning to fray (as if cause and effect could be untangled so easily) is unknowable. My suspicion is that drink intruded earlier rather than later, that it contributed to the precipitous decline in his productivity (sixteen new songs in 1851, four in 1852, and five in 1853) and that Foster's friends and family were in deep denial. There's something fishy about Susan Pentland Robinson's story of Foster's prostration by nicotine poisoning during that steamboat excursion to New Orleans. Surely liquor was more likely than a stogie to have laid him low.

Morrison Foster's account of a brawl in which Stephen intervened arouses similar suspicions:

> One night as he was returning home from Pittsburgh to Allegheny, he found at the end of the bridge two brutes abusing and beating a drunken

man. He of course interfered, and fought them both, rough and tumble, all over the street. He managed to pick up a piece of a board in the scramble, with which he beat one almost senseless and chased the other ingloriously from the field. A knife wound on the cheek, received in the encounter, left a scar which went with him to his grave.[10]

Presumably Morrison was relating the story Stephen had told when he staggered home bleeding. No witnesses confirmed it, and even Morrison's account wobbled. According to his daughter, the drunk was a black man and the board, with a nail in it, was wielded by one of the attackers, not by Stephen. How do we know that Stephen wasn't the drunken man? That a knife gashed his cheek in a fight, rather than a nail in a fall? George Cooper, Foster's collaborator during the last couple of years of his life, said Foster had told him that he had been scarred by the "jagged edge" of the lip of a bottle he had raised to his mouth while "out with a serenading party one night."[11] The scar that curved from Foster's lip deeply into his left cheek carved a lifelong question mark.

Stephen Foster's granddaughter recounted a family story about another occasion when Stephen came home with an unwelcome surprise. He had been out all night playing music with friends. "When they were assisting one another home in the wee, small hours of the morning, they passed the old Allegheny marketplace," according to Jessie Welsh Rose, and felt "the necessity for a peace offering of some kind for their respective and presumably unconciliatory wives." So Stephen showed up at his doorstep clutching to his chest a live, honking goose. " 'Oh, Jinny,' he called, 'see the nice goose I have for you, honey.' " Jane Foster was unable to tell "tother from which," and both geese were cooked.[12]

One of the friends with whom Stephen Foster hung out was Charles Shiras. The abolitionist poet and journalist had already collaborated with Henry Kleber on "My Mother, I Obey"; now he contributed the lyrics to Foster's song, "Annie My Own Love," copyrighted in May 1853, just as Stephen and Jane were breaking up. Shiras's daughter, who called Stephen "Uncle," remembered that he "drank very hard" and that her grandmother, "like all mothers, did not want my father to associate with him nor put his name on the 'Nigger Songs.' " Morrison Foster wrote that Stephen would have gladly collaborated with Shiras more frequently, but his "style of poetry was too heavy and sombre for Stephen's muse." "Annie My Own Love" is certainly lugubrious ("By Death, unrelenting, /

She's freed from her vow, / And Annie, my own love, / Is gone from me now . . ."), but no more so than many of Foster's other genteel tearjerkers.[13]

Another joint effort has not survived. On November 9, 1853, a play by Charles Shiras premiered in Pittsburgh and ran for six nights. *The Invisible Prince; or, The War with the Amazons* was billed as a "Grand Original Fairy Spectacle," but it was not all *that* original. It was based on the same seventeenth-century French fairy tale, the Comtesse D'Aulnoy's *Le Prince Lutin*, as J. R. Planché's extravaganza *The Invisible Prince; or, The Island of Tranquil Delights*. Much as William Dempster's setting of *The May Queen* had earlier inspired Shiras and Foster to pen additional stanzas, the British playwright's popular burlesque may have prompted Shiras to try his hand at dramaturgy. The Pittsburgh *Daily Morning Post* commended Shiras's dialogue as "spirited, very often witty" and said the play "exceeds in point of dramatic merit any spectacle that has ever been produced in this city." The music did not merit a mention, even though the preview in the previous day's *Post* had described *The Invisible Prince* as "the joint production of two of our townsmen," the second being Stephen Foster.[14]

The composer of "What Must a Fairy's Dream Be?" may have found a "Fairy Spectacle" congenial, but perhaps Foster only contributed some arrangements. His involvement does not seem to have been deep enough to draw him back from New York City, where he had been living for several months by then. There's no indication he was at the premiere or at the benefit performance for Shiras attended by "friends—and gentlemen—and scholars—/ Who love the man that wrote of 'Dimes and Dollars.'" (So a poem delivered at the benefit described the audience, which included Morrison Foster, Richard Cowan, and Henry Kleber.)[15]

The Invisible Prince soon surrendered the stage to Pittsburgh's first production of *Uncle Tom's Cabin*, with some of the same actors in the cast and three Foster songs in the score.[16] The composer didn't come home for that event, either.

Foster moved to New York City in the summer of 1853, but he had reconnoitered it the previous winter. On January 29, *The Musical World and New York Musical Times* noted,

We were recently visited by a celebrated Pittsburgher, namely, Stephen C. Foster, Esq., the author of most of the popular Ethiopian melodies now afloat—such for example, as Nelly Bly; Oh! boys carry me 'long; Uncle Ned; the Old Folks at Home. . . .

With studied casualness, and probably at Foster's instigation, the journal blew E. P. Christy's cover credit as the composer of "Old Folks." (The editorial "we" was probably the *Musical World*'s editor, Richard Storrs Willis, Nathaniel Parker Willis's younger brother and composer of the Christmas carol, "It Came Upon a Midnight Clear.") Foster had broken his word, and there followed a second betrayal by the man who had once promised to "unite" with Christy "in every effort to encourage a taste" for blackface. The article continued:

> Mr. Foster possesses more than ordinary abilities as a composer; and we hope he will soon realize enough from his Ethiopian melodies to enable him to afford to drop them and turn his attention to the production of a higher kind of music. Much of his music is now excellent, but being wedded to negro idioms it is, of course, discarded by many who would otherwise gladly welcome it to their pianos. We were glad to learn from Mr. F. that he intends to devote himself principally hereafter to the production of "White men's" music.

It's ironic that Foster was being urged to abandon his low-down Ethiopian ways even as his blackface songs were winning acceptance in more elevated musical circles. Firth, Pond is reputed to have commissioned a portrait of Foster from Thomas Hicks, a relation of Edward (*Peaceable Kingdom*) Hicks. The younger Hicks had studied with Thomas Couture in Paris, and his distinguished subjects included Longfellow, Oliver Wendell Holmes, William Cullen Bryant and Harriet Beecher Stowe.[17] In the following months, "Old Folks at Home" and other Foster melodies would worm their way into the crowd-pleasing repertories of Louis Moreau Gottschalk and (take a deep breath) Louis George Maurice Adolphe Roch Albert Abel Antonio Alexandre Noé Jean Lucien Daniel Eugène Joseph-le-brun Joseph-Barême Thomas Thomas Thomas-Thomas Pierre Arbon Pierre-Maurel Barthélemi Artus Alphonse Bertrand Dieudonné Emanuel Josué Vincent Luc Michel Jules-de-la-plane Jules-Bazin Julio César Jullien.

Foster may well have been in New York City when Gottschalk returned after twelve years abroad on January 10, 1853, disembarking with a grand piano and his Andalusian manservant, Ramon.[18] Gottschalk was not the first virtuoso pianist to barnstorm the United States. Leopold de Meyer and Henri Herz, among others, preceded him, and the plethora of pianists had tried some Americans' patience. An 1853 editorial in the Pittsburgh *Evening Chronicle*, for instance, deplored "the adulation and toddyism [sic] lavished upon every Piano-Forte player of any talent," and ridiculed "each fresher greater Signor Pound-the-keys" who

> rattled and splurged and hammered and tinkled and growled through three or four musical compositions with long-line names, fill[ing] his pockets for one night's work with as many dollars as three-fourths of the community earn in a year. . . .[19]

Gottschalk pounded the keys, too. Richard Storrs Willis, who attended Gottschalk's first private soirée in New York City with his brother, likened the pianist's fingers to "a row of disconnected and perfectly independent little hammers." (By one account, however, he lacked the fingernails to execute a proper glissando because he bit them to the quick.) Never mind that Gottschalk's parents were an English-born German Jew and a French refugee from Haiti. Or that his upbringing in Creole New Orleans and his education in Paris prompted a Frenchman to declare him *"français d'esprit, de coeur, de goût et d'habitudes."* Gottschalk was the first *American* Signor Pound-the-keys, and he was warmly welcomed as such.[20]

His first public concerts in New York included his own compositions based on Creole melodies, *"Le Bananier"* and *"Bamboula."* European audiences had been captivated by the exoticism of these pieces, which were far more deeply rooted in African-American music than Foster's blackface. There were more blacks in Gottschalk's childhood household than in Foster's and many more in New Orleans than in Pittsburgh. Well into the twentieth century, even some African-American critics assumed Gottschalk was a mulatto.[21]

No sooner did Gottschalk go on the road, however, than he incorporated, on March 19, 1853, at the second of two concerts in Louisville, "Oh! Susanna," "Old Folks at Home," and, possibly, "My Old Kentucky Home" into a "grand national symphony" entitled *National Glory*. The pastiche had been renamed *American Reminiscences* by October, when Gottschalk played it in Boston.[22]

Soon Gottschalk was performing another piano piece, "The Banjo," that prefigured the swaggering rhythms of ragtime and jazz and finished with a rapid-fire rendition of "Camptown Races." The sheet music urges the pianist on from triple to quadruple *fortissimo: velocissimo, tutta la forza, prestissimo,* and *ben martellato* (R. S. Willis wasn't kidding about those hammers).[23]

Slowly peeling off his doeskin gloves in emulation of Liszt before he played, Gottschalk was a highly theatrical performer. He was a shrinking violet, however, compared to the " 'ombog" Jullien, to whom a flunky brought out on a silver salver a pair of white kid gloves and a jeweled baton whenever the flamboyant French maestro prepared to conduct Beethoven.[24]

Jullien arrived in New York City in August, 1853, with twenty-three musicians, hired more and rented Castle Garden to stage the kind of program music and "pops" concert that Philippe Musard had originated in Europe and Frank Johnson had introduced in America. Jullien, however, worked on a scale as gargantuan as his full name (which honored his thirty-six godfathers, all members of the orchestra in his native Sisteron, France). For his so-called monster concerts he advertised the world's biggest bass drum, its largest ophicleide (a deep-toned, keyed bugle) and a soprano able to sing three notes higher than Jenny Lind. On September 5 he introduced *American Quadrille,* a symphony in five movements based on American themes. To the delight of New York's b'hoys and to the chagrin of Boston's Brahmins, the third movement's theme was "Old Folks at Home." Love it or leave it, Stephen Foster's music had become an emblem of America.[25]

"My Old Kentucky Home" was published by Firth, Pond the same month as the *Musical World* item welcoming Foster to New York. It was advertised on its cover as No. 20 of "Foster's Plantation Melodies." Seven months later, No. 21 came out, with a significant change in the wording. It was still "sung by Christy's Minstrels," but now these were "Fosters *American* Melodies." It was a claim as bold and all-embracing as Berry Gordy's motto for Motown Records, "The Sound of Young America." The difference between black music and blackface is massive, obviously; still Foster, like Gordy, wanted to cross over, to transcend racial categories and restrictions. He had graduated from Ethiopian to plantation to American songs.

There was, of course, a "Young America" before Motown, a literary and political movement in the late 1840s and early 1850s that championed American culture and conquest. Melville and Whitman were among its recruits. As writers wrestled with the nature of American identity and art, so did composers and their critics. In the pages of the *New York Tribune* and in a controversial lecture series at New York's Metropolitan Hall, William Henry Fry, the composer of the grand opera *Leonora* and *Santa Claus (Christmas Symphony)*, challenged American music to declare its independence and kick over the Old World's aristocratic traces in the name of New World democracy. Foster may have attended one of these lectures during his visit to New York in the winter of 1853. He certainly read about them, for the January 19 *Musical World* excerpted one of them extensively, and Foster referred to Fry in a letter that appeared in the February 26 issue.

Stephen had returned to Pittsburgh, but he had not abandoned his publicity campaign in the *Musical World*, which had followed up its January notice with another item. In reply to a query from a reader named "Harry" (one suspects Harry may have been Stephen), the journal explained:

> S.C. Foster is the author of the "Old Folks at Home." E.P. Christy probably bought the song and the right to be considered its author at the same time, and the publishers of course put his name to it, thinking he was the composer; but such things always "come out" sooner or later.[26]

A week later, in the February 26 issue, a letter from S. C. Foster took R. S. Willis to task for having written that the "leading note, or 7th of the scale, may not be doubled, and must resolve upward to the 8th." Nitpicking for no other reason than to see his name once again in print, Foster argued obtusely that unwary readers might mistake Willis's wording and confuse the "seventh of the *scale*," which Willis had clearly indicated, with the interval of the minor seventh. Foster had become a convert, for the moment at least, to P. T. Barnum's faith in "advertising and blowing my own trumpet, beating the gongs, drums, & c. to attract attention."[27]

Then Foster turned to Fry, who had spoken at length in a January 4 lecture Foster might have attended about the "different qualities and capacities of the masculine and feminine voice."[28] "Might we not have a musical gender?" Foster asked. With that, he tried to parade more learning and wit than he possessed by distinguishing between masculine fifths, which suggest "trumpets, and 'the big wars that make ambition virtue,' " and the feminine mystique of "the conciliating *third*, and the complaining, though gentle (minor) *seventh*."

Foster was not an intellectual, and it would be preposterous to claim that his songs were self-conscious salvos in the culture wars of the mid-nineteenth century, but they were on the fringe of the fray. Indeed, one critic of Young America jeered that its emblem should be Jim Crow, since the only thing unique about American culture was Ethiopian minstrelsy.[29]

After such a contextual build-up it is anticlimactic, even comical, to confess that Foster's American Melody No. 21 is "Old Dog Tray":

> Old dog Tray's ever faithful,
> Grief cannot drive him away,
> He's gentle, he is kind;
> I'll never, never find
> A better friend than old dog Tray.

But this corniest of all Foster's songs was extraordinarily successful, selling as many as a thousand copies a week.[30] When Foster tallied his royalties in 1857, the $1,080.25 he had received for "Old Dog Tray" was exceeded only by "My Old Kentucky Home" ($1,372.06) and "Old Folks at Home" ($1,647.46).

Foster's first big hit that was neither written in blackface dialect nor about the South was "White men's music," to be sure, though perhaps not "the higher kind" that Richard Storrs Willis had in mind. Its origins are definitely Old World. "Old Dog Tray" traces its pedigree to Robert Burns's song "The Winter It Is Past" and Thomas Campbell's "The Harper," one of the poems that won the then-young Scotsman acclaim as Burns's worthy successor.[31]

"Old Dog Tray" was more than just a literary exercise, however. Morrison Foster wrote that Tray was based on "a handsome setter dog" that had been given to Stephen, which he used to watch playing with children on the East Common.[32] One can easily imagine Foster gazing out the window of his study at the park as he wrote of "merry forms I've seen / Upon the village green, / Sporting with my old dog Tray." One can also imagine this ode to canine fidelity as a rebuke to Jane Foster. Unlike his wife, "ever faithful" Tray would never leave him.

According to Stephen's granddaughter, Foster played "a few bars" of the song at a neighbor's house and jotted them down on a piece of paper he left behind there. Months later he returned after a business trip to New York. (If this story is true, that trip might have been his visit to the *Musical World* offices in the winter of 1852–53.) Only then, at his host's urging, did Foster complete the song.[33] If Foster did indeed abandon "Old Dog Tray" for a spell, it may have been because he realized he was plagiarizing himself. The tempos are different, but the time signature (2/4), the key (G), and the first six notes of "Old Dog Tray" are identical to those of "Oh! Lemuel!" That a blackface melody could do double duty as "White men's music" suggests how skillful Foster had become at synthesizing different styles—and how much Anglo-Scots-Irish rather than African-American music hid beneath minstrelsy's burnt cork. Sung by minstrels and maidens, "Old Dog Tray" was equally at home on the stage and in the parlor.

In "Old Memories," the song that followed "Old Dog Tray" in his sketchbook, Foster worked in yet another style. The key is the same, and so is the autumnal nostalgia for vanished youth and loved ones, but Foster shifted to waltz time and a legato bel canto vocal line that would have done Donizetti proud.

"Sontag in opera with Salvi Seffaroni &c. next week," Stephen wrote Morrison from New York City on July 8, 1853.[34] Perhaps he saw Henrietta Sontag in Donizetti's *Lucia di Lammermoor*, *L'Elisir d'Amore*, or *La Fille du Regiment*—though "the beautiful pink lady" was "slightly worn," Henry James reminisced, Sontag's "clear bird-notes" received "thunderous applause"—or Balbina Steffanone in *La Favorita* or *Lucrezia Borgia*. All these Donizetti operas were presented at Castle Garden in the summer of 1853 by Max Maretzek, who later wrote caustically that the tenor Lorenzo Salvi "believed himself to be the Louis Quatorze of the lyric drama."[35]

"But for the opera, I could never have written *Leaves of Grass*," wrote Whitman, with whom Foster may well have rubbed shoulders in Castle Garden's $1.00 seats, spellbound like the poet by

> Italia's peerless compositions.
>
> Across the stage with pallor on her face, yet lurid passion,
> Stalks Norma brandishing the dagger in her hand.
>
> I see poor crazed Lucia's eyes' unnatural gleam,
> Her hair down her back falls loose and dishevel'd.

It was an era when arias were popular songs, when Italian airs were churned out by street-corner organ-grinders so ubiquitous—an estimated 4,382 plied the streets of Manhattan alone—that George Templeton Strong yearned for a special "cockroach powder" to "exterminate" them.[36]

From street corners to steamboats: In the spring of 1853, after selling the *James Millingar*, Dunning Foster became the captain (though not the owner) of a smaller sidewheeler christened the *Norma*. In October of that year, Henry Kleber published "The Opera Schottisch." The following month, he joined Morrison Foster, Richard Cowan, Robert McKnight, and other enthusiastic Pittsburghers in signing a petition inviting a touring opera company to tarry and stage one more performance. The company acceded and repeated *Lucrezia Borgia*.[37]

The year before, Alexander Wheelock Thayer, a music scholar who later wrote a massive biography of Beethoven, traveled west and noted that in Pittsburgh and along the Ohio River there seemed "to be no assortment of good pianoforte music to be found, and I was asked several times for a list of pieces, which at the same time are easy and yet worthy of the name classical." Young ladies in particular, he wrote in *Dwight's Journal of Music*, expressed "a craving for something beyond"; their "natural taste" spurned "the namby pamby airs with the old hacknied 'tum, tum, tum' accompaniment." Why, Thayer asked,

> cannot some of our music publishing periodicals sometimes give a page or two of *real* music? Why should not Graham or Godey sometimes give an Andante from Beethoven or Haydn, instead of a 'Lament on our dead Pussey,' by the sentimental Mr. Jones?[38]

A similar sense of an unsatisfied market out there, as well as Stephen Foster's ambition to distinguish himself in the field of "White men's music," prompted Firth, Pond and Foster to undertake *The Social Orchestra*, a compendium of seventy-three arrangements for flute, violin, piano, and other instruments of popular, operatic, and classical airs. When the eighty-four-page collection appeared in late January 1854, its cover promoted Foster as the author of "Old Kentucky Home," "Massa's in de Cold Ground," "Farewell My Lilly Dear," and "The Old Folks at Home" (though Christy is credited inside). In addition to instrumental arrangements of and variations on some of his songs (including a lovely solo rhapsody, based on "Massa's in de Cold Ground," entitled "Anadolia"), Foster contributed "Jenny's Own Schottisch," presumably in tribute to his wife; "Irene," a tune that would reappear five years later as the melody of "Linger in Blissful Repose"; and a set of four new quadrilles and a jig.[39]

But Donizetti composed as much of *The Social Orchestra* as Foster: thirteen tunes, including six from *Lucia*. The selection makes several obligatory nods to blackface, such as the ditty "Commence Ye Darkies All," but these are outnumbered by arrangements of Jullien, Abt, Mozart (an aria from *The Magic Flute*), Schubert (the song *"La Sérénade"* is the famous *"Ständchen"* from Schubert's *Schwanengesang*), and even a waltz erroneously attributed to Beethoven.[40]

The Social Orchestra, in sum, tended to shun the minstrel stage for the more respectable pleasures of playing (and dancing, as many of the pieces were waltzes, polkas, schottisches, quicksteps, and quadrilles) in the parlor. It catered to the cozy snobbery of Richard Storrs Willis, who declared the "music of private life" "a thousand times more enjoyable than public music." The collection's introduction identifies Foster as "a gentleman of acknowledged musical taste," but many of his arrangements, which proceed from solos to duets to trios to quartets, are quite rudimentary. *The Musical World and New York Musical Times*, while applauding the goal of "improving the taste of the community for social music," noted that the parts for second violin, written entirely in doubled chords, were "tedious and troublesome." Still, the reviewer hoped that this would not be Foster's "only work of the kind which he will find the public calling for at his hands."[41]

The Social Orchestra was indeed popular and reprinted repeatedly. But Foster never followed up its success, probably because he was paid so little (a flat fee of $150) for what must have been an extraordinary amount of work for a songwriter with little experience as an arranger. (Perhaps he was assisted by Kleber, who also contributed a polka and two schottisches.) Especially now that Foster had negotiated a new contract with Firth, Pond, in May 1853, which increased his royalties on new songs from 8 to 10 percent, writing original songs was more profitable than arranging old ones.[42] Although a 10 percent royalty was generous for that era (when Gottschalk received the same from a Philadelphia publisher, it was considered "unusual"), Foster was having difficulties making ends meet amid the diversions of New York City.[43]

Chapter Twenty-two

"HEARD ANYTHING FROM STEPHEN LATELY?"

*L*ife in New York was exhilarating. In addition to the opera at Castle Garden, Foster enjoyed the horse races under the striped canvas tent of Franconi's Hippodrome at Madison Square. The posh saloon of the new Taylor's International Hotel on the corner of Broadway and Franklin was *"great,"* Stephen wrote Morrison, and the young Henry and William James, who often stopped there for ice cream on their way back from the dentist, agreed.[1]

Not only Stephen Foster and the James boys but Walt Whitman and Mark Twain (who arrived in New York that year with ten dollars tucked in the lining of his coat) were awed by America's first world's fair. It was held in the Crystal Palace, the ill-fated iron-and-glass pleasure dome that not even Barnum could save from bankruptcy the following year. The Exhibition of the Industry of All Nations included a newfangled violin, shaped somewhat like a guitar, that William Sidney Mount had designed and patented, but Henry James was most impressed by the statuary. Whitman, who cruised the Crystal Palace day and night in a slouch hat, was more attracted to the young men.[2]

In 1853 Firth, Pond published "The Crystal Schottisch," with a handsome lithograph of the palace on its cover. The piano piece's author, "Wm. Byerly," was probably another of Foster's playful pseudonyms, since according to his account book he received $44.06 in royalties for it. Foster included arrangements of this tune and "Byerly's Waltz" in *The Social Orchestra* and may have left a clue to Byerly's identity on the back of a manuscript arrangement for vocal quartet of "I Would Not Die in Spring Time." On the reverse sheet he wrote "Music by Byerley," a line of a waltz and, upside down at the bottom of the page, another line of music and the words: "When You Reply Anser true / You need not the name for you surely Know who— / Trio to the medley waltz by byerley."[3]

Foster savored to the fullest what Henry James would recall as "the queer empty dusty smelly New York of midsummer." On his twenty-seventh birthday, he took the ferry to Staten Island and visited "Vin" Smith. The younger sister of Brother William's second wife, Lavinia Smith would later wed Brother William's boss, J. Edgar Thomson.[4]

But life in New York was also costly, all the more so because Foster was presumably sending at least some money to Jane and Marion in Lewistown. Foster's songs were selling. Stephen wrote Morrison in July 1853 that Firth, Pond "have just rendered my account which is over five hundred dollars, and that for the dullest season of the year." While his publishers owed Foster royalties, he owed them money, too, for advances he had received in the form of promissory notes. While he was still in Allegheny City, Stephen had given Morrison one such note to repay a $125 debt. Now he had to write Morrison to ask for the note back. "I am not living expensively," he assured his brother, "and I hope it will not be long before I can pay you back the amt."

"I am getting along first rate," Stephen wrote, but his separation from his wife and daughter troubled him.[5] Tellingly, all of the original songs he published between December 13, 1853, and the following June were about families. "Little Ella" and "Ellen Bayne" (copyrighted December 13, 1853, and February 3, 1854, respectively) sing sweet praises of a beloved daughter. Little Ella is an "earthly cherub" whose redemptive powers as well as her name recall Harriet Beecher Stowe's little Eva. "Ellen Bayne" is a lullaby reassuring a child of her parents' abiding love. (That Foster spelled the girl's last name "Bane" throughout the drafts in his sketchbook suggests he may have been nagged by guilt on this score.) *The Musical World* complimented its "easy and graceful melody" but did not remark that "Ellen Bayne" is the first Foster parlor ballad with a harmonized chorus. Foster wrote it for two voices, possibly a mother's and a father's, but the chorus also made the song especially amenable to minstrel performance, and Christy added the song to his repertory. The parlor and the stage, private and public, were continuing to converge.[6]

"Willie We Have Missed You" (copyrighted March 4, 1854) tells the treacly tale of a husband's reunion with his wife and children on Christmas Eve—a holiday Stephen may well have not spent with his family three months earlier. There's no suggestion in the first draft in Foster's sketchbook that Willie is returning on a special night like Christmas Eve, or that he's been away for more than one evening, out on a bender. "How bitterly I grieve," Willie's wife upbraids him in a second draft, "When I know not where you roam." In the song as finally published, Foster left it unclear why and for how long Willie had been absent, blurred the inference that he'd been out on a tear and fantasized that he (Foster) could reunite with his family without a word of rebuke from a grateful wife.

During these months Foster also wrote his first song explicitly about alcohol, although it would not be published until much later, with different words. "No life so dull but hath some hours of pleasur," Foster wrote in his sketchbook, "No heart so poor but hath some hidden treasur." Then his handwriting nearly doubled in size, turning into a loose scrawl, as if he had indeed been drinking:

> No heart so bright
> But finds its night
> [or]
> blight
> When the bowl goes round
> When the bowl goes round

"Jeanie with the Light Brown Hair" (copyrighted June 5, 1854) shares the same key (F), time signature (4/4), and tempo (*moderato*) as "Willie We Have Missed You," and begins with nearly the same eleven notes. "Jeanie" also echoes a melodic motif from "Ellen Bayne," underscoring how intimately interrelated this suite of family songs is.[7]

In Foster's sketchbook, Jeanie was Jennie, his nickname for his wife (as in "Jenny's Own Schottisch"), and in the first draft of "Jeanie with the Light Brown Hair," Jennie was dead. "I long for Jennie but her form lies low," Foster wrote, ending some of his words with violent, daggerlike downstrokes rarely seen in his handwriting, and then he changed "her form" to "she now." Her fingers were "snowy" with the chill of death (or at least of a frigid relationship), not "gentle" as in the published version. A faint echo of "The Raven" survives in the second verse's "Never more to find her. . . ." Foster, in other words, went from wishing his wife were dead to wishing they were reunited.[8]

For "Jeanie" is not a corpse. Like Jane Foster (and Stephen, for that matter), she has "strayed / Far from the fond hearts round her native glade." Like most of the females in Foster's lyrics, however, she is certainly incorporeal. "Borne, like a vapor, on the summer air" at the beginning of "Jeanie with the Light Brown Hair," at its end she is "Floating, like a vapor, in the soft summer air." The song is static, stuck eternally but ever so artfully on one note (well, two) of estrangement and of yearning to overcome that estrangement.

Most of the artfulness lies in the music, in the illusion of movement the piano accompaniment creates by alternating soft, hymnlike chords, gently rippling arpeggios and a music-box tinkle. The high point, dramatically, is the vocal cadenza that introduces the chorus, when the singer ad-libs his (or her) way up and over an octave, from C to high D, and then falls back to high C—as if, in an excess of passion and yearning, the singer had overshot the mark and then recovered. So persnickety about his music that he lectured even Christy about following it precisely, note for note, Foster had marked a vocal passage *ad lib* only twice before —in "Mary Loves the Flowers" and "Ah! May the Red Rose Live Alway!"—and never to such eloquent effect as in "Jeanie with the Light Brown Hair."

"Jeanie" is usually interpreted straightforwardly as a song about Jane Foster, but the dangling participles of the second verse encourage a more complex reading:

> I hear her melodies, like joys gone by
> Sighing round my heart o'er the fond hopes that die:
> Sighing like the night wind and sobbing like the rain,
> Wailing for the lost one that comes not again. . . .

Who is sighing and sobbing here, and for whom? The singer and the song, the lover and the beloved, have become so entangled syntactically (graphologically, too: the capital I's and J's in Foster's sketchbook are nearly indistinguishable) that "the lost one" could be Jane, Stephen, their daughter Marion—and/or the muse, which Foster may have felt was abandoning him just as Jane had. The next song Foster wrote, "Come with Thy Sweet Voice Again," is a pendant of sorts to "Jeanie" and uses the same device of overreaching an octave and then subsiding. Here the singer clearly addresses a disembodied and nameless muse, imploring her to return "with the music that wells from thy soul."

In a year that saw him publish only four new songs, Foster may well have feared that his inspiration was slipping. Moreover, none of these would sell as well as "Old Dog Tray" or his plantation melodies. In 1854, a Philadelphia publisher, Fisher & Brother, paid Foster $110 for "the sole and exclusive right to publish, apart from the music, the words of all the Negro Songs written by Stephen C. Foster, Esq." A series of four song-sters, entitled *Christy's Plantation Melodies*, highlighted Foster's contributions but included many other songs, among them an early version of "The Yellow Rose of Texas" ("She's the sweetest girl of colour / That this darkey ever knew").[9]

Although they continued to be popular, Foster was no longer writing "Negro Songs." And he paid a price for it. When Foster added up his royalties in 1857, "Ellen Bayne" had earned $642.34; "Willie We Have Missed You," $497.77; "Jeanie," only $217.80; and "Come with Thy Sweet Voice Again," a mere $54.33. This despite the fact that all but the last sold for thirty-eight cents rather than the twenty-five cents his earlier songs had fetched and were illustrated on their covers with elaborate lithographs: Ellen Bayne, pensive in pantalettes; Willie embracing his long-suffering wife in a cameo aglow with moonlight, a candle and a crackling fire; Jeanie clasping her hands as if in prayer, a simpering Madonna with a cross at her throat. Firth, Pond was going all out to advertise "The Song Writer of America," and publishing sheet-music arrangements of most of his songs for guitar, but the market for Foster's new family songs was only fair to middling.[10]

Although at least one minstrel troupe performed "Jeanie" and alluded in a blackface song to "that lubly Jenne with a luxriant head of wool," the New York *Herald* noted that "Jeanie" was "decidedly not a negro melody": "The music is very clever, but the least said about the words, the better for the poet." Not until the twentieth century, when it was recorded by Al Jolson and the Irish tenor John McCormack, featured in the 1940 Hollywood "biopic" *Swanee River*, and widely broadcast during a dispute between radio stations and ASCAP, did "Jeanie with the Light Brown Hair" become a popular favorite.[11]

Aboard the *Norma* near Vicksburg, Mississippi, Dunning Foster wrote fretfully to Morrison:

> Have you heard anything from Stephen lately, it is a subject of much anxiety to me notwithstanding his foolish and unaccountable course,—I hope he will continue to make a comfortable living for himself. . . . [12]

What Dunning meant by Stephen's "course" is as ambiguous and tantalizing as their sister Henrietta's reference the year before to Jane Foster's "course of conduct." He could have been referring to Stephen's decision to become a full-time, professional songwriter, to his removal to New York, to his separation from Jane—or, by this time, to their reconciliation. Sometime in the winter or spring of 1854, Jane and Marion rejoined Stephen, and together they set up housekeeping in a brick row house in Hoboken, New Jersey. It was probably just about the time he was writing "Jeanie," because on the page following those drafts in his sketchbook, as if that song's dream had come true, he wrote five lines under the heading, "Hoboken." Jane Foster's *Book of Common Prayer*, published in 1854, bears the same inscription in *her* hand.[13]

Jane and Marion may have initially lodged with Stephen in Manhattan. According to an early Foster biographer, Jane spoke to a reporter more than twenty years afterward of "boarding on Sixth Avenue." She told her granddaughter an anecdote that had occurred "when they had not yet gone to housekeeping, and were boarding in one of the old brownstone front houses so common in New York in the fifties." It seems that the landlady was so parsimonious with her fare that the self-sacrificing Episcopal minister who carved and dished out the main course often ended up with nothing on his own plate. After a few weeks, Stephen could not stomach such stinginess and stormed out, refusing to lodge there any longer.[14]

What impelled Stephen across the Hudson was probably not indignation so much as the considerations that have always induced young families of modest means to leave New York. Hoboken's directory for 1854–1855 listed "Stephen C. Foster, music composer, 233 Bloomfield" among the 6,211 residents of a town in transition. Earlier, Hoboken had been a summer resort and day-trippers' picnic spot, extolled by Frances Trollope as a "little Eden," the birthplace of both the aristocratic New York Yacht Club and plebeian baseball. Not only the Knickerbocker Giants but Dan Emmett and other minstrels played at Hoboken's Elysian

Fields. Jim Crow jumped over there (in one version of the song) "to hab a promenade / An dar [he] see de pretty gals, / Drinking de Lemonade." Walt Whitman loafed there, "enjoying picnics or jigs or a good game of baseball." [15]

Now Hoboken was well on its way to becoming a year-round suburb. "Generally speaking, the dwellings . . . [in] Hoboken are of the better class," the city directory boasted, "and it would be scarcely possible to find a more healthy location." Hoboken harbored "neither gambling halls nor houses of infamy," claimed another booster of local real estate. Served by three ferries, it was a short ride but safe distance from New York City, that "Babylon . . . famous for its dirty streets, the reign of disorder. . . ." [16] In other words, Hoboken was a great place to raise a family armed with a new *Book of Common Prayer*.

The Fosters lived on a newly developed middle-class block. Thanks to their location on the northeast corner of Bloomfield and Sixth Streets, the Fosters' parlor had windows on two sides. Afternoon light and a marble fireplace, one of three in the house, must have made it a cozy room. If Foster's sketchbook is any indication, however, it was not a happy household. Hoboken, he wrote, was

> Where wranglers bid you to their scenes of strife
> In wrong conception of your plan of life
> One hour of pain will flood the measure
> That years would fail to fill with pleasure.

Although Jane and Stephen had reconciled, she may not have become reconciled to her husband's "plan of life," his insistence on pursuing a career that seemed incapable of supporting a family. Or to his drinking, if the lyrics to "Pass the Bowl Around" had any basis in Foster's actual behavior.

The Fosters kept house in Hoboken for less than a year. In October 1854 Stephen returned to Allegheny City, taking his parents and siblings by surprise. His mother was in Philadelphia, attending a wedding, and visiting with friends and Brother William, who had been promoted the previous year to vice president of the Pennsylvania Railroad. She had just sent a letter to Stephen in New York when she received one from him informing her of his return home. "Tell Stephen," she wrote Morrison, "I hope to find him at home when I come, to help make it more like one, which I verily think I shall greatly treasure when I get back to it."[17]

There's a strong likelihood that Stephen came back alone. His mother's letter asked Morrison to give her love to "dear Stephen" and "your Father," but made no mention of her daughter-in-law or granddaughter, even though three-year-old Marion would presumably have been on Eliza's mind if she were eager to make the house on East Common more like a home.

Previous biographers of Foster have assumed that his wife and daughter accompanied him back to Allegheny City and resumed residence there without a hitch. Homesickness, they say, rather than marital discord ended their stay in Hoboken. But photographs and transcripts of three letters in the Foster Hall Collection, uncatalogued and never before published under orders from Morrison Foster's daughter, Evelyn Foster Morneweck, suggest this was not the case.

The letters were written by James Buchanan, the oldest offspring of Ann Eliza Foster Buchanan and the Rev. Edward Young Buchanan. James was reading law with a Pittsburgh attorney and boarding on East Common. His famous uncle and namesake, who had lost the 1852 Democratic presidential nomination to Franklin Pierce and was now his ambassador in London, was paying his expenses. When Eliza Foster returned from Philadelphia to Allegheny City, she brought with her twenty-year-old James, who had been visiting his parents at Rev. Buchanan's new parish just outside Philadelphia.

Eliza Foster and her grandson arrived in Allegheny "in perfect safety," James Buchanan wrote home on October 26. "Uncle Stephen intends remaining in Pittsburg this Winter I think. His wife will not be here however. I believe he wants to get her out to Youngstown with Aunt Henrietta."[18] This might be interpreted to mean that Stephen had returned to Allegheny with Jane and Marion, were it not for a letter that James Buchanan wrote his father three weeks later:

The announcement of the arrival of my Aunt Jane in Pittsburg seems to have created quite a stir betwixt you and mother. I was surprised at the movement myself from some expressions of horror which I had heard dropped concerning that individual, but to tell the truth I never have found out what the nature of her sin was. Certain it is that she is now fairly fixed and at her ease in Allegheny and every one (Aunt Henrietta included who is here now with her daughter Mary who in turn having suffered for the last two months with fever and ague was brought here to be recuperated) all, I say, unite in the endeavor to appear perfectly oblivious to all that is past. The heroine of this story is greatly to be commended for the propriety of her conduct. I judge she remains at home entirely. I don't think Uncle Morrison is much to blame in this matter. Grandmother loves her son Stephen with a wildness of which you can hardly form a conception, and I verily believe Uncle Morrison conceded purely for her sake.[19]

Was Jane Foster a sinner, a heroine, or both? Had she initially refused to return with Stephen to Allegheny, or had her brother-in-law Morrison, who was now a town councilman and had a reputation to protect, initially barred her from East Common? Possibly both occurred. As always, Jane Foster is a cipher, and one can fill in the blank of her behavior with any speculation. Maybe Jane loved Hoboken, didn't feel the least bit homesick, hated the notion of moving back in with her in-laws and dug in her heels. Perhaps she had had an affair, or asked for a divorce, or simply insisted that Stephen get a day job. Whatever she had done, she had shamed and outraged the Foster family. Yet Stephen, who had earlier wanted to live apart from Jane—he in Allegheny and she in Youngstown—now wanted to live with her. He enlisted his doting mother's support, overcame Morrison's objections, and once again the family was crowded under the same roof in Allegheny City.

"All are well at Grandmother's if we may except Uncle Morrison who has had a return of Neuralgia which was quite violent at first but does not at present interfere with his business," James Buchanan wrote on December 15. "Uncle Stephen is still composing as usual his last being a very good song. It seems that he with some others are going to give a concert in Allegheny for the benefit of the poor."[20]

Chapter Twenty-three

HARD TIMES

Distress was widespread in Allegheny City and Pittsburgh in 1854. Unemployment had reached unprecedented levels that spring, and in the summer cholera struck once again, killing four hundred people in just two weeks. The Fosters took in a boarder, a young minister, to help make ends meet in the already crowded house on East Common. It was hard times not only in Pennsylvania that year. In New York City, Irish dock workers battled African-American strike-breakers on the waterfront, Dan Emmett concocted "A Negro Extrava-ganza" for Charles White's Minstrels entitled *Hard Times*, and George Templeton Strong noted in December that *"Hard Times"* were "the gen-eral subject of talk. No sign yet of any let-up on their hardness." In England, meanwhile, Charles Dickens's novel, *Hard Times*, was serialized from April to August.[1]

The "very good song" by Uncle Stephen that young James Buchanan mentioned in his December 15 letter to his father was probably "Hard Times Come Again No More." (No reference in the local papers to Foster's participation in a benefit for the poor, however, has been found.) Firth, Pond registered the song's title page for copyright on December 16, and deposited the complete song on January 17, 1855. It was, Firth, Pond advertised, "just the song for the times," and one reviewer noted that "if the *hard times* continue," the song, "intrinsically one of the best productions of S.C. Foster's prolific pen," would "have a run equal to *Old Folks at Home*."[2]

Foster need not have read Dickens in order to write "Hard Times Come Again No More." "Hard Times" had already come "a knocking at the door" in "My Old Kentucky Home." But a tally of volumes inside Stephen Foster's sketchbook includes Dickens's previous novel, *Bleak House*, and it's likely that Foster devoured *Hard Times* as avidly as the rest of Dickens's vast American readership. Dickens's descriptions of the imaginary Coketown—"a town of machinery and tall chimneys, out of which interminable serpents of smoke trailed themselves forever and ever, and never got uncoiled"—must have reminded Foster of Pittsburgh, and the circus performer Signor Jupe, with his dog-and-pony act and "Shakespearean quips and retorts," was a dead ringer for Dan Rice.[3]

Literary inspiration and the economic hardship all around him may have encouraged Foster to write "Hard Times Come Again No More." To these sources might well be added a third: the example and memory of Charles Shiras, who had died of consumption in July while his friend and sometime collaborator was still in Hoboken. A few pages before "Hard Times" in Foster's sketchbook appears a lyric that never became a published song. "The Robin and the Butterfly" is a confused and uncharacteristic expression of economic resentment in which a butterfly menaces a robin eating worms because the butterfly, recently a caterpillar, "has many a friend in wormdom left." Foster crossed out these lines in the final draft:

> There's many a Robin and many a Ben
> Who eats more victuals than worthier men
> Who spends his days in robbin' the poor
> No better a Robin than this one, I'm sure.

Shades of Shiras and "Dimes and dollars! dollars and dimes! / An empty pocket's the worst of crimes!" Foster's execrable pun may have made the poet roll over in his grave and laugh once again "with a groan, / In an unearthly tone."

"Hard Times Come Again No More," on the other hand, is one of Foster's greatest songs, and the one that has been most widely revived in recent years. Stephen's "sympathies" were "always with the lowly and the poor," according to Morrison, who told how his brother stayed throughout a stormy night at the nearby house of "a poor working man," consoling the grief-stricken parents of a little girl who had been run over and slain by a wagon.[4] In "Hard Times Come Again No More" those sympathies found their most explicit expression:

> Let us pause in life's pleasures and count its many tears,
> While we all sup sorrow with the poor:
> There's a song that will linger forever in our ears;
> Oh! Hard Times, come again no more.
> Chorus:
> 'Tis the song, the sigh of the weary;
> Hard Times, Hard Times, come again no more:
> Many days you have lingered around my cabin door;
> Oh! Hard Times, come again no more.

"Hard Times" is exceptional and haunting because the "sigh" is not the singer's or his beloved's, for a change. For once Foster was able to venture outside himself and see other people looking at him, their pinched faces pressed against the window pane:

> While we seek mirth and beauty, and music light and gay,
> There are frail forms fainting at the door;
> Though their voices are silent, their pleading looks will say
> Oh! Hard Times, come again no more.

Poverty, not sentimentality, makes the "pale drooping maiden" languish in the third verse. And, despite the rustic "cabin door," the poverty seems to have an urban air. It feels immediate and close at hand, not distant and displaced on a faraway plantation. It's as if Foster, who never wrote about Pittsburgh, who always preferred rural fantasy to urban realism, suddenly looked out a restaurant window and recognized, with a jolt, another world.

It was the world, for instance, of David Gilmour Blythe, a tall, gaunt, red-headed scarecrow of a man who wandered in and out of Pittsburgh and painted about this time (roughly 1854–1858) a somber canvas entitled *Hard Times*, in which a squat constable grabs a glum wretch by the scruff of his frayed jacket. Blythe had little in common with Foster except genius, a weakness for drink, and an early death. He was an American

Daumier whose pictures drew crowds to the windows of J. J. Gillespie's art gallery, where Pittsburgh's hoi polloi gaped at sardonic caricatures of themselves. While Foster composed songs about cherubs frolicking in pastoral dells, Blythe painted sallow, oafish street urchins sucking on cigars—the smoke and ash of their stogies the very smoke and ash of Pittsburgh itself. Blythe painted the world that Foster's music usually tried to evade, the lumpen proletariat into which the shabby-genteel Foster family had a horror of falling, and which the nearby Carnegies were grimly determined to rise above. Yet this once, in "Hard Times Come Again No More," Blythe's world and Stephen Foster's coincided.[5]

Morrison Foster wrote that "Hard Times," like "Oh! Boys, Carry Me 'Long," contained echoes of "the church of shouting colored people" to which Stephen Foster had been taken as a child. But there's nothing overtly African-American about the melody of "Hard Times Come Again No More" or the four-part harmony of its chorus. It's the social realism and mournful moralizing of the lyrics, so unusual for Foster, that have encouraged people to attribute atypical origins to the song.

"Hard Times Come Again No More" was the most recent song cited in a new contract Foster signed with Firth, Pond on December 21, 1854. The two surviving copies of the contract—three dense pages containing eighteen "Articles" and a numbing procession of parties of the first part (Firth, Pond) and parties of the second part (Foster)—are written in Foster's own meticulous, bookkeeper's hand, as if the party of the second part had dictated his own terms.[6]

The terms seem reasonable. Foster was to receive 10 percent of the retail price Firth, Pond charged for every new Foster song as well as for twelve songs copyrighted within the past three years, including "My Old Kentucky Home," "Old Dog Tray," and "Jeanie." For eighteen songs copyrighted between 1849 and 1852, Foster would receive an 8 percent royalty. For every sale of a sheet-music arrangement of a Foster song, past, present, or future, for voice and guitar or exclusively for instruments, the party of the second part would receive 1.5 cents. For a number of instrumental arrangements by other hands of Foster songs, including Henry Kleber's "Home Schottisch for four hands," the composer would collect a penny royalty.

And so it goes, the contract droning on predictably until Article Sixteenth, which declares "null and void" the contracts of December 3, 1849, and May 5, 1853, and any agreements granting Firth, Pond the "sole and exclusive" right to publish Foster's music. This suggests that Foster's 1853 contract, of which no copy survives, had given Firth, Pond exclusivity—a distinction the publisher advertised as late as November 1854.[7] Although Foster had not published a new song elsewhere since "Laura Lee," a parlor ballad, with Benteen back in 1851, suddenly he was free once again to shop around. The irony is that once Foster was free to seek other outlets he had little to sell.

The day after Firth, Pond deposited "Hard Times Come Again No More" for copyright, on January 18, 1855, a stroke felled Eliza Foster. She was stricken while walking down Pittsburgh's Marbury Street, staggered to the nearest house and rang the bell. The servant who answered heard a groan from the parlor, where Eliza had dragged herself and collapsed on a settee. By the time a doctor arrived, she was dead. An obituary in the Pittsburgh *Daily Union* identified her as Miss Eliza C. Foster; another overlooked her husband, the two-term mayor of Allegheny City, while mentioning Stephen and Morrison. She was buried in Allegheny Cemetery, not far from the paradise lost of her beloved White Cottage, on the afternoon before her sixty-seventh birthday.[8]

Stephen Foster's love for his mother, Morrison later wrote, "amounted to adoration." Still, short as always on cash, he chipped in only seven dollars to bury her and settle her accounts while each of his brothers contributed twenty-eight or thirty dollars. It was Stephen who assumed responsibility, however, with the help of two servants, for the household on East Common. Morrison was often away on business, sometimes visiting Brother William in Philadelphia; Henry had moved with his wife Mary and their two children into his mother-in-law's home in Lawrenceville; Dunning, whenever the "infernal cough" he had contracted in the Mexican War would allow him, still piloted the *Norma.* These comings and (mostly) goings left Stephen in charge of the house and his invalid father.[9]

In March, Stephen wrote his sister Henrietta in Ohio that "Pa's health is excellent. . . . I have taken great care to see that he is treated with regularity and system." In a P.S. suggesting that mourning had not put a damper on his rekindled marriage, Stephen added, "Jane sends her love. She is making summer dresses for Marion."[10]

Stephen, on the other hand, was making little new music. Due to his new responsibilities, grief or, most likely, a combination of both, Foster published only four songs during the rest of 1855. The first two of these, both copyrighted by Firth, Pond on June 28, suggest that his mother was much on his mind. "Some Folks" and "Come Where My Love Lies Dreaming" share the same key (F) and are both marked *moderato*, but otherwise they seem like diametrically opposed responses to Eliza Foster's death. While "Come Where My Love Lies Dreaming," the most ambitious and complex song Foster ever composed (as well as, at sixty-eight measures, one of his longest), seems more than half in love with easeful death, the trifling "Some Folks" kicks up its heels and dances on the grave to a polka beat.

"Come Where My Love Lies Dreaming," labeled a *Serenade, per voci sole*, is an a cappella "quartette" for mixed voices that develops and amplifies Foster's vocal duets (especially "Wilt Thou Be Gone, Love?") and draws on his experience arranging instrumental quartets for *The Social Orchestra*. The previous year, William Henry Fry, thumping the tub for American music, had crowed that "negro minstrel bands draw nightly crowds of devotees to their temples, while a German four-part *Lied* . . . is unknown." Foster's four-part *lied* was his boldest bid for classical European respectability, and listeners have detected in "Come Where My Love Lies Dreaming" echoes of Schubert, Rossini, and, closer to home, Henry Kleber (whose daughter said the song's ending was his idea).[11]

"Come Where My Love Lies Dreaming" is unique among Foster's works in that it forsakes conventional verses and choruses. "Through-composed" rather than strophic, the song unfolds in discrete sections, including a brand-new melody, or "middle eight," that appears unexpectedly halfway through the song, and a theatrical coda. Legato passages are punctuated by staccato ones in which every voice save the soprano's repeats a percussive "come" eight times consecutively. Instead of developing or progressing, the song flows and eddies as if it were a New Age idyll, and the words keep repeating like a mesmerizing mantra: "Come where my love lies dreaming, / Dreaming the happy hours away."

But come, come, come, come where? To the beloved's bedside or to her grave? While he still had command of his faculties, William Barclay Foster pasted into his scrapbook a creepy poem entitled "Lines on a Sleeping Wife":

> Delicious task—to sit and watch
>   The breathing of a sleeping wife,

And mark the features of that state
Dividing death from life![12]

Part of the fascination with the line dividing life and death is the yearning to cross it—a fascination and yearning that Stephen Foster shared with his era, which entertained itself with spiritualist, table-rapping séances and converted graveyards into artfully landscaped pleasure gardens. "Come Where My Love Lies Dreaming" is a siren's song from the cemetery, a come-hither from what the cultural critic Ann Douglas has called the "Disney World for the mortuary imagination of Victorian America."[13]

Its sumptuous, intertwining harmonies are also fun to sing and play, which is why "Come Where My Love Lies Dreaming" enjoyed considerable popularity well into the twentieth century. It's hard to imagine, given the song's lulling spell, but Nicholas Young's brass band, the successor to Henry Kleber's local ensemble, played "Come Where My Love Lies Dreaming" as a sprightly quickstep. According to a member of the band, Foster gave Young many of his songs, which his group was the first to play. Brass bands flourished in the 1850s and were an expanding new market for sheet music. In December 1854, Firth, Pond advertised twenty-four new brass band arrangements, six of them Foster songs.[14]

"Some Folks" is a fiddle-dee-dee rebuke to the lugubriousness of "Come Where My Love Lies Dreaming":

> Some folks like to sigh,
> Some folks do, some folks do,
> Some folks long to die,—
> But that's not me nor you.

The lighthearted irreverence of the lyrics suggests blackface, but the idiom seems to hark back to England, and so does the tripping melody of the unison chorus:

> Long live the merry merry heart
> That laughs by night and day,
> Like the Queen of Mirth,—
> No matter what some folks say.

The song, of course, protests too much. If anyone ever liked to sigh, it was Stephen Foster, and his title here inevitably recalls "Old Folks," which lamented, "take me to my kind old mudder." That Foster was still troubled by the death of his mother is suggested by the page in his sketchbook immediately following "Come Where My Love Lies Dreaming" and "Some Folks." Beneath the title, "I See thee Still in my dreams," Foster doodled an entire page of arrows and fishhooks, and the capital letter "F" becomes a barb, too. Two of the arrows are crossed in an emblem of love and war. Foster would return to this title a couple of years later and write a song about his mother. In his dreams he still saw his love who lay dreaming, but how can we tell the dreamer from the dream? It would be an oversimplification, however, to interpret these doodles as a demonstration that Foster was hooked and impaled on his mother's memory. What's most striking is the aggression in these bristling barbs, the anger that Foster's music usually denies and, in its dreaminess, evades—unless all the dead females and all the dead African Americans in Foster's songs amount to the ultimate expression of hostility.[15]

Was Foster mad at a) his mother for leaving him? b) his father for not leaving him? c) his wife for their marital problems? d) himself for those marital problems and/or his financial problems and/or his drinking problem? Perhaps e) all of the above.

On July 27, 1855, after more than four years of incapacitation, one of the people at whom Stephen Foster was probably angriest finally died at the age of seventy-five. If William Barclay Foster was conscious during those last months, the unexpected death of his wife must have been a crushing blow. His youngest child was now master of the house, but he was still a tenant, and he was falling behind in the rent he owed Brother William. Stephen started keeping an account book that year, which is an invaluable record of his affairs from 1855 to 1860. The account book notes out-of-pocket expenses for home repairs such as replacing a spigot —seventy-five cents. It also shows that the one hundred dollar loan Brother William had given Stephen back in 1850 had accrued $33.50 in interest by October 1, 1855. Twelve days later, Stephen sent him a check for sixty-four dollars, which was more likely six months' rent than a partial repayment of the loan.[16]

A poem by Lydia Sigourney that William Barclay Foster had clipped and saved began, " 'I'll pay my rent in music,' said a Thrush / Who took his lodgings 'neath my eaves in spring."[17] But Stephen Foster's financial problems did not prod him to become more prolific. He published only two more songs in 1855. From his sketchbook he exhumed "The Village Maiden," which he had all but completed three years earlier, and sent it to Firth, Pond. The song's "requiem soft and low" for a provincial bride had acquired a new meaning since the death of his mother.

Then Foster exercised the right he had negotiated the previous year to publish elsewhere. In November, Miller & Beacham, a Baltimore firm that advertised itself as the successor to F. D. Benteen, copyrighted "Comrades, Fill No Glass for Me," which returned to the theme of the unpublished "When the Bowl Goes Round." It's a cautionary confession that reflects on the disappointment and pain the singer's drinking has caused his family:

> When I was young I felt the tide
>   Of aspirations undefiled,
> But manhood's years have wronged the pride
>   My parents centered in their child.
> Then, by a mother's sacred tear,
> By all that memory should revere,
> Though boon companions ye may be—
> Oh! comrades, fill no glass for me.

Writing so shortly after the loss of both his parents, Stephen Foster did not invoke a "mother's sacred tear" lightly. But if the song acknowledges one of his father's favorite causes, temperance, it does not embrace it. The singer declines a drink this time around, but he doesn't promise or pretend to reform. The somber mood of "blighted fortune, health and fame" is akin to that of David Gilmour Blythe's painting, *Temperance Pledge*, in which a man ponders a paper pledge and the neck of a bottle. His face is so careworn that it may be too late for his decision to make much difference. Robert Nevin, who was a druggist, later wrote that no one knew better than he how earnestly but ineffectually Foster had wrestled with his drinking problem, "resorting to all the remedial expedients which professional skill [presumably Nevin's] or his own experience could suggest, but never entirely delivering himself from its inexorable mastery."[18]

Foster published just one song in 1856. Deaths continued to depress him. On March 31, his brother Dunning died of consumption. Stephen, Henry, and Morrison brought his body back from Cincinnati aboard the steamboat *Philadelphia*.[19] Brother William's second wife, Elizabeth, died

in October. Stephen was also distracted by politics, and in 1856 he beat
the drum for his late father's other favorite cause: the Democratic Party.
Before Stephen joined the parade, however, he wrote "Gentle Annie," a
sentimental song steeped in Thomas Moore and Irish and Scottish balladry. "Thou wilt come no more, gentle Annie," the singer mourns
(there's that "no more" again), "Like a flower thy spirit did depart." The
first line of the melody makes that by now long-familiar leap ("gentle
An-NIE"), although it falls just short of the octave in "Old Folks at
Home," and the chorus asks,

> Shall we never more behold thee;
> Never hear thy winning voice again
> When the Springtime comes, gentle Annie,
> When the wild flowers are scattered o'er the plain?

If there was a "real-life" Annie, she may have been Annie Jenkins, the
neighbors' child who was struck and killed by a wagon, or Annie Evans,
Oliver Evans's granddaughter and a Foster cousin, who died after a long
illness.[20]

"Gentle Annie" was sufficiently successful for Firth, Pond to issue the
Gentle Annie Melodist in 1858. Although this songster included "Old
Folks at Home," Foster's publisher was trying to reposition him and
appeal to a more genteel and female audience than the market for the
1854 series, *Christy's Plantation Melodies*. The preface introduced Foster
as "the most popular song writer of the present day," citing "charming
melodies" such as "Old Dog Tray," "Jeanie with the Light Brown Hair,"
and "Ellen Bayne" but not a single blackface song. In addition to six
Foster compositions, the songster featured ballads by Moore and Burns,
and other Irish and Scottish songs.

The new marketing strategy evidently worked, because *Gentle Annie
Melodist No. 2* followed in 1859. In its preface, Firth, Pond called the
success of *No. 1* "unprecedented" and predicted that its sales, already
more than thirty thousand, would "undoubtedly" reach one hundred
thousand. Foster didn't see a penny of those profits, because by then he
had sold all the rights to his earlier songs. Before taking that momentous
step, however, Foster put aside commercial composing in 1856 for campaign songwriting. Pennsylvania was front and center on the national
stage in a presidential election year, and Foster helped write the score.

Chapter Twenty-four

POLITICS AND
PUNKINS

*O*n February 22, 1856, Washington's birthday, opponents of slavery or its expansion gathered from twenty-four states at Pittsburgh's Lafayette Hall to call for the formation of a national Republican Party. Andrew Carnegie, too young to vote but already vehemently opposed to slavery, felt "lost in admiration" as he watched the delegates stroll about Pittsburgh. (Martin Delany, on the other hand, had despaired of the black man's prospects in the United States. That very month, he and his family emigrated to Canada.)[1]

In June, the Republicans convened in Philadelphia and nominated their first presidential candidate, John C. Frémont. "Free Speech, Free Press, Free Soil, Free Men, Frémont and Victory" was the Republicans' cry, which the Democrats, nominating James Buchanan on the seventeenth ballot in Cincinnati, derided as a call for "free niggers and freebooters." It was a scabrous campaign, in which Republicans mocked Buchanan's bachelorhood ("Who ever heard in all his life, / Of a candidate without a wife?") and bruited it about that a Democratic victory would inflate the price of a slave from two thousand to five thousand dollars. The Democrats gave worse than they got, denouncing the "Black" Republicans as "Nigger Worshippers" and "Woolly Heads," and Frémont as a bastard (which he was) and a Catholic (which the Episcopalian Pathfinder was not).[2]

Stephen Foster's invective was not exceptional when he maligned a Republican rally in his sketchbook as an assembly of "niggers and ruffians and / raccoons and fools." Walt Whitman was scarcely more charitable when he anathematized supporters of Buchanan (and Millard Fillmore, the Know-Nothing candidate) as

> spies, blowers, electioneers, body snatchers, bawlers, bribers, compromisers, runaways, lobbyers, sponges, ruined sports, expelled gamblers, policy backers, monte dealers, duelists, carriers of concealed weapons, blind men, deaf men, pimpled men, scarred inside with the vile disorder, gaudy outside with gold chains from the people's money and harlot's money twisted together; crawling, serpentine men, the lousy combings and born freedom sellers of the earth.[3]

Although related to Buchanan by marriage, Foster did not rally to his support because of close personal ties. Buchanan kept his in-laws at arm's length and was cool toward his younger brother, Edward, the minister who had married Ann Eliza Foster. Harriet Lane, James Buchanan's favorite niece and mistress of ceremonies at the White House during his presidency, wrote that Edward's "kinsmen are too well acquainted with his want of wisdom, energy, decision, judgment, sentiment & feeling."[4]

Envious and resentful, Edward Buchanan visited Wheatland, James Buchanan's estate outside Lancaster, Pennsylvania, infrequently. When the president-to-be's namesake and nephew was studying law and living with the Fosters on East Common, his mother, Ann Eliza Foster Buchanan, wrote Morrison that she "was unwilling that James' Uncle should feel that he was in any way assisting my family. . . ." When Democrats recaptured the White House from the Whigs in 1853 and Henry Foster sought a new political appointment, "The Sage of Wheatland" condescended to write a letter of introduction on his behalf to President Franklin Pierce, but he declined to intervene more actively, and Henry was left out in the cold.[5]

Stephen Foster's enthusiasm for the Democratic ticket was more likely a somewhat guilty genuflection toward his late father, as well as an honest expression of his own deep conservatism. When Buchanan said that "the object of my administration will be to destroy any sectional party, North or South, and harmonize all sections of the Union under a national and conservative government, as it was fifty years ago," it struck a responsive chord, right down to the musical metaphor in "harmonize," in a composer who dwelled reluctantly in the industrial Pittsburgh of the present and dreamed in his lyrics of a Southern or pastoral past.[6]

Stephen Foster entered the fray on August 6, 1856, with the formation of the Allegheny Buchanan Glee Club—Morrison Foster, Treasurer; Stephen Foster, Musical Director. William Hamilton, who served with Stephen on the committees "to select Instrumental Performers" and to "solicit subscriptions to defray the expenses of the club during the campaign," later recalled that it was "a very hot campaign." So hot that when the club marched through the streets, it was accompanied by "a body guard of sometimes 50, sometimes 100 men, who joined in the chorus." When rival glee clubs and their corteges clashed, volunteer fire companies often joined the donnybrook.[7]

One such altercation occurred when the Allegheny Buchanan Glee Club, returning from a rally in outlying East Liberty, paused in Lawrenceville to serenade a sympathetic household with a Stephen Foster song. Billy Hamilton was singing the lead when a stranger in the crowd insisted on joining him and mangling the melody. An annoyed Hamilton motioned to one of the bodyguards to urge the man to confine himself to the choruses—which the bodyguard did by knocking the stranger to the ground not just once, but twice. Firemen poured out of their company headquarters across the street and started throwing punches. "In a twinkling," Hamilton remembered,

> our peaceful body of serenaders was transformed into a howling mob. Foster, his brother, myself and other vocalists hastened out of the crowd. We were all too small for our ages and had no business around where any fighting was going on. We always left that to our body guard, and they protected us most effectually in that case. None of us were hurt, and few of the members of the guard suffered, but the firemen were completely routed and driven back into their headquarters. They had tackled the wrong crowd that time.

Perhaps the Foster song Hamilton was singing before fists started flying was "The White House Chair," which denounced the Know-Nothings ("We'll have no dark designing band / To rule with secret sway"), defended the South against Republican aspersions ("We'll not outlaw the land that holds / The bones of Washington") and urged, in its chorus:

> Then come ye men from ev'ry state
>   Our creed is broad and fair;
> Buchanan is our candidate,
>   And we'll put him in the White House Chair.

The *Pittsburgh Morning Post,* the city's major Democratic paper, printed a version of Foster's lyrics, without music, on September 29, 1856.

"The White House Chair" was tame compared to Foster's other surviving campaign song. Possibly because the lyrics were so nasty, the *Morning Post* did not name their author when it published, on September 26, "The Abolition Show," to be sung to the popular British music hall melody, "Villikins and His Dinah" (which evolved into the American "folk" tune, "Sweet Betsy from Pike").

Republicans had staged a "monster parade" in Pittsburgh on September 17, and "The Great Baby Show," as he entitled it in his sketchbook, was Foster's scornful counterattack. The printed version omitted the word "niggers" (". . . and ruffians and / raccoons and fools") from the draft in Foster's sketchbook, and tried to restore at least a measure of decorum:

> On the Seventeenth day of September, you know,
> Took place in our city the great Frémont show;
> They shut up the factories and let the schools out,
> For the children will all vote for Frémont, no doubt.
> Chorus:
> Sing tu ral lal lu ral lal lu ral lal lay. . . .

Either the *Post* or Foster himself toned down the sketchbook's more scathing

> On the Seventeenth day of September, you know,
> Took place in our city the great baby show;
> They shut up the factories and let out the schools
> For the Seventeenth day was the day of all fools.

Foster let loose in his sketchbook with racist and misogynist ridicule:

> They had gemmen ob color to join in their games
> And jokers and clowns of all ages and names

> They had pop guns and tin pans and all kinds of toys
> And a very fine party of women and boys.

(The *Post*'s version skirted sexism by eliminating the women.)

Forgetting that his own bread had been buttered on the dark side, the composer of "Way Down Souf" and "My Brodder Gum" mocked the Republican rally as a minstrel show:

> Now was it not Kind in these good simple clowns
> To amuse all the children in both of our towns
> To shut up their work shops and spend all their money
> To black up their faces, get tight and be funny.

What drove Stephen Foster to such uncharacteristically vehement racism? What incensed a college dropout and songwriter to defend strict school hours and factory shifts, and to shoot himself in the foot with a potshot at minstrelsy? The anger and frustration Foster felt at the loss of his parents and his own financial difficulties may have found a temporary focus and outlet in politics. He was also agitated, I suspect, by his own ambivalence about blackface and "White men's music," as well as by his conflicted feelings about the presidential campaign in which he had become embroiled. It was his late father who had been passionate about politics, and it was his brother Morrison, a devoted Democrat, who had drawn the essentially apolitical Stephen into the campaign. Although Harriet Beecher Stowe and the implicitly antislavery themes of some of his own songs had not converted Stephen Foster to outright abolitionism, he could not in good conscience condone the peculiar institution that Buchanan pledged to respect in order to preserve the Union. Foster could not acknowledge the appeal of the Republicans' free soil platform, however, without betraying his family (Henrietta was as ardent and active a Democrat as Morrison). When an argument is weak, the best and sometimes the only defense is a strong offense. So Stephen Foster lashed out.

Foster's feelings about the 1856 campaign were mixed, and so was his music, which Frémont and Fillmore supporters appropriated as freely as the "Buchaneers." Republicans set campaign songs to the tunes of "Nelly Bly," "My Old Kentucky Home," and "Camptown Races."[8] Although Buchanan carried his native state, an unusually big turnout gave the nod in Allegheny County to Frémont. The large Republican margin attests that Stephen Foster was acting out of familial loyalty rather than following local fashion when he enlisted in the campaign. Well before a diarrhea-stricken Buchanan dragged himself to the White House (like many other guests, the president-elect had contracted the dreaded "National Hotel disease" while residing there), Foster seemed glad to be over and done with politicking. A newspaper account mentions Morrison Foster, but not Stephen, among those making preparations for a torchlight parade of glee clubs celebrating the Democrats' "glorious victory in Pennsylvania."[9]

In a January 16, 1857, letter to Billy Hamilton, Stephen dismissed politics with a one-sentence shrug: "We have had another little political brush behind the election of Mayor, but there was very little excitement." Foster was much more interested in discussing music with Hamilton, whom he hailed with hearty humor as "the great North American ballad singer," and in sharing the domestic details of life on the East Common, where Morrison was once again domiciled. Henry Kleber was giving a concert, Stephen wrote, and had offered him

> the post of *first anvil* player in the "Anvil Chorus" from a new opera. I was unwilling to go through the course of training and dieting requisite for the undertaking, and consequently declined. I understand he has sent to Europe for a "first anvil."[10]

The new opera was Verdi's *Il Trovatore*, of course, which Max Maretzek had given its American premiere in New York in May 1855. "The Anvil Chorus" was an immediate hit. Three weeks before Foster wrote Hamilton, Gottschalk and his friendly rival virtuoso, "Old Arpeggio" Sigismund Thalberg, had played a thunderous two-piano version to cap their New York concert seasons.[11] By disparaging the European role of "first anvil" in a letter to "the great North American baritone," Foster was taking sides, however tongue-in-cheek, in the transatlantic culture wars.

"Mrs. F. and Miss Maggie are quite well," Foster reported of Jane and Marion, the latter having apparently acquired a new nickname. The mundane geniality of this letter to Billy Hamilton makes it worth quoting at length, for it shows that Foster, despite his preoccupation with songwriting and his problems with alcohol, money, and marriage, could also enjoy himself. The Gloomy Gus sadness of so many of his songs too easily overshadows the Ordinary Joe aspects of Foster's everyday life.

I am much obliged to you for that dog, "Rattrap" as we call him, on account of his well known ferocity toward those animals. You must pardon me if I inform you that he is now with us no more. He continued to devour shoes, stockings, spools, the Cat and everything else that he could find lying around loose. At last we held a council of war, and thought we would put him in the cellar. There he stayed for three weeks and howled all the time, and would have howled until now if I had not let him out. I was afraid the neighbors would inform on us for keeping a nuisance. Solitary confinement did not agree with him. He lost his appetite. Then I gave him some garlic as you had instructed me. This gave him a sort of diarrhea, and he got into Mit's [Morrison's] room and relieved himself on his bed, then he scattered his dirty shirts over the floor, sprinkled his shoes and played hob generally. This performance seemed to bring him to his appetite, for that same evening he stole a whole beef steak off the Kitchen table and swallowed it all raw. We concluded that this was too much to stand even from "Friendships offering," so I made up my mind to trade him off. John Little had a friend in Chicago who wanted just such a dog, so he gave me a very fine Scotch terrier eighteen months old for him. "Trap" is enjoying the lakebreezes. *I am very much obliged to you for that dog.*

Foster also wrote Hamilton that he had not yet seen a "puff" that he hoped would appear shortly in the *Cincinnati Gazette*. When the article ran six days later, Foster wrote its author a letter that said in so many words: I am very much obliged to you for that article. For the first time since he had made a stab at self-promotion four years earlier in the pages of *The Musical World*, Foster seemed to be heeding the advice P. T. Barnum would shortly deliver in his popular lecture, "The Art of Money Getting." "Advertise your business," Barnum urged everyone: "lawyers, doctors, shoemakers, artists, blacksmiths, showmen, opera singers, railroad presidents, and college professors." [12]

John B. Russell (no relation to Henry) was a veteran printer and journalist whose home Foster had often visited when he lived in Cincinnati. [13] His article mistook Foster's middle initial in the very first sentence (just as Foster's first published song, "Open Thy Lattice Love," was attributed to L. C. Foster), but otherwise his lead was highly complimentary:

If popularity is any test of merit, to Stephen E. Foster's Melodies must be assigned a high rank. Probably no man's ideas have been more often repeated, when we consider singing, playing, whistling, etc. . . . It is hardly too much to assert, there is not a family in the country where any musical taste exists, that has not been cheered with the melody of his songs. In fact they are sung all over the civilized world, the sea-coast cities of China not excepted.[14]

This may have been puffery, but it also happened to be true.

Russell then proceeded to describe Foster's publishing career, acknowledging as the source for "the main facts" his fellow Cincinnatian, W. C. Peters, "one of the first to discover the extraordinary talent of Mr. Foster, and who has been from the first to last, his firm friend and advisor." Foster had not had any dealings with Peters for more than six years, which may be why Russell reported vaguely, and erroneously, that Foster "resides somewhere near Pittsburgh and has always contented himself, we think, with a moderate clerkship and a small per centage on the sale of his songs." This may also be why Russell concentrated on the early blackface songs Foster had written when he was in league with Peters: "Uncle Ned," "Oh! Susanna," and "Camptown Races." Foster's ballads, and everything he had published in the past three years, were relegated to little more than a footnote. Russell's article was picked up by the Boston-based *Dwight's Journal of Music* and condensed to a one-paragraph brief that appeared on March 21 under the headline "WHO WROTE THE NEGRO SONGS."[15]

Foster recognized that Russell's article was almost an obituary, observing with gallows humor: "I am beginning to think, since reading it, that I am 'some punkins' and that the Nation will have to put on crape, when I take my flight to a higher (or lower) sphere." His thank-you note to Russell ended on a cheerful note, however: "How a man likes to show these little flattering testimonials to his wife! If it were not for that, the benefits to me of your kind and friendly action would be half lost."[16]

The day before Foster wrote Russell, he tallied another kind of testimonial that may not have been nearly so pleasing to Jane. He listed thirty-six compositions that Firth, Pond had copyrighted and, in his careful bookkeeper's hand, recorded how much he had received in royalties for each of them. The list was in roughly descending order of profitability, topped by " 'Old Folks,' and all arrangements" ($1,647.46) and reaching rock-bottom with the 1851 song with lyrics by the pseudonymous Wm. Cullen Crookshank, "Once I Loved Thee, Mary Dear" ($8.00). Beneath this column of figures he appended $150 for *The Social Orchestra*, $10 "for arranging," and a note that the royalty figures included $15 each for

"Old Folks" and "Farewell My Lilly Dear" from E. P. Christy, and $10 for each of four other songs that Christy had been given first crack at performing. If you add all these figures up (which Foster did not on this sheet of paper), they come to $9,596.96. That's how much money Foster had earned from all his work that Firth, Pond had published from "Dolcy Jones" in 1849 to "Gentle Annie" the previous April.[17]

In Foster's account book is a similar list, compiled later in 1857, of royalties from sixteen works copyrighted by F. D. Benteen, headed by "Camptown Races" ($101.25). Below these appears $110 from Fisher & Brother, who had purchased the rights to reprint Foster's lyrics in the songster series, *Christy's Plantation Melodies*. Add these amounts to the Firth, Pond figure, and it turns out that Foster earned $10,168.81 from his music in a little more than seven years.

Although Foster's average income of somewhat over $1,400 a year is appalling in light of his work's international popularity—P. T. Barnum guaranteed Jenny Lind $1,000 a night—it was not an inconsequential sum by the standard of the era. When Andrew Carnegie was promoted to superintendent of the Pittsburgh Division of the Pennsylvania Railroad in 1859, his annual salary was raised to $1,500.[18] But averages can be deceiving. In the previous three years, Foster had published only four of the fifteen songs that had earned one hundred dollars or more. Just one had been copyrighted in 1855 ("Hard Times Come Again No More") and none in 1856. As the hits dwindled, so, inevitably, did Foster's income.

Foster added a second column of figures to his January 27 Firth, Pond accounting, listing each song's "computed future value to me." "Old Folks at Home," he estimated, was good for another $100 in royalties. His hopes were highest for his newest song, "Gentle Annie," which had earned $39.08 already, and he expected it would eventually fetch $500 more. A quarter of the songs were either so old or so feeble that Foster pegged their future royalties at a dollar apiece. Foster added up these figures and arrived at $2,786.77.

On March 14, he entered in his account book $1,872.28 received from Firth, Pond for "Copyrights in full till date." He had sold to them his interest in all the music they had published—"Old Folks at Home," "My Old Kentucky Home," "Jeanie with the Light Brown Hair," songs of incalculable value—for roughly two-thirds of his own myopic estimate of their eternal worth. (If not eternal, at least for twenty-eight years, which is how long copyright law at the time protected literary and musical compositions, with an option to renew copyright for an additional fourteen years.) This might qualify as the worst business deal in the history of the popular music business had Foster not given "Oh! Susanna" to Peters for free. Foster cut a similar deal with Benteen, selling all future rights to "Camptown Races," "Ah! May the Red Rose Live Alway!," and fourteen other songs for two hundred dollars.

A couple of years later, *The Knickerbocker* magazine took pride in the revolution that had occurred in American sheet-music publishing:

> Reprints of English works used to form the staple of a publisher's issues, but, with the increase of musical cultivation among us, multitudes of composers have been developed, and our sheet-music publishers now do mostly a copyright business. Many of these copyrights are very valuable.[19]

No one among the "multitudes of composers" had contributed more to this revolution than Foster. George Root demanded and persisted until he received $1,200 from a publisher for the rights to just one song, "Rosalie, the Prairie Flower," which he had written in emulation of Foster.[20] Yet Foster sold his own copyrights for pottage.

Chapter Twenty-five

WHEN THE MUSE
IS MISSING

Part of the impetus for Foster's fire sale of his copyrights must have been the impending loss of the house on East Common, which Brother William sold on April 1, 1857. Stephen, Jane, and Marion moved across the river to Pittsburgh and started boarding, for eleven dollars a week and later twelve dollars, at the Eagle Hotel, by the railroad tracks at the corner of Liberty and Seventh Streets.

At the age of thirty, Foster lost his home soon after losing his parents. In an eerie way he was repeating and reliving the traumas of his childhood, when he was deprived of the White Cottage and Charlotte. The shattering experience must have contributed to his songwriter's block. His inability to compose new songs forced him, in desperation, to settle for whatever money he could get for his old ones. He returned to the song title he had written in his sketchbook a year or so earlier, revised it and sent to Firth, Pond "I See Her Still in My Dreams." Copyrighted on June 8, 1857, it was the first song Foster had published in fourteen months, and it would be the last for another ten. Foster, whose sole source of income was his music, was able to come up with only one "new" song in two years. And it was not even a good song. Clearly it was his mother who haunted Foster's dreams, but instead of rising to the emotional occasion, Foster ducked it, composing a vapid, generic melody.

According to Foster's account book, the song earned him sixty-five dollars, and that included the twenty-five for which, seven months later, he sold Firth, Pond all future rights to it.

That sale was part of a new contract Foster negotiated during a brief visit to New York—Foster's account book indicates that Firth, Pond reimbursed him $43.75 in traveling expenses. This contract, dated February 9, 1858, was Foster's fourth with the firm. Unlike the surviving copies of the previous, December 21, 1854, contract, it is not written in Foster's script, suggesting that this time Firth, Pond rather than Foster had the upper hand. It's simpler than the previous contract and shorter, but not sweeter. No doubt the economic panic of 1857, in which banks suspended specie payment and many factories and railroads went bust, contributed to its asperity.[1]

Once again, the party of the first part guaranteed Foster a 10 percent royalty on all new vocal compositions (there were no old compositions in which the party of the second part still owned an interest). For guitar and voice arrangements, however, he would be paid only 1 cent, compared to the previous contract's 1.5 cents. (Surely it was not coincidental that Foster published few arrangements for guitar after this.)

Article 4 (there were seven in all, compared to eighteen in the previous contract) relinquished to Firth, Pond for twenty-five dollars all future rights to any music it had previously published. Firth, Pond had issued just one song by Foster since he had sold them the rights to all his past work, so this could only mean "I See Her Still in My Dreams."

Article 5 promised to advance Foster a minimum of one hundred dollars against royalties upon receipt of each new song, up to a total of twelve songs a year. Thus Foster would be guaranteed a minimum annual income of $1,200 if he managed to write a song a month—this at a point in his life when he was lucky if he wrote one song a year.

Article 6 granted Firth, Pond exclusive publication rights, which it had not enjoyed under the previous contract, to all Foster's compositions until August 9, 1860, two and one-half years hence.

Foster was no longer in a position to dictate terms, but at least he had negotiated a fresh start. Getting down—and back—to business, in December, 1857, he had rented a piano from Charlotte Blume (not, curiously, from his friend Henry Kleber), a piano dealer on Wood Street. He paid her four dollars a month, though his account book suggests that at one point he may have given her sheet music, presumably his own, in lieu of cash. Foster installed the piano in an office he rented at 112 and 114 Smithfield Street, three and a half blocks from the Eagle Hotel. The Pittsburgh business directory listed Stephen C. Foster at that address, in a category all by himself, Music Composer, between Mineral Water Manufacturers and Master Cementer.[2]

Foster managed to publish five songs in 1858, but they did not come easily. He devoted nine pages in his sketchbook to working out the words for "Lula Is Gone" and eight pages to its follow-up, "Where Has Lula Gone?" It was hardly worth the effort. The first song's initial draft strongly suggested that Lula (an echo of Poe's "Ulalume"?) was dead. So do the opening words of the published version, set to a melodic line that repeatedly trips and falls down the scale as if heartbroken. Yet it turns out that Lula hasn't gone to her grave but merely on vacation to Florida or some other clime "by orange blossoms shaded / Where summer lingers ever on the air." Even after it becomes clear that Lula will return, however, the singer continues to wallow in woe. Although "Lula Is Gone" seems ludicrous today, it was the most successful song Foster wrote during the next couple of years, earning $182.07 in royalties. Foster quickly capitalized on this modest success with "Where Has Lula Gone?," advertised on the cover of the sheet music as "a companion to the popular song."

All the females in the songs Foster published in 1858 are dead, departed, or dreaming. "Linger in Blissful Repose," billed as a serenade on its cover, is a bel canto lullaby in 3/4 time that Foster had published as an instrumental solo entitled "Irene" in *The Social Orchestra*. The lyrics to its two brief verses are an unexceptional echo of "Come Where My Love Lies Dreaming": "Dreaming, dreaming, unfettered by the day, / In melody, in melody I'll breathe I'll breathe my soul away." That "melody," however, is gorgeous. Foster never composed anything more deeply imbued with the spirit of Italian opera than this song's final measures, which waft up the scale as if on wings of song and then burst into breathtaking appoggiatura and ornament.

Foster may have been striving for an equally operatic effect in "My Loved One and My Own or Eva," where the singer holds the first syllable of Eva's name on one keening high note for an entire measure. This ballad may have originated in an attempt to write another song based on *Uncle Tom's Cabin*, perhaps with theatrical productions in mind.

"Sadly to Mine Heart Appealing," the last of Foster's songs to be copyrighted in 1858, set to music lines by Elizabeth Sheridan Carey, a minor Irish poet. Foster probably came across her poem in *Littell's Living Age,* a Boston-based reader's digest of sorts that printed reviews and excerpts, mostly from the British press. If the sheet music did not credit Carey, her misty-eyed nostalgia for "Forms departed" and "Smiles long vanish'd" might easily be mistaken for one of Foster's own lyrics. The nostalgia is triggered by hearing an old Scottish melody, "that old familiar lay." Foster dedicated the song, as he did "Farewell! Old Cottage" and a "Gallopade and Waltz" that has not survived, to an old familiar friend, Mrs. Harry Woods, the surviving Keller sister. Mrs. Woods was a pianist as well as a singer—Foster is said to have enjoyed playing the German rosewood piano she purchased from Henry Kleber—and probably appreciated the musical prank Foster played in "Sadly to Mine Heart Appealing." For the song is a joke, a play not on words but on tunes.[3]

The opening measures of the melody are certainly familiar but, far from being Scottish, they're German: the first bars of *"Ständchen"* from Schubert's *Schwanengesang* (D.957), which Foster had arranged for a quartet in *The Social Orchestra.* That's not the last laugh, however. On October 22, 1858, Stephen wrote to Morrison, who had moved to Philadelphia to assist Brother William in his business affairs. "If you have the book containing Scotch melodies I wish you could send it to me," Stephen requested. He had dispatched "Sadly to Mine Heart Appealing" to Firth, Pond, he explained, but "would like to select an old tune for the introductory symphony." There's no evidence Morrison ever sent Stephen the book, which survives with Morrison's name inscribed on the title page. *The National Melodies of Scotland; United to the Songs of Robert Burns, Allan Ramsay, and Other Eminent Lyric Poets* . . . does not include the air Foster eventually chose, "Robin Adair," to which Burns had set his poem, "Phyllis the Fair." The "symphony" introducing "Sadly to Mine Heart Appealing" consists of four measures of *"Ständchen"* followed by four bars of "Robin Adair." Foster wittily spliced Scottish and German traditions, a lay and a lied.[4]

Foster displayed another kind of playfulness the following month on a pleasure trip with Jane, Marion, and his niece, Henrietta's daughter Mary Wick, aboard the steamboat *Ida May,* on which Billy Hamilton clerked. "We will stirr old John McClellan up in Cincinnati, make the children sing and bring in Billy's bass voice," Stephen wrote Morrison on the eve of his departure. "The trip will be a recreation and variety for me." No account survives of a singalong at the residence of Col. John B. McClelland, an executive with the Little Miami Railroad whom Foster had known during his sojourn in Cincinnati, but Billy Hamilton recalled a more impromptu concert.[5]

One chilly evening Hamilton and Foster called on Cons. Miller, river editor of the *Commercial Gazette*. On their way back to the *Ida May*, they encountered a party of serenaders singing a "strangely familiar" melody that turned out to be "Come Where My Love Lies Dreaming." They were "bungling" it, in Hamilton's opinion, so Foster and he "chimed in. Naturally they regarded us as intruders, and when the song was finished demanded what right we had to interfere. . . ."

Hamilton asked if they knew the song's composer. The young men replied "Stephen C. Foster," but said they did not know him personally. Hamilton tried to rectify that, but the serenaders refused to believe that his companion was the songwriter and accused them of being "impostors."

"The situation began to grow alarming, and we were in danger of having a lively set-to," Hamilton recalled. But the serenade did not turn into a slugfest like the one that had sent Hamilton and Foster running for cover in Lawrenceville two years earlier. Hamilton asked if the young men knew Cons. Miller. They did, so he proposed visiting his office. When Miller vouched for their identities, "[n]othing was too good for us," Hamilton said, and they "spent the balance of the evening in their company serenading."[6]

Hamilton also recollected that on their way to Cincinnati, Foster "wrote and composed" the song, "Parthenia to Ingomar." Jean Davenport had appeared as Parthenia in a traveling production of *Ingomar, the Barbarian*, a "beautiful romantic play" adapted from the German that was performed in Pittsburgh on November 5, 1858, shortly before Foster embarked on the *Ida May*. The well-known English actress's star turn inspired Foster, but it did not inspire him enough. The words to Foster's ballad, copyrighted April 4, 1859, are credited to William Henry McCarthy, a pressman at the *Pittsburgh Daily Dispatch* with whom Foster collaborated on three songs during the winter and spring of 1859. None of their joint efforts—the others were "Linda Has Departed" and "For Thee, Love, for Thee"—is memorable. Although his account book shows that Foster scrupulously split his royalties on these songs fifty-fifty with McCarthy, he cannot have been terribly pleased with the partnership. Otherwise he would not have devoted six pages in his sketchbook to reworking the lyrics to "For Thee, Love, for Thee," lyrics for which McCarthy received credit and at least $10.57 in royalties.[7]

Casting about for words other than his own, Foster also composed a lovely setting of Richard Henry Wilde's "My Life Is Like the Summer Rose," which he retitled, after a variant on Wilde's last line, "None Shall Weep a Tear for Me."[8] "Far better verses are to be found in every second newspaper," Poe sneered, but Wilde's poem had been popular for forty years, widely anthologized, often parodied and set to music as recently as 1857. Wilde, a Georgia lawyer, congressman, and connoisseur of Italian literature, had been born in Dublin, and "My Life Is Like the Summer Rose" is rooted in the tradition of Thomas Moore and "The Last Rose of Summer" as deeply as Foster's own "Ah! May the Red Rose Live Alway!" A year earlier, Foster had revisited Burns, the master of Scottish song, in "Sadly to Mine Heart Appealing." Now he paid tribute anew to Moore, the master of Irish song. It was as if, no longer sure in what direction, if any, his own music was headed, Foster wanted to retrace its origins.[9]

Surely Foster read with mixed emotions "Who Writes Our Songs?," an article about him that was widely reprinted. The piece originally ran on April 22, 1859, in William Cullen Bryant's New York *Evening Post*.[10] Its unbylined author, W. F. Williams, was more closely acquainted than John Russell with the details of Foster's life and enjoyed his cooperation, quoting "a private letter" from Foster recalling his delight upon receiving one hundred dollars for the song he wrote after "Oh! Susanna." The lead probably made Foster feel "some punkins" once again:

> The musical composer who really furnishes the great majority of our songs, and whose productions have the widest popularity among the masses of our people, is known to very few of them, even by reputation. The new melodies that greet the public ear month after month, and are sung, whistled and hummed by thousands—that are thumped on pianofortes, thrummed on banjoes, breathed on flutes, tortured into variations, and enjoy a wide, though after all, evanescent popularity, are chiefly the product of one fertile brain—and that brain, as Mr. Micawber would say, is the brain appertaining to Stephen C. Foster.

It had been a long time since new Foster melodies had pleased the public "month after month," and the author mingled high praise with condescension. By harping, as Russell had, on Foster's personal obscurity and the popularity of his older plantation melodies, the writer painted a portrait of the artist as past his prime. Yet "as Mr. Foster is still young, he may improve and elevate his style, till he attains a musical reputation that will be more than ephemeral."

Not only Foster's reputation but his residence seemed transitory at the end of the 1850s. According to his account book, after a year's stay he stopped boarding at the Eagle Hotel in April 1858. Then a gap occurs during which he owed a William and James Murdock forty dollars for "5 quarters" rent, possibly for his office space but conceivably for living quarters. By September he was paying a Mrs. Johnston nine dollars a week (three dollars less than at the Eagle Hotel). On one of the drafts for "Where Has Lula Gone?" in his sketchbook, Foster noted "Johnston a/c $117." That would add up to thirteen weeks. Then another blank, from the excursion to Cincinnati through the Christmas holidays, until February 26, 1859, when Foster began boarding with Mrs. A. Miller for $9.50 a week, raised to $10.50 in May. It's not entirely clear from his account book that Foster ever fully paid what he owed this landlady—or the Murdocks, for that matter. In the last half of 1858 he earned only $178.50 in royalties, chiefly from the two "Lula" songs' sales of 3,700 copies. In all of 1859, he earned just $267.05.[11]

Stephen Foster's relations expressed anxiety about his whereabouts and welfare in this world and in the next. In May 1858, his niece, Lidie Wick, wrote Morrison Foster, asking whether "Uncle Steve" had "moved yet" and wishing that "perhaps they would make us a visit before they went away." The next year, Lidie's mother, Henrietta, voiced her concern that neither Stephen (nor Morrison, for that matter) had joined the church and booked passage on "the Ark of Safety."[12]

Just as Stephen seemed to be slipping out of sight, the first photographs of him that have survived were taken. On June 13, 1859, he sent one to Morrison in Philadelphia, explaining in the accompanying letter, "Yesterday my neighbor who has the Daguerreotype establishment invited me to have my picture taken. I think it is rather good. . . ." The two subtly different ambrotypes that have been preserved were probably made by D. M. Coates, who maintained a studio at the same 112–114 Smithfield address where Foster rented an office. In both likenesses Foster poses rather stiffly. His dark eyes, dark hair, dark tie, and dark suit make him seem forbiddingly formal, but two incongruities confuse that first impression: the scar that furrows his cheek and the tuft of pale hair that almost looks as if it had been pasted beneath his lower lip. The scar suggests suffering and the tuft of hair, frivolity: "Hard Times Come Again No More" and "Doo-dah!"[13]

A ferrotype that was probably made within the next year or so presents a more sentimental Foster. He has shaved the lip hair, and his face seems softer, more rounded. His gaze and his pose are more open, less tense. He's all dressed up in a gleaming white shirtfront and a dandy's elegant waistcoat and coat, but his shirt collar seems two sizes too big and his cravat as well as his posture are slightly askew, as if he still felt a boyish tentativeness about putting himself on display.[14]

"I sent off a first rate song that other day to Firth, Pond & Co.," Stephen wrote Morrison in the 1859 letter accompanying his ambrotype. Quite likely that song was "Fairy-Belle," the first he had set to his own words in nearly a year:

> The pride of the village and the fairest in the dell
> Is the queen of my song and her name is Fairy-Belle;
> The sound of her light step may be heard upon the hill
> Like the fall of the snow-drop or the dripping of the rill. . . .

"So many copies of this song have been sold," observed *The Knickerbocker* magazine of "Fairy-Belle,"

> that we suppose our lady friends may all have copies; if any have not, they
> should get it; it is one of those easy, taking melodies so quickly learned,
> and so simply beautiful that its popularity is not surprising.[15]

Presumably these were the lady friends whom *Godey's Lady's Book* advised that it was socially acceptable to be seen carrying music in the street. A bundle of groceries would be unspeakably vulgar, but "[a] roll of music looks so perfectly *genteel*. It announces that you can not only play, but can also afford to get all the novelties as they appear."[16]

"Fairy-Belle" is a trifle, yet it invokes Foster's muse, "the queen of my song," at a time when he was trying to salvage his capsized career and write productively once again. It was followed immediately by another invocation of the muse, also marked *moderato*, in the same key (C) and 4/4 time: "Thou Art the Queen of My Song." Just as "Come Where My

Love Lies Dreaming" and "Some Folks" were flip sides of Foster's response to his mother's death, written consecutively in the same key and time signature, "Fairy-Belle" and "Thou Art the Queen of My Song" are opposing though not necessarily mutually exclusive accounts of Foster's musical inspiration or want of it.

In "Fairy-Belle," the muse comes all too easily, prattling sweet nothings; Foster's melodic facility would always enable him to confect cookie-cutter tunes and superficial sentiments. "Thou Art the Queen of My Song" draws more deeply from the wellspring of Foster's creativity and comes up empty. This muse is long gone and seems unlikely ever to return:

> I long for thee; must I long and long in vain?
> I sigh for thee; wilt thou come not back again?

The song reaches a poignant climax in the penultimate phrase of each verse, "Pride of my early years." Foster clings to that "Pride" for an extra beat and dramatizes the fragile half-life of "early" by dividing its syllables with a wide interval and flinging away the second of them with a fleeting eighth note. As 1860 dawned and the Civil War loomed, Foster would make a last-ditch attempt to recapture that pride.

Chapter Twenty-six

ALMOST A SPIRITUAL

*O*n the spring of 1860, a teenager fresh out of school in Mount Sterling, Kentucky, hopped a steamboat to Pittsburgh. Making his way through the early-morning mist and industrial murk, John Alexander Joyce checked into a tavern near Lafayette Hall. He had one hundred dollars in the pocket of his one good suit of clothes, and he hoped to learn how to earn more by studying bookkeeping at a local business college.

But the bright lights (even in the smog), big city, and the drinking buddies he fell in with dazzled the seventeen-year-old Irish immigrant. Stagestruck and eager to try his luck as "a minstrel song and dance man and Shakespearean poetical 'prodigy,'" Joyce rented the Lafayette for one night and plastered Pittsburgh with handbills. The program they advertised included "Darky Songs" by Stephen Foster.

On the stage where the Republican Party had met four years earlier, Joyce "danced a shuffle or a jig to the music of the small string band" and was swept away by a liberating rapture, the kind of out-of-body experience and out-of-skin kick that blackface and black music, from minstrelsy to jazz to rock 'n' roll, have historically provided white folks. "The more I danced, sang, and spouted," Joyce recalled forty years later, the wilder grew that impromptu audience, and after an hour and a half, from sheer exhaustion, I bowed myself out through the wings, rang down the curtain, and left the house for the tavern, not even stopping to share the few dollars that the ticket-seller had in his box. . . .

My peculiar eccentricities must have entertained and strangely impressed the audience, for, as a matter of fact, my brain became suddenly unbalanced, and King Lear in all his wild ravings of lunacy was never more deranged than myself. That . . . audience . . . to this day may not know, that they once paid money to hear a living lunatic on the mimic stage of life.[1]

Compare Joyce in 1860 to Hoagy Carmichael in 1919. A "hot Negro band" from Louisville was playing a dance at his Bloomington, Indiana, high school, when all of a sudden Carmichael shouted, "I'm a Congo medicine man!" He and his dancing partner

whirled and wilted to the floor. . . . It was a breakdown, an insane dancing madness brought on by music—new, disjointed, unorganized music, full of screaming blue notes and a solid beat. We pioneers of it all broke down. I behaved to give the impression that I was imbalanced. And I think I was. . . .

Jazz maniacs were being born and I was one of them.[2]

Stephen Foster would not have recognized the word "jazz" in Carmichael's account, but Americans had been "breaking down" before Foster was born. If Foster happened to catch Joyce's act at the Lafayette, he probably saw something of his younger self in Joyce, another restless bookkeeper bewitched by minstrelsy, exactly half Foster's age (and also born, coincidentally, on the Fourth of July).

Joyce claimed that Foster was there. The songwriter had met him a few days before the concert, Joyce wrote, and introduced him "to some of his 'boon companions,' who indulged in social cheer till after the noon of night." Foster "and a few of his intimate chums" showed up at the Lafayette and were "lavish in their applause, leading off with hands and feet when I made a hit with one of his own songs. . . ."

Joyce made his claim in the *Washington Post* in 1900, during the same spate of national publicity when Foster's statue was unveiled in Pittsburgh that refreshed Susan Pentland Robinson's and Morrison Foster's recollections of Stephen's visit to Bardstown. Just as Morrison indicated that

Stephen was "an occasional visitor" to Federal Hill after neglecting to indicate this in the biography he had published only four years earlier, Joyce had previously recalled his rave-up in a memoir, *A Checkered Life*, that made no mention of Foster.[3] Since Joyce's "checkered life" included stints in a mental hospital and in prison (for conspiring with tax-dodging liquor distillers while working as an Internal Revenue agent in the Grant administration), he is hardly a reliable source. Yet Joyce touched on two timely topics: drinking and "Darky Songs."

Joyce insisted in the *Post* that Foster "did not indulge very much himself in Bacchanalian eccentricities, [but] we youngsters made up for his conservative conduct." Still, if Joyce is to be believed, once again Foster was out with the boys after midnight as he had been with the Cincinnati serenaders in 1858 and on that evening in Allegheny when his goose was cooked the morning after.

On February 9, 1860, Firth, Pond copyrighted Foster's "The Wife":

> He'll come home, he'll not forget me,
> For his word is always true.
> He's gone to sup the deadly cup,
> And while the long night through,
> He's gone to quaff,
> And talk and laugh
> To while the drear night through:
> He'll come home, he'll not forget me,
> For his word is always true.

In "Willie We Have Missed You," which was a song about drinking only by implication and in its first, unpublished draft, Willie returns. Here the temperance theme is more overt but unresolved, since "The Wife" never reveals whether the errant husband does indeed stumble home. Foster was teasing his audience, toying with the conventions of monitory melo-dramas like Monk Lewis's lyric for Henry Russell's "The Gambler's Wife," in which the gambler returns at four in the morning to discover that the wife and child he has neglected froze to death at three. While "The Wife" dramatizes female fears, it also indulges male fantasies with professions of stand-by-your-man fidelity:

> My heart may break,
> But for his sake
> I'll do all I can do.

Tammy Wynette's signature song, cowritten a century later by a man—her producer, Billy Sherrill—is cut from the same cloth coat of self-sacrifice: "But if you love him, / You'll forgive him, / Even though he's hard to understand."[4]

It was also just about the time of Joyce's visit to Pittsburgh and his renditions of Foster's old "Darky Songs" that Foster published, for the first time in eight years, a new one. Marked "Moderately fast," "The Glendy Burk" is a jaunty departure from the snail's pace at which most of Foster's ballads had been creeping. It returns to the key of "Oh! Susanna" (G) and to its lyrics in a chorus that begins "Ho! for Lou'-siana!" (where the singer of "Oh! Susanna" was "gwine"). The rhythm of the chorus also recalls that of "Ring, Ring de Banjo!"

The song is retrospective in other ways, too. The steamboat *Glendy Burke* (never a sure speller, Foster dropped the "e") had been built in Jefferson, Indiana, in 1851, and named for a New Orleans banker, merchant, and legislator, Glenn D. Burke, with whom Morrison Foster had done business back in 1843. Times had changed since "Oh! Susanna," however, and railroads had overtaken steamboats as the swiftest means of transport. Unlike the *Telegraph No. 1* and *No. 2*, which had been going strong when Foster immortalized them, the *Glendy Burke* was no longer even afloat. In 1855, the 425-ton side-wheel packet hit a snag and broke up near Cairo. Its wreckage damaged other vessels for decades. Foster's "mighty fast boat" was nothing but a navigational hazard.[5]

"The Glendy Burk" is written in light, streamlined dialect. No "niggers" or "darkeys" are on board. Yet why publish a blackface song at all in May 1860, in the ominous and widening wake of John Brown's execution and Lincoln's nomination for the presidency? Martin Delany, who had known John Brown, was implicated but never charged in the attack on Harper's Ferry because he was overseas at the time, negotiating a treaty with the Alake of Abeokuta to permit African Americans to settle among the Egba people in what is now Nigeria. Delany had pointedly parodied "Oh! Susanna" and other Foster songs in the chapters of his novel, *Blake*, that appeared serially in 1859.[6] Now Foster was returning to the scene of the crimes with "The Glendy Burk." Its melody is sprightly but its lyric is malarkey. This was no time for a black deckhand to be going downriver, inviting his "lady love" "back to de sunny old south."

That Foster would publish three more plantation melodies as the Civil War simmered does not seem quite so anomalous when one recalls that

Ethiopian delineators enjoyed their first flush of popularity in the early 1830s, coincidental with Nat Turner's uprising and the appearance of William Lloyd Garrison's *Liberator*. "Minstrelsy was most popular when the black group seemed most threatening," one critic, Berndt Ostendorf, has observed. "In minstrelsy America buried a deep fear under laughter."[7] Any white American (the number must have been minuscule) who read *Blake*'s parting shot—"Woe be unto those devils of whites, I say!"—had reason to fear.

Two of Foster's other belated plantation melodies are decidedly minor. "Down Among the Cane-Brakes," a woe-is-me ballad in conventional English, may not be a plantation melody at all. Apart from the echo of "Uncle Ned," whose "fingers were long like de cane in the brake," and the mention in the chorus of "the Mississippi shore" (which does not appear in the sketchbook's first draft and seems to have been an after-thought), nothing indicates that the song is about life down South, much less about black life there.

"Don't Bet Your Money on de Shanghai," written in dialect and set to a frisky 2/4 tempo like "The Glendy Burk," tries to do for cockfighting what "Camptown Races" did for the track:

> De Shanghai chicken when you put him in de pit
> He'll eat a loaf of bread up but he can't fight a bit
> De Shanghai fiddle is a funny little thing
> And ebry time you tune him up he goes ching! ching!

Foster may have been familiar with "Crow Out Shanghai," a minstrel ditty full of topical references to the prohibitionist Maine Law, P. T. Barnum, and Manifest Destiny's designs on Cuba.[8] "Don't Bet Your Money on de Shanghai" sounds antique by comparison, its melody like a creaky Scots-Irish reel. Firth, Pond's proofreader may have made an edi-torial comment of his own on the first edition's cover, which reads "Plantntion Song."

The fourth blackface song Foster wrote during his flurry of renewed interest is one of his most memorable, and infamous, compositions in any genre. Like "Down Among the Cane-Brakes," "Old Black Joe" harks back to "Uncle Ned." Once again, an old man is going gently into that night. The song is not written in dialect, however, and it distills the world-weariness of many of Foster's previous songs, parlor ballads as well as blackface. Not only is Old Black Joe the singer of "Old Folks at Home" and the Uncle Tom figure in "My Old Kentucky Home," but take away the "black" and an allusion to "the cotton fields" and Joe could be white —the singer of "Old Dog Tray," for example. Compare

> The forms I call'd my own
> Have vanished one by one,
> The lov'd ones, the dear ones have all passed away,
> Their happy smiles have flown,
> Their gentle voices gone . . .
>
> ("Old Dog Tray")

to

> Why do I weep when my heart should feel no pain
> Why do I sigh that my friends come not again
> Grieving for forms now departed long ago?
>
> ("Old Black Joe")

Yet the bluntness of Joe's blackness and his docility also reduce Old Black Joe to the status of Old Dog Tray rather than its owner, to simply another white man's possession prized solely for its loyalty. Only a year before, an apologist for slavery had described his attendance at the death-bed of a beloved slave. "Thanky, Mass'r Jesus" were Aunt Marie's last words, but the writer, Edward A. Pollard, had the last say:

> . . . [S]eldom is it, that the slave is left to meet his death as the white pauper in his rags and desolation. His master and mistress and the white family are always by to visit him in this great need of humanity. Indeed, when an old, loved slave (as Aunt Marie was), who has grown up with the family, the handmaiden of the old when they were young, and the mammy of the young before they have grown old in worldly care, is taken away by the equal hand of death, it evokes a sympathy and grief that many a white, saintly soul of your Northern Pharisees might envy, when he leaves the world unhonored and unwept.[9]

"Old Black Joe" epitomizes Foster's racial condescension, which is all too easily exaggerated and caricatured by distorting the chorus's dialogue with the dead into a slave's cringing obedience, like the dog's in the old RCA Victor logo, to His Master's Voice(s):

> I'm coming, I'm coming, for my head is bending low;
> I hear those gentle voices calling, "Old Black Joe."

Listeners are right to detect in "Old Black Joe" the servility of a "house nigger," for that's what the original Joe evidently was: a servant (though not, in Pennsylvania, a slave) in the McDowell household. According to Jane and Stephen Foster's granddaughter, Jessie Welsh Rose, Joe was

> an old colored man who drove for Dr. McDowell for many years. He also had some household duties, such as admitting visitors in the evenings. All through the sweetheart days Joe watched Foster come and go, presenting to "Miss Jenny" with much shuffling of feet and many broad grins his and other admirers' bouquets. . . .
> "Some day I am going to put you in a song," he told Joe. . . . The old man was gone when the day of inspiration came. . . .[10]

But there is more to "Old Black Joe" than broad grins and shuffling feet. In *The Souls of Black Folk,* after referring to America, perhaps inadvertently, as "the foster land," W. E. B. Du Bois singled out "Old Folks at Home" and "Old Black Joe" for praise. Exempting them from "the debasements and imitations" of "minstrel" and "coon" songs, he called them "songs of white America [that] have been distinctively influenced by the slave songs or have incorporated whole phrases of Negro melody." [11]

Despite its demeaning stereotypes, "Old Black Joe" comes closest of Foster's famous songs to the African-American spiritual, and it approaches that tradition with sympathy and respect. The affinity lies deeper than the verbal coincidences—"coming" and "low"—that link the choruses of "Old Black Joe" and "Swing Low, Sweet Chariot" ("coming for to carry me home"). James Weldon Johnson, who penned the lyrics for "Lift Every Voice and Sing," the African-American national anthem, wrote that "Go Down, Moses" and other spirituals "contain more than mere melody; there is sounded in them that elusive undertone, the note in music which is not heard with the ears." Morrison's memoir notwithstanding, Stephen Foster may not have been taken as a child to a church of "shouting colored people," and "Old Black Joe" certainly doesn't shout. But it does sound a little like what a British visitor to Pittsburgh reported hearing in a black Methodist church in 1848 before the shouting started, when, right after the sermon, worshipers sang "their own peculiarly soft and melancholy airs." Its soft melancholy and elusive undertone, rather than any formal musical correspondence, make "Old Black Joe" almost a spiritual.[12]

Chapter Twenty-seven

ALL IN THE FAMILY

Shortly after John Joyce's wild night at Lafayette Hall, the "living lunatic on the mimic stage of life" was confined to a real lunatic asylum for a couple of months. And sometime during the spring of 1860 the Fosters moved to Warren, Ohio, planning to visit Henrietta briefly there before heading to New York City.[1]

Morrison Foster had married on February 23 and had already moved to Cleveland, where he had landed a job in the branch office of Pittsburgh's Juniata Iron Works. His departure left Stephen two fewer reasons to remain in Pittsburgh, because it deprived him not only of a brother (Henry was the only other Foster left in Pittsburgh) but also of a singer. Morrison's bride, Jessie Lightner, was a contralto who had rehearsed many of Stephen's songs and taken the pleasure cruise to New Orleans aboard the *James Millingar*.

Nine days after the wedding, there was not just one less Foster in Pittsburgh, but one less on earth. Brother William, who had been too ill to make it to the ceremony, died in Philadelphia, of an infected carbuncle on the back of his neck. Brother William's two children were left orphans, since their mother, his second wife, had died in 1856. It's a testament to how high Brother William had risen in the world and in the hierarchy of the Pennsylvania Railroad, the nation's biggest railroad and soon the world's largest private business firm, that the line's president, J. Edgar Thomson, became the children's guardian and immediately incorporated a coal company to manage some property Brother William had left his offspring.[2]

Thomson had married the younger sister of Brother William's second wife—the "Vin" Smith whom Stephen had visited on Staten Island in 1853, and to whom he would "respectfully" dedicate a winsome love song in 1861. (Unfortunately, the respect did not extend to the proper spelling of Lavinia's married name, which the cover of "Molly Dear Good Night" rendered as Mrs. J. Edgar Thompson.) Another bond between the Foster family and the Pennsylvania Railroad would be formed when Alexander Johnston Cassatt, the railroad executive who would mastermind New York City's Penn Station, married a daughter of Ann Eliza Foster and Edward Buchanan. (Marie Lois Buchanan Cassatt got along poorly with her sister-in-law, the painter Mary Cassatt.)[3] Despite his penury and preindustrial nostalgia, Stephen Foster lived in close proximity and consanguinity to a juggernaut of modern capitalism.

A special funeral car draped in black bore Brother William's body to Pittsburgh, and every station it passed flew its flag at half-mast. The cortege included Thomas Scott, who would succeed Brother William as vice president of the Pennsylvania Railroad and had recently appointed Andrew Carnegie superintendent of its Pittsburgh Division. "Scott's Andy," as J. Edgar Thomson had called him when he first met Thomas's protégé, was well on his way to becoming as intimately associated with Thomson and Scott as Brother William had been earlier in their careers.[4]

On April 26, the *Trumbull Democrat* noted that Foster was visiting friends in that Ohio county. "Mr. Foster has probably contributed more than any other American writer to the list of popular songs, during the past ten years," the weekly paper observed, adding to that list a song he didn't write, the Scottish ballad, "Annie Laurie." The following day Stephen wrote Morrison from Warren that "Jane and Marion are well, also Etty's family." They were planning to go to New York "very soon," and to see Morrison in Cleveland on their way.[5]

In the meantime they were staying at the Gaskill House, Warren's swankest hotel and first four-story building. One of the proprietor's daughters later recalled that Stephen "would sit in the big public parlor on the second floor in the evening and play and sing." Sometimes she and Marion would dance in the grand ballroom and Stephen would watch from the doorway and applaud. He "always wore a high silk hat and was gentle and kind to us." Mrs. Foster, on the other hand, "never left her room"; Marion "always took her meals up to her."[6]

Foster published a dozen songs in 1860, more than in any single year since 1851. "I have written two songs since I have been in Warren and have two underway," Stephen wrote Morrison on April 27, "but do not feel inclined to send them off half made up."

Panic may finally have unblocked Foster's writing. His bookkeeping shows that his account with Firth, Pond was overdrawn by $1,396.64, and his 1858 contract with them would expire in August. Unable to pay even for his laundry—"little washing bills &c., which are, you know, the most perplexing"—Stephen began his letter to Morrison with a plea for a loan, "immediately":

> Please send me by return mail $12—I have received from F.P. & Co. a letter stating that they cannot advance me any more money till I send them the songs now due them (about two as I make the calculation) as our present arrangement is about expiring. They show a disposition to renew agreement, but, very properly require payment in music before any new arrangement.

A month later, it was not just his laundry but his lodgings Foster could no longer afford. On May 31, he wrote Morrison:

> Herewith I send you a draft on Firth Pond & Co. for $50—which I wish you to *hold for ten days,* and, if you can conveniently, please send me the amount by return mail. There will be no trouble about payment of the draft. I have only one song to finish in the time mentioned. I desire you to pay Mr. Shoenberger (the landlord) at the end of the month as I engaged to do, and have told him that I would pay him when I hear from Cleveland.[7]

The songs Foster was sending to Firth, Pond were a mixed bag. His sketchbook intersperses plantation and parlor songs. Sometimes Foster would switch genres in midstream, abandoning temporarily a draft in blackface dialect to turn to one in genteel English. Mourning two dead little girls, one dead female of unknown age, and one maiden languishing for unknown reasons, the four Firth, Pond parlor ballads of 1860 are lachrymose even by the maudlin standard of the era.

"Poor Drooping Maiden" plucks out of her economic context the "pale drooping maiden who toils her life away" in "Hard Times Come Again No More." Why, the singer asks, is she cooped up "in a dreary home, / Bound to a weary doom," when outside the birds are chirping on this "bright bright summer's day"? If Foster had written "loom" instead of "doom," he might have provided an answer similar to the one the more politically engaged Hutchinsons proffered in songs of economic protest like "The Song of the Shirt" and "Hannah's at the Window Binding Shoes." But perhaps he was thinking of his wife, immured in her hotel room.

"Cora Dean" sings the praises of the fairest of all "Long Island's lovely daughters," who "reposes" in her grave "down by the calm blue sea." This song sounds positively chipper compared to "Under the Willow She's Sleeping," which a mother croons over her daughter's grave. John Mahon, a friend of Foster's, wrote that the songwriter had told him that Marion had inspired "Under the Willow She's Sleeping." Marion, "who had her mother's auburn hair and fair complexion," Mahon wrote, had been missing for several hours. Stephen eventually found her asleep beneath a willow tree.

> He stood a few moments, as if spellbound, watching "the beautiful vision," as he called it, and exclaimed:
> "Under the willows she's laid with care!" and before awaking her sketched the first notes of the melody on his thumb-nail, as was his wont. Aye, and often he sang that melody in my rooms, being particularly pathetic in the first line of the chorus: "Fair, fair, and golden hair." Once my wife said to him:
> "Well, I think, Mr. Foster, it was a strange thing for you to write that song as if it were a lament for a dead child."
> "Ah!" said he, "I then for the first time realized the extraordinary beauty of my little darling, and thought what a horror it would be to me if I had found her dead instead of asleep. But in the line 'There's where my darling lies dreaming' I show my feelings. The words are poetical, and may be understood either of death or of sleep, or of both."[8]

His mother, his wife, and his daughter, women and girls, death and dreams blurred in Foster's imagination. Lydia Sigourney was not the only one "to overlook the apparently trivial distinction between the living and the dead female."[9]

"Virginia Belle," the fourth Firth, Pond parlor ballad of 1860, inters the previous year's "Fairy-Belle." She "was our little laughing darling," as "lythe as any fairy, / Winning hearts with fairy spell," but "she bereft us / When she left us," and now Virginia Belle is dead. It's all too easy to ridicule these songs, but the corpse-in-the-cradle threnodies of Sigourney, Felicia Hemans, and other professional mourners outsold more vigorous verse. Catering to this market, Foster drew on his own increasingly funereal fantasies.

The public wasn't buying, however. On July 1, 1860, Foster added up the royalties he had received for the sixteen songs Firth, Pond had published in the two and a half years since he had sold them (and F. D. Benteen) his interest in all his previous work. The total came to only $731.25. Even more ominous, the very first song Foster had published under the new dispensation, "Lula Is Gone," had been by far his biggest seller. It had been downhill ever since, with only one other song, "Fairy-Belle," earning more than $100. His recent parlor ballads had garnered $13.75 apiece, and "The Glendy Burk" had done scarcely better: $21.25. Foster's return to blackface had not been rewarded with a return to his old sales figures.

At the bottom of this page in his account book, beneath the dismal tally in ink, Foster wrote in pencil, "Nelly was a Lady—" and left after the hyphen a poignant blank. That represented how much he had received in royalties for a song that had been far more popular than any of those listed above it, a song he had sold outright to Firth, Pond for fifty copies of the sheet music eleven years ago.

On August 9, Foster listed these sixteen songs again and wrote, "1600." That's what he sold his rights to them for: one hundred dollars a song. But Foster did not sacrifice quite so much as he had the last time he cleared the books with Firth, Pond. "Poor Drooping Maiden" was never going to perk up anybody's balance sheet, and several of these songs were unlikely ever to earn more than one hundred dollars in royalties. ("Old Black Joe" was not included in the deal, for it was not published until November.)

At least this act of desperation enabled Foster to eliminate his debt of nearly $1,400 to Firth, Pond, and Foster had another iron in the fire, an arrangement with *Clark's School Visitor*, a nineteenth-century *Weekly Reader* (though a monthly) that claimed "the largest circulation of any educational journal in America" and offered schoolchildren "choice Stories, Readings, Poems, Dialogues, Music, Puzzles, &c., &c." Its July 1860 issue also included a ballad, "Jenny's Coming o'er the Green," "written and composed expressly for Clark's School Visitor, by Stephen C. Foster." The lad who had howled like a Comanche and fled on his first day at school was now to "contribute . . . *original music* to the Visitor."[10]

The magazine promised "a beautiful *Album*" with her name in gold leaf on its cover to the girl under seventeen, and "a *Gold pen*, with silver case" to the boy under sixteen, who sent in "the best original Composition." Foster received a little more for his contributions—four hundred dollars for six songs, three of which appeared in 1860.[11] That's less than the one hundred dollars Firth, Pond paid for even his worst songs. Once again, Foster had struck a bad bargain, especially since some of these songs, which were subsequently published in sheet music form without any additional payment to Foster, proved more popular than many of his Firth, Pond ballads.

"Jenny's Coming o'er the Green," for example, became so well known that four years later the very first song in a songster, *George Christy's Essence of Old Kentucky*, was a cruel parody by J. F. Poole entitled "Whiskey in Decanter Clean."[12] The first draft in Foster's sketchbook begins, "Little Jenny's seventeen," but later drafts and the published version omit her age. According to John Mahon, Foster said he had changed the line to mollify Jane, who resented Stephen's attraction to "a young girl named Jennie (platonic, of course)." Evidently the allusion was a source of continuing marital discord, because forty years later Jane insisted that one song Stephen "never published was 'Jennie's Only Seventeen.' " On the other hand, "Jenny's Coming o'er the Green" was by one account Stephen's favorite song in his final years, and on those rare occasions when he sang publicly, he would sing it "almost invariably." In any event, Stephen never bothered to change the lines in the second verse, "She is younger far than me,— / Why do I love her so?" There's a hint of Humbert Humbert in this and other Foster songs for juveniles, and it was creeping into his songs for adults as well. At least this Lolita was still alive, "coming o'er the green" rather than buried beneath it.[13]

While "Jenny's Coming o'er the Green" is a light Irish air, "Beautiful Child of Song," the second song to appear in *Clark's School Visitor*, features the languid piano triplets and legato vocal line of Foster's more Italianate compositions. Its lyric is yet another invocation of Foster's child/woman/muse in the manner of "Come with Thy Sweet Voice Again," "Thou Art the Queen of My Song," and "Fairy-Belle."

Foster's third song for schoolchildren, printed in the December 1860

Clark's, is far more disturbing. The page in Foster's sketchbook on which it begins provides a psychoanalytical field day. At the top are lines that read more like a poem than song lyrics:

> If in my trembling wayward path
> To the land of love or the land of wrath
> If I should reach the doubtful goal
> Before his steadfast earnest soul
> Least at the bitter trying end
> He dies without one poet friend
> Now I'm that friend, he'd wish no other
> Carve on his tomb these words—"my brother"

Brother William was dead or dying. (Since the pages in the sketchbook are undated, there's no way of knowing precisely when Foster wrote anything in it.) He was surely on Stephen's mind, and certainly a "steadfast earnest soul." Perhaps Stephen was also thinking of Morrison, another steady, shoulder-to-the-wheel sibling on whom he could usually depend for a loan.

A space follows, and then these lines, written in a larger, looser hand that makes them leap out:

> Make peace with your mother
> take leave of your mother
> That is a gentleman and
> my brother

It's his mother more than his brother(s) who haunts Foster, whom he can't let go. Five years after her death, he sees her still in his dreams.

Then Foster makes another leap, from dead mother to dead father:

> Tis my father's song and he can't live long
> Every one knows he wrote it
> I've been down at the hotel steps
> And all the gentlemen bought it

Only this fragment made its way into a song, for it is the first version of the chorus of "The Little Ballad Girl," a lurid tearjerker unlike anything Foster had written before, and his last song to be copyrighted in 1860.

The girl in the finished song is a "Fairy-Belle" muse, "dressed with care . . . / With fairy slippers and golden hair," but she's not in fairyland anymore. Peddling her dying father's sheet music to "a heartless, motley crowd," she's been cast out into an indistinct urban setting like that of "Hard Times Come Again No More"—or the mean streets of Five Points. The child is accosted by a leering man who asks to light his cigar with one of the sheet music pages. The insult to her father's craft is also a sexual affront to the girl. (Sometimes a cigar is more than just a cigar. . . .) The child drops the music and bursts into tears as the wind sends the sheets "blowing around, / All soiled and scattered and strewn on the ground."

The imagery of sexual defilement seems more appropriate to Victorian pornography than to the schoolroom or parlor. It's as if Foster's muse had been raped, his talent prostituted, and he recognized not only that his career and his life were nearing their end, but also that he was the author of their doom:

> 'Tis my father's song,
> And he can't live long;
> Everyone knows that he wrote it. . . .

Although the sketchbook suggests that "The Little Ballad Girl" originated in Foster's mourning over the past and the loss of his mother and brother, it ended up as an eerily accurate premonition of what befell Foster after he shepherded Jane and Marion into a stagecoach, doffed his high silk hat, waved goodbye to Warren, and set off one last time for New York City.[14]

Chapter Twenty-eight

"INFERNAL SWISH-SWISH!"

The Fosters arrived in New York during the fall of 1860, a time of tumult across the nation. No sooner had Pittsburgh given a greater percentage of its vote to Lincoln than any other American metropolis (the only municipality he carried by an even greater margin was Allegheny City) than it rose up in near-rebellion against the outgoing Democratic administration. Buchanan's secretary of war, John B. Floyd, ordered 125 cannons shipped to the Gulf Coast from the arsenal on William Barclay Foster's old Lawrenceville land. Rightly suspicious of Floyd (a Virginian who would become a Confederate general), Pittsburghers threatened to sink the steamboat on which the guns were to be transported, and the order was countermanded by Attorney General Edwin M. Stanton, an adopted son of Pittsburgh who had practiced law there for nine years.[1]

Long before Buchanan retreated from the White House to Wheatland and the bottle ("He was no single bottle man, either," wrote one of his cronies. "He would dispose of two or three at a sitting, beginning with a stiff jorum of cognac and finishing off with a couple of glasses of old rye"), the lame duck was denounced as a Benedict Arnold and a "cowardly old imbecile." Even a visiting foreigner, Anthony Trollope, called the man for whom Stephen Foster had written campaign songs four years earlier a "traitor to the country whose servant he was and whose pay he received."

The Philadelphia parsonage in which the president's youngest brother and the songwriter's oldest sister lived was stoned, their children jeered on their way to school.[2]

Philadelphians found other targets as well. They showered Dan Rice with eggs and hisses when his circus came to town. Branded by one paper as the "Chameleon Clown," who "talks 'secesh' in the South, and union in the North," Rice never fully recaptured the popularity he had enjoyed before the war.[3]

In New York City, Mayor Fernando Wood talked up secession. When police seized nearly a thousand muskets bound for Georgia in another underhanded deal engineered by John Floyd, the city's reaction was diametrically opposed to Pittsburgh's. Wood apologized, and the guns were eventually released to rebel hands. Meanwhile Wood's Minstrels, the blackface troupe led by the mayor's brother Henry, regaled Brooklyn audiences with their rendition of "Dixie's Land," a hit song written by Dan Emmett that began, "I wish I was in de land ob cotton. . . ."[4]

Foster, who would soon be selling songs to Henry Wood, did not rally round any flag for a long while. None of the dozen songs he published in 1860 and only one of the fifteen copyrighted in 1861 refers to politics or the war. "I'll Be a Soldier," published in August 1861, treats the prospect of conflict as unlikely and unreal. The introductory "symphony" interrupts the *mezzo-forte* melody with a passage marked "drums" that rapidly repeats one double-octave chord fourteen times, but the tattoo is *piano*, as if it were a distant rumor. The verses have a toy-soldier air, an almost nursery-rhyme naiveté: "I'll be a soldier and march to the drum, / And lie in my tent when the night shadows come; / I'll be a soldier with knapsack and gun. . . ." Three days after the song was copyrighted, the Union's alarming defeat in the first Battle of Bull Run awakened everyone to the bloody reality of war.

"No dainty rhymes or sentimental love verses for you terrible year," Whitman wrote in "Eighteen Sixty-One,"

> Not you as some pale poetling seated at a desk lisping cadenzas piano,
> But as a strong man erect, clothed in blue clothes, advancing, carrying a
>   rifle on your shoulder. . . .[5]

Even by standards less strident than Whitman's, Foster was a poor drooping poetling.

Where the Fosters lodged when they arrived in New York is uncertain.

Stephen's movements from late 1860 on are difficult to track, for he no longer kept an account book that survives, and his sketchbook peters out as well. The Fosters were boarding on Greene Street by the time Stephen met John Mahon, an Irish journalist whose 1877 reminiscence, already cited in snatches, is one of the most reliable accounts of Foster's second stint in New York.[6]

When the bartender at Windust's Restaurant whispered to Mahon that the stranger at the rail was "the great songwriter!," Stephen Foster was "very neatly dressed in a blue swallow-tailed coat [and a] silk hat"— probably the same topper he had worn in Warren. Mahon harbored musical aspirations of his own, and the two quickly became friends, Foster often composing on the piano in Mahon's lodgings at 311 Henry Street.

One day Foster felt dejected because Firth, Pond had declined one of his songs, "Our Bright, Bright Summer Days Are Gone." (The ballad is a pretty pallid piece of work, but Firth, Pond published worse.) Sitting at Mahon's piano, Foster rewrote the song from memory, handed Mahon the music, and asked him to try to sell it to his own publisher, John Daly —"and take what he will give you."

Mahon did not divulge what Daly, whose office was on nearby Grand Street, gave him, only that it was "not a tithe of what Foster got in his better days . . . [but] still considered handsome." Copyrighted on June 4, 1861, "Our Bright, Bright Summer Days Are Gone" was the first of seventeen Foster songs (including "I'll Be a Soldier" the following month) that John J. Daly published. His firm was known among song-writers as "a sort of clearing house for rejected MSS."[7] He ran a strictly cash-and-carry business, and Foster was increasingly hard-up for cash.

According to Mahon, Foster said he had an annual income of $1,200, which came from a contract with Firth, Pond to write ten songs a year for eight hundred dollars, and an agreement to provide six songs a year for four hundred dollars to a Philadelphia publisher, Lee & Walker. This isn't too far off from the $1,500 another New York friend said Foster had claimed he was making.[8] But Firth, Pond published only four songs by Foster in 1861 and just two in 1862. Lee & Walker seemed to have an agreement with *Clark's School Visitor*, which was published in Philadelphia, to reprint Foster's contributions to the monthly in sheet music form, but only "Jenny's Coming o'er the Green" came out under Lee & Walker's imprint. The five additional songs Foster wrote for *Clark's*—one of them a duet, "Mine Is the Mourning Heart," that Stephen taught Mahon's ten-year-old daughter to sing with him—were published by other houses.[9] In other words, if Foster had contracts, his publishers didn't honor them, he didn't fulfill them—or both.

Foster was no longer bound by an exclusive agreement with Firth, Pond. If he was free to publish elsewhere, however, his old house was also free to reject his compositions, and it did so frequently. Foster published widely but not well in New York, writing more prolifically than ever before and appearing under more imprints. In 1861, Horace Waters as well as John Daly began to issue his music. Flooding the market with inferior work reduced his income to a trickle, however, and he was no longer able to command royalties. Even if he had, they probably could not have kept up with New York City's inflationary Civil War economy, in which, by one estimate, retail prices rose 43 percent from 1860 to July 1863.[10]

Fully a third of the fifteen songs Foster published in 1861 are lugubrious ballads about dead or dying children. The crying jag was kicked off by lines a minor poet and children's author named Mary Bynon Reese had written after the Irish steamer *Hungarian* sank, without survivors, off Nova Scotia in February 1860. Foster set the poem to music for *Clark's Visitor*, and the ghastly echo in "Lizzie Dies To-Night" of "Old Folks at Home"—the same D-to-high-D leap in "Lizzie DIES" as in "Swa-NEE," the same Scottish snap on "MO-tthheerr" as "RIB-bbeerr"—reminds one how far he had fallen, from startling originality into recycled hackdom. There may not have been a dry eye in classrooms across America as schoolchildren lisped poor Lizzie's fate, but their tears would have been better spent on the deterioration of Foster's talent.

The third verse of "Lizzie Dies To-night" reveals that the girl's imminent death is but the most recent in a long-running series:

> I'm thinking, Mother, of the time
> When little Willie died,
> We laid him down with bursting hearts,
> My father's tomb beside.

This and memories of the deaths of his own father and half brother William may have prompted Foster to write the words as well as music to "Our Willie Dear Is Dying," which, like "Willie We Have Missed You" and "The Wife," is sung by a woman to a husband who is absent and presumed drinking. This time Willie is their child on his deathbed. The chorus shifts from the verse's 2/4 time to a more impassioned 6/8 as the woman urges her husband to return before Willie expires, but she doesn't have the confidence, however deluded, expressed in "The Wife" that he will come home.

"Our Willie Dear Is Dying" was written for the stage, not the schoolroom, and it was sung, according to the cover of the sheet music, by Gustavus Geary, a popular performer who specialized in Thomas Moore ballads. Number 54 in Firth, Pond's series of "Foster's Melodies" was the first since No. 21, "Ellen Bayne" back in 1854, to be advertised as sung by someone, as if Foster's name alone could no longer sell a song. Then it was E. P. Christy; now it was Geary, who, with his daughter Mina, shared a bill with Tom Thumb afternoons and evenings at Hope Chapel but probably couldn't squeeze into the miniature carriage that bore the General from his hotel to the theater.[11]

Foster wrung the last sob from this infanticidal cycle with "Little Belle Blair" ("We have made a grave for little Belle Blair . . ."), a reprise of "Gentle Annie" with a four-part chorus amenable to the minstrel stage. Foster dedicated it to Napoleon W. Gould, a guitarist who had performed with Christy's, Bryant's, and Campbell's Minstrels (and who would appear onstage with Gustavus Geary in December 1861, a month after "Little Belle Blair" was copyrighted).[12]

In the early autumn Foster published "Farewell Mother Dear" and "Farewell Sweet Mother," in which a dying daughter and a dying child urge their mothers not to weep because they will be reunited in heaven. Mothers were on Foster's mind, for he also wrote "Oh! Tell Me of My Mother," in which the singer asks an older woman about his (or her) dead mother.

Ignoring Firth, Pond's warning way back in 1849 about composers "who write too much & too fast," Foster published indiscriminately and indistinguishably, producing melodies on automatic pilot and lyrics by free association. Mahon wrote that he had seen Foster "stop in the street, take a pencil out of his pocket, mark a stave on his left thumb-nail, and write three or four starting notes." Asked what he was doing, Foster would explain "there is so much music running through my brain that I will miss it unless I put a note or two down to jog my memory."

As for lyrics, each verse of "A Penny for Your Thoughts!" ends,

". . . Jenny Dow, that lives beyond the hill." The next song Foster published, in January 1862, was "Little Jenny Dow," which begins, "Little Jenny Dow lives beyond the mill. . . ."

By this time Jenny Dow/Jane McDowell Foster was probably living way beyond the mill, for she and Marion moved back to Pennsylvania sometime before July 1861. The separation from his family may have prompted the chorus of "Why Have My Loved Ones Gone?," copyrighted on August 5:

> Why have my loved ones gone,
> Gone to return no more—
> Calmly gliding o'er a Summer sea
> Whilst I'm left plodding on the shore?

Significantly, Foster (or his publisher, Horace Waters) dedicated this song to a singing *family*, the Tremaines.

"Over the Calm Lake Gliding Song," which may have suggested or been suggested by the line in "Why Have My Loved Ones Gone?," is the title Foster gave to two of the last pages in his sketchbook. He covered them with cartoons slightly reminiscent of Hugh Lofting's line drawings for his Doctor Dolittle books and dedicated them to Amelia, a girl whose adventures with Stephen they illustrate. Foster probably made these drawings in New York City, for one of the captions explains that Stephen and Amelia are "going to the 7 sisters." *The Seven Sisters*, with an all-female cast, was an "operatic, spectacular, diabolical, musical, terpsichorean, farcical burletta" that ran on Broadway from November 26, 1860, through August 10 the following summer. Perhaps because a "leg drama" was not appropriate entertainment for a young girl, or because Stephen was entertaining another man's daughter with these sketches, they end on a guilty note, with a drawing of a "Policeman after Stephen & Amelia."[13]

Jane and Marion joined Jane's mother and Jane's sister Agnes in Lewistown. Agnes McDowell had wed a Dr. Cummings there and had borne two or three children (she would have five before a train struck Dr. Cummings's buggy and left her a widow). Marion attended school while Jane, it would seem, came and went. According to Jane's granddaughter, Jessie Welsh Rose, Jane tried, with the help of Morrison Foster and her sister Marion's husband, John Scully, "to put her husband upon his feet

—a futile effort." How frequently this effort took Jane back to New York is anyone's guess. John Scully, younger brother of the diarist Charles Scully, also lent Jane financial support while she trained for a job.[14]

It's unclear precisely when, but eventually Jane Foster became the Pennsylvania Railroad's telegraph operator in Greensburg, about thirty-three miles east of Pittsburgh. That's 135 miles west of Lewistown, so Marion was probably left at times with her grandmother and aunt. Jane Foster boarded at the Fisher House, a downtown Greensburg hotel, and later moved to the corner of Grove and Palmer Streets.[15]

Greensburg is where Andrew Carnegie was working as a telegrapher when a lightning bolt knocked him off his stool. And it was through Carnegie, now head of the Pennsylvania Railroad's Pittsburgh Division, that Jane Foster landed her position. In his autobiography, Carnegie congratulated himself on being "the first to employ young women as telegraph operators in the United States upon railroads, or perhaps in any branch." One of these, his cousin Maria Hogan, ran a training school of sorts in her office at the Pittsburgh freight station, and Jane Foster was probably among her pupils. "Our experience was that young women operators were more to be relied upon than young men," Carnegie wrote, neglecting to add that they were also cheaper. "Among all the new occupations invaded by women I do not know of any better suited for them than that of telegraph operator."[16]

The wife of the man who wrote "Doo-dah!" spent a decade or more tapping dot-dash, dot-dash.

In September 1861, Jane wrote Morrison from Lewistown, where she had been spending "a couple of months," and pleaded for a ten-dollar loan so she could revisit New York. ". . . I am now beginning to feel very uneasy about Steve, and he has not at present the money to send me," she confided. ". . . I wish to go back to him immediately, and indeed it is very necessary that I should be with him."[17]

She received the money within a week and wrote:

> When I arrive in New York I will deliver your message to 'Steve.' Marion
> is well & sends her love to you, she goes to school every day and she is
> very attentive to her studies & is a most excellent child in every respect.[18]

How long Jane remained with Stephen on this return visit, and whether she brought Marion with her, are unknown.

By 1862, Foster could no longer afford to ignore the war, because songs about it were becoming big sellers. George Root, who had imitated Foster in songs like "The Hazel Dell" and "Rosalie, the Prairie Flower," had stolen a march on everyone by publishing "The First Gun Is Fired! May God Protect the Right!" just three days after Fort Sumter was bombarded. He followed it with songs whose success was longer-lived: "The Vacant Chair," "The Battle Cry of Freedom," "Just Before the Battle, Mother," and "Tramp! Tramp! Tramp!" Gottschalk performed and published an arrangement of "The Battle Cry of Freedom," appropriating it as eagerly as he had absorbed "Oh! Susanna" and "Camptown Races" a decade earlier. Root's call to "rally 'round the flag," Gottschalk wrote, "ought to become our national air."[19]

Root made money from his music, too—"Tramp! Tramp! Tramp!" alone earned $10,000—because he was a principal in the Chicago publishing house of Root & Cady.[20] Half a century ahead of Irving Berlin, Root recognized that the surest way to protect and maximize a songwriter's income was to own it and publish it oneself. (Would that Foster or one of his "practical business men" brothers had been so savvy!) As their publisher, Root also profited from the hits of probably the North's second most successful Civil War songwriter, Henry Clay Work, the composer of "Kingdom Coming," "Wake, Nicodemus!," and "Marching Through Georgia."

The war was such a compelling subject, politically and emotionally as well as commercially, that it roused even John Hill Hewitt, now in his sixties and a staunch supporter of the Confederacy, to write his most popular songs since "The Minstrel's Return'd from the War" in the 1820s: "All Quiet Along the Potomac Tonight" and "Somebody's Darling."

Foster wanted no part of the war. According to a friend, the only time Foster lost his temper was

> when a returned soldier began to describe the noise of a shell in action. Foster disliked the disruption of the ties that held the negroes to their masters & of which he had written so many songs. So . . . when Mr. Soldier-man imitated the noise of a shell, Foster would say: "George, let's get out, there's that blanks [by which the writer meant "expletive deleted"], with his infernal *Swish-Swish!*" I can't stand the fellow![21]

Foster loathed military bluster. His siblings in Ohio, Henrietta in Warren and Morrison in Cleveland, were Copperhead Democrats vehemently opposed to the war. In a long letter to the editor of the *Cleveland*

Plain Dealer, Morrison warned in 1861 that "dissolving the Union in an insane quarrel over the negro slave" would be the economic ruination of the North.[22]

But eventually Stephen Foster had to change his tune. Three weeks after the slaughter at Shiloh (the North's name for the battle, Pittsburg Landing, must have rung ominously in Foster's ear), Firth, Pond copyrighted "That's What's the Matter." Assuming once again that Foster's name needed a boost, the publishers touted the song on the cover of the sheet music as "Dan Bryant's Celebrated Song, as sung by him with great success." If there is any truth in this advertising, it was a stroke of good fortune for Foster. Bryant's Minstrels, run by Dan Bryant (born Daniel Webster O'Brien) and also featuring his brothers Jerry and Neil, were the longest-running (and, for a stretch during the 1861–1862 season, the only running) minstrel show in New York. They held the stage for more than nine years at Mechanics' Hall, where Christy's Minstrels had performed for a decade, and they were Christy's successors as the preeminent blackface troupe. In 1862 their cast occasionally included Napoleon Gould as well as Dan Emmett, who had originally written "Dixie's Land" for Bryant's Minstrels in 1859.[23]

"That's What's the Matter" begins by agreeing rather querulously with Walt Whitman that this is no time for silly love songs:

> We live in hard and stirring times,
> Too sad for mirth, too rough for rhymes;
> For songs of peace have lost their chimes,
> And that's what's the matter!

The song scolds the Confederacy's "rebel crew" as if they were naughty boys, delights in their comeuppance at Shiloh, and praises the iron-clad *Monitor* and its true-blue captain, John Ericsson. Since it had been built and launched in Brooklyn, the *Monitor* was a source of special pride to New Yorkers (and perhaps of additional pride to Foster because its guns had been manufactured in Pittsburgh).[24]

Blackface singers had written and improvised political squibs ever since "Jim Crow," and military commentary goes back even further, to Micah Hawkins's "Backside Albany." "That's What's the Matter" is not written in blackface dialect, however, and Dan Bryant, who sometimes appeared as the Irishman he was, may not have sung it that way, either.

Many of Henry Clay Work's hit songs were in dialect, which suggests that Foster might have returned profitably to blackface. Work was an abolitionist who relished the irony of a blackface song ridiculing "massa" rather than slaves. He inverted blackface, subverting the racism it often reinforced. But none of the war songs for which Foster wrote the words is in dialect. Sedulously avoiding any suggestion of race in either form or content, his lyrics defend the Union but do not oppose slavery; in fact, they never even mention it.

"That's What's the Matter" was soon followed by "Better Times Are Coming," which exudes the chin-up cheer and optimism of Foster's early song, "There's a Good Time Coming." It sings the praises of Lincoln, his cabinet and his entire military command, mentioning nineteen officers, including Captain Ericsson, as it calls the roll in rote rhyme. There's a sense here—as there is not in the more spirited "That's What's the Matter"—that Foster was merely going through the motions. Surely his heart was not in his bland paean to the man he had excoriated six years earlier: "General Fremont the path-finder never lags behind. . . ."

"Better Times Are Coming" has a chorus for soprano, alto, tenor and bass, suggesting that Foster wrote it with the family parlor in mind. Two years later, a musical journal observed that the Civil War was a singularly family affair:

> . . . while the war literature of other nations abounds in love songs, ours is almost exempt from them; and while in the terrible struggle of the French revolution the chief appeal was made to glory and liberty, our soldiers go into battle and do nobly and steadily their duty evoking the blessings of mothers and sisters.
>
> But not only the words but the music itself strongly point to the ties by which the families are bound together. Almost all the songs published are concluded by a chorus of four voices. . . . There are few families in the country who can not and do not make up a quartet. This not only shows a satisfactory state of musical culture in the country, but also the deep-felt want of association and social enjoyment.[25]

Foster's next war song lacked the harmonized chorus, but its sentiment exemplifies the journal's point. "Was My Brother in the Battle" is a plaintive ballad that falters down the scale as a sister or younger brother asks of a returning soldier a question whose answer the singer suspects and fears: "Tell me, tell me weary soldier, will he never come again, / Did he suffer 'mid the wounded or die among the slain?"

Foster returned to a more anthemic mode with "We Are Coming Father Abraam 300,000 More," one of many musical settings of lines that appeared in the New York *Evening Post* after Lincoln's call, on July 12, 1862, for 300,000 additional volunteers:

> We are coming Father Abraam three hundred
> thousand more,
> From Mississippi's winding stream and from
> New England's shore. . . .

The poem was originally published anonymously, leading many to assume that the *Post*'s editor, William Cullen Bryant, had written it, but the author was James Sloane Gibbons, a wealthy New York banker, Quaker, and abolitionist. Nearly as many songwriters as soldiers answered the call, for the poem inspired songs by Patrick Gilmore, Luther Emerson, Nathan Barker, Augustus Cull, A. B. Irving, S. J. Adams, L. S. Burditt, George R. Pulton, J. A. Getze, and, composing answers to those songs, William Bradbury and George Root.[26]

Foster's setting, "respectfully dedicated to the President of the United States," is clearly superior to the one by Gilmore, the brass bandleader who wrote "When Johnny Comes Marching Home"; its rhythm is more varied and its melody richer. But Emerson, a composer chiefly of hymns who had studied briefly with Root, wrote by far the most popular version, although, to a modern ear, it does not enjoy a clear musical advantage over Foster's.[27] Perhaps what made the difference was that a major national publisher, Oliver Ditson, issued Emerson's song while Foster's was brought out by S. T. Gordon, a cheapjack New York outfit to which Foster had just started selling material. In any event, Foster's failure illustrates how little good his name still did him. S. T. Gordon published another war song in a similar vein, "We've a Million in the Field," with lyrics as well as music by Foster.

The last war song for which Foster wrote the words was copyrighted on February 14, 1863, probably in anticipation of Washington's Birthday. The singer is a veteran of the Revolutionary War who boasts that he "handled a gun / Where noble deeds were done, / For the name of my commander was George Washington." The second verse strays into "Old

Dog Tray" and "Old Black Joe" nostalgia for days and dear ones of old, but the third returns to the war, grumping about Lincoln's dismissal of George McClellan as head of the Army of the Potomac, and his dithering appointment of Ambrose Burnside and then Fighting Joe Hooker to replace him:

> You've had many Generals from over the land,
> You've tried one by one and you're still at a stand,
> But when *I* took the field we had *one* in command.

Foster's songs about the war failed, for the most part, because he couldn't get into the spirit of it. He could not update his music, so eloquently expressive of the late 1840s and 1850s, to the martial beat of the 1860s. His inability was partly political, largely temperamental and increasingly psychological and even physiological as he became more self-absorbed and self-destructive. The analogy may seem farfetched, but in some respects Foster's experience during the Civil War resembles the effect of the Vietnam War on Brian Wilson's music and behavior. In both cases it's insufficient to blame the songwriter's decline entirely on the exhaustion of his creative powers or the debilitating effects of drink or drugs. The Beach Boy who had never surfed and the songwriter who had never visited the Deep South when he wrote most of his plantation melodies could no longer sustain their fantasies or share them with the rest of the world when the rude reality of war kicked sand in everyone's face.

In his "dark night of the soul" Foster tried, like F. Scott Fitzgerald, "to refuse to face things as long as possible by retiring into an infantile dream."[28] Among the other songs he published in 1862 were "A Dream of My Mother and My Home," "Slumber My Darling" (for "thy mother is near"), "No One to Love," "No Home, No Home," "I'll Be Home Tomorrow," and "Happy Hours at Home." Adapting the melody of his old Buchanan campaign song, "The White House Chair," he contributed his last song to *Clark's School Visitor,* "The Merry, Merry Month of May," and he wrote another ditty that was ostensibly for adults, with tenor and bass parts in the chorus, but which one can imagine only schoolchildren singing: "Merry Little Birds Are We" ("Twit, twit, twee, / Twit, twit, twee").

On June 30, 1862, Jane Foster wrote from Lewistown to Morrison, thanking him profusely for five dollars he had sent her and for the clothing he had sent Stephen. The swallow-tailed coat and top hat were surely threadbare by now, but according to Foster's niece, Evelyn Foster Morneweck, Stephen didn't wear the clothing—he sold it for drink. Stephen's granddaughter wrote that Morrison reproached him, saying that if *he* went about looking so shabbily, he'd be afraid of being insulted. "Mitty," Stephen replied wearily, "don't worry so about me. No gentleman will insult me, and no other can."[29]

Jane Foster wrote this letter to Morrison after leaving Stephen in New York, where she may have spent only days or (far less likely) the better part of a year if she stayed when she visited him in the fall of 1861. "He was well," she wrote, "& publishes once in a long while with Pond."

It's ironic that even though Foster published sixteen songs in 1862, the only one he wrote that year which is remembered today is the one Firth, Pond didn't publish: "Beautiful Dreamer." Possibly the delay was caused by the imminent dissolution of Firth, Pond, since the principals went their separate ways in January 1863. William A. Pond & Co. continued business in the old office at 547 Broadway while Firth, Son & Co. set up shop a few doors away at 563 Broadway. Pond did not publish "Beautiful Dreamer" until March 10, 1864; perhaps he never would have issued it if Foster's demise had not presented an opportunity to exploit. "Beautiful Dreamer" was "the last song ever written" by Foster, Pond claimed, "composed but a few days previous to his death." The copyright line on the sheet music seems to have been altered, however, and to have originally read 1862.[30]

Although "Beautiful Dreamer" was not Foster's last song, it is still a kind of musical culmination that seems to review and cap his career. It is a serenade like the very first song he published, "Open Thy Lattice Love," and the two songs share the same imagery of starlight on a midnight sea, as well as triple meter. In contrast to the 6/8 of "Open Thy Lattice Love," however, "Beautiful Dreamer" is written in 9/8, a signature he had used only once before, in seven measures of the *Clark's School Visitor* duet he sang with little Annie Mahon, "Mine Is the Mourning Heart." And the marine imagery in "Beautiful Dreamer" is more ominous: those mermaids "chaunting the wild lorelie" are luring sailors to their death. The caressing, cloying triplets of the arpeggiated piano accompaniment, on the other hand, recall Foster's fondness in the 1850s for bel canto opera. The dreamer, "queen of my song," is the muse of

"Come with Thy Sweet Voice Again" and "Thou Art the Queen of My Song," the sleeping (or dead) woman in "Come Where My Love Lies Dreaming."

It is all but impossible to hear "Beautiful Dreamer" with fresh ears today. Incessant repetition and parody have reduced it to kitsch, a cheap laugh for a few bars on the soundtrack of *Natural Born Killers*. The appoggiatura in the last line, the checked-sob quaver in "awa-ake unto me," is the quintessence of cornball. But if you listen very closely, you may detect a dissonant murmur. For this is a song about dissolution. The moon reflects like a mirror on a world of dewdrops and vapors, streamlets and seas, where everything seeps, flows, and evaporates into everything else. And the ultimate dissolution is death. Even if Foster was not familiar with the original poem by Heine, whose popularity rivaled Longfellow's, he surely knew "Die Lorelei" from Friedrich Silcher's if not Liszt's setting of the German poet's melancholy homage to the temptress of the Rhine, a Jeanie with light blond hair who groomed her golden tresses with a golden comb as she sang. "Beautiful Dreamer" is a siren song beckoning its singer not to dash against the rocks, but to melt into the sea of its own melody. The lapping of waves makes another, quieter kind of *Swish-Swish*.[31]

Chapter Twenty-nine

RUM AND RELIGION

I am very well and have been working quite industriously," Stephen wrote his brother Henry on December 6, 1862, "but pay, in these times, especially in music, is very poor."[1] Foster was indeed working industriously. In 1863 he would publish forty-nine songs (though in a couple of instances these consisted of one tune with two different sets of lyrics), almost a quarter of his entire life's output. Although their quantity is astounding, the quality of these songs is generally inferior. Indifference as well as indigence expedited Foster's mass production of melodies. He no longer cared enough to labor over the songs he was cranking out, and he seldom wrote his own lyrics anymore, relying as he never had in his greatest compositions on other people's words.

His factory was a bar in the backroom of a shabby German grocery store in the Bowery, on the corner of Chrystie and Hester streets. Although Lord and Taylor's resplendent marble emporium was only a block away, a select committee of the New York State Assembly aptly described much of the neighborhood surrounding Foster when it reported of a Hester Street tenement: "The place literally swarmed with life, but life of so abject and squalid a character as to scarcely merit the name."[2]

"[T]he Liquor Grocery squats like a venomous toad," warned the journalist George G. Foster (no relation to Stephen, though he did play the flute) in one of his lurid urban exposés, "upon the corner of a block of miserable poor-men's dwellings, crowded and overrunning with families, deprived of air and wholesome sunshine, and disseminates its venom on all around." Of all the "dens of dissipation" in the city, George Foster wrote, liquor groceries were "the most pernicious," overcharging the poor for small quantities of inferior and adulterated food, and encouraging them to squander on equally inferior and adulterated drink what they should have spent elsewhere on dinner. There were some two thousand of these "filthy holes" in New York when George Foster wrote in 1849, and two groceries—John Lankenau's and Henry Sieckmann's—at the intersection of Chrystie and Hester when Stephen Foster hung out there in 1862 and 1863.[3]

It was in one of these establishments that George W. Birdseye, a minor journalist and versifier, met Foster in late 1862. Four and a half years later, he wrote that Foster's "soft brown eyes" were "somewhat dimmed by dissipation" and that he wore "an old glazed cap" with a peak. Morrison took great offense at Birdseye's sensationalistic account of his brother's "insatiable appetite for liquor."[4] But Birdseye registered the diffidence and distractedness that Stephen's friends had noted back in Pittsburgh:

> He would walk, talk, eat and drink with you, and yet always seem distant, maintaining an awkward dignity. . . . Whether it was a natural bashfulness, or a voluntary reserve, I cannot say, but those who knew him most intimately were never familiar.

Foster "slept in an old lodging-house in the Bowery," Birdseye said, but spent most of his time in that "dark grocery bar-room," where he would

> take a sheet of brown wrapping-paper from the counter, and seating himself at a little drinking-table, or more probably a bean-box, rapidly jot down a few bars of some sweet air . . . , whistling the passage over and over again, modifying it until he felt satisfied.

Some of the tunes Foster whistled were hymns. As his life hit rock-bottom, Foster, who had never expressed much interest in religion, who had resisted the urgings of his sisters Ann Eliza and Henrietta to join the church, wrote nearly thirty songs for Sunday schools. He hadn't found God, but he had found a publisher.

Horace Waters was a Maine Yankee whose faith in the Lord was rewarded by the fortune he made when *The Sabbath-School Bell,* his collection of hymns for Sunday school classes, sold an unprecedented 170,000 copies within fourteen months of its publication in 1859. "[P]robably the most influential Sunday school songbook ever published in the United States," in one scholar's judgment, *The Sabbath-School Bell* was revolutionary because it all but ignored the distinction between sacred and secular music.[5]

Only six years earlier, in 1853, Thomas Hastings, composer of the tune of "Rock of Ages" ("cleft for me") and himself the editor of a popular Sunday school songbook, had expressed outrage that "Old Folks at Home" had been outfitted with new, religious lyrics for Sunday school classes. Popular tunes filled children's minds with "poisonous trash," he fulminated: "merry dances, street ballads, bacchanalian songs, and negro melodies, often tricked with parodies which, by a double power of association, bring wicked and irreverent thoughts to mind!"[6]

But why should the devil have all the good tunes? Waters embraced the more vigorous rhythms, sentimental lyrics, even the Scottish snap and, above all, the refrains of popular music. The harmonized choruses that had crossed over from minstrelsy to the parlor ballad were now crossing over once again, this time into church school. "Choruses are proverbially contagious," Waters wrote, "and many a boy and girl who can hardly be persuaded to sing an entire tune, will join in the sweep of a full chorus with zest and advantage."[7]

Waters borrowed popular melodies, too. When the inevitable *Sabbath-School Bell No. 2* came out in 1860, it included "Sorrow Shall Come No More" (set to the melody of "Hard Times Come Again No More") and "We Love the Happy School" (set to the melody of "Some Folks"), both arranged by Augustus Cull. So it was quite natural, after he started publishing some of Foster's secular songs (beginning in 1861 with "Why Have My Loved Ones Gone?"), for Waters to recruit Foster for religious songwriting as well. Who was more highly qualified to bring popular music into the Sunday schoolroom? And his work for *Clark's School Visitor* had already nudged Foster in the right direction.

Given America's high infant and juvenile mortality rates, death cast a long shadow over Sunday school lessons. "Remember, dear children," warned "Little Lessons for Little Folks" in *Youth's Companion 1*, "that a large proportion of you *must* appear in eternity before your twentieth year!"[8] Since Foster had recently written several songs about the deaths of children, it was easy for him to dash off "Bury Me in the Morning, Mother," "Little Ella's an Angel!," "Suffer Little Children to Come unto Me," and "Willie's Gone to Heaven" (in which Willie jumps an octave to "Hea-VEN!" in a startling leap of faith).

Waters copyrighted these songs on January 31, 1863, and sold them as single sheets for three cents a song (two dollars for a hundred). Later in the year he brought out two collections, *Waters' Golden Harp for Sunday Schools* and *The Athenaeum Collection of Hymns and Tunes for Church and Sunday School*, which included, in addition to "Bury Me in the Morning, Mother" and "Little Ella's an Angel!," nineteen more melodies by Foster. For many of these Foster did not write the lyrics, which are furnished by more orthodox authors, chiefly Mary Ann Kidder, who had translated "Some Folks" into "We Love the Sunday School" and must have been quite a taskmistress. In one of these hymns she scolds, "Don't be idle little children/ . . . Labor for the Sunday School." (Mrs. Kidder drove no one harder than herself: by the time she died in 1905, she had written a thousand hymns.)[9] One text in *The Athenaeum Collection* is a poem, "Imperishable," commonly attributed to Charles Dickens.[10] Retitled "The Pure, the Bright, the Beautiful" ("These things can never die"), it provides an optimistic antidote to the dolor of Foster's early ballad, "Ah! May the Red Rose Live Alway!" ("Why should the beautiful die?"). "The Beautiful Shore" is a fully developed hymn that could bear revival, but many of Foster's settings are elementary sketches, some as brief as eight bars, that make his contributions to *Clark's School Visitor* seem sophisticated by comparison.

In much the same way that he wrote religious songs without joining the church, Foster mesmerized a temperance meeting without taking the pledge. Assigned as a reporter to cover one such gathering in the Bowery, John Mahon took Foster along with him. When members of the audience were asked to sing, Mahon, without revealing Foster's identity, suggested that he sing "Hard Times Come Again No More." Foster "could remember the music of all his songs," according to Mahon, but "the only song whose words he could recollect" was "Hard Times." George Birdseye wrote that Foster often entertained "the forlorn-looking *habitués*" of the grocery barroom with "Hard Times," singing it "with a pathos that a state of semi-inebriation often lends the voice." Foster's rendition didn't leave a dry eye at the temperance rally, either, and Mahon wrote that he seemed to recall "something stronger than lemonade was improvised somewhere for Foster and myself during the recess."

Waters published Foster but, as a fervent abolitionist and teetotaler, he can hardly have approved of him. According to Birdseye, Foster was treated rudely at a publisher's office that was probably Waters's at 481 Broadway. When he went to ask for a few copies of one of his songs (Birdseye thought it was "Why Have My Loved Ones Gone?"), Foster was refused and "left the store with tears rolling down his cheeks."

This story is lent credence by the recollections of a young woman who worked for Waters. Interviewed years later, Mrs. Parkhurst Duer said that one day

> a poorly dressed, very dejected looking man came in, and leaned against the counter by the door. I noticed he looked ill and weak. No one spoke to him. A clerk laughed and said:
> "Steve looks down and out."
> Then they all laughed, and the poor man saw them laughing at him.

When she asked who the man was, the snickering clerk replied, "Stephen Foster": "He is only a vagabond, don't go near him."

> I walked over to him, put out my hand, and asked, "Is this Mr. Foster?"
> He took my hand and replied: "Yes, the wreck of Stephen Foster." [11]

Foster's remark, like his claim that "no gentleman will insult me, and no other can," sounds too stagy to be true, as if Mrs. Duer had rehearsed and improved it over the years. But Foster wrote in "Bury Me in the Morning, Mother" of being laid to rest "Where the murmuring winds will mourn, mother, / The wreck that death has made."

On a raw, snowy day in the winter of 1862–63, a notary who lived behind or over his father's fancy-goods store at nearby 176½ Bowery ventured gingerly into the liquor grocery. George Cooper had been studying law with Chester A. Arthur, later president of the United States, but poetry appealed more vividly than torts to the young man's imagination. He had been contributing to literary magazines since he was sixteen, and now he was looking for Foster, with some lines he "fondly hoped might be wedded to immortal melody." [12]

Foster looked them over, drew from his pocket a creased sheet of music paper, and smoothed it out over an upturned cheese box. Ignoring the conversation and curiosity of the drinkers around him, he began to compose.

> The melody was soon dotted down, and the piano accompaniment followed as quickly. When in doubt as to a proper note of said accompaniment, [his] right hand . . . would run up and down imaginary piano keys upon the cheese box. . . . "Now for a publisher!" exclaimed Foster, as the finishing touches were made to the song, and some sand was gathered from the floor by the manuscript, in the form of a scoop, to hasten the drying of the ink.

Cooper and an overcoatless Foster were trudging through the slush along Broadway between the offices of Horace Waters and Firth, Pond (which by this time may have become simply Pond) when Henry Wood called out from the entrance of his new Minstrel Hall opposite the St. Nicholas Hotel.[13] "Hello, Steve!" Wood said, eyeing the rolled-up manuscript. "What have you got there? Something new?" Wood's company, which included veteran troupers like Frank Brower, was giving Bryant's Minstrels a real run for their money, and it was rehearsing that very moment. One of the musicians ran through the song and Wood promptly bought it, for ten dollars on the spot and fifteen dollars more to be paid at the box office that evening.

The words to "Willie Has Gone to the War" (a name Cooper may have chosen to appeal to the author of "Willie My Brave," "Willie We Have Missed You," and "Our Willie Dear Is Dying") were no more immortal than the melody to which they were set, but Foster and Cooper were off and running. Foster called Cooper "the left wing of the song factory," and together they produced more than twenty songs in little over a year.[14]

Foster may have seen a younger version of himself in his junior partner. The reluctant law student was twenty-two or twenty-three, the same age Foster had been when he abandoned bookkeeping for songwriting. Cooper became Foster's protégé, but Foster was too far gone to be very fatherly. Indeed, their roles were often reversed, as when Cooper gave

Foster clothes (perhaps from his real father's store). Like the clothing Morrison sent, Stephen sold or discarded it.

Foster and Cooper wrote many kinds of songs, including two hymns for Horace Waters, but the lion's share were about the war. Cooper was a private in Company B of the Twenty-Second Regiment of New York's National Guard—the "Union Grays," as they were known until the similarity of their uniforms (gray with scarlet trim and white piping) to those of the Confederate artillery persuaded them to change their garb. Cooper had been on active but not particularly eventful guard duty in Baltimore and Harper's Ferry during the summer of 1862. The regiment had returned to New York City on September 2, just in time to avoid surrender when Stonewall Jackson captured Harper's Ferry two weeks later. Cooper would not be called to serve again until June 19, 1863, and then for less than two months, so he had lots of time on his hands in which to work with, learn from, and care for Foster.[15]

Cooper echoed familiar Foster themes in their war songs, following up "Was My Brother in the Battle?," for instance, with "Bring My Brother Back to Me." "For the Dear Old Flag I Die!" is ostensibly based on the last words of "a brave little drummer boy" struck down at Gettysburg. The lad's plea to his distant mother, "dry your weeping eye," could have been penned a decade earlier by Foster himself. ("Give This to Mother," a song advertised as "Stephen C. Foster's last musical Idea," was published a year after Foster's death. This time, the drummer boy was dying on "one of the Battle fields near Washington"; with his last breath he pulled a locket from his neck and begged a comrade to give it to his mother.)[16] "When This Dreadful War Is Ended" may have been an attempt to cash in on the success of Henry Tucker and Charles Carroll Sawyer's "When This Cruel War Is Over," which sold nearly a million copies and so unmanned the troops, Yanks and Rebels alike, who heard it that some generals prohibited its performance.[17] Two Foster-Cooper collaborations, "The Soldier's Home" and "My Boy Is Coming from the War," jerk cheap tears by revealing only in their last verses that the soldiers in question are dead.

Foster's melodies for these songs seem as pro forma as Cooper's lyrics. How deeply Foster detested the war's "infernal *Swish-Swish!*" is suggested by a song he published in 1863 with lyrics of his own. He had written "I'll Be a Soldier," but "I'd Be a Fairy," which he may have dug out of his trunk, reveals where his true feelings lay. Harking back to early ballads like "What Must a Fairy's Dream Be?" (and Peter K. Moran's "I'll Be a Fairy"), the ditty was so flagrantly untimely that it amounted to a protest song.

Cooper turned to the blackface dialect that Foster had forsaken in a nasty piece of work entitled "A Soldier in the Colored Brigade." At the war's outset, Martin Delany had tried to raise a unit of black Zouaves. Failing that, he helped recruit African Americans for the famous Fifty-Fourth Massachusetts Volunteers. His eldest son, Toussaint, joined the regiment which was celebrated in the 1989 film, *Glory*. When another African-American regiment from Massachusetts, the Fifty-Fifth, had to pass through New York City on its way to the front, its commander was so fearful of a hostile reception that he requested special protection. When New York's Union League Club sponsored a black regiment, it couldn't find a landlord who would rent space to the recruiters or a band that would march with the soldiers.[18]

"A Soldier in the Colored Brigade" pandered to such prejudice by deriding a black volunteer, "Wid musket on [his] shoulder and banjo in [his] hand," who promises his sweetheart he'll return to marry her and "raise up picanninnies for de Colored Brigade / Ninnies! Ninnies for de Colored Brigade." The lyric is a complete about-face from "Backside Albany," in which the overt object of ridicule was not the blackface singer, but his foes. Preferring black slaves to black soldiers, the song also condemns the Emancipation Proclamation:

> Some say dey lub de darkey and dey want him to be free
> I s'pec dey only fooling and dey better let him be.
> For him dey'd brake dis Union which de're forefadders hab made,
> Worth more dan twenty millions ob de Colored Brigade.

Foster had always been a conservative Democrat. No matter how much sympathy his songs had expressed for African Americans, there's no reason to suppose he did not share Morrison and Henrietta's Copperhead views. "A Soldier in the Colored Brigade" was copyrighted on May 27, 1863, at the height of the controversy over former Ohio Congressman Clement L. Vallandigham. Only two days earlier, Union cavalry had escorted the outspoken Peace Democrat, convicted of disloyalty by a military tribunal, to exile behind Confederate lines. Vallandigham was an occasional guest at Morrison's Cleveland home, and Henrietta fired off verses on Vallandigham's behalf: "Tho' banished, and branded as a traitor, thou art, / Yet still dost thou live in the people's great heart." Former Pennsylvania governor William Bigler, whom Stephen Foster had hurrahed in an 1851 campaign jingle, shared Vallandigham's vehement opposition to the war and conferred with him. Many New Yorkers, including Fernando Wood and Governor Horatio Seymour, rallied to his support as well, and Vallandigham ran for governor of Ohio while in exile. Democrats tarred his opponent as a "fat Knight of the corps d'Afrique"—a soldier, in other words, in the colored brigade. Henrietta set a campaign song to the tune of Stephen's "Better Days Are Coming":

> The Dictator Lincoln has put us under ban,
> He has exiled Vallandigham for speaking like a man.
> He scoffs at the people's rights, we are no longer free,
> Unless we stop the despot who strikes at liberty.[19]

Ohioans ignored Henrietta's call to "cast [their] votes or die!" and rejected Vallandigham overwhelmingly.

Cooper's most distinctive collaborations with Foster are a cluster of songs that look ahead to variety shows, to the Gilded Age and even the Gay Nineties, rather than back to the minstrel stage and prewar parlors. Written mostly in 6/8 and marked *vivace* rather than Foster's beloved *moderato*, they're wordier, wittier and more theatrical than Foster's previous songs. Drawing on elements of minstrelsy and the British music hall, vaudeville was beginning to emerge. The man who would be crowned its first king, Tony Pastor, was already presenting live entertainment at a New York City bar. Cooper would later become one of Pastor's best friends, and write material for one of Pastor's discoveries, Lillian Russell.[20]

Foster himself composed or arranged a song performed by Pastor that makes fun of the explosive proliferation of popular music Foster did so much to detonate. "The Song of All Songs" strings together in half-sensical sentences song titles ranging from "Oft in the Stilly Night" to "Root, Hog or Die!," including Tucker and Sawyer's "When This Cruel War Is Over" and Foster's own "Jenny's Coming o'er the Green." These verses, reproduced in *Tony Pastor's New Comic Irish Songster* and attributed there to Pastor, may actually have been written by John F. Poole, who parodied "Jenny's Coming o'er the Green" as "Whiskey in Decanter Clean" for George Christy and contributed "No Irish Need Apply" to Pastor's songster.[21]

John Mahon as well as George Cooper may have heightened Foster's interest in the theater, for many of Mahon's friends were actors. Foster played and sang at the wedding of Mahon's oldest daughter, where the guests included George F. Boniface, his wife, his sister-in-law Kate Newton, and John Nunan. All four were in the company at the New Bowery Theatre, just around the corner from Foster's backroom barroom. Talk and peanuts flowed freely as the company presented *Hamlet, The Devil in the Bowery,* and *The Perilous Adventures of the Great Exploring Expedition to the North Pole* to a pit one reviewer described as "jammed with democracy, unwashed and unterrified." Foster arranged the piano accompaniment to a song Mahon composed in tribute to Kate Newton, "Our Darling Kate"; perhaps "Katy Bell," a Foster-Cooper collaboration, was also inspired by the versatile actress, who appeared in everything from *Much Ado About Nothing* to *A Terrible Secret, or, the Mysteries of Free Masonry.*[22]

Under the pen name Velsor Brush, Walt Whitman wrote in 1862 that life on the Bowery was "more pungent. Things are in their working-day clothes, more democratic, with a broader, jauntier swing, and in a more direct contact with vulgar life." The very title of one Foster-Cooper song, "Kissing in the Dark," swings with a jaunty familiarity that Foster never permitted in his own lyrics.[23]

Some of Foster's collaborations with Cooper are overtly theatrical, describing comic encounters and dialogue between the sexes. In "Larry's Good Bye," even the war is good for a joke as sly Norah sweet-talks Larry into marrying her before he departs for battle. A finicky young woman rejects so many suitors in "There Are Plenty of Fish in the Sea" that she dooms herself to spinsterdom. "If You've Only Got a Moustache" jests in lingo which sounds quite modern that anyone who grows one "will be all the rage with girls."

Cooper and Foster are both clean-shaven in a tintype made of them together. Foster's suit, possibly lent him by Cooper, is baggy, and there are bags under his eyes as well. Foster holds an envelope in his left hand, as if he were discussing business or a lyric with Cooper, whose eyes seem uncomfortably averted, gazing off into the distance.

A diminutive tintype portrait, about an inch square, seems to have been made of Foster on the same occasion. (Although Cooper recollected more than half a century later that their portrait was made in 1863, these may well have been "the pictures" to which Stephen Foster referred—and for which he requested money—in his December 6, 1862, letter to his brother Henry.)[24] Age has thinned Foster's lips but not his unkempt hair, a stray strand of which droops over his forehead. His brows droop, too, over eyes that seem weary, wary, and haunted. It's the face of a man who no longer expects much from life or from himself.

Two of Foster's collaborations with Cooper turn a subject he had always treated as melodrama into situation comedy as a wife confronts a husband lurching home late at night. "What, you tell me you're sober, you wretch you . . . !" declares the tippler's better half in "My Wife Is a Most Knowing Woman." A duet, "Mr. and Mrs. Brown," even stage-directs hiccoughs: "And if I could have sooner come (*hic*) / I'd been here (*hic*) before." Both songs have happy endings, in which the husband swears (however unconvincingly) that he'll never touch another drop and reconciles with his wife.

In real life, the unreconciled Foster had little appetite except for alcohol. He "drank constantly," according to Cooper, but "was never intoxicated. He was indifferent to food, often making a meal of apples or turnips from the grocery shop, peeling them with a large pocket-knife." The bartender in the back of the grocery where Foster spent most of his time in "not very delectable society" served him "rum" concocted "from French spirits and brown sugar, and . . . kept in a keg." (According to George Foster, liquor grocery rum was "the fieriest New England, sweet-ened and corrupted.")[25]

Uncorking a lyric he had worked on in his sketchbook when he lived in Hoboken a decade earlier, Stephen Foster collaborated with Cooper on a drinking song, "While the Bowl Goes Round." Cooper ultimately rejected the words "as not likely to suit the general public" and came up with new ones about yet another Jenny: "Did you see dear Jenny June / When the meadows were in tune. . . ." According to the sheet music published by Firth, Son & Co., "Jenny June" was sung "with great suc-cess" by one C. Henry, a lesser light amid the stars in Wood's Minstrels. "While the Bowl Goes Round," with nearly the identical melody, was published seven years later by John Daly, at whose office Foster may have left—or lost—a copy of the original manuscript.[26]

Birdseye and Cooper agree that Foster slept in cheap lodgings on the Bowery, Cooper specifying the address as No. 15.[27] The young woman who took pity on Foster in Horace Waters's office later recalled that he had a bed in a cellar on Elizabeth Street, just a block off Bowery. Wher-ever he ended up for the night, it may have resembled the scene David

Gilmour Blythe painted in *Art versus Law*, his sardonic self-portrait of 1859 or 1860. With two canvases under his arm and a palette and brushes in his hand, the painter climbs the stairs to his studio in Pittsburgh's Denny Building to find it padlocked. A notice on the door advertises its availability to anyone who can pay the rent and utilities. Like his finances, the artist's clothes are in disarray: His hat is dented, his coat ripped, his pants patched. His beard and hair are long and unkempt. Is it art or the law that has reduced him to such wretchedness? A bottle on a staved-in barrel and broken crockery on the landing suggest another culprit.[28]

Chapter Thirty

LAST PALL

The smoke that darkened the Manhattan sky in the sweltering July of 1863 was not the smudge of industry and barbecue that had greeted Stephen Foster's birth thirty-seven years earlier. It was the pall of insurrection as rioters protesting conscription torched two draft offices (one of them on Grand Street, near Foster's haunts), the Second Avenue armory, the Union Steam Works, and, most despicably, the Colored Orphan Asylum. As the targets of the mob's wrath expanded from the premises of the draft to the residences of the rich (including the author of the verses, "We Are Coming Father Abraam") and the persons of unfortunate African Americans, the war's "infernal *Swish-Swish!*" was no longer faraway shells—it was howitzer fire on East Nineteenth Street and black corpses swaying from neighborhood lampposts.[1]

Estimates of the death toll in the Draft Riots of July 13–17 range from 105 to 128; by any count they were the most deadly riots our nation has ever seen, claiming twice as many lives as the violence in Los Angeles after the acquittal of Rodney King's assailants in 1992. They began after the Lincoln administration, having concluded that Father Abraam's call for still more volunteers would not suffice, pushed through the first federal conscription bill in March 1863. Any man between the ages of twenty and thirty-five, and any unmarried man between thirty-five and forty-five, could be called to military service if his name were drawn in a lottery conducted in each congressional district.

Over thirty-five and, though separated, still wed, Foster had nothing to worry about, but many other poor men complained bitterly that the brunt of the act fell unfairly on them. As the third day of violence drew to a close, John Vance Lauderdale, a young surgical intern at Bellevue, watched from his window in the teaching hospital as a drunken rioter reeled down the avenue and declared, echoing the title of a Stephen Foster song, "A poor man had to be drafted and go to the war, but a rich man could pay his money and stay at home. Thats whats the matter."[2]

The affluent could pay three hundred dollars for an exemption or hire a substitute to dodge minié balls at Chickamauga. That's what Andrew Carnegie did. After a brief stint supervising railroad repair under Tom Scott, his mentor who was now assistant secretary of war, sunstroke sent Carnegie home to Pittsburgh, where he decided he'd rather make money than war. He made $42,260.67 in 1863, and when he was drafted in 1864, the fervent abolitionist paid an Irish immigrant $850 to fight the good fight for him.[3]

Poor Irish Americans represented the majority of the rioters, starting with members of the Black Joke Engine Company, No. 33. Infuriated that their status as volunteer firemen—b'hoys of the first order, like the legendary Mose—did not exempt them from the draft, they ignited the violence when they set fire to a draft office and ignored pleas to douse the flames. It was galling to many Irish that they were being forced, in the aftermath of the Emancipation Proclamation, to fight on blacks' behalf. Irish and African Americans were locked in a bitter struggle for a toehold on the bottom rung of America's economic ladder.

By the time the Twenty-second Regiment of New York's National Guard returned to the city on July 18, the riots had been suppressed by massive military force, and a sullen, apprehensive peace prevailed. George Cooper's regiment was not released even though it had just marched 170 miles in less than three weeks on ten days' rations without a change of clothing as it helped chase Robert E. Lee back to Virginia after Gettysburg. Instead the troops had to guard their own armory, and then the Croton Aqueduct, against fellow New Yorkers. Not until September 15 were they all sent home.[4]

The five days of rioting can only have been nightmarish for Foster as arson, looting, and soldiers with fixed bayonets swept up and down Grand

Street. (One local bartender poured oil on the flames but saved his saloon from the torch by treating the rioters to free drinks.) The sky, darkened here by smoke, fitfully illuminated there by flames, must have reminded Foster of the great fire that had engulfed Pittsburgh when he was in his teens. Perhaps the racial violence recalled the melee after Frank Johnson's concert in Allegheny.

Foster had devoted his life to writing music for the millions. Now, not only were millions no longer buying it, but the people, the vast popular audience his work had inspired and united, were dividing and destroying each other: South against North, poor against rich, white against black. The Draft Riots were a brutal repudiation of Foster's music, the best of which, even Frederick Douglass admitted, had encouraged sympathy for black suffering. If they were an endorsement of his politics, the worst of which had encouraged indifference to black suffering, surely Foster found cold comfort in such chilling vindication. "All this," wrote attorney Joseph Choate, who sheltered four African Americans in his home during the riots, "is the natural fruits of the doctrine of Seymour, Wood, and Vallandigham."[5]

Scribbling hymns for a religion in which he had little faith (and for a publisher who treated him with un-Christian contempt), tossing off songs about a war in which he believed even less, Foster lost his voice before he lost his life. ". . . [T]here was not an 'I' anymore," as F. Scott Fitzgerald wrote of *his* crack-up, "—not a basis on which I could organize my self-respect. . . ."[6] It's easy (though frightful) to imagine Foster, his eyes stinging with smoke, his ears ringing with gunfire and shouts of "Kill the niggers," stumbling down Chrystie Street into the rifle sights of a hundred Lord and Taylor employees barricaded behind packing cases. (Although Brooks Brothers was pillaged, Lord and Taylor's makeshift ramparts were not breached.) But it's hard to imagine how, at this point, Foster could ever have recovered his music, his audience, or his self-respect.

Louis Moreau Gottschalk rushed back to New York when he learned that the house in which he had been staying on West Fourteenth Street was endangered. Though a Southerner with a French accent, he had given his all for the Union, including a patriotic pastiche entitled *The Union* that quoted "The Star-Spangled Banner," "Hail Columbia," and "Yankee Doodle." (Its subtitle, *"Paraphrase de Concert,"* betrayed Gottschalk's lingering linguistic confusion.) By the end of 1863, the pianist had grossed enough money from tirelessly barnstorming the

Northern states to buy a house of his own on East Thirty-first Street. As
Foster fell ever deeper into impoverished anonymity, Gottschalk enjoyed
sleigh rides through unfinished Central Park, treated urchins to sugar
plums, and mingled with the demimonde in the blue room at the tony
La Maison Dorée. He cut a familiar, romantic figure as he promenaded
down Fifth Avenue, wrapped in an elegant Spanish cloak and a wreath
of cigar smoke.[7]

Few New Yorkers recognized their shabby fellow-passenger as Foster
jostled up and down Broadway in a crowded horse-drawn omnibus. He
took the rattling ride often, Foster told Cooper, because it "stirred up
melodies in his mind." Family and old friends tried in vain to persuade
Foster to leave New York. Ann Eliza Buchanan sent her younger son,
Edward, to see Stephen, but Eddie returned empty-handed.[8] Morrison
Foster seems to have set out on a rescue mission in the late summer or
fall of 1863. In October, Jane Foster wrote from Lewistown to Morrison
that she felt "relieved . . . about Steve when I read your letter: If you can
persuade him to return to Cleveland with you I am sure that all will soon
be well with him again."[9] But the next time Morrison and Jane saw
Stephen was in New York, and Stephen was dead.

On Saturday night, January 9, 1864, Foster turned in early at the hotel
where he was staying at No. 30 on the Bowery, at the corner of Bayard
Street. He had not been feeling well, and according to John Mahon, one
of the reasons he had written the piano accompaniment to Mahon's
song, "Darling Kate," was for the money to rent (or continue to rent) a
decent room in which to recuperate.[10]

The building had seen better times and other names: the North American Hotel, the Moss Hotel, the New England Hotel. "Supercilious
youths, at the new Delmonico's, or the huge pale-faced Fifth avenue,
will, of course, turn up their noses at restauration and a night's repose in
the Bowery, near Bayard street," Whitman wrote in 1862, mentioning
the New England Hotel by name.

> But what do you care, you full-blooded samples from the rural districts,
> and from marine bays and sounds, as you eat your hearty dinner or supper,
> or, early retiring, sleep without demur, having deposited a well-stuffed
> pocket-book in the safe in the office, or haply under your pillow?

(Whitman admitted, however, that some of those pocket-books were
picked clean by morning.)

Thirty-one years earlier, according to Dan Emmett, the North American Hotel had spawned the Virginia Minstrels. "The public houses along here used to be filled winters with the circus-men, showmen, &c.," Whitman wrote. "You will see a few driblets of such remaining; but the former and peculiar glories of the neighborhood . . . seem to have taken to themselves wings." Stephen Foster was just a driblet, but No. 30 had not yet fallen into utter disrepute. Henry Foster would be relieved and somewhat surprised to discover that it was "a very respectable Hotel." [11]

On Sunday morning, Foster spoke to a chambermaid at his door and then, as he turned back into his room, fell "as if he had been shot," striking a wash basin or chamberpot that cut a deep gash in his neck. (Flash back to the broken crockery on the landing in Blythe's *Art versus Law*.) George Cooper and a doctor were sent for. When Cooper, who lived only four blocks away, arrived on the scene, he found Foster lying naked ("Steve never wore any night-clothes") with a cut throat, a bruised forehead and "a bad burn on his thigh." The tin boiler used for making hot drinks in the liquor grocery had overturned a few days earlier and scalded Foster "terribly," but he had neglected to tend his wound. Looking up with the same "wonderful big brown eyes" that Birdseye had remarked on, Foster whispered to Cooper, "I'm done for" and "begged for a drink, but before I could get it for him, the doctor . . . arrived and forbade it." [12]

Years later, Cooper recalled a trivial yet vivid detail that seems grotesquely apt, considering the importance of the color line in Foster's music. The doctor was stitching up Foster's throat when a "horrified" Cooper noticed that he was using black rather than white thread.

> "Haven't you any white thread," I asked, and he said no, he had picked up the first thing he could find. I decided the doctor was not much good and I went down stairs and got Steve a big drink of rum, . . . which seemed to help him a lot. [13]

Cooper and the doctor hurried Foster into a carriage and off to Bellevue, which was overcrowded even then, unsanitary, and almost as famous for the size of its rats as for the superiority of its surgeons. He was admitted by John Vance Lauderdale, the intern who had observed the Draft Riots from his window and tended their victims as well as some of their instigators. Lauderdale was a bit of a musician himself. He took guitar lessons from one of his patients, who "in his more palmy days" had played with Jullien, and he was impressed by the man whom Bellevue's register correctly listed as "Composer" even if it misspelled his name ("Forster, Stephen") and mistook his age ("thirty-nine"). Cooper and the doctor had managed to dress Foster, because Bellevue records indicate he was wearing "Coat. Pants. Vest. Hat. Shoes. Overcoat."[14]

When Cooper visited Foster on Monday or Tuesday, "he said nothing had been done for him, and he couldn't eat the food." Unable to stomach the meat and potatoes he was offered, Foster requested "some raspberry vinegar to cool [his] throat." He also asked Cooper to contact Morrison Foster, whom Cooper wrote on January 12:

> Your brother Stephen I am sorry to inform you is lying in Bellvue Hospital in this city very sick. He desires me to ask you to send him some pecuniary assistance as his means are very low. If possible, he would like to see you in person.

Cooper also telegrammed Henry Foster that Stephen "wishes to see you."[15]

Before either brother could respond, on Wednesday, January 13, an apparently improving Stephen was propped up in bed and fed some soup. Although he seemed cheerful as his wounds were being cleaned and his bandages changed, wordlessly he fainted dead away. By the time Cooper arrived for a visit, either later that day or the next, his body had already been moved to the morgue. The attendant, an old man smoking a pipe, told Cooper he could search among the coffins for his friend's corpse. Foster's coffin lay under three others. "Stephen is dead," Cooper telegraphed Morrison Foster on January 14 (sending Henry Foster a similar wire). "Come on."[16]

What killed Stephen Foster? Drinking too much and eating too little had reduced him to a medically tenuous state that hemorrhaging exacerbated. Foster may also have continued to drink, for alcohol was readily available at Bellevue. Lauderdale wrote to his sister of gin smuggled to a patient inside a roast chicken and of a whiskey bottle baked in a loaf of bread. The suddenness of Foster's death suggests, among other possibilities, a heart attack, heart arrhythmia, a stroke, or a pulmonary embolism, but the proximate cause of death is less important than its origins.[17]

If, as F. Scott Fitzgerald remarked, there are no second acts in American lives, it's true for very different reasons in this century from the last.[18] Many popular artists in the twentieth century—from Fitzgerald himself to Jack Kerouac, Hank Williams, Marilyn Monroe, Elvis Presley, Jean Michel Basquiat, and Kurt Cobain—have gone to pieces because they couldn't cope with success. More popular artists in the nineteenth century, such as Foster, Poe, and David Gilmour Blythe, fell apart because they couldn't deal with failure.

Poe didn't write books, it must be remembered—he wrote for and edited magazines. He had the foresight to recognize in its American infancy a great organ of popular culture. "The whole tendency of the age," he said, "is Magazine-ward."[19] But he paid a price for being ahead of his time, since the magazine industry was not yet sufficiently developed and organized to provide many of the people who stoked it with an adequate living. "The Raven" was as great a hit in 1845 as "Oh! Susanna" three years later, but neither stocked the larder for long.

In a similar fashion, Foster saw the potential of popular music, and staked his life and livelihood on it. But it would be another decade or so before pop music became so big a business that one could support a family solely by writing it. By then it would be too late for Foster, though not for George Cooper, who enjoyed a reasonably prosperous career writing lyrics for roughly as many songs—more than two hundred—as Foster paupered himself composing in a lifetime that wasn't half so long.

Aggravating their alcoholism, their precocious understanding and premature embrace of popular culture helped speed both Poe and Foster to early graves. What Baudelaire wrote of Poe applies to Foster as well with an uncanniness that Poe himself might have appreciated: "This death was almost a suicide, a suicide prepared for a long time."[20]

Henry Foster met Morrison Foster and Jane Foster on Saturday, January 16 at the St. Nicholas Hotel. It was probably Morrison who had notified Jane of her husband's hospitalization and/or death. At the undertaker's on Broome Street, she fell on her knees before Stephen's iron coffin, according to Cooper, "and remained for a long time."[21]

Henry reassured his sister Ann Eliza in a letter that they had "found everything connected with Stevey's life and death in New York much better than we expected." George Cooper was "as fine a little gentleman as I ever met," and Stephen "did not owe the Landlord a cent or any one else that we know of." Morrison paid Stephen's hospital bill, which amounted to $1.25, and collected his belongings. In addition to thirty-eight cents in pennies and scrip, Stephen's worn brown leather purse contained a piece of paper, an irregular trapezoid no more than three inches long that might have been torn from an account book or ledger, on which he had written in pencil a song title or fragment of a lyric, "dear friends and gentle hearts." [22]

The Adams Express Company—which had paid Andrew Carnegie his first-ever stock dividend, on ten shares bought with six hundred dollars borrowed from relatives and Tom Scott—transported Stephen Foster's body without charge. J. Edgar Thomson, formerly Brother William's boss and for a year longer Carnegie's, provided free passage on the Pennsylvania Railroad for the casket's escort. Fortunately, the main party missed the train and had to take a later one. On Sunday, January 17, while Henry, Morrison, and Jane awaited a connection in Philadelphia, the train carrying Stephen's body and his nephew, Edward Buchanan, derailed between Lewistown and Greensburg on a stretch of track Brother William had laid fifteen years earlier. A couple of cars plunged into the Little Juniata River, but the casket and Eddie were unscathed. [23]

Foster's funeral service was held where he had been baptized and wed, at Pittsburgh's Trinity Episcopal Church. The Rev. C. E. Swope concluded his eulogy with "the hope that the deceased had joined in singing an heavenly anthem which would never end." Henry Kleber conducted the choir in Edward Harwood's century old English setting of Alexander Pope's poem, "The Dying Christian to His Soul." No. 191 in the Episcopal hymnal, it concluded, "O Grave! where is thy Victory? / O Death! where is thy Sting?" Then, with "a power and pathos" a reporter for the *Pittsburgh Post* had "never heard excelled and rarely equalled," Kleber sang, in his tenor that had often joined Stephen's baritone, an aria from Handel's oratorio, *Joseph and his Brethren*. [24]

Kleber's program might have seemed inappropriately antiquated and High-Church to send off the composer of "Willie's Gone to Heaven" and "Tell Me of the Angels, Mother," but he selected shrewdly. The siren call of Pope's seraphs in Harwood's passage marked *affettuoso* ("Hark, Hark, Hark, Hark, they whisper, angels say, / Sister spirit, come away") could have been those gentle voices calling Old Black Joe. And Stephen Foster, like Joseph, had been a favored young son, a dreamer and interpreter of dreams, his music a coat of many colors, a crazy-quilt of blackface, bathos, and beauty. To wrench out of its original context an observation by Ralph Ellison, the "clashing of styles" in Foster's music, "interwoven of many strands," "sounded an integrative, vernacular note" that testified to Foster's "essential 'Americanness.' " But Stephen had not flourished in New York as Joseph had in Egypt, and he had become a burden to his older brothers rather than their savior.[25]

The funeral cortege proceeded to Allegheny Cemetery, where a brass band performed "Come Where My Love Lies Dreaming" and "Old Folks at Home." Henry Foster felt "completely overcome by *his loss* and the beautiful music," but relieved that his "anxiety" about his brother was *"now all over."* Buried to the left of his father (Dunning Foster already flanked their mother) in the family plot where Charlotte had been reinterred, little more than a mile from the cottage in which he had been born, Stephen was home at last.[26]

New York noted Foster's passing belatedly in scattered obituaries. *The Round Table*, a weekly cultural report, observed that

> Foster possessed a fund of plaintive melody which, had it coursed through more respected channels in art, might have given him a proud position as a composer. As it was, he can hardly be said to have been more than an amateur writer. We believe that he was only tolerably acquainted with the rules of composition, and in putting his ideas upon paper did so rather as a recreation, for he was engaged in some active mercantile calling until within a short period before his death.[27]

So much for America's first full-time professional songwriter!

Yet *The Round Table* obituary, which George Cooper mailed to Morrison Foster and called "the best article I have yet seen on your brother's death," also praised Foster's "true humor" and "genuine pathos": "While he made us laugh at his caricatures, he seldom failed to awaken our sympathies in Sambo's behalf." By infusing with "a poetic aroma" "the inodorous idea suggested by [minstrelsy's] aggravating twang and grotesque description," Foster elevated popular taste. He "revolutionized" and "emancipated" it when he forsook "negro melody" for "light-complexioned themes": "Here, after he had washed away a deal of absolute dirt and rubbish, Foster's mission as a reformer ended."[28]

In death just as when he still lived, Foster was trapped in a double bind: urged to abandon blackface and commended for doing so, yet remembered chiefly for the songs he had written before he "reformed." Even as *The Round Table* saluted Foster's shift from the plantation to the parlor, it wrote him off as "a name that was once a household word throughout our land," the "leading negro-melodist—the representative of a short-lived school of popular music peculiar to this country." Foster might as well have died a decade earlier.

Foster would have had to live a decade longer in order to write all the songs that were advertised as his "last" composition. Touting them as "the two songs Foster wrote just before he died," Horace Waters rushed out "When Old Friends Were Here," a collaboration with Cooper, and "She Was All the World to Me," with lachrymose lyrics by a Dr. Duffy. William Pond, as noted earlier, dusted off "Beautiful Dreamer" and claimed it was "composed but a few days previous to his death." P. A. Wundermann, a New York publisher who had not brought out anything by Foster while he was still alive, prefaced "Give This to Mother" with a note, "Three days after, he handed us *this his last composition* . . . death summoned him to his last account." John Mahon sold "Our Darling Kate," his tribute to the actress Kate Newton, to *Demorest's Illustrated Monthly*, which presented the piano accompaniment as "Foster's last musical effort" and claimed that its purchase had been "a very costly affair." [29]

Four years later, in 1869, George Cooper published "Dearer than Life!" in the same magazine. Foster had called on him "[s]ome three weeks before his death," Cooper explained. As they chatted, Foster improvised on the piano and, "dotting down this melody, presented it to me as a memento of our friendship." [30]

Cooper also warned readers of *Demorest's* that some of Foster's "posthumous compositions . . . were not genuine, but frauds upon a credulous public." One such fake was "Little Mac! Little Mac! You're the Very Man," a campaign song for George McClellan, who did not win the Democratic presidential nomination until seven months after Foster's death. Published in Philadelphia as Stephen's work and copyrighted in his daughter Marion's name, the song, which splices the tunes of "Nelly Bly" and "Better Times Are Coming" and sneers at Lincoln's "nigger proclamations," is now thought to have been the handiwork of his sister Henrietta. [31]

But amid the flotsam that appeared in the wake of his death surfaced several songs that were unquestionably Foster's—doubly so because he composed their words as well as their music. Since Foster wrote so few lyrics during the last couple of years of his life, relying not only on

Cooper but for one-shots on obscure versifiers such as Dr. Duffy, Francis D. Murtha ("Oh! Why Am I So Happy?"), and James D. Byrne ("There Was a Time"), it's tempting to read autobiographical significance into these ballads. An additional inducement is that all but one of them lack a harmonized chorus, so they seem intimate if not outright confessional. Going . . . going . . . gone is the explicit theme of "When Dear Friends Are Gone," "The Voices That Are Gone," "Tell Me Love of Thy Early Dreams" (which ends, "Gone, gone in the past"), and "Kiss Me Dear Mother Ere I Die." Yet the songs consider death with a kind of acquiescent calm.

The first of them to be issued, "Sitting by My Own Cabin Door," falls down the scale in its opening measures, but instead of languishing there, it picks itself up, dusts itself off, and bounces right back up an octave. "[N]ow I calmly glide through life," the singer observes, whereas only a couple of years earlier, in the desolated "Why Have My Loved Ones Gone?," it was the family that had abandoned him that "Calmly glid[ed] o'er a Summer sea," leaving the singer to moan alone.

> I've had my hours of grief and mirth,
>   And felt the tear drops pour,
> But nothing grieves me now on earth,
>   For I'm sitting by my own cabin door.

Not even the war disturbs the singer's equanimity ("No sounds of battle round me ring"), for he's found his way back home, even if only in his mind—or in the liquor grocery. Indeed, "Sitting by My Own Cabin Door" resembles James Taylor's "Carolina in My Mind," another song written by a substance abuser amid a fierce conflict, the Vietnam War.

John Daly brought out "Sitting by My Own Cabin Door" in April 1864. In May, along with "Give This to Mother," P. A. Wundermann published "When Dear Friends Are Gone," misspelling Foster's name as "Stephan" on the sheet-music cover. There are no "gentle hearts" in this song, but the title inevitably recalls the "dear friends" on the slip of paper in Foster's purse. Those friends have vanished, like the "early dreams" in "Tell Me Love of Thy Early Dreams," which Daly published in August. Both songs seem restrained; far from being tear-streaked, they're tempered by a stoic simplicity. "Tell Me Love of Thy Early Dreams" accepts with a philosophical shrug the fate that gave the younger Foster fits: "Know'st thou not that the fairest flowers, / Bloom but to decay?"

"The Voices That Are Gone," which William Pond published in 1865, is a lento waltz that proceeds almost in lockstep, one note for each syllable, until it suddenly swirls in a repeated melodic phrase: "Memory bri-ings the past befo-ore me"; "Then like mu-usic heard when drea-eaming." Music, memory and dreams dance off into the sunset as the "voices that are gone" summon the singer as sweetly as those "gentle voices" called Old Black Joe.

In 1869, Pond issued "Kiss Me Mother Ere I Die." It's a mere snippet of a song: The melody is only sixteen measures long, and the two verses repeat the same last four lines, as if they were a chorus. Appoggiatura, more frequently and emphatically notated than in any other song Foster wrote, wrack these four lines with sobs, yet this is not just another tearjerker. It is a prayer, as "Lifes chilling close is now drawing near," for forgiveness:

> I have been wayward unto thee
> Now I can feel it painfully
> Patient and kind were thou to me
> Kiss me dear mother ere I die.

Foster's five last songs compose an eloquent epitaph.

AFTERWORD

On June 1864, five months after Stephen Foster's death, Dan Rice's circus came to Washington. If *Dan Rice's Great American Humorist Song Book*, a songster he had published the year before, reflected his repertory, during his performances he may have sung either "Good Old Baltimore" or "A Peep at Washington" to the tune of "Oh! Susanna." And if Rice's own claims reflected the truth (a much bigger "if"), Abe and Mary Lincoln visited his tent.

Rice would fall in and out of debt, and off and on the wagon, many times during his long life, but he kept in touch with his boyhood friend Morrison Foster. When Rice was "saved" in St. Louis by the famed evangelist Dwight Moody in 1879, his conversion was front-page news. In 1884, Rice wrote Morrison from Florida, where he was lecturing and organizing Dan Rice Temperance Clubs. After his death in 1900, a vicious rumor circulated that the water pitcher on the podium from which Rice extolled abstinence was filled with gin. But Rice had always preferred bourbon.[1]

In August 1864, Andrew Kloman, a brilliant Prussian-born engineer, purchased the White Cottage and tore down what remained of the original frame house in which Stephen Foster had been born, replacing it with a brick mansion. He was then a competitor of Andrew Carnegie's, but soon he became one of his partners in the iron and steel conglomerate that would surpass even the Pennsylvania Railroad as a corporate colossus. Although eventually they had a bitter falling out, Carnegie praised Kloman's "good heart" and "great mechanical brain."[2]

On December 6 and 7, 1864, Louis Moreau Gottschalk played to an "immense crowd" in Pittsburgh. Gottschalk was at the height of his fame and proud of it. "For ten years," he crowed in his journal, "a whole generation of young girls has played my pieces."[3]

Unfortunately, young girls would soon be his downfall. Ten months later, while performing in the San Francisco Bay area, Gottschalk and a companion took two students from Oakland Female College on a carriage ride and didn't return to the campus until 2:30 in the morning. The scandal was such that Gottschalk fled to Latin America, never to return to his native land. In 1869, shortly after his left hand sounded the death-knell octaves in *"Morte!! (She Is Dead),"* one of his recent compositions, Gottschalk collapsed during a concert in Rio de Janeiro. He died weeks later of appendicitis.[4]

In February 1865, Martin Delany obtained an interview with Abraham Lincoln and proposed forming a separate army of blacks, commanded by black officers. Referred to Secretary of War Stanton, Delany became the first African-American field major commissioned in the United States Army. But by then the war was nearly over, and Delany ended up working with the Freedmen's Bureau in South Carolina. Delany seemed erratic in his later years as he veered from campaigning for a former Confederate general as governor of South Carolina to supporting an ill-fated back-to-Africa movement among frustrated Southern blacks. He died in 1885, still a proud and fascinating race man. "I thank God for making me a man simply," Frederick Douglass is purported to have said, "but Delany always thanks him for making him a *black man.*"[5]

In March 1865, Andrew Carnegie resigned from the Pennsylvania Railroad. In 1867, like Stephen Foster before him, he moved to New York City. He had learned in his adopted city the flinty lessons that Foster had spurned in his hometown, a cradle of America's Industrial Revolution and modern capitalism. While Stephen Foster felt that he had been booted from heaven shortly after his birth, Carnegie eventually acquired it on earth. Instead of building castles in the sky, he bought them in Scotland. Six years before his death in 1919, he wrote of his "deep regrets that one isn't allowed to live here in this *heaven on earth forever,* which it is to me." Ablaze with the flames of his own ovens and mills, Pittsburgh was, by comparison, "H——l with the lid off," but Carnegie always professed to be "in heart a devoted son" of the "dear old smoky" inferno. He persuaded Benjamin Harrison to appoint to the Supreme Court his fishing buddy George Shiras, the nephew of Stephen's friend Charles. When Morrison Foster published his brief biography and collection of his brother's songs, Carnegie ordered a hundred copies, reminding Morrison in a letter of the time "when you and I were boys."[6]

In 1867, Harriet Beecher Stowe, America's first millionaire novelist, bought a cottage and an orange grove in Mandarin, Florida, and began to spend the winters there. *Palmetto Leaves*, her best-selling collection of sketches and essays about Florida, helped popularize the state as a winter haven. Mandarin was on the St. John's River, but the Suwannee enjoyed its day in the Sunshine State when "Old Folks at Home" was declared Florida's official song in 1935.[7]

In 1869, grieving over the death of his young bride, George Cooper wrote a lyric that Henry Tucker, the composer of "When This Cruel War Is Over," set to music. "Sweet Genevieve" became by far the biggest hit of Cooper's long career, and enjoyed a revival of popularity shortly before his death in 1927. (It was sung as late as 1941 by seven nutty professors in Howard Hawks's screwball comedy, *Ball of Fire*.) Cooper had learned a lot from Foster, but not enough: he sold Tucker his interest in the song for five dollars.[8]

Lightning killed Henry Foster in 1870 when it struck the largest refinery tank at the Eclipse Oil Works, where he worked as a clerk, and ignited the worst conflagration in the Pittsburgh area since the great fire of 1845. One obituary called Henry "a quiet, unobtrusive gentleman" whom death overtook "where he was ever to be found—at his post."[9]

Morrison Foster, the sole surviving Foster brother, returned from Cleveland to Allegheny City that same year. Jane Foster came back from Greensburg about this time, too. Remarried to Matthew D. Wiley, a baggage and express agent she presumably met on the job, she worked as a telegrapher at the Pennsylvania Railroad's Allegheny depot. Jane's life remains as blank as many of the pages in the diary she kept sporadically in 1871 and all but abandoned by August. Even had she been so inclined, she might never have found time to write. For a while she supported not only her mother and her daughter, but also her widowed sister Agnes and *her* five children. Then she raised her daughter Marion's first two children, Jessie and Matthew Wiley Welsh, from infancy.[10]

Grandmother and grandchildren lived much of their lives together until one cold morning in 1903. The seventy-three-year-old Jane was dozing by the fire when a spark set her clothing aflame. Jessie, now Mrs. Alexander D. Rose, heard her screams and extinguished the flames, but it was too late: Stephen Foster's Jeanie died that night, having survived him by thirty-nine years.[11]

By then Jane and Marion had received more than $4,199.24 in royalties and reprint permissions from Stephen Foster's songs. In 1879, when the original twenty-eight-year copyrights of "Old Folks at Home" and other songs started coming up for optional fourteen-year renewals, Morrison negotiated three-cent royalties on Jane and Marion's behalf.[12]

Henrietta Foster Wick Thornton died in 1879, and Ann Eliza Foster Buchanan in 1891, leaving Morrison the only living Foster sibling. His first wife, Jessie Lightner, died in 1882, and in 1886 he married Rebecca Snowden, granddaughter of the mayor of Pittsburgh and editor-publisher of the *Mercury* who had presided with William Barclay Foster over the Fourth of July festivities in Lawrenceville during which Stephen Foster was born. In 1895, Morrison built a frame house in the Pittsburgh suburb of Edgewood, dubbed it the White Cottage and while living there composed his memoir of Stephen. When he died in 1904, his last word was "Ma!"[13]

Marion Foster, Stephen's daughter, married Walter Welsh, with whom she had three children. After living in St. Louis and Chicago, she returned to Pittsburgh and, in 1914, moved into the mansion Andrew Kloman had built on the site of the White Cottage. A local philanthropist had bought the house at 3600 Penn Avenue and given it to the city of Pittsburgh as a shrine to Foster, with the understanding that Marion and other descendants could live there as caretakers. (Caretakers were replaced by undertakers when the deteriorated home was eventually returned to the descendants of its donor and converted, in 1950, into a funeral home.)

Marion Foster Welch (as she preferred to spell her married name) lived in the Stephen C. Foster Memorial Home, joined by her children Jessie Rose and Matthew Welsh, until her death in 1935. "I've always had to live in turmoil & excitement & hard work," she wrote a friend, and poverty did indeed compel her to teach piano lessons well into her seventies. She became convinced that she had been cheated of property that was rightfully hers and tried repeatedly to recover it, nursing her resentment and expectations for decades. Oddly and pathetically, it wasn't her father's music she sought to reclaim. It was her grandfather's land, the site of the arsenal not far from 3600 Penn Avenue, which William Barclay Foster had sold to the government in 1814. After the arsenal was abandoned in 1901 and converted to peacetime uses, Marion insisted that her grandfather had donated the arsenal site as he had a nearby plot for a soldiers' cemetery, that the conditions of the nearly century-old gift had been violated, and that either the land or fifty thousand dollars (how she arrived at this figure is unclear) was due her. Like her grandfather before her, she sought redress again and again: before Morrison's death in 1904, in 1909, in 1925 and thereafter. And, like her grandfather, again and again she failed.[14]

Unfortunately for Marion, the most precious property she had inherited, Stephen Foster's music, was now in the public domain. And that's where it remains: not just every American's patrimony, but a global inheritance. The copyrights are registered in the soul Charles Ives wrote about in one of *his* most eloquent songs, "The Things Our Fathers Loved (And the Greatest of These Was Liberty)," which includes a melodic shard from "My Old Kentucky Home":

> I think there must be a place in the soul all made of tunes, of tunes of long ago. . . .[15]

Sources and Acknowledgments

Although their paths crossed, there's no evidence Stephen Foster actually encountered Louis Moreau Gottschalk or Martin Delany—and no hard proof he ever even met Andrew Carnegie, Dan Rice, or, for that matter, E. P. Christy. These and other characters appear in this narrative not only to provide contrast and context, dramatizing the alternatives and opportunities that confronted Foster, but also to enable us, by means of triangulation, to zero in on the elusive Foster, much of whose life is otherwise utterly blank. Mortified by his failed marriage, his drunkenness, and his sorry end, Foster's family—notably Morrison—destroyed most of his letters, of which fewer than thirty survive, while preserving all their own. (Jane Foster Wiley, on the other hand, seems to have destroyed nearly everything.) The ironic result is that the negligible lives of Stephen Foster's parents and siblings are better documented than his own.

Having burned many of Stephen's letters, Morrison Foster became the keeper of his brother's flame, and with Morrison's death, his daughter, Evelyn Foster Morneweck, picked up the torch. Not wishing to impugn the integrity of her father's memoir, Morneweck withheld some information from Foster's chief biographer, John Tasker Howard, and doctored it in her own *Chronicles of Stephen Foster's Family*. Her book and Howard's *Stephen Foster: America's Troubadour* are invaluable but occasionally misleading, so whenever possible I have double-checked everything they contain against the original documents and made silent (for the most part) emendations.

Most of those documents are in the Foster Hall Collection of the Center for American Music at the University of Pittsburgh. This extraordinary archive was established in 1931 by Josiah Kirby Lilly and subsequently moved from the pharmaceutical magnate's native Indianapolis to Pittsburgh. Formerly known as the Stephen Foster Memorial, the center makes its extensive holdings available to amateur enthusiasts as well as to scholars not just of Foster but of all American music. The center deserves support as far-ranging as its holdings.

No one who has read this book will mistake me for a scholar, certainly not for a musicologist. If the pluses of my broader historical and cultural inquiries are not outweighed by the minus of my musicological inexpertise, it's because I've depended heavily on and stolen shamelessly from Stephen Saunders and Deane L. Root's authoritative *The Music of Stephen Foster: A Critical Edition;* William W. Austin's *"Susanna," "Jeanie," and "The Old Folks at Home": The Songs of Stephen C. Foster from His Time to Ours;* Hans Nathan's *Dan Emmett and the Rise of Early Negro Minstrelsy;* Charles Hamm's *Yesterdays: Popular Song in America;* Eileen Southern's *The Music of Black Americans: A History;* and the late Vera Brodsky Lawrence's encyclopedic two-volume *Strong on Music: The New York Music Scene in the Days of George Templeton Strong.*

Robert McKnight and Charles Scully are Pittsburgh's George Templeton Strong and Philip Hone. Their surviving diaries, in the University of Pittsburgh's Darlington Memorial Library, richly deserve transcription and publication so that others can mine them as I have.

Further afield, I am indebted to a couple of recent biographies—Kenneth Silverman's of Edgar Allan Poe, Joan Hedrick's of Harriet Beecher Stowe—to a couple of older ones—the late Joseph Frazier Wall's of Andrew Carnegie and Alfred Frankenstein's compendious *William Sidney Mount*—and, as models of biographical craft, to everything Justin Kaplan has ever written.

This is a book about places almost as much as it is about people, so let me begin to thank the many others who have contributed to it in geographical order:

In Pittsburgh, Gerry and Bill Bair; Jean and Clarke Thomas; the late C. Rollo Turner; Dr. John Folmar; Lynne Wohleber of the Episcopal Diocese of Pittsburgh's Diocesan Historical Commission; Charles E. Aston, Jr. and the staff of the University of Pittsburgh's Darlington Memorial Library; Corey Seeman and the staff of the Historical Society of Western Pennsylvania's library; Louise Lippincott at the Carnegie Museum of Art; Kathie Logan and the staff of the Carnegie Library of Pittsburgh; Kathy Miller at the Center for American Music; and Fletcher

Hodges, Leona Sellin, and Don McGrath when it was still the Stephen Foster Memorial.

Elsewhere in Pennsylvania, Alfred Maass of New Milford, Robert B. Van Atta of Greensburg, Joan Weir of the Bradford County Historical Society, the Mifflin County Historical Society, Chambersburg's Kittochtinny Historical Society and Coyle Free Library, and the Pennsylvania State Library.

In Cincinnati, Laura L. Chace and the staff at the Cincinnati Historical Society Library, and Abby S. Schwartz at the Taft Museum.

For information about Foster and his relatives in the environs of Youngstown, Ohio, Carol Willsey Bell, Michael J. Hill, Marian Kutlesa, and James P. Struthers, whose great-great-great-grandfather took Stephen Foster hunting "for the possum and the coon."

In Bardstown, Kentucky, the indomitable Erleen Johnson.

In New York, Dr. Stuart Feder for his psychoanalytical insights; Dr. Daniel Roses for his medical insights; Thomas Hampson, Carla Maria Verdino-Süllwold and Maurice Peress for their musical insights; Louise Erpelding for her graphological insights; Peter Quinn, Ben Gerson, Stephen Holden, and Gregg Geller for their friendly advice and persistent encouragement; Michael Leonard of the Church of Jesus Christ of Latter-Day Saints and Peter Josyph for their helpfulness; and the staffs of the New-York Historical Society Library and the New York Public Library's Central Research Library, the Schomburg Center for Research in Black Culture, and the Performing Arts Research Center at Lincoln Center.

I'd also like to thank my former colleagues at *Newsday/New York Newsday* for allowing me to take a month's leave to conduct research.

In New Jersey, the public libraries of Hoboken and Montclair, and Montclair State University's Harry A. Sprague Library.

Among Foster family descendants, Richard K. Foster, Sarah Foster, Marshall Foster Reed, Jr., Arthur Hull, Gail Foster Hull Healy, and Bill Healy. And, for his help in contacting some of them, Douglas Jimerson.

For providing me with tapes of out-of-print recordings, I would like to thank James Isaacs, New World Records, and Kathy Kim of the Smithsonian Collection of Recordings.

And, for various and sundry, J. Hoberman, Mark Kaplan, Vance and Gerald Lauderdale, Ben Ortiz at Bridgeport's Barnum Museum, Fred Dahlinger at Circus World Museum, Philip B. Kunhardt III and Peter W.

Sources and Acknowledgments

Kunhardt, Anne Underwood for taking me into her home (where Foster lived in Hoboken), and Randy Richman (who owns it).

Among the scholars who unselfishly shared their expertise and research with an undocumented alien in the academic worlds of musicology and cultural studies are David Carlyon (Dan Rice); Dale Cockrell at Vanderbilt (G. W. Dixon); Eric Lott at the University of Virginia (blackface generally); Robert Levine at the University of Maryland (Martin Delany); N. Lee Orr at Emory (John Hill Hewitt); Tom Riis, director of the American Music Research Center, University of Colorado at Boulder (the theatrical history of *Uncle Tom's Cabin*); John Spitzer at the Peabody Conservatory (the publishing history of "Oh! Susanna"); and Samuel A. Floyd, director of the Center for Black Music Research, Columbia College-Chicago (African-American music).

I'll always be grateful to Ann Patty and Elaine Pfefferblit for their original enthusiasm for this project, and to Bob Bender, my editor, for picking up the ball without missing a beat.

The two people who made this book possible are Gloria Loomis, my agent, and Dr. Deane L. Root, curator of the Foster Hall Collection and director of the Center for American Music. I owe everything to her faith, his generosity and the tireless efforts of both of them on my behalf. Deane read every word of this book—even the thousands that eventually went by the wayside. The errors that remain are all mine.

Finally, I'd like to thank my mother, Roberta Emerson, for going to Bardstown with me; my mother-in-law, Jean O'Meara, for going to the Stephen Foster Memorial in White Springs, Florida, for me; and my wife and daughter for putting up with me (and Stephen Foster).

NOTES

In the footnotes that follow, FHC stands for the Foster Hall Collection in Stephen Foster Hall, at the Center for American Music, University Library System, University of Pittsburgh. Whenever possible, catalogue numbers, usually preceded by a "C" or "A," are also indicated.

INTRODUCTION

1. Archer Butler Hulbert, *Forty-Niners: The Chronicle of the California Trail* (Boston: Little, Brown, 1931), 260, 167–68.

2. *The Knickerbocker* 33, no. 3 (March 1849): 273–74; B. H. Mills, *The Temperance Manual* (St. Louis: Edwards & Bushnell, 1859), 164–66; "Editorial notes—Music," *Putnam's* 6, no. 32 (August 1855): 222; William W. Austin, *"Susanna," "Jeanie," and "The Old Folks at Home": The Songs of Stephen C. Foster from His Time to Ours*, 2d ed. (Urbana: University of Illinois Press, 1989), 31, citing Bayard Taylor, "The Magic of Music," *National Intelligencer*, reprinted from *Dwight's Journal of Music* 3 (1853): 131; Bayard Taylor, " 'Old Zip Coon' and 'Uncle Ned' among the Arabs," *American Musical Review and Choral Advocate* 3, no. 8 (1 August 1852): 118.

3. Thomas Collier Platt, *The Autobiography of Thomas Collier Platt*, compiled and ed. by Louis J. Lang (New York: B. W. Dodge & Co., 1910), 10.

4. "Jingle Bells or the One Horse Open Sleigh," *Popular Songs of Nineteenth-Century America*, ed. Richard Jackson (New York: Dover, 1976), 93–96.

5. *The Anti-Slavery Harp: Collection of Songs for Anti-Slavery Meetings*, ed. William W. Brown, 3d ed. (Boston: Bela Marsh, 1851), 9–10.

6. "Letter from a Teacher at the South," *Dwight's Journal of Music*, 26 February 1853, reprinted in *What They Heard: Music in America, 1852-1881, From the Pages of "Dwight's Journal of Music,"* ed. Irving Sablosky (Baton Rouge: University of Louisiana Press, 1986), 261.

7. Eileen Southern, *The Music of Black Americans: A History*, 2d ed. (New York: Norton, 1983), 226, 232, 237–38; Tom Fletcher, *100 Years of the Negro in Show Business* (New York: Burdge & Co., 1954; reprint, New York: Da Capo, 1984), 62, 69.

8. W. C. Handy, *Father of the Blues* (New York: Macmillan, 1941; reprint, New York: Da Capo, 1991), 35, 149.

9. Maurice Peress, "Dvorak and African-American Musicians, 1892–1895," *Black Music Research Bulletin* 12, no. 2 (Fall 1990): 26–27; Charles Ives, *Memos*, ed. John Kirkpatrick (New York: Norton, 1972), 115; Austin, 319; Stuart Feder, *Charles Ives: "My Father's Song"—A Psychoanalytic Biography* (New Haven: Yale University Press, 1992), 51.

10. Herbert G. Goldman, *Jolson: The Legend Comes to Life* (New York: Oxford University Press, 1988), 16, 367–68, 392–93.

11. Laurence Bergreen, *As Thousands Cheer: The Life of Irving Berlin* (New York: Viking, 1990), 40-41; Edward A. Berlin, *Ragtime: A Musical and Cultural History* (Berkeley: University of California Press, 1980), 66–67; John Kisch and Edward Mapp, *A Separate Cinema: Fifty Years of Black-Cast Posters* (New York: Farrar, Straus and Giroux, 1992), 28. Ellington's recording of "Swanee Shuffle" has been reissued on Duke Ellington and His Orchestra, *Jubilee Stomp*, Bluebird 66038–2). For "Swanee River Rhapsody," see John Edward Hasse, *Beyond Category: The Life and Genius of Duke Ellington* (New York: Simon & Schuster, 1993), 125.

12. Goldman, 110; Deena Rosenberg, *Fascinating Rhythm: The Collaboration of George and Ira Gershwin* (New York: Dutton, 1991), 39.

13. Hoagy Carmichael with Stephen Longstreet, *Sometimes I Wonder: The Story of Hoagy Carmichael* (New York: Farrar, Straus and Giroux, 1965), 132–134, 151.

14. "Old Black Joe" and "Old Folks at Home" have been reissued on *The Complete Tommy Dorsey, Volume VIII/1938–1939*, Bluebird AXM2–5586, and Tommy Dorsey, *Yes, Indeed!*, Bluebird 9987–1–RB, respectively. Waller's "Oh! Susanna" and Armstrong's "Old Folks at Home" are on Fats Waller, *Fine Arabian Stuff: Original 1939 Recordings*, Deluxe DE 601, and *The Mills Brothers 1936–1940*, Jazz Roots, CD 56072.

15. Syd Straw, *Surprise*, Virgin Records America 7 91266–1; Kate and Anna McGarrigle and other artists, *Songs of the Civil War*, Columbia CK 48607; Emmylou Harris, *Emmylou Harris & the Nash Ramblers at the Ryman*, Reprise 4–26664; Bob Dylan, *Good As I Been to You*, Columbia CK 53200; Thomas Hampson, *American Dreamer: Songs of Stephen Foster*, Angel CDC 0777 7 54621 2 8.

16. Neil Baldwin, *Edison: Inventing the Century* (New York: Hyperion, 1995), 97, 397–98; Walt Whitman, "Starting from Paumanok," ll.29–30, *The Collected Writings of Walt Whitman*, ed. Gay Wilson Allen and Sculley Bradley; *Leaves of Grass: A Textual Variorum of the Printed Poems*, ed. Sculley Bradley, Harold W. Blodgett, Arthur Golden and William White, vol. 2 (New York: New York University Press, 1980), 274–75. Unless otherwise noted, all subsequent references to the poetry and prose of Walt Whitman will be to the multi-volume New York University Press *Collected Writings*.

17. Unless otherwise noted, every citation in this book of a Stephen Foster song, its music or its lyrics is drawn from Steven Saunders and Deane L. Root's definitive *The Music of Stephen Foster: A Critical Edition*, 2 vols. (Washington: Smithsonian Institution Press, 1990). These citations will not be footnoted.

18. Mark Twain, *Adventures of Huckleberry Finn, Mississippi Writings* (New York: Library of America, 1982), 841.

19. "Note Book," *Chronicle of Higher Education* 43, no. 10 (1 November 1996): A41.

20. Jan DeGaetani, Leslie Guinn and Gilbert Kalish, *Songs by Stephen Foster,* 2 vols., Elektra/Nonesuch H–71268 and H–71333 (all of vol. 1 and portions of vol. 2 have been reissued as Elektra/Nonesuch 9 79158–2); Ken Emerson, "Stepping Out With Stephen Foster," *New York Times,* 3 December 1995.

21. Melvin Patrick Ely, *The Adventures of Amos 'n' Andy: A Social History of an American Phenomenon* (New York: Free Press, 1991), 45–46.

22. Whitman, "By Blue Ontario's Shore," l.219, *Collected Writings; Leaves of Grass,* 1: 204.

Chapter 1: American Eden

1. Samuel Jones, *Pittsburgh in the Year Eighteen Hundred and Twenty-Six, Containing Sketches Topographical, Historical and Statistical; Together With a Directory of the City, and a View of its Various Manufactures, Population, Improvements, &c.* (Pittsburgh: Johnston & Stockton, 1826; reprint, New York: Arno Press and the New York Times, 1970), 6–7, 11, 21.

2. Walter Blair and Franklin J. Meine, eds., *Half Horse Half Alligator: The Growth of the Mike Fink Legend* (Chicago: University of Chicago Press, 1956; reprint, New York: Arno Press, 1977), 3, 13–14, 257–59.

3. Samuel Jones, 39, 46; *Narrative of Richard Lee Mason in the Pioneer West in 1819* (New York: n.p., n.d.), 19–20; quoted in William Treat Upton, *Anthony Philip Heinrich: A Nineteenth-Century Composer in America* (New York: Columbia University Press, 1939), 21.

4. John Tasker Howard, *America's Troubadour,* rev. ed. (New York: Thomas Y. Crowell, 1953), 6. According to Evelyn Foster Morneweck, *Chronicles of Stephen Foster's Family* (Pittsburgh: University of Pittsburgh Press, 1944), 1: 10, it was 121 acres.

5. *Butler Sentinel,* 11 November 1826 (FHC, C390); *Pittsburgh Mercury,* 12 July 1826.

6. Morrison Foster, *Biography, Songs and Musical Compositions of Stephen C. Foster* (Pittsburgh: Percy F. Smith, 1896, reprinted as *My Brother Stephen* [Indianapolis: Foster Hall Library, 1923]), 18; Frank Donovan, *River Boats of America* (New York: Thomas Y. Crowell, 1966), 49; Louis C. Hunter, with the assistance of Beatrice Jones Hunter, *Steamboats on the Western Rivers: An Economic and Technological History* (Cambridge, Mass.: Harvard University Press, 1949; reprint, New York: Octagon, 1969), 13–17; Alfred A. Maass, "Brownsville's Steamboat *Enterprize* and Pittsburgh's Supply of General Jackson's Army," *Pittsburgh History* 77, no. 1 (Spring 1994): 22–29. A written copy of William Barclay Foster's appointment is preserved in his account book (FHC).

7. Frederick Marryat, *A Diary in America, With Remarks on Its Institutions,* ed. Sydney Jackman (New York: Knopf, 1962), 57.

8. *Pittsburgh Mercury*, 12 July 1826.

9. Ann Eliza Buchanan to Morrison Foster, 5 March 1872 (FHC, C461).

10. Robert Wray, "Abandonment of the Allegheny Arsenal," *Pittsburgh Gazette*, 12 January 1902 (FHC, C900); Stefan Lorant, *Pittsburgh: The Story of an American City*, rev. ed. (Lenox, Mass.: Authors Edition, Inc., 1975), 80; Ann Eliza Buchanan to Morrison Foster, 5 March 1872 (FHC, C461).

11. Eliza C. Foster, "Sketches and Incidents by Eliza C. Foster" (FHC, C386), 68, 120. This memoir survives in the form of a handwritten transcription by Eliza's adoring and extremely protective son, Morrison. The whereabouts of the original, if it still exists, are unknown, so the accuracy and completeness of the transcription cannot be verified. If not utterly trustworthy, it's a fascinating document nonetheless.

12. Morneweck, 1: 45; Annie Clark Miller, *Chronicles of Families, Houses and Estates of Pittsburgh and Its Environs* (Pittsburgh: n.p., 1927), 47–49.

13. Samuel Jones, 12.

14. Eliza C. Foster to Charlotte Foster, 2 November 1821 (FHC, C393).

15. William Barclay Foster, Jr.'s illegitimacy was a family secret that Evelyn Foster Morneweck, Stephen Foster's niece, insisted his biographer, John Tasker Howard, respect. Howard divulged the story in a rough draft of his uncompleted, untitled autobiography, a copy of which is now in FHC. It is corroborated by Morneweck's correspondence (Evelyn Foster Morneweck to William Thornton, 1 July 1944 [FHC]), and by her nephew, Richard K. Foster (telephone conversations, January 1996).

16. William Bender Wilson, "History of the Pennsylvania Railroad Company, with Plan of Organization, Portraits of Officials and Biographical Sketches— William B. Foster, Jr.," *Railroad Men's News* 9, no. 8 (August 1897): 260; Madeline Sadler Waggoner, *The Long Haul West: The Great Canal Era, 1817–1850* (New York: Putnam, 1958), 194; Harry Sinclair Drago, *Canal Days in America: The History and Romance of Old Towpaths and Waterways* (New York: Clarkson N. Potter, 1972), 141.

17. The following genealogical information, except where noted otherwise, is taken from Morneweck, 1: 2–5, and 2: 607–17 (appendix I).

18. Morrison Foster, 9.

19. Lorant, 540.

20. Leland D. Baldwin, *Pittsburgh: The Story of a City 1750–1865* (Pittsburgh: University of Pittsburgh Press, 1937; reprint, Pittsburgh: University of Pittsburgh Press, 1981), 148.

21. Morrison Foster, 10–11.

22. The following genealogical information is drawn from Morneweck, 1: 4–5, and 2: 616–17 (appendix I).

23. George Rogers Taylor, *The Transportation Revolution 1815–1860*, vol. 4 of *The Economic History of the United States* (New York: Holt, Rinehart and Winston, 1951), 66; Carroll W. Pursell, Jr., *Early Stationary Steam Engines in America: A Study in the Migration of a Technology* (Washington, D.C.: Smithsonian Institution Press, 1969), 47, 62–67; Morrison Foster, 11.

24. *The Franklin (County, Pa.) Repository*, 17 November 1807.

25. Eliza C. Foster, "Sketches," 1.

26. The ledger is in the collection of the Historical Society of Western Pennsylvania.

27. Leland Baldwin, 151–52; Eliza C. Foster, "Sketches," 53–54.

28. Eliza C. Foster, "Sketches," 15–16.

29. Michael Fitzgibbon Holt, *Forging a Majority: The Formation of the Republican Party in Pittsburgh, 1848–1860* (New Haven: Yale University Press, 1969), 18; Lorant, 70; Pursell, 62.

30. *The Honest Man's Extra Almanac, No. 1 For 1813* (Pittsburgh: R. & J. Patterson, 1813); Morneweck, 2: 6–7.

31. James Birtley McNair, *McNair, McNear and McNeir Genealogies: Supplement 1955* (Los Angeles: self-published, 1955), 235; James M. Riddle, *The Pittsburgh Directory for 1815 . . .* (Pittsburgh: James M. Riddle, 1815; reprint, Pittsburgh: Colonial Trust Company, 1905), 119.

32. Andrew Carnegie, *The Autobiography of Andrew Carnegie* (Boston: Houghton Mifflin, 1920; reprint, Boston: Northeastern University Press, 1986), 91–92; Annie Clark Miller, 101.

33. Eliza C. Foster, "Sketches," 143; Lavinia Day to Eliza C. Foster, 23 June 1822 (FHC, C606).

34. Eliza C. Foster, "Sketches," 143–44.

35. William B. Foster to Eliza C. Foster, 20 January 1826 (FHC, C594).

36. Morrison Foster, 19.

37. Morneweck, 1: 11.

38. Eliza C. Foster, "Sketches," 16.

39. Ibid., 84.

40. *Pittsburgh Mercury*, 12 July 1826.

CHAPTER 2: A FATHER'S FALL

1. John A. Stephens and William McClellan, "Henry Russell," *The New Grove Dictionary of American Music*, ed. H. Wiley Hitchcock and Stanley Sadie (London: Macmillan, 1986), 4: 11.

2. Howard, 115.

3. Eliza C. Foster, "Sketches," 142–46.

4. Ann Eliza Foster to William Barclay Foster, 23 March 1828 (FHC, C595); Morneweck, 1: 53.

5. William B. Foster, Jr. to William B. and Eliza C. Foster, 9 June 1838 (FHC, C664).

6. William B. Foster to William B. Foster, Jr., 16 June 1838 (FHC, C665).

7. Undated clipping from the *Pittsburgh Mercury* in William B. Foster's unpaginated scrapbook (FHC, C390). In the margin is written, in ink, "Oct. 23, 1822" and "by A. Sidney Mountain, Atty. at Law Pittsburgh." This quote differs somewhat from the version in Morrison Foster (9) that is repeated by Morneweck (1: 8) and Howard (9).

8. The best account of this complex affair is in Howard (10–11).

9. Undated newspaper clipping, labeled in ink: "Wm B. Foster's Speech in Penna Legislature," in William B. Foster's scrapbook (FHC, C390).

10. William B. Foster to William B. Foster, Jr., 1 June 1833 (FHC, C619).

11. Ibid., 14 July 1834 (FHC, C628).

12. Ibid., 4 April 1833 (FHC, C639), 31 May 1840 (FHC, C691), 30 March 1842 (FHC, C513). In this last letter, the words "filed my application for the benefit of the general Bankrupt law, it has occured to me that, since objections may be raised on the ground of my having" are crossed out in pencil, and the paragraph in which they appear is marked, also in pencil, "omit." Presumably the censor was Morneweck, who not only omitted this paragraph and all mention of its contents from her *Chronicles of Stephen Foster's Family,* but also may have withheld the original from John Tasker Howard, who does not refer to it in his biography, although he quotes (19) a subsequent passage from the letter.

13. Eliza C. Foster to William B. Foster, Jr., 14 August 1841 (FHC, C708).

14. Quoted in "Early Voting," *Pittsburg Leader,* 8 January 1888 (FHC, C900).

15. William B. Foster to Eliza C. Foster, 20 January 1826 (FHC, C594); Ian R. Tyrrell, *Sobering Up: From Temperance to Prohibition in Antebellum America, 1800–1860* (Westport, Conn.: Greenwood Press, 1979), 61; Lloyd L. Sponholtz, "Pittsburgh and Temperance, 1830–1850," *The Western Pennsylvania Magazine* 46, no. 4 (October 1963): 351; William B. Foster to William B. Foster, Jr., 8 February 1833 (FHC, C616).

16. Henrietta Angelica Foster Wick Thornton to William Foster Thornton, 7 June 1865 (FHC, C879). (This is a typed transcription, presumably by Evelyn Foster Morneweck.)

CHAPTER 3: DEATH AND THE MAIDEN

1. Eliza C. Foster, "Sketches," 96.

2. Ibid., 82–90.

3. William Evens's scrapbooks, vol. 1 (vols. 1–4 of these unpaginated scrapbooks compiled by a Pittsburgh music maven are preserved in Pittsburgh's Carnegie Library; vol. 5 is in the Darlington Memorial Library, University of Pittsburgh Libraries); David Barron, "Anthony Philip Heinrich," *New Grove Dictionary of American Music,* 2: 361; E. G. Baynham, "The Early Development of Music in Pittsburgh" (Ph.D. diss., University of Pittsburgh, 1944), 44–45; Richard C. Wade, *The Urban Frontier: The Rise of Western Cities, 1790–1830* (Cambridge, Mass.: Harvard University Press, 1959; reprinted as *The Urban Frontier: Pioneer Life in Early Pittsburgh, Cincinnati, Lexington, Louisville, and St. Louis* [Chicago: University of Chicago Press/Phoenix, n.d.]), 260.

4. Wade, 190–96; Charlotte Foster to William B. Foster, Jr., 13 June 1828 (FHC, C409).

5. Timothy Flint, *Knickerbocker* 2 (1833): 292, quoted in Daniel Aaron, *Cincinnati, Queen City of the West: 1819–1838* (Columbus: Ohio State University Press, 1992), 260.

6. Frances Trollope, *Domestic Manners of the Americans* (London: Century, 1984), 49–50.

7. Ibid., 147, 60. For more about the Bazaar, see Teresa Ransom, *Fanny Trollope: A Remarkable Life* (New York: St. Martin's Press, 1995), 54–63.

8. Morneweck, 2: 614 (appendix I).

9. Charlotte Foster to William B. Foster, 21 June 1828 (FHC, C407).

10. Ibid.

11. William B. Foster to Charlotte Foster, 26 June 1828 (FHC, C406).

12. Charlotte Foster to William B. Foster, 3 July 1828 (FHC, C405).

13. Charlotte Foster to Eliza C. Foster, 12 August 1828 (FHC, C402).

14. Charlotte Foster to William B. Foster, 26 September 1828 (FHC, C399).

15. Randall Capps, *The Rowan Story: From Federal Hill to My Old Kentucky Home* (Bowling Green, Ky.: Homestead Press, 1976), 25; Charlotte Foster to William B. Foster, 26 September 1828 (FHC, C399).

16. Charlotte Foster to William B. Foster, 26 September 1828 (FHC, C399); William B. Foster to Charlotte Foster, 7 September 1828 (FHC, C400).

17. Charlotte Foster to Eliza C. Foster, 12 October 1828 (FHC, C396). The Rowan who proposed marriage to Charlotte has previously been identified as Judge Rowan's youngest son, John Rowan, Jr. (Morneweck, 1: 65–66; Howard, 36–37; Capps, 20). But Charlotte described her suitor as "about 25" and "the eldest" of the two Rowan sons still at home (Charlotte Foster to Eliza C. Foster, 12 October 1828). Atkinson Hill Rowan, born in 1803, was 25 in 1828, while his younger brother John was 21. I am grateful to Erleen Johnson of Bardstown, Kentucky, for pointing this out in a 13 February 1996 telephone conversation.

18. Charlotte Foster to Eliza C. Foster, 27 October 1828 (FHC, C395).

19. Eliza C. Foster to Charlotte Foster, 4 October 1828 (FHC, C397); Morneweck, 1: 68.

20. A note by Evelyn Foster Morneweck (FHC, C443) indicates that this remark appears in a letter from Ann Eliza to Charlotte Foster in the summer of 1829. The letter's whereabouts are unknown.

21. Atkinson Hill Rowan to Ann Eliza Foster, 19 November 1829 (FHC, C451).

22. Ann Douglas, *The Feminization of American Culture* (New York: Knopf, 1977), 200–226; Twain, *Huckleberry Finn*, 725.

23. Harriet Beecher Stowe to Sarah Allen, 2 December 1850, Harriet Beecher Stowe Collection, University of Virginia, quoted in Joan D. Hedrick, *Harriet Beecher Stowe: A Life* (New York: Oxford University Press, 1994), 191–92.

24. Eliza C. Foster to William B. Foster, Jr., 14 May 1832 (FHC, A306).

CHAPTER 4: THE CRYING GAME

1. "There's nothing true but Heaven, a Favorite Song from Moore's Sacred Melodies Composed by O. Shaw," 6th ed. (Providence: published by the author, 1829). A lovely and faithful rendition of the song, by soprano Susan Belling and fortepianist Harriet Wingreen, appears on *The Flowering of Vocal Music in America, Volume 2*, New World Records NW 231.

2. For information about Shaw, see Charles Hamm, *Yesterdays: Popular Song in America* (New York: Norton, 1983), 95–99.

3. Ibid., 12; Austin, 146.

4. Charlotte's cousin, Caroline Grace, wrote her in April, 1828, that her (Caroline's) father "says he would give anything to hear you play the Swiss Waltz again" (Morneweck, 1: 50). For Moran, see J. Bunker Clark and Eve R. Meyer, "Peter K. Moran," *New Grove Dictionary of American Music*, 3: 269–70.

5. Hamm, *Yesterdays*, appendix 2, 481–82; Kenneth Silverman, *Edgar A. Poe: Mournful and Never-ending Remembrance* (New York: HarperCollins, 1991), 142; Edgar Allan Poe, "The Poetic Principle," *Essays, Miscellanies*, vol. 14, *The Complete Works of Edgar Allan Poe*, ed. James A. Harrison (New York: Crowell, 1902; reprint, New York: AMS, 1965), 282; S.A. Ferrall, *A Ramble of Six Thousand Miles Through the United States of America* (London, 1832), 10, quoted in Nicholas E. Tawa, *Sweet Songs for Gentle Americans: The Parlor Song in America, 1790–1860* (Bowling Green, Ohio: Bowling Green University Popular Press, 1980), 21.

6. Nicholas Tawa, *A Music for the Millions: Antebellum Democratic Attitudes and the Birth of American Popular Music* (New York: Pendragon, 1984), 2.

7. Scott C. Martin, "Leisure in Southwestern Pennsylvania, 1800–1850" (Ph.D. diss., University of Pittsburgh, 1990), 64.

8. See, for instance, Leonard L. Richards, *Gentlemen of Property and Standing: Anti-Abolition Mobs in Jacksonian America* (New York: Oxford University Press, 1971), 71–73; Dorothy Miller, *The Life and Work of David G. Blythe* (Pittsburgh: University of Pittsburgh Press, 1950), 42.

9. Whitman, "Starting from Paumanok," ll.258–59, "Song of Myself," l.478, *Collected Writings; Leaves of Grass*, 2: 288, 1: 30.

10. George Gershwin, introduction, *George Gershwin's Songbook*, ed. and revised by Herman Wasserman (New York: Simon & Schuster, 1941), unpaginated; Elizabeth Wurtzel, "Fight the Power," *The New Yorker*, 28 September 1992, 110.

11. *The Singer's Own Book: A Well-Selected Collection of the Most Popular Sentimental, Amatory, Patriotic, Naval, and Comic Songs* (Philadelphia: Key & Biddle, 1832), 6; *Grigg's Southern and Western Songster: Being a Choice Collection of the Most Fashionable Songs, Many of Which Are Original* (Philadelphia: J. Grigg, 1833), 174–75. The first president to be introduced by "Hail to the Chief," incidentally, was James Polk in 1845. See Austin, 129.

12. Daniel Drake, *Malaria in the Interior Valley of North America: A Selection from A Systematic Treatise, Historical, Etiological, and Practical, on the Principal Diseases of the Interior Valley of North America, As They Appear in the Caucasian, African, Indian, and Esquimaux Varieties of Its Population* (Cincinnati: 1850; reprint, ed. Norman Levine, Urbana: University of Illinois Press, 1964), 700; Whitman, *Democratic Vistas, Collected Writings, Prose Works 1892*, 2: 408.

13. Hamm, *Yesterdays*, 44–46.

14. Stephen Stills, "Love the One You're With," *Stephen Stills*, Atlantic SD 7202; The Isley Brothers, "Love the One You're With," *Timeless*, T–Neck KZ2

35650; Thomas Moore, *Moore's Irish Melodies with Symphonies and Arrangements by Sir John Stevenson, Mus. Doc. and Sir Henry Bishop* (Dublin: M. H. Gill & Son, 1891; reprint, Wilmington, Del.: Michael Glazier, Inc., 1981), 82–83.

15. W. C. Handy, "St. Louis Blues," on Bessie Smith, *The Complete Recordings, Vol. 2*, Columbia/Legacy C2K 4741; Hugh Prestwood, "Hard Rock Bottom of Your Heart," on Randy Travis, *No Holdin' Back*, Warner Bros. 9 25988–1; *Moore's Irish Melodies*, 234–35.

16. Saunders and Root, 1: 467.

17. Hamm, *Yesterdays*, 55–57, 59–60; Morneweck, 2: 495.

18. Hamm, *Yesterdays*, 54.

19. *Moore's Irish Melodies*, "Oh the Shamrock!," 114–15; Peter Quennell, introduction to *The Journal of Thomas Moore 1818–1841*, ed. Peter Quennell (New York: Macmillan, 1964), xi.

20. "A Talk About Popular Songs," *Putnam's Monthly Magazine of American Literature, Science and Art* 7, no. 4 (April 1856): 409.

21. George F. Root, *The Story of a Musical Life: An Autobiography* (Cincinnati: 1891; reprint, New York: Da Capo, 1970), 18.

22. Henry Russell, *Cheer! Boys, Cheer! Memories of Men and Music* (London: John Macqueen, 1895), 26–27; Austin, 17.

23. Russell, 60–61.

24. Charles Hamm, liner notes to Clifford Jackson and William Bolcom's *An Evening with Henry Russell*, Nonesuch H–71338.

25. John H. Hewitt, *Shadows on the Wall or Glimpses of the Past. A Retrospect of the Past Fifty Years* (Baltimore: Turnbull Brothers, 1877), 81–82.

26. James Fenimore Cooper, *Home as Found* (New York: Capricorn, 1961), 212.

27. Vera Brodsky Lawrence, *Strong on Music: The New York Music Scene in the Days of George Templeton Strong, 1836–1875*, vol. 1, *Resonances 1836–1850* (New York: Oxford University Press, 1988), 68.

28. Russell, 234.

CHAPTER 5: OUT OF THE MOUTHS OF BABES

1. Richard D. Wetzel, "Harmony Society," *New Grove Dictionary of American Music*, 2: 326.

2. Morrison Foster, 31. For Peters, see Richard D. Wetzel, *Frontier Musicians on the Connoquenessing, Wabash, and Ohio: A History of the Music and Musicians of George Rapp's Harmony Society 1805–1906* (Athens: Ohio University Press, 1976), 74–89.

3. Morrison Foster, 31. For "the centrality of music in nineteenth-century female education," see Julia Eklund Koza, "Music and References to Music in *Godey's Lady's Book*, 1830–77" (Ph.D. diss., University of Minnesota, 1988), 314.

4. Henrietta Foster to William B. Foster, 16 June 1832 (FHC, C615); Morneweck, 1: 77–79.

5. Morrison Foster, 24.

6. Verna L. Cowin, *Pittsburgh Archaeological Resources and National Register Survey* (Pittsburgh: Carnegie Museum of Natural History, Pennsylvania Historical and Museum Commission, Pittsburgh Department of City Planning, 1985), 322; Holt, 24–25; Charles Fenno Hoffman, *A Winter in the West* (New York: Harper & Bros., 1835), 1: 79.

7. For the source of Andrew Jackson's distrust—Buchanan's slippery role in the disputed presidential election of 1826—see Philip Shriver Klein, *President James Buchanan: A Biography* (University Park: Pennsylvania State University Press, 1962), 49–59.

8. William B. Foster to William B. Foster, Jr., 10 April 1833 (FHC, C639).

9. Eliza C. Foster to William B. Foster, 9 July 1833 (FHC, A307); Eliza C. Foster to William B. Foster, Jr., 7 July 1833 (FHC, unnumbered copy).

10. William B. Foster to William B. Foster, Jr., 14 July 1834 (FHC, C628).

11. Morrison Foster, 23–24.

12. William B. Foster to William B. Foster, Jr., 7 December 1834 (FHC, C631).

13. Ibid., 30 October 1835 (FHC, C637); William B. Foster to Eliza C. Foster, 10 March 1836 (FHC, C638); William B. Foster to William B. Foster, Jr., 20 February 1837 (FHC, C592); William B. Foster to William B. Foster, Jr., 5 May 1837 (FHC, C641); J. W. F. White, "The Judiciary of Allegheny County," *The Pennsylvania Magazine of History and Biography* 7 (1883): 161; William B. Foster to William B. Foster, Jr., 13 May 1838 (FHC, C661); William B. Foster to William B. Foster, Jr., 16 April 1838 (FHC, C660).

14. Eliza C. Foster to William B. Foster, Jr., 16 June 1837 (FHC, C647).

15. Morrison Foster, 27.

16. Eliza C. Foster to Henrietta Foster, 21 September 1836 (FHC, unnumbered).

17. George C. D. Odell, *Annals of the New York Stage* (New York: Columbia University Press, 1929–49), 3: 38; Philip B., Jr., Philip B. III and Peter W. Kunhardt, *P. T. Barnum: America's Greatest Showman* (New York: Knopf, 1995), 139–40.

18. Morrison Foster, 25–26.

19. Frances Trollope, 110–11.

20. "My Long-Tail Blue" (New York: Atwill's Music Saloon, ca. 1827), reprinted in S. Foster Damon, *Series of Old American Songs* (Providence: Brown University Library, 1936), song no. 14.

21. "Coal Black Rose" (New York: Firth & Hall, ca. 1827), reprinted in Damon, song no. 13.

22. The complete texts of most letters by Stephen Foster are reprinted in Calvin Elliker's *Stephen Collins Foster: A Guide to Research* (New York: Garland, 1988). Where possible, citations of Stephen Foster's correspondence will include, in addition to their FHC catalog numbers, the appropriate page in Elliker. This letter (FHC, A343) is reprinted in Elliker, 89.

CHAPTER 6: JUMPING JIM CROW

1. *The Singer's Own Book*, 6; *The Parlour Companion, or, Polite Song Book, Comprising a Choice Selection of Fashionable and Popular Songs* . . . (Philadelphia: A. I. Dickinson, 1836), 1: iii–iv.

2. Sidney Smith, *Edinburgh Review* 33 (January 1820): 79, quoted by John S. Whitley and Arnold Goldman in their introduction to Charles Dickens, *American Notes for General Circulation* (London: Penguin, 1989), 14.

3. Molly N. Ramshaw, "Jump, Jim Crow! A Biographical Sketch of Thomas D. Rice (1808–1860)," *The Theatre Annual* 17 (1960): 44; Iver Bernstein, *The New York City Draft Riots: Their Significance for American Society and Politics in the Age of the Civil War* (New York: Oxford University Press, 1990), 149.

4. Oscar Wegelin, "Micah Hawkins and The Saw-Mill," *The Magazine of History* 32, no. 127 (1927): 157, quoted in Vera Brodsky Lawrence, "Micah Hawkins, the Pied Piper of Catherine Slip," *The New-York Historical Society Quarterly* 62, no. 2 (1978): 143.

5. William J. Mahar, " 'Backside Albany' and Early Blackface Minstrelsy: A Contextual Study of America's First Blackface Song," *American Music* 6, no. 1 (Spring 1988): 9; Lawrence, "Micah Hawkins," 151. The song's lyrics are printed in full in Mahar, 3–4.

6. The text of "Massa Georgee Washington and General La Fayette" is reprinted in Lester S. Levy, *Grace Notes in American History: Popular Sheet Music from 1820 to 1900* (Norman: University of Oklahoma Press, 1967), 294–96.

7. Lawrence, "Micah Hawkins," 157–59.

8. Dixon's state of birth and considerable other background information about him are drawn from Dale Cockrell, *Demons of Disorder: Early Blackface Minstrels and Their World* (New York: Cambridge University Press, 1997), portions of which the author kindly showed me in manuscript.

9. Constance Rourke, *American Humor: A Study of the National Character* (New York: Harcourt Brace, 1931; reprint, New York: Harcourt Brace Jovanovich, 1959), 98.

10. Odell, 3: 472.

11. "Zip Coon" (New York: Atwill's Music Saloon, 1834); Damon, song no. 20. Eric Lott comments on the phallic imagery in blackface lyrics and sheet music illustrations in *Love and Theft: Blackface Minstrelsy and the American Working Class* (New York: Oxford University Press, 1993), 120–21.

12. The contemporary singer-songwriter Michelle Shocked underscores Disney's debt to blackface by appending a few choruses of "Zip-A-Dee-Doo-Dah" to her version of "Jump Jim Crow" on *Arkansas Traveler*, Mercury 314 512 101–2.

13. Howard L. Sacks and Judith Rose Sacks, *Way Up North in Dixie: A Black Family's Claim to the Confederate Anthem* (Washington, D.C.: Smithsonian Institution Press, 1993), 158.

14. Laurence Hutton, *Curiosities of the American Stage* (New York: Harper &

Bros., 1891), 122; Joseph N. Ireland, *Records of the New York Stage from 1750 to 1860* (New York: 1866; reprint, New York: Benjamin Blom, 1966), 1: 586; Robert W. Johannsen, *To the Halls of the Montezumas: The Mexican War in the American Imagination* (New York: Oxford University Press, 1985), 230–31; T. Allston Brown, *History of the American Stage* (1870; reprint, New York: Benjamin Blom, 1969), 101–2. Cockrell (*op. cit.*) explores Dixon's journalistic career in fascinating detail.

15. There are a number of conflicting accounts of the origins of "Jim Crow." The most convincing one is summarized by Ramshaw, 38–39.

16. Ramshaw, 40.

17. Robert Peebles Nevin, "Stephen C. Foster and Negro Minstrelsy," *Atlantic Monthly* 20, no. 121 (November 1867): 610.

18. Odell, 4: 233, 238–9; Ramshaw, 42–46; James H. Dorman, "The Strange Career of Jim Crow Rice," *Journal of Social History* 3, no. 2 (Winter 1969–70): 116; *The Knickerbocker* 16 (July 1840): 84, quoted in Ramshaw, 45.

19. "Zip Coon" (New York: J. L. Hewitt, ca. 1830–1835), in *Popular Songs of Nineteenth-Century America*, 260.

20. Martin, 49–50.

21. Sean Wilentz, *Chants Democratic: New York City and the Rise of the American Working Class, 1788–1850* (New York: Oxford University Press, 1984), 265; Bernstein, 149–50.

22. William B. Foster to William B. Foster, Jr., 1 October 1841 (FHC, C597).

23. Clarence Rollo Turner, "Black Pittsburgh: A Social History, 1790–1840" (A Census Compilation prepared for the Friday Evening Urban Historians Group, Department of History, University of Pittsburgh, March 1974), 3.

24. Victor Ullman, *Martin R. Delany: The Beginnings of Black Nationalism* (Boston: Beacon, 1971), 4, 256; Kwame Toure in an interview with the author, 1993; Martin Delany, "The International Policy of the World towards the African Race," reprinted in Frank A. Rollin [Mrs. Frances E. Rollin Whipper], *Life and Public Services of Martin R. Delany* (Boston: 1883; reprint, New York: Arno Press and the New York Times, 1969), 317–26.

25. Martin R. Delany, *Blake or The Huts of America,* ed. Floyd J. Miller (Boston: Beacon, 1970), 313; Ullman, 114; Elizar Wright to Beriah Green, 4 October 1833 (Elizar Wright Papers, Library of Congress), quoted in Ann Greenwood Wilmoth, "Pittsburgh and the Blacks: A Short History, 1780–1875" (Ph.D. diss., Pennsylvania State University, 1975), 74–75.

26. Ullman, 29–31; Wilmoth, 21–22.

27. Wilmoth, 122–23; William B. Foster to William B. Foster, Jr., 18 August 1838 (FHC, C667).

28. P. T. Barnum, *Struggles and Triumphs: or, Forty Years' Recollections of P. T. Barnum* (Buffalo: The Courier Company, 1882), 89–91.

29. "Jim Crow" (New York: E. Riley, n.d.), verses xxxvii–xxxix.

30. David R. Roediger, *The Wages of Whiteness: Race and the Making of the American Working Class* (London: Verso, 1991), 66.

31. "Long, Long Ago" (New York: Firth & Hall, n.d.), *Popular Songs of Nineteenth-Century America*, 119–20.

32. "Long Time Ago" (New York: Gèorge Endicott, 1836); Damon, song no. 18.

33. Noah M. Ludlow, *Dramatic Life as I Found It* (St. Louis: 1880; reprint, Bronx, N.Y.: Benjamin Blom, 1966), 533.

34. Barnum's account of this incident is drawn from *Struggles and Triumphs*, 106–9. Another, somewhat contradictory account appears in White, 176. The two versions are not reconciled in A. H. Saxon's definitive biography, *P. T. Barnum: The Legend and the Man* (New York: Columbia University Press, 1989), 82, 356 n. 11.

35. Cincinnati *Daily Times*, 23 October 1848, quoted in Charles R. Wyrick, "Concerts and Criticism in Cincinnati, 1840–1850" (Ph.D. diss., University of Cincinnati, 1965), 125; Marian Hannah Winter, "Juba and American Minstrelsy," *Chronicles of the American Dance*, ed. Paul Magriel (New York: Henry Holt, 1948), 47.

36. Dickens, *American Notes*, 139.

37. Winter, 45.

38. William S. McFeeley, *Frederick Douglass* (New York: Norton, 1991), 82.

39. Charles K. Jones and Lorenzo K. Greenwich II, eds., *A Choice Collection of the Works of Francis Johnson* (New York: Point Two Publications, 1982–1987), 1: 40–45, 106; Southern, 108–109.

40. See Jones and Greenwich, 2: 223; Southern, 113; Samuel A. Floyd, Jr. and Marsha J. Reisser, "Social Dance Music of Black Composers in the Nineteenth Century and the Emergence of Classic Ragtime," *The Black Perspective in Music* 8, no. 2 (Fall 1980): 175.

41. Robert Waln, Jr., *The Hermit in America on a Visit to Philadelphia* (Philadelphia: M. Thomas, 1819), 155.

42. For the suggestion that Johnson may have provoked "Jim Brown," and for this version of the lyrics, see Sam Dennison, *Scandalize My Name: Black Imagery in American Popular Music* (New York: Garland, 1982), 71–72.

43. Martin R. Delany, *The Condition, Elevation, Emigration and Destiny of the Colored People of the United States* (Philadelphia: 1852; reprint, New York: Arno Press and The New York Times, 1968), 83; *Pittsburgh Gazette*, 26 November 1830. For information about John Julius I am indebted to the research and generosity of the late Clarence Rollo Turner.

44. George G. Foster, *New York Gaslight and Other Urban Sketches*, ed. and introduced by Stuart M. Blumin (Berkeley: University of California Press, 1990), 141–45; David Crockett [pseud.], *An Account of Col. Crockett's Tour to the North and Down East . . .* , 10th ed. (Philadelphia: E. L. Carey and A. Hart, 1837), 48.

45. Martha B. Pike, "Catching the Tune: Music and William Sidney Mount," in *Catching the Tune: Music and William Sidney Mount*, ed. Janice Gray Armstrong (Stony Brook, N.Y.: The Museums at Stony Brook, 1984), 13; Thomas F.

De Voe, *The Market Book* (1862; reprint, New York: Burt Franklin, 1969), 344, quoted in Lott, 41–43.

46. Mark Twain, *Life on the Mississippi, Mississippi Writings*, 244.

47. Robert C. Toll, *Blacking Up: The Minstrel Show in Nineteenth-Century America* (New York: Oxford University Press, 1974), 27, 44; Dennison, 27, 48.

48. Eliza C. Foster, "Sketches and Incidents," 139; Evelyn Foster Morneweck to Helen Mistrik, 5 August 1939 (FHC); Morrison Foster, 49–50; Morneweck, 1: 103.

49. Morneweck, 1: 103; William B. Foster to William B. Foster, Jr., 14 July 1834 (FHC, C628); William B. Foster to Henrietta Foster Wick, 9 April 1842 (FHC, A313).

50. This verse is reprinted in Levy, 91.

51. *An Account of Col. Crockett's Tour*, 33; Charles K. Wolfe, "Crockett and Nineteenth-Century Music," in *Crockett at Two Hundred*, ed. Michael A. Lofaro and Joe Cummings (Knoxville: University of Tennessee Press, 1989), 83; *Crockett's Free-and-Easy Song Book: Comic, Sentimental, Amatory, Sporting, African, Scotch, Irish, Western and Texian, National, Military, Naval, and Anacreontic . . .* (Philadelphia: Kay & Troutman, 1846).

52. Blair and Meine, 62; *The Comic Tradition in America: An Anthology of American Humor*, ed. Kenneth S. Lynn (Garden City, N.Y.: Anchor, 1958), 155; David Crockett, *A Narrative of the Life of David Crockett* (Philadelphia: E. L. Carey and A. Hart, 1834; reprint, Lincoln: University of Nebraska Press, 1987), 195–200.

53. "Dan Rice's Impromptu," *Dan Rice's Great American Humorist Song Book* (n.p., 1863), 31–32; George G. Foster, *New York Gaslight and Other Urban Sketches*, 170.

CHAPTER 7: "I PREFER NOT TO"

1. For information about Struthers I am indebted to the research and assistance of James P. Struthers, his great-great-great grandson, and Marian Kutlesa, secretary of the Struthers Historical Society Museum. A transcript of John Struthers, Jr.'s application for a pension (General Services Administration, National Archives and Records Service, File Designation John Struthers R–18262) was especially helpful.

2. William Galbraith-Smith to Evelyn Foster Morneweck, 25 October 1939 (FHC), quoting the 14 January 1846 *Western Reserve Chronicle*; William B. Foster to William B. Foster, Jr., 24 March 1840 (FHC, C689); Morneweck, 1: 164–66; Morrison Foster, 50–51; William B. Foster to Morrison Foster, 12 January 1840 (FHC, C685).

3. Henrietta Foster Wick to William B. Foster, Jr., 29 September 1839 (FHC, C683).

4. Morrison Foster, 50–51.

5. William B. Foster to William B. Foster, Jr., 14 August 1837 (FHC, C651).

6. Ibid., 17 February 1841 (FHC, C699), 27 February 1841 (FHC, C702).

7. Ibid., 23 October 1839 (FHC, C684), 24 March 1840 (FHC, C689).

8. Eliza C. Foster to William B. Foster, Jr., 7 August 1840 (FHC, C692).

9. James Buchanan to James Clark, 31 January 1839 (FHC, C738).

10. William B. Foster to Morrison Foster, 12 January 1840 (FHC, C685).

11. Eliza C. Foster to Morrison Foster, 21 January 1840 (FHC, C686).

12. *Pennsylvania Reporter*, 21 January 1840; Charles B. Scully, Journal No. 6 (MS diary for the year 1843; Darlington Memorial Library, University of Pittsburgh Libraries), 26 May 1843, 111; Wyrick, 129–30.

The Rainers were not the first act billed as the Tyrolese Minstrels to tour Pennsylvania. The duo of Carl and Friedel Schnepf preceded them in the winter of 1832–33. Tarrying in Pittsburgh, one of them gave guitar lessons to Sarah Collins, for whose dead brother Stephen Collins Foster had been named. A transcription of an 11 February 1833 letter relating this, from Mary Anderson in Pittsburgh to Espy L. Anderson in Bedford, Pa., is pasted into the copy in Pittsburgh's Carnegie Library of Sarepta Kussart's *The Early History of the Fifteenth Ward of the City of Pittsburgh* (Bellevue/Pittsburgh: Suburban Printing, 1925). See also, Evens's scrapbook no. 1.

13. When the mayor of Philadelphia insisted that blacks not be admitted to a Hutchinsons concert because their antislavery anthems might provoke a disturbance, the singers refused and left town. See Hamm, *Yesterdays*, 153.

14. Hans Nathan, *Dan Emmett and the Rise of Early Negro Minstrelsy* (Norman: University of Oklahoma Press, 1962), 158; John Anthony Stephens, *Henry Russell in America: Chutzpah and Huzzah* (Ph.D. diss., University of Illinois at Urbana-Champaign, 1975), 88; Robert B. Winans, "Early Minstrel Show Music 1843–1852," *Musical Theater in America: Papers and Proceedings of the Conference on the Musical Theater in America*, ed. Glenn Loney (Westport, Conn.: Greenwood Press, 1984), 80; *Cincinnati Atlas*, 5 May 1849, reprinted in Wyrick, 120.

15. The account of Athens Academy is derived from Louise Welles Murray's *A History of Old Tioga Point and Early Athens Pennsylvania* (Athens, Pa.: n.p., 1908), 548–53; her daughter, Elsie Murray's *Stephen C. Foster at Athens: His First Composition* (Athens, Pa.: Tioga Point Museum, 1941), 5–18; and R. M. Welles's "The Old Athens Academy," *Bradford County Historical Society Annual* (Towanda, Pa.), no. 5 (1911): 22–36.

16. A. H. Kingsbury, "The Old Towanda Academy," *Bradford County Historical Society Annual* (Towanda, Pa.), no. 4 (1910): 16, 19.

17. Stephen Foster to William B. Foster, Jr., 9 November 1840 (FHC, A344; Elliker, 89–90).

18. Stephen Foster to William B. Foster, Jr., undated (FHC, A345; Elliker, 90).

19. Welles, 32–33.

20. Kingsbury, 21.

21. Because Stephen Foster's letter from Towanda is undated, it can't be synchronized with Henry's whereabouts exactly.

22. Stephen Foster to William B. Foster, Jr., undated (FHC, A345; Elliker, 90).

23. Welles, 34; Elsie Murray, 6.

24. Saunders and Root, 2: 494.

25. Morrison Foster, 32.

26. Elsie Murray, 10.

27. Stephen Foster to William B. Foster, Jr., 24 July 1841 (FHC, A346; Elliker, 91).

28. Ibid., 28 August 1841 (FHC, A347; Elliker, 92).

29. Eliza C. Foster to William B. Foster, Jr., 14 August 1841 (FHC, C708).

30. William B. Foster to William B. Foster, Jr., 3 September 1841 (FHC, A315).

31. Isaac Harris, *Harris' Business Directory of the Cities of Pittsburgh & Allegheny* (Pittsburgh: A. A. Anderson, 1844), 19, and an advertisement on an unnumbered page; Eliza C. Foster to William B. Foster, Jr., 7 August 1840 (FHC, C692); William B. Foster to William B. Foster, Jr., 15 May 1841 (FHC, C706), 3 September 1841 (FHC, A315).

32. Stephen Foster to William B. Foster, Jr., 28 August 1841 (FHC, A347; Elliker, 93); William B. Foster to William B. Foster, Jr., 23 October 1839 (FHC, C684); Herman Melville, "Bartleby, the Scrivener," *Pierre, Israel Potter, The Piazza Tales* . . . (New York: Library of America, 1984), 645.

CHAPTER 8: O TEMPERANCE, O MORES!

1. Charles Cist, *Cincinnati in 1841: Its Early Annals and Future Prospects* (Cincinnati: Charles Cist, 1841), 237.

2. Ullman, 26, 40–45.

3. Russell, 178–80.

4. John F. Coleman, *The Disruption of the Pennsylvania Democracy 1848–1860* (Harrisburg, Pa.: The Pennsylvania Historical and Museum Commission, 1975), 13, 159; William B. Foster to William B. Foster, Jr., 16 November 1840 (FHC, C696); White, 178–79; Sponholtz, 351; William B. Foster to William B. Foster, Jr., 30 March 1841 (FHC, C703).

5. William B. Foster to William B. Foster, Jr., 22 November 1841 (FHC, C602).

6. Clipping dated 25 January 1842 in William B. Foster's scrapbook (FHC, C390); William B. Foster to William B. Foster, Jr., 30 March 1842 (FHC, C513).

7. Judge John E. Parke, *Recollections of Seventy Years and Historical Gleanings of Allegheny, Pennsylvania* (Boston: Rand, Avery, 1886), 364; *Pittsburgh Daily Morning Post*, 11 and 13 January 1843; Scully (10 January 1843), 9.

8. William B. Foster to William B. Foster, Jr., 30 March 1842 (FHC, C513).

9. J. P. Carter, "Ole Pee Dee" (Boston: Keith's Publishing House, 1844), reprinted in Nathan, 469–70.

10. Dickens, *American Notes*, 200; Charles Dickens to John Forster, 1, 2, 3 and 4 April 1842, *The Letters of Charles Dickens* (Pilgrim Edition), ed. Madeline House, Graham Story, Kathleen Tillotson; associate ed., Noel C. Peyrouton, vol. 3 (1842–1843) (Oxford: Clarendon Press, 1974), 178.

11. Eliza C. Foster to Henrietta Foster Wick, 14 February 1842 (FHC, un-numbered); Eliza C. Foster to Henrietta Foster Wick, 5 March 1842 (FHC, C518); Eliza C. Foster to Henrietta Foster Wick, 9 April 1842 (FHC, A304); Frederick Douglass, *My Bondage and My Freedom* (Miller, Orton & Mulligan, 1855; reprint, New York: Dover, 1969), 63.

12. Eliza C. Foster to William B. Foster, 11 March 1842 (FHC, C517).

13. Eliza C. Foster to William B. Foster, Jr., 6 May 1842 (FHC, C509).

14. Ibid., 3 September 1842 (FHC, C499).

15. William B. Foster to Henrietta Foster Wick, 29 October 1842 (FHC, A314).

16. Eliza C. Foster to William B. Foster, Jr., 14 August 1841 (FHC, C708); Eliza C. Foster to William B. Foster, Jr., 16 September 1841 (FHC, C596).

17. Tyrrell, 160–63; Sponholtz, 355.

18. Fredrika Bremer, *The Homes of the New World: Impressions of America* (New York: Harper Bros., 1853; reprint, New York: Negro Universities Press, 1968), 1: 508.

19. William B. Foster to William B. Foster, Jr., 3 September 1841 (FHC, A315); "King Alcohol," performed by the New Hutchinson Family Singers on *Homespun America*, Vox Box SYBX 5309.

20. Ullman, 27.

21. Morneweck, 1: 261; Wyrick, 134–35.

22. *Pittsburgh Daily Morning Post*, 11 May 1843; Waln, 155; Southern, 110; Jones and Greenwich, 2: 210–14.

23. This account of the melee in Allegheny and its aftermath is drawn from the *Pittsburgh Daily Morning Post*, 18–20 May 1843; Scully (18 May 1843), 107; Evens's scrapbook no. 1; Morneweck, 1: 261–64; Parke, 76–77; and Wilmoth, 23.

24. Scully (16–19 May 1843), 104–8.

25. Jones and Greenwich, 2: 232 (citing Philadelphia *Public Ledger*, 10 April 1844), 75, 37; Southern, 110.

26. Morrison Foster, 33.

27. Jones and Greenwich, 2: 163 (citing Samuel Manning Welch, *Home History: Recollections of Buffalo During the Decade From 1830 to 1840, or Fifty Years Since*); Dan Emmett, "The Fine Old Colored Gentleman" (Boston: Chas. H. Keith, ca. 1843), reprinted in Dennison, 99–100. An abridged version of the song is performed on *The Early Minstrel Show*, New World Records NW 338.

CHAPTER 9: "GENUINE NEGRO FUN"

1. Max Maretzek, *Crotchets and Quavers or Revelations of an Opera Manager in America* (New York: S. French, 1855; reprint, New York: Da Capo, 1966), 18; Lawrence, *Strong on Music*, 1: 157; Nathan, 158.

2. Nathan, 115–17; Robert E. McDowell, "Bones and the Man: Toward a History of Bones Playing," *Journal of American Culture* 5, no. 1 (Spring, 1982): 38.

3. Winans, 73.

4. Gershwin (unpaginated).

5. Karen Linn, *That Half-Barbaric Twang: The Banjo in American Popular Culture* (Urbana: University of Illinois Press, 1994), 2, 15; John Dixon Long, *Pictures of Slavery* . . . (Philadelphia: n.p., 1857), 17, quoted in Southern, 202; "Enthusiastic Eloquence," *The Works of Mark Twain, Early Tales & Sketches*, vol. 2 (1864–1865), ed. Edgar Marquess Branch and Robert H. Hirst (Berkeley: University of California Press, 1981): 235.

6. Deena Rosenberg, 26–27; Nathan, 120; Herman Melville, *Moby-Dick, Redburn, White-Jacket, Moby-Dick* (New York: Library of America, 1983), 1107–11; Mel Watkins, *On the Real Side: Laughing, Lying, and Signifying—The Underground Tradition of African-American Humor That Transformed American Culture, From Slavery to Richard Pryor* (New York: Touchstone, 1995), 309–14.

7. "American Popular Ballads," *The Round Table* 1, no. 8 (6 February 1864): 117.

8. Lawrence, *Strong on Music*, 1: 232; *Cincinnati Atlas*, 1 February 1844, reprinted in Wyrick, 120.

9. H. P. Grattan, "The Origins of the Christy's Minstrels," *The Theatre: A Monthly Review of the Drama, Music and the Fine Arts*, 1 March 1882, 130–31; Carl Wittke, *Tambo and Bones: A History of the American Minstrel Stage* (Durham, N.C.: Duke University Press, 1930), 215; "Memoir," *Christy's Plantation Melodies* (Philadelphia: Fisher & Brother, 1854), v–vi.

10. Lawrence, *Strong on Music*, 1: 415; Wyrick, 120; *Cincinnati Gazette*, 26 August 1843, quoted in Wyrick, 117–18; Baynham, 230; Edward LeRoy Rice, *Monarchs of Minstrelsy, from "Daddy" Rice to Date* (New York: Kenny, 1911), 19–20; Nathan, 151–52.

11. New York *Herald*, 29 April 1846, quoted in Lawrence, *Strong on Music*, 1: 417; Nathan, 128–29; Tawa, *Sweet Songs*, 176.

12. Tawa, *Sweet Songs*, 73, 93–99; Winans, 83–93; *The Autobiography of Mark Twain*, ed. Charles Neider (New York: Harper Perennial, 1990), 61; Hamm, *Yesterdays*, 126, 136–38.

13. Nathan, 120, 130–31; Wyrick, 120.

14. "Miss Lucy Long" (New York: James L. Hewitt, 1842); Damon, song no. 31.

15. Ivor Guest, *Fanny Elssler* (Middletown, Conn.: Wesleyan University Press, 1970), 73–76, 133–54.

16. James Sanford, "Miss Lucy Neale" (Philadelphia: A. Fiot, 1844); Damon, song no. 40. Both "Miss Lucy Long" and "Miss Lucy Neale" are performed on *The Early Minstrel Show*, where "Lucy Neal" is credited to J. P. Carter.

17. Douglas, 254.

18. Meade Minnigerode, *The Fabulous Forties* (New York: Putnam's, 1924),

127, quoted in Wittke, 51; P. T. Barnum to *New York Ledger* publisher Robert Bonner, 5 February 1862, *Selected Letters of P. T. Barnum*, ed. A.H. Saxon (New York: Columbia University Press, 1983), 116; Matilda Despard, "Music in New York Thirty Years Ago," *Harper's New Monthly Magazine* 67, no. 237 (June 1878): 120. The cover of *Christy's Plantation Melodies* credits Christy as the author of "Lucy Long" and "Lucy Neal," and as the "originator of Ethiopian minstrelsy."

Minstrelsy's considerable following among the middle class, families and females is scanted in the otherwise excellent sociocultural studies, David R. Roediger's *The Wages of Whiteness: Race and the Making of the American Working Class* and Eric Lott's *Love and Theft: Blackface Minstrelsy and the American Working Class.*

19. Grattan, 131; Mark Twain to Tom Hood and George Routledge and Sons, 10 March 1873, reprinted in Gustavus D. Pike, *The Singing Campaign for Ten Thousand Pounds; or, The Jubilee Singers in Great Britain*, rev. ed. (New York: American Missionary Society, 1875), 14–15, quoted in Shelley Fisher Fishkin, *Was Huck Black? Mark Twain and African-American Voices* (New York: Oxford University Press, 1993), 92.

20. Nathan, 120, citing playbills of Brinley Hall (Worcester, Mass., March 20, 21, 22, 1843); *Christy's Plantation Melodies*, vi.

21. Cockrell; Ramshaw, 46; Nathan, 110–11, 71 n. 3 (citing the *New York Clipper*, 13 April 1878), 115; Linn, 2.

22. Pike, "Catching the Tune: Music and William Sidney Mount," *Catching the Tune*, 33; Alfred Frankenstein, *William Sidney Mount* (New York: Harry N. Abrams, 1975), 141 (quoting a January 1846 diary entry) and 61 (quoting a 17 January 1841 letter from Robert Mount to W. S. Mount).

23. "Black folk sang the minstrel songs just as did the whites," according to Eileen Southern "Here was a kind of curious interaction. The minstrel songs, originally inspired by genuine slave songs, were altered and adapted by white minstrels to the taste of white America in the nineteenth century, and then were taken back again by black folk for further adaptation to their musical taste. Thus the songs passed back into the folk tradition from which they had come" (95).

24. "A Scholar Finds Huck Finn's Voice in Twain's Writing About a Black Youth," *New York Times*, 7 July 1992; Fishkin, 4–5.

25. Twain's 29 November 1874 *New York Times* article is both reproduced in facsimile and reprinted in the text of Fishkin, 21 and 252, respectively.

26. Southern, 115; *Popular Songs of Nineteenth-Century America*, 110–14, 273–74; Robert A. Gerson, *Music in Philadelphia* (Philadelphia: University of Pennsylvania Press, 1940; reprint, Westport, Conn.: Greenwood Press, 1970), 110.

27. Alain Locke, *The Negro and His Music* (Washington, D.C.: The Associates in Negro Folk Education, 1936; reprint, New York: Arno Press and The New York Times, 1969), 90.

CHAPTER 10: PIGEON WING AND MOONBEAMS

1. George H. Thurston, *Allegheny County's Hundred Years* (Pittsburgh: A. A. Anderson & Son, 1888), 306; Erasmus Wilson, *History of Pittsburg* (Chicago: H. R. Cornell, 1898), 868. Most of the information in this biographical sketch of Kleber is drawn from Jean W. Thomas's unpublished 1991 paper, "Henry Kleber: Musical Entrepreneur of Nineteenth Century Pittsburgh," which the author graciously lent me. A copy is in the Historical Society of Western Pennsylvania.

2. Robert McKnight, diaries, vol. 2, 13 March 1847 (manuscript diaries in the Darlington Memorial Library, University of Pittsburgh Libraries).

3. Samuel Fahnestock, *Fahnestock's Pittsburgh Directory for 1850; Containing the Names of the Inhabitants of Pittsburgh, Allegheny, & Vicinity, Their Occupation, Places of Business and Dwelling Houses; also, a List of the Public Offices, Banks, &c* (Pittsburgh: George Parkin & Co., 1850), 53 and unpaginated advertisement.

4. Thomas, 11; undated clipping in William Evens's scrapbook no. 1.

5. Morrison Foster, 31.

6. Henry Ward Beecher, *Seven Lectures to Young Men, on Various Important Subjects; Delivered Before the Young Men of Indianapolis, Indiana, During the Winter of 1843–4* (Indianapolis: Thomas B. Cutler, 1844), 193, quoted in Karen Halttunen, *Confidence Men and Painted Women: A Study of Middle-class Culture in America, 1830–1870* (New Haven: Yale University Press, 1982), 23.

7. This account of Dan Rice's early career is drawn from David James Carlyon, "Dan Rice's Aspirational Project: The Nineteenth-Century Circus Clown and Middle-Class Formation" (Ph.D. diss., Northwestern University, 1993); John C. Kunzog, *The One-Horse Show: The Life and Times of Dan Rice, Circus Jester and Philanthropist—A Chronicle of Early Circus Days* (Jamestown, N.Y.: John C. Kunzog, 1962), 1–37; and John Culhane, *The American Circus: An Illustrated History* (New York: Henry Holt/Owl, 1991), 47–68. Carlyon was extremely generous with his time and advice, correcting many errors.

8. Dan Rice to Morrison Foster, 17 June 1843 (FHC).

9. Odell, 4: 420; Carlyon, 49–53, 314–15; Twain, *Huckleberry Finn*, 770–71; Culhane, 47–48.

10. Morrison Foster, 36.

11. Jones and Greenwich, 1: 18.

12. *Cincinnati Daily Times*, 20 December 1844, reprinted in *The People's Paper*, 21 December 1844, and quoted in Wyrick, 26.

13. The catalogue of river craft comes from Frank Donovan, *River Boats of America* (New York: Thomas Y. Crowell, 1966), 7.

14. Scully (21 July and 3 August 1843), 144–45, 176–77. Examples of serenading's popularity in other cities are given in Tawa, *Sweet Songs*, 28.

15. *Pittsburgh Morning Chronicle*, 6 May 1842, quoted in Martin, 246.

16. Foster's poem is in FHC and reprinted in Elliker, 80–81.

17. Morrison Foster, 34; Morrison Foster to S. Reed Johnston, 14 February 1886 (FHC).

18. Lawrence, *Strong on Music*, 1: 324.

19. Eliot Feld provided just such an interpretation in his choreography of "Open Thy Lattice Love" in *Doo Dah Day (no possum, no sop, no taters)*, an extended dance piece set to Stephen Foster songs that premiered at New York City's Joyce Theater in 1994. The "Open Thy Lattice Love" segment was a rubbery duet in which the female dancer splayed her legs lewdly and comically before the couple made the beast with two backs and then with two bellies as they intertwined and undulated across the floor.

"Sometimes it seems overly cultured to disguise lust as love," Feld told me in a 1995 interview. "I think [Foster] must have had a hard-on—or if he didn't, he wanted to. Did he do it straight? Did he not suggest or understand that 'lattice' has sexual innuendo? If he didn't know, it doesn't mean it wasn't there."

20. John Spitzer, " 'Oh! Susanna': Oral Transmission and Tune Transformation," *Journal of the American Musicological Society* 47, no. 1 (1994): 110, n. 42.

21. Virginia Writers' Project, *The Negro in Virginia* (New York: Hastings House, 1940), 92, quoted in Lynne Fauley Emery, *Black Dance from 1619 to Today*, rev. ed. (London: Dance Books, 1988), 90.

22. Ramshaw, 44; *The Kentucky Minstrel and Jersey Warbler: Being a Choice Selection of Coon Melodies* (Philadelphia: Robinson and Peterson, 1844), 10–11; *The Anti-Slavery Harp*, 36–37. Lavern Baker's "Jim Dandy" is on *Soul on Fire: The Best of LaVern Baker*, Atlantic CD 82311. Larry Williams's "Short Fat Fannie" is on *The Specialty Story*, Specialty 5SPCD–412–2.

23. Dennison, 99–100.

24. F. M. Brower, "Old Joe" (Boston: C. H. Keith, 1844), reprinted in Nathan, 457–59. This song as well as "Old Uncle Ned" are performed, along with "The Fine Old Colored Gentleman," on *The Early Minstrel Show*.

25. Frederick Douglass, "The Anti-Slavery Movement, lecture delivered before the Rochester Ladies' Anti-Slavery Society, January, 1855," *The Life and Writings of Frederick Douglass*, ed. Philip S. Foner, vol. 2, *Pre-Civil War Decade 1850–1860* (New York: International Publishers, 1950): 356–57.

26. Delany, *Blake*, 105–6.

27. Lott, 188–90; Thomas F. Gossett, *"Uncle Tom's Cabin" and American Culture* (Dallas: Southern Methodist University Press, 1985), 172.

28. John Updike, *Buchanan Dying: A Play* (New York: Knopf, 1974), 259; Harriet Beecher Stowe to Catherine Beecher, ca. 1850–1851, Beecher Family Papers, Sterling Memorial Library, Yale University, quoted in Hedrick, 205.

How curious that Updike, for all his meticulous descriptions of Pennsylvania, and of the popular music that provides the soundtracks of his characters' lives, has never, to my knowledge, mentioned Stephen Foster, not even in his two books concerning Foster's brother-in-law, *Buchanan Dying* and *Memories of the Ford Administration* (New York: Knopf, 1992)!

29. Morrison Foster, 34.

CHAPTER 11: PITTSBURGH IN RUINS

1. Wall's two small oil paintings are in the collection of the Carnegie Museum of Art, Pittsburgh. The Pittsburgh fire is described in Thurston, 54–55; Leland Baldwin, 228–30; Lorant, 110–11.

2. Morneweck, 1: 281.

3. Rollin, 48–49; Ullman, 45, 48–49, 60.

4. Norman Ware, *The Industrial Worker 1840–1860* (Boston: Houghton Mifflin, 1924; reprint, Chicago: Quadrangle, 1964), 141–42.

5. Isaac Harris, 75.

6. Coleman, 17; William Bender Wilson, 260–62; Stewart H. Holbrook, *The Story of American Railroads* (New York: Bonanza Books, 1947; reprint, New York: American Legacy Press, 1981), 82–83.

7. Morneweck, 1: 287–89; Raymond Walters, *Stephen Foster: Youth's Golden Gleam* (Princeton: Princeton University Press, 1936), 12; Fletcher Hodges, Jr., "Stephen Foster—Cincinnatian and American," *Bulletin of the Historical and Philosophical Society of Ohio* 8, no. 2 (April, 1950): 88.

8. Stephen Foster to Ann Eliza Foster Buchanan, 15 September 1845 (FHC, A335; Elliker, 93); Henry Foster to Morrison Foster, 16 March 1846 (FHC, C488).

9. Johannsen, 11, 27.

10. Stephen Foster to Ann Eliza Foster Buchanan, 15 September 1845 (FHC, A335; Elliker, 93).

11. Henry C. Watson, *New York Evening Signal*, 3 February 1841, quoted in Lawrence, *Strong on Music*, 1: 143; *Cincinnati Atlas*, 9 April 1846, quoted in Wyrick, 83; Morrison Foster, 38; Morneweck, 1: 439–40.

12. Lawrence, *Strong on Music*, 1: 490; Nathaniel Hawthorne, *The English Notebooks, Our Old Home, and English Note-Books* (Boston, Cambridge, Mass.: Houghton, Mifflin, Riverside Press, 1898), 2: 232.

13. Douglass, *My Bondage and My Freedom*, 366; *The Book of Brothers, or The History of the Hutchinson Family* (New York: "published by and for the Hutchinson Family," 1852), 16.

14. The Hutchinsons' version of "There's a Good Time Coming," its "symphonies & accompaniments" attributed to E. L. White, was published by Oliver Ditson (Boston: 1846). It can be heard on *There's a Good Time Coming and Other Songs of the Hutchinson Family as Performed at the Smithsonian Institution* (Smithsonian Collection N020) and compared to Foster's version on Jan DeGaetani, Leslie Guinn and Gilbert Kalish, *Songs by Stephen Foster* (Elektra/Nonesuch H–71268).

15. Scully (21 July 1843), 144–45.

16. John B. Russell, "Foster's Music," *Cincinnati Daily Gazette*, 22 January 1857.

CHAPTER 12: HOG HEAVEN

1. Charles Dickens to John Forster, 4 April 1842, *Letters*, 3: 182; Lady Emmeline Stuart Wortley, *Travels in the United States, etc., During 1849 and 1850* (London: Richard Bentley, 1851), 1: 169.

2. Charles Cist, *Sketches and Statistics of Cincinnati in 1851* (Cincinnati: Wm. H. Moore & Co., 1851), 228, 44–45, 83, 184, 252; *Cincinnati: A Guide to the Queen City and Its Neighbors*, compiled by workers of the Writers' Program of the Work Projects Administration in the State of Ohio (Cincinnati: The Wiesen-Hart Press, 1943), 7, 39; Holt, 21; *Cincinnati: The Queen City*, bicentennial ed. (Cincinnati: The Cincinnati Historical Society, 1988), 44; Steven J. Ross, *Workers On the Edge: Work, Leisure, and Politics in Industrializing Cincinnati, 1788–1890* (New York: Columbia University Press, 1985), 72, 78; Nathan, 109; Leonard P. Curry, *The Free Black in Urban America 1800–1850: The Shadow of the Dream* (Chicago: University of Chicago Press, 1981), 245.

3. William Jay, *Miscellaneous Writings on Slavery* (Boston: J. P. Jewett, 1853), 373, quoted in Frank U. Quillen, *The Color Line in Ohio: A History of Race Prejudice in a Typical Northern State* (Ann Arbor: University of Michigan Press, 1913), 45; Wilmoth, 25; Curry, 91.

4. Ross, 50–51; *Cincinnati: A Guide to the Queen City*, 42.

5. Dickens, *American Notes*, 207.

6. *Williams' Cincinnati Directory and Business Advertiser, for 1849–50* (Cincinnati: C. S. Williams, 1849), additions and corrections; *Cincinnati Daily Enquirer*, 14 April 1848.

7. The daguerreotypes, in the collection of the Public Library of Cincinnati and Hamilton County, are reproduced in a fold-out format in Graydon DeCamp, *The Grand Old Lady of Vine Street* (Cincinnati: Cincinnati Enquirer, 1991).

8. Newspaper advertisements for these and other boats and destinations are reproduced in Walters, facing p. 11; Morrison Foster, 35.

9. Whitman, *Democratic Vistas, Collected Writings, Prose Works 1892*, 2: 384–85.

10. *View of Cincinnati from Covington, Kentucky* is in the collection of the Cincinnati Historical Society. It is discussed in Joseph D. Ketner, *The Emergence of the African-American Artist Robert S. Duncanson 1821–1872* (Columbia: University of Missouri Press, 1993), 40. For relations between Avery and Duncanson, see Ketner, 25–27, 44–45. For Avery, see Rollin, 49–50; Ullman, 70; Morneweck, 1: 210–11.

11. Hedrick, 119–21.

12. Levi Coffin, *Reminiscences of Levi Coffin* (Cincinnati: Robert Clarke, 1898; reprint, New York: Arno Press and the New York Times, 1968) 286–89; Carter G. Woodson, "The Negroes of Cincinnati Prior to the Civil War," *The Journal of Negro History* 1, no. 1 (January 1916): 19–20; James Oliver Horton, *Free People of Color: Inside the African American Community* (Washington, D.C.: Smithsonian Institution Press, 1993), 129 and 137, citing Joana C. Colcord,

compiler, *Roll and Go: Songs of American Sailormen* (Indianapolis: Bobbs-Merrill, 1924), 17; Charles Thomas Hickok, *The Negro in Ohio, 1802–1870* (Cleveland: Williams Publishing & Electric, 1896; reprint, New York: AMS, 1975), 70.

13. Hunter, 450; Southern, 147–49.

14. Bremer, 2: 176.

15. Frederick Law Olmsted, *A Journey in the Seaboard Slave States, with Remarks on Their Economy* (New York: Dix & Edwards, 1856; reprint, New York: Negro Universities Press, 1968), 606–7.

16. Delany, *Blake*, 100–101.

17. Scully (May 26, 1843), 111.

18. Ullman, 76–81; John Burt, "The Poet of the Iron City: Charles P. Shiras (1824–1854)," *Carnegie Magazine* 67, no. 7 (January–February 1987): 21–22.

19. Delany's gripping account of this incident appeared in the *North Star*, 28 January 1848. It is quoted at length in Ullman, 93–95, and a complete transcription was kindly provided to me by Robert Levine, who has collected Delany's essays and letters in *"Stand Still and See the Salvation": A Martin R. Delany Reader* (Chapel Hill: University of North Carolina Press, in press).

20. *Cincinnati Daily Enquirer*, 11 and 14 May 1848.

21. Ibid., 11 and 14 April 1848; Carlyon, 290–91.

22. This account of the role of music in the Mexican War is taken from Johannsen, 53–54, 118, 230–40.

CHAPTER 13: ICE CREAM AND THE ANNIHILATION OF TIME AND SPACE

1. Ernest C. Krohn, "Nelson Kneass: Minstrel Singer and Composer," *Yearbook for Inter-American Musical Research* 7 (1971): 22.

2. *Pittsburgh Daily Gazette and Advertiser*, 9 August 1847.

3. Krohn, 20–21.

4. Ibid., 22; Wyrick, 122–24; Katherine P. Preston, *Opera on the Road: Traveling Opera Troupes in the United States, 1825–60* (Urbana: University of Illinois Press: 1993), 321, 327 n. 3, 328 n. 13, 366 n. 6; Nevin, 613; *Pittsburgh Daily Commercial Journal*, 19 August 1847.

5. *Pittsburgh Daily Gazette*, 3 and 4 September 1847; *Pittsburgh Daily Commercial Journal*, 31 August 1847; *Pittsburgh Daily Morning Post*, 4 September 1847; Morrison Foster, 37.

6. *Pittsburgh Daily Morning Post*, 6, 7, and 8 September 1847; *The Pittsburgh Daily Gazette*, 9 September 1847.

7. *Pittsburgh Daily Commercial Journal*, 8 September 1847.

8. Nevin, 613; Morrison Foster, 37; "Wake Up Jake," written and composed by Geo. Holman (Baltimore: W. C. Peters, 1848); *Wood's Minstrels Songs: Containing a Selection of the most Popular Choruses, Quartettes, Trios, Duets, Glees, Songs, Parodies, Burlesques, Conundrums, etc., etc.* (New York: Dick & Fitzgerald, 1855).

9. In *My Brother Stephen*, Morrison Foster wrote that it was "one of the

troupe" (37). However, in a penciled note in the margin of his copy of Robert Nevin's *Atlantic Monthly* article, preserved in FHC, Morrison indicated there were "two vagabonds." Could these have been Kneass and Holman? Nevin wrote that the would-be thief was Kneass, and Kneass alone (613).

10. Krohn, 37; *Popular Songs of Nineteenth-Century America,* 265.

11. *Pittsburgh Daily Commercial Journal,* 19 August 1847; Morneweck, 1: 315; *Cincinnati Daily Enquirer,* 21 January 1848. "I'll Be a Fairy" (New York: P. K. Moran, ca. 1822), with words by W. Roscoe, begins, "I'll be a fairy and drink the dew, / . . . And sleep in the violet's tender blue. . . ." Foster's lyric starts with the questions, "What must a fairy's dream be, / Who drinks of the morning dew? / Would she think to fly til she reach'd the sky / And bathe in its lakes of blue . . . ?"

12. *Pittsburgh Daily Commercial Journal,* 11 September 1847; *Pittsburgh Daily Morning Post,* 11 September 1847; John M. Belohlavek, *George Mifflin Dallas: Jacksonian Patrician* (University Park: Pennsylvania State University Press, 1977), 126–30.

13. Morrison Foster said his brother wrote "Oh! Susanna" "while in Cincinnati" (35). John Tasker Howard thought it more likely he wrote it in Pittsburgh (136).

14. The fourth verse does not appear in the W. C. Peters edition of 30 December 1848 that, according to Saunders and Root, "represents the published form in which Foster intended the song to reach the marketplace" (1: 461). It occurs, however, in many other sheet music versions. This one is taken from the 25 February 1848 edition, published by C. Holt, Jr. in New York, "Sung by G.N. Christy of the Christy Minstrels," without any credit or attribution to Foster. It is reprinted in *Popular Songs of Nineteenth-Century America,* 152–55.

15. "Jim Along Josey" (New York: Firth & Hall, 1840); Damon, song no. 24.

16. "Ole Tare River" (Boston: Henry Prentiss, 1840); Damon, song no. 27.

17. "Brack Eyed Susianna" (Philadelphia: Fiot, 1846), reprinted in part in Tawa, *A Music for the Millions,* 171.

18. William Francis Allen, Charles Pickard Ware and Lucy McKim Garrison, eds., *Slave Songs of the United States* (New York: A. Simpson, 1867), 89; Charles Hamm, *Music in the New World* (New York: W. W. Norton, 1983), 138.

19. Nicholas Tawa, review of *"Susanna," "Jeanie," and "The Old Folks at Home": The Songs of Stephen Foster from His Time to Ours,* by William W. Austin, *Yearbook for Inter-American Musical Research* 11 (1975), 220; Tawa, *Sweet Songs,* 197 n. 87; Austin, 10. The anticipation of "Oh! Susanna" is audible in the performance of "Mary Blane" on *The Early Minstrel Show.*

20. Foster originally entitled his song "Susanna," but as early as February 1848 it was published in an unauthorized edition as "Oh! Susanna," and Foster eventually acquiesced. See Saunders and Root, 1: 461; Howard, 141; Spitzer, 90–117, 132–33.

21. The manuscript is an arrangement for vocal quartet of "I Would Not Die in Spring Time" (FHC, A354).

22. Howard, 144; Austin, 7; Hamm, *Yesterdays,* 210.

23. Hunter, 24, 307 n, 407–8.

24. Donovan, 118; Delany, *Blake,* 122.

25. Whitman, "To a Locomotive in Winter," l.13, *Collected Writings, Leaves of Grass and Selected Prose,* 3: 666; Andrew Carnegie, *Triumphant Democracy, or Fifty Years' March of the Republic* (New York, 1886), quoted in Joseph Frazier Wall, *Andrew Carnegie* (New York: Oxford University Press, 1970; reprint, Pittsburgh: University of Pittsburgh Press, 1989), 443; Charles Dickens, *The Life and Adventures of Martin Chuzzlewit,* ed. Margaret Cantwell (Oxford, Eng.: Clarendon, 1982), 406.

26. Hunter, 286; Scully (March 18, 1843), 61.

27. *North Star,* 28 January 1848; Hunter, 537.

28. Hunter, 485–89.

29. S. Frederick Starr, *Bamboula! The Life and Times of Louis Moreau Gottschalk* (New York: Oxford University Press, 1995), 50.

30. Cist, *Sketches and Statistics of Cincinnati in 1851,* 310.

31. John Steele Gordon, "The Man Who Invented Mass Media," *Audacity* 4, no. 1 (Fall 1995): 39.

32. Delany, *Blake,* 143.

33. *Pittsburgh Daily Morning Post,* 4 September 1847.

34. Scully (May 17, 1843), 105–6.

35. Ibid. (March 18, 1843), 61.

36. Henry David Thoreau, *Walden,* ed. J. Lyndon Shanley (Princeton: Princeton University Press, 1971), 53, 174.

37. Herman Melville, "Cock-A-Doodle-Doo!," *Pierre, Israel Potter, The Piazza Tales . . . ,* 1205.

38. Walters, 20–22; Dunning Foster to Morrison Foster, 29 December 1848 (FHC, C483).

39. J. S. Holliday, *The World Rushed In: The California Gold Rush Experience* (New York: Touchstone, 1983), 92.

40. Hulbert, 238.

41. Bayard Taylor, *El Dorado; or, Adventures in the Path of Empire* (New York: G. P. Putnam, 1850; reprint, New York: Knopf, 1949), 208–9, quoted in Holliday, 322.

42. Whitman, *Democratic Vistas, Prose Works 1892,* 2: 388.

CHAPTER 14: WHISTLED ON THE WIND

1. *Pittsburgh Daily Morning Post,* 13 and 14 September 1847.

2. Lawrence, *Strong on Music,* 1: 542.

3. See Lawrence W. Levine, *Highbrow/Lowbrow: The Emergence of Cultural Hierarchy in America* (Cambridge, Mass.: Harvard University Press, 1988).

4. Wyrick, 105; clipping from the *Pittsburg Press,* dated in pencil "June, 1895" (FHC, C764).

5. Stephen Foster to William E. Millet, 25 May 1849 (Elliker, 94).

6. Wyrick, 119, 123; Howard, 140; Spitzer, 91.

7. Nevin, 614; Morrison Foster, 35. Nevin cited a letter that has not survived in which Stephen Foster allegedly wrote that he had been given two $50 bills for "Oh! Susanna": ". . . [I]magine my delight in receiving one hundred dollars in cash!" The letter as quoted by Nevin is puzzling, since it states that "Oh! Susanna" "was not successful." Nevin may have misquoted, misunderstood or not seen the actual letter, which was originally quoted in "Who Writes Our Songs?," an unsigned article by W. F. Williams in the 22 April 1859 *New York Evening Post*. (Williams revealed his identity in a 26 January 1864 letter to Morrison Foster [FHC, C856].) As quoted by Williams, the letter seemed to suggest that Foster had been paid $100 for the song that Peters published *after* "Oh! Susanna." That song was probably the unsuccessful "Away Down Souf."

8. Hewitt, 66.

9. Russell, 198–99.

10. Root, 4, 83.

11. Charles E. Rosenberg, *The Cholera Years: The United States in 1832, 1849, and 1866* (Chicago: University of Chicago Press, 1987), 1–2; Carol Brink, *Harps in the Wind: The Story of the Singing Hutchinsons* (New York: Macmillan, 1947), 138–39; Dunning Foster to Morrison Foster, 29 December 1848 (FHC, C483).

12. Dunning Foster to Morrison Foster, 13 January 1849 (FHC, C482); Stephen Foster to Morrison Foster, 27 April 1849 (FHC, C583). The second letter survives in the form of a transcript handwritten in 1865 by Morrison Foster, who sent the original letter to Louis J. Cist of St. Louis, a collector who had been a bank teller in Cincinnati when Stephen Foster lived there.

13. Dunning Foster to Morrison Foster, 13 January 1849; Morneweck, 1: 94; Morrison Foster, 41.

14. Stephen Foster to Morrison Foster, 27 April 1849; John Dizikes, *Opera in America: A Cultural History* (New Haven: Yale University Press, 1993), 111; Lawrence, *Strong on Music*, 1: 461–64.

15. Wyrick, 90–92, 105–6, 32, 78–81; Lawrence, *Strong on Music*, 1: 467; Lawrence, *Strong on Music*, vol. 2, *Reverberations: 1850–1856* (Chicago: University of Chicago Press, 1995), 64–65, 78.

16. A slightly different version of "Summer Longings" had appeared a few weeks earlier in the 21 April 1849 *Cincinnati Atlas* (see Walters, 93), but Foster's sheet music credits *The Home Journal*.

17. Harriet Beecher Stowe to Sarah Buckingham Beecher, 9 March 1849, quoted in Hedrick, 186.

18. Walters, 36.

19. Stephen Foster to Morrison Foster, 27 April 1849.

20. For the tangled tale of "Nelly Was a Lady" and Firth, Pond, see Saunders and Root, 1: 462; Howard, 153; Morneweck, 1: 353.

21. Firth, Pond to Stephen Foster, 12 September 1849 (FHC).

22. Morrison Foster to Louis J. Cist, 27 February 1865 (FHC, C583).

23. J. A. Turner, "Jessie Was a Fair One," *The Singer's Companion* (New York: n.p., 1854), quoted in Tawa, *Sweet Songs*, 94.

24. Frankenstein, 245.

CHAPTER 15: JENNIE WITH THE LIGHT BROWN HAIR

1. *Daily Commercial Journal*, 18 August 1847; Fahnestock, 32. William B. Foster's account book is in FHC.

2. The undated daguerreotype, marked "McClees," "Phila," and "copy," is in FHC. According to Floyd and Marion Rinhart's *The American Daguerreotype* (Athens: University of Georgia Press, 1981), J. E. McClees, in partnership with Washington L. Germon, was active in Philadelphia from 1847 to 1855. Although William Foster does not look well, the image was probably made before the spring of 1851, since there is no record of his leaving Allegheny City after the stroke he suffered at that time.

3. Stephen Foster's account book is in FHC.

4. For the relation between Andrew McDowell and Martin Delany, see Rollin (46) and Ullman (5, 20).

5. Abby Barlow to Charlotte Foster, 3 March 1826 (FHC, C425). Although Morneweck wrote (1: 349) that Jane Denny Porter was "of Chambersburg" and was married there by Rev. David Denny, the 27 July 1824 *Franklin (County, Pa.) Repository* noted that she was "late of Pittsburgh" and married in Lewistown on July 13 by a Reverend Woods. Morneweck (1: 349) and Howard (157) wrote that the McDowells had six daughters, while *Biographical Annals of Franklin County Pennsylvania* (Chambersburg, Pa.: 1905; reprint, Chambersburg, Pa.: The Print Peddler, 1978) suggests there were seven.

6. Dunning Foster to Morrison Foster, 13 January 1849.

7. For Mary Anderson's letter, see chap. 7, n. 12.

8. Jessie Welsh Rose, "His Widow's Memories of Foster's Life Are Recalled by Granddaughter," *Pittsburgh Sunday Post*, 4 July 1926 (FHC, C771). For more about Foster's fascination with hair, see Austin, 224–25. "Jennie with the Light Brown Hair" appears in Foster's unpaginated sketchbook of lyrics, music and doodles from 1851 through 1860, in FHC. This volume will be referred to in subsequent notes as Sketchbook.

9. Morrison Foster, 8; Nevin, 615.

10. Rose, "His Widow's Memories."

11. Stephen Foster to Ann Eliza Foster Buchanan, 16 July 1850 (FHC, A336; Elliker, 95).

12. Agnes McDowell to Marion McDowell Scully, 23 July 1850 (FHC). For "callithumpians" and the American version of the charivari, see Susan G. Davis, *Parades and Power: Street Theatre in Nineteenth-Century Philadelphia* (Philadelphia: Temple University Press, 1986), 77–78, 97–98; Lott, 136–38; Cockrell. I'm grateful to Deane Root for drawing my attention to the phenomenon.

13. Holt, *Forging a Majority*, 52, 88.

14. Ibid., 111; Michael Fitzgibbon Holt, "Change and Conflict: Politics in Pittsburgh, 1850–1865," *David Gilmour Blythe's Pittsburgh: 1850–1865. An All-Day Public Forum Saturday, May 9, 1981* (Pittsburgh: Museum of Art, Carnegie Institute, 1981), 53; Leland Baldwin, 295–99; Tyrrell, 265.

15. Holt, *Forging a Majority*, 29, 89.

16. "The Redemption of Labor" and "The Popular Credo" are to be found in Charles P. Shiras, *The Redemption of Labor, and Other Poems* (Pittsburgh: W. H. Whitney, 1852).

17. George Shiras, *Justice George Shiras Jr. of Pittsburgh: A Chronicle of his Family, Life and Times*, ed. and completed by Winfield Shiras (Pittsburgh: University of Pittsburgh Press, 1953), 3-16; Burt, 20.

18. Carnegie, 12, 28–29, 37; Wall, 79–81.

19. Andrew Carnegie, "The Advantages of Poverty," *Nineteenth Century* 29, (March 1891); reprint, *The Gospel of Wealth*, ed. Edward C. Kirkland (Cambridge, Mass.: Belknap/Harvard University Press, 1962), 64, quoted in Wall, 393; Carnegie, *Autobiography*, 38.

20. Carnegie, *Autobiography*, 34, 57.

21. William B. Foster to William B. Foster, Jr., 23 October 1839 (FHC, C684).

22. Carnegie, *Autobiography*, 335.

23. Morrison Foster, 37.

CHAPTER 16: GWINE TO WRITE ALL NIGHT

1. Nevin, 615; Stephen Foster to Ann Eliza Foster Buchanan, 16 July 1850 (FHC, A336; Elliker, 95).

2. Stephen Foster to E. P. Christy, 23 February 1850 (Library of Congress; Elliker, 94).

3. The poem and Kleber advertisement appear in William Evens's scrapbook no. 1; the Swiss Bell Ringers' notice is in scrapbook no. 4.

4. Timothy Flint, "Mike Fink: The Last of the Boatmen," *The Western Monthly Review*, July 1829, quoted in Blair and Meine, 60.

5. Pike, *Catching the Tune*, 12.

6. *New York Herald*, 3 February 1850, quoted in Lawrence, *Strong on Music*, 2: 125.

7. Kussart, 37.

8. Deane Root, interviewed by author, 23 May 1996; *Hutchinson's Republican Songster*, ed. John W. Hutchinson (New York: Hutchinson, 1860), 15, quoted in Austin, 34.

9. The title and title page of "Angelina Baker" were registered on February 18, 1850, but the entire song was not copyrighted until March 18. See Saunders and Root, 1: 465.

10. *The Beatles* (the "White Album"), Apple SWBO 101.

11. Hugh Henry Brackenridge, *Modern Chivalry: Containing the Adventures of Captain John Farrago and Teague O'Reagan, His Servant*, ed. Lewis Leary (New Haven: College & University Press, 1965), 29–34.

12. Henry Marie Brackenridge, *Recollections of Persons and Places in the West* (Philadelphia: Lippincott, 1868), 62.

13. Martin, 163–65; Morneweck, 2: 377.

14. Alan A. Siegel, *Out of Our Past: A History of Irvington, New Jersey*

(Irvington, N.J.: Irvington Centennial Committee, 1974), 104–6; *Camptown Pennsylvania 1792–1975* (Wyalusing, Pa.: Camptown Civic Club, 1975), 18.

15. Winter, 45–46; Frankenstein, 62–63.

16. *Christy's Plantation Melodies*, Second Songster, 40–41.

17. Wittke, 73; *Pittsburgh Daily Gazette*, 1 and 6 August 1849; Wyrick, 125–127; Damon, notes for song no. 39.

18. Dickens, *American Notes*, 216; W. C. Handy, *Father of the Blues*, DRG SL 5192.

19. *Pittsburgh Gazette*, 1 October 1850.

20. Rollin, 76.

21. Charles Shiras, 67.

22. Wilmoth, 110.

23. Ullman, 113–17; *Blacks at Harvard: A Documentary History of African-American Experience at Harvard and Radcliffe*, ed. Werner Sollers, Caldwell Titcomb, and Thomas Underwood (New York: New York University Press, 1993), 19–31.

24. Ullman, 123.

CHAPTER 17: THE RAVEN AND THE NIGHTINGALE

1. Susan Warner, *The Wide, Wide World* (originally pub. under the pseudonym Elizabeth Wetherell, New York: G. P. Putnam, 1850; reprint, New York: Feminist Press, 1987), 182.

2. Baynham, 216; Evens's scrapbook no. 1; Lawrence, *Strong on Music*, 1: 488–89, 600; N. Lee Orr, "John Hill Hewitt: Bard of the Confederacy," *American Music Research Center Journal* 4 (1994): 46, 53; Herbert Holl, "Some Versions of Pastoral in American Music" (Ph.D. diss., University of Texas at Austin, 1980), 70–71.

3. For a discussion of gender and voice in Foster's songs, see Susan Key, "Sound and Sentimentality: Nostalgia in the Songs of Stephen Foster," *American Music* 3, no. 2 (Summer 1995): 145–66.

4. For the division between men as public performers and women as private consumers of music, see Vicki Lynn Eaklor, "Music in American Society, 1815–1860: An Intellectual History" (Ph.D. diss., Washington University, 1982), 135–36.

5. Richard L. Bushman, *The Refinement of America: Persons, Houses, Cities* (New York: Vintage, 1993), 251–52, 262–65.

6. "Go, lovely Rose!," Attwood's Canzonet, with words by Waller, in *The Musical Library*, vol. 2 (London: Charles Knight, 1835), in Evens's scrapbook no. 3.

7. For a discussion of the musical origins and inspirations of "Ah! May the Red Rose Live Alway!" and "The Voice of By Gone Days," see Hamm, *Yesterdays*, 205–6, 219.

8. Carl Bode, *The Anatomy of Popular Culture 1840-1861* (Berkeley: University of California Press, 1960), 274; Twain, *Huckleberry Finn*, 725; *Grigg's Southern and Western Songster*, 174.

9. Ellen Morgan Frisbee, *Henry Sylvester Cornwell, Poet of Fancy: A Memoir* (New London, Conn.: Ellen Morgan Fisher, 1905), 12, 15 (citing the Springfield [presumably Mass.] *Republican*). The royalty figure is from Stephen Foster's account book (FHC).

10. Frisbee, 8, 16; Harold Vincent Milligan, *Stephen Collins Foster: A Biography* (New York: G. Schirmer, 1920), 104.

11. Silverman, 237–38; Poe, "The Philosophy of Composition," *Complete Works*, 14: 198.

12. Austin, 156; *The Poetical Works of James Gates Percival with a Biographical Sketch* (Boston: Ticknor and Fields, 1859); Saunders and Root, 1: 470; Henrietta Foster to William B. Foster, Jr., 30 April 1836 (FHC, typed transcript, presumably by Evelyn Foster Morneweck).

13. Stephens, 105; Tawa, *Music for the Millions*, 167.

14. Saunders and Root, 1: xxiii; Howard, 184–85. Both versions of "I Would Not Die in Winter," with music credited to Stephen Glover (Philadelphia: Edward L. Walker, 1851) and to J. H. Milton (Philadelphia: Lee & Walker, 1851), are in the Special Collections of the Lincoln Center Library of the Performing Arts, New York Public Library. Hewitt's "I Would Not Die at All" (Baltimore: G. Willig Jr., 1852) is in the Hewitt archive at Emory University.

15. Rollin, 68; Ullman, 28.

16. Undated clipping, Evens's scrapbook no. 1.

17. *Pittsburgh Gazette*, 22 April 1851, reprinted from the *Cincinnati Gazette*; Barnum, *Struggles and Triumphs*, 290; Lawrence, *Strong on Music*, 2: 38–39 (unless otherwise noted, the account that follows of Jenny Lind's arrival and appearances in New York is drawn from Lawrence, vol. 2); Dizikes, 128.

18. *There's a Good Time Coming and Other Songs of the Hutchinson Family.*

19. Lawrence, *Strong on Music*, 1: 303.

20. *Dwight's Journal of Music*, 7 February 1857, quoted in Preston, 311.

21. Rollo G. Silver, "Whitman in 1850: Three Uncollected Articles," *American Literature* 19, no. 4 (January 1948): 303–5, quoted in Justin Kaplan, *Walt Whitman: A Life* (New York: Touchstone, 1986), 177.

22. Evens's scrapbook no. 1; Henry Kleber, "The Opera Scottisch" (New York: Firth, Pond, 1853); *Pittsburgh Gazette*, 21 April 1851.

23. C. G. Rosenberg, *Jenny Lind in America* (New York: Stringer & Townsend, 1851), 215. Unless otherwise noted, this account of Jenny Lind's visit to Pittsburgh is drawn from newspaper clippings, most of them unidentified and undated, in Evens's scrapbook no. 1.

24. Louis Moreau Gottschalk, *Notes of a Pianist*, ed. Jeanne Behrend (New York: Knopf, 1964), 46.

25. Wall, 101, citing a 22 June 1851 letter in the Andrew Carnegie Papers, vol. 1, Library of Congress; Emily Dickinson to Austin Dickinson, 6 July 1851, *The Letters of Emily Dickinson*, ed. Thomas H. Johnson, associate ed. Theodora Ward (Cambridge, Mass.: Belknap/Harvard University Press, 1958), 1: 121.

26. *Pittsburgh Daily Gazette*, 16 April 1852; Evens's scrapbook no. 1; Dizikes, 111.

27. *Pittsburgh Daily Gazette*, 16 April 1852.

28. Tawa, *Sweet Songs*, 202; Edward F. Kravitt, "Franz Wilhelm Abt," *The New Grove Dictionary of Music and Musicians*, ed. Stanley Sadie (London: Macmillan, 1980), 29. See also, Hamm, *Yesterdays*, 195–98.

29. Kays Gary, "Elvis Defends Low-Down Style," *Charlotte Observer*, 27 June 1956, quoted in Peter Guralnick, *Last Train to Memphis: The Rise of Elvis Presley* (Boston: Little, Brown, 1994), 289.

CHAPTER 18: FROM BLACKS TO FOLKS

1. Stephen Foster to E. P. Christy, 12 June 1851. This letter, the original MS. of which is in the Henry E. Huntington Library, San Marino, California, is reprinted in full in Elliker, 95–96.

2. Foster's 20 June 1851 letter to E. P. Christy is in the Henry E. Huntington Library, and reprinted in Elliker, 96.

3. J. William Pope, quoted in the *Pittsburgh Sunday Press*, 23 June 1895 (FHC, C764); Ives, *Memos*, 115.

4. Scott Joplin, Exercise No. 6, *School of Ragtime* (New York: Scott Joplin, 1908), quoted in Berlin, 77.

5. Jacob Little, *The Musical World and Times* 7, no. 9 (29 October 1853): 68.

6. Stephen Foster to E. P. Christy, 20 June 1851.

7. Ibid., 25 May 1852 (FHC; Elliker, 97); Morrison Foster, 47–48; John Mahon, "Last Years of Stephen C. Foster," *New York Clipper*, 17 or 24 March 1877, reprinted in *Foster Hall Bulletin* 10 (May 1934): 4. Howard argues persuasively for the lower figure of $15 (195–200).

8. "Ole Pee Dee," written and composed by J. P. Carter (Boston: Keith's Publishing House, 1844), reprinted in Nathan, 469–70.

9. Morrison Foster, 47.

10. *New York* [*Clipper?*], 3 March 1877, preserved in Morrison Foster's scrapbook (FHC); Henry James, *A Small Boy and Others*, in *Henry James: Autobiography*, ed. Frederick W. Dupee (Princeton, N.J.: Princeton University Press, 1983), 91; T. Allston Brown, 1: 72.

11. Lawrence, *Strong on Music*, 2: 273–74.

12. John Sullivan Dwight, *Dwight's Journal of Music*, 22 October 1853, reprinted in *What They Heard*, 39–40.

13. *Negro Year Book: An Annual Encyclopedia of the Negro*, 1931–1932, ed. Monroe N. Work (Tuskegee, Ala.: Tuskegee Institute, 1931), 445.

14. Little, *op. cit.*, 48.

15. Stephen Foster to E. P. Christy, 25 May 1852 (FHC; Elliker, 97).

CHAPTER 19: POSSUM FAT AND FLOWRETS

1. *Moore's Irish Melodies*, 164–65.

2. Delany, *Blake*, 105.

3. Frederick Way, Jr., *Way's Packet Directory, 1848–1983* (Athens: Ohio University Press, 1983), 241.

4. Richard Cowan wrote Morrison Foster in 1853 that "when we reached the warm latitudes we used to sit on deck to enjoy the moonlight and the sight of the negroes burning the brush and the cotton stalks at the plantations" (quoted in Howard, 169). In the same letter Cowan also mentioned singing "Old Folks at Home" and "Wilt Thou Be Gone, Love?"

5. Poe, "To Helen" ("I saw thee once . . ."), ll.26–28, *Poetry and Tales* (New York: Library of America, 1984), 96.

6. *Pittsburg Press*, 5 June 1895 (FHC, C771).

7. Way, 13.

8. Capps, 55, 97 n. 18.

9. *Pittsburg Press*, 12 September 1900; notation on a 29 August 1900 letter from Gilbert L. Eberhart to Morrison Foster (FHC).

10. Capps, 87–88, quoting the *Kentucky Standard*, 19 February 1925.

11. Erleen Johnson, "Writer has no doubts Foster was here," *Kentucky Standard*, 7 June 1985; Mrs. Will S. Hays to Josiah K. Lilly, 14 and 20 August 1931 (FHC); Robert V. Remini, *Henry Clay: Statesman for the Union* (New York: Norton, 1991), 774–81. Johnson's article is the most impressive marshaling of evidence that Foster visited Federal Hill, and it is noteworthy that she doesn't insist he did so in 1852.

CHAPTER 20: A SHOCK OF RECOGNITION

1. Whitman, "House of Friends," *Collected Writings, The Early Poems and the Fiction*, 36–37.

2. Edward Raymond Turner, *The Negro in Pennsylvania: Slavery—Servitude —Freedom, 1639–1861* (Washington: 1911; reprint, New York: Arno, 1969), 240–43; Klein, 217–18.

3. Holt, *Forging a Majority*, 102; Wilmoth, 90; Hedrick, vii–viii; Gossett, 164; Andrew Carnegie to George Lauder, 12 November 1855, quoted in Wall, 100.

4. Harriet Beecher Stowe, *Uncle Tom's Cabin*, in *Three Novels: Uncle Tom's Cabin or, Life among the Lowly, The Minister's Wooing, Oldtown Folks* (New York: Library of America, 1982), 13; see also p. 278.

5. *New York Daily Times*, 18 September 1852, quoted in Hedrick, 211.

6. Stowe, 67.

7. Ibid., 345, 307.

8. Ibid., 336; Morneweck, 2: 419–20.

9. Florine Thayer McCray, *The Life-Work of the Author of Uncle Tom's Cabin* (New York: Funk & Wagnalls, 1889), 106, cited in Gossett, 211; Stowe, 489.

10. Stowe, 486.

11. Levy, 125–37; Stephens, 97, 99, 100, 108; Evens's scrapbook no. 1; Ketner, 46–49.

12. Stowe, 391.

13. Poe, "The Philosophy of Composition," *Complete Works*, 14: 200.

14. *Moore's Irish Melodies*, 24–25.

15. *The American Songster, Containing a Choice Selection of about One Hundred and Fifty Modern and Popular Songs*, ed. John Kenedy (Baltimore: John Kenedy, 1835), 15–16; Emily Dickinson to Abiah Root, 25 September 1845, *The Letters of Emily Dickinson*, 1: 18; Tawa, *Music for the Millions*, 45, 123; Tawa, *Sweet Songs*, 129.

16. All quotations are from Poe, *Poetry and Tales*.

17. Allen *et al.*, *Slave Songs of the United States*, 46.

18. "No More Auction Block for Me," Gustavus D. Pike, *The Jubilee Singers* . . . (Boston: 1873), 186, reproduced in Southern, 159–60. Robeson's performance can be heard on *The Power and the Glory*, Columbia/Legacy CK 47337. Dylan's is on *The Bootleg Series 1961–1991 (Rare and Unreleased)*, vol. 1, Columbia 47382, and John Bauldie relates "No More Auction Block" to "Blowin' in the Wind" in his liner notes for this set (6–8).

19. Charlotte Foster to Eliza C. Foster, 12 August 1828 (FHC, C402).

20. Joseph Kaye, "Famous First Nights: 'Uncle Tom's Cabin,'" *Theatre Magazine* (August 1929): 26; Gossett, 260.

21. Harry Birdoff, *The World's Greatest Hit* (New York: S. F. Vanni, 1947), 24.

22. Ramshaw, 46; Krohn, 28–29; James, 91; T. Allston Brown, 1: 72.

23. Gossett, 269–71; T. Allston Brown, 1: 312; Cordelia Howard Macdonald, "Memoirs of the Original Little Eva," *Educational Theatre Journal* 8, no. 4: 273.

24. George L. Aiken and George C. Howard, *Uncle Tom's Cabin*, ed. Thomas Riis, vol. 5 in *Nineteenth-Century American Musical Theater*, general editor, Deane L. Root (New York: Garland, 1994), 49.

25. Lawrence, *Strong on Music*, 2: 437 n. 173.

26. *Pittsburgh Daily Morning Post*, 17 November 1853.

CHAPTER 21: WHITE MEN'S MUSIC

1. Henrietta Foster Wick Thornton to Morrison Foster, 21 June 1853 (FHC, C532).

2. Jane McDowell's move to Lewistown is described in a 7 July 1926 letter from Jessie Welsh Rose, her great-granddaughter, to William H. Stevenson. A copy of the letter is on file at the Mifflin County (Pa.) Historical Society. An approximate date for the move is suggested by the disappearance of Jane McDowell's name from city directories for Pittsburgh and Allegheny City after 1850 (it reappears in 1860–61). Rev. James S. Woods's long residence in Lewistown is described in a "Historical Souvenir Booklet," *One Hundred and Fiftieth Anniversary of the Presbyterian Congregation of Lewistown* (Lewistown, 1935).

3. Henrietta Foster Wick Thornton to Morrison Foster, 21 June 1853 (FHC, C532).

4. James Buchanan to Edward Young Buchanan, 15 November 1854, typed transcript (FHC).

5. Mahon, 6.

6. According to John Tasker Howard's draft of his memoirs (FHC, p. B 57), Evelyn Foster Morneweck told him that this is what Stephen Foster's siblings had felt.

7. Peter Quinn, *Banished Children of Eve* (New York: Viking Penguin, 1994).

8. Nevin, 615.

9. Rose, "His Widow's Memories."

10. Morrison Foster, 39.

11. Evelyn Foster Morneweck to Rhea L. Larrabee, 9 February 1940 (FHC); "Massa's in de Cold Ground," *New York Evening Sun,* 12 October 1888.

12. Rose, "His Widow's Memories."

13. George Shiras, 16–19; Morrison Foster to S. Reed Johnston, 14 February 1886 (FHC).

14. *Pittsburgh Daily Morning Post,* 9 and 11 November 1853. See also, Edward G. Fletcher, "Stephen Collins Foster, Dramatic Collaborator," *The Colophon,* new series, vol. 1, no. 1 (Summer 1935): 34–35; and Morneweck, 2: 432–35.

15. *Pittsburgh Daily Morning Post,* 12 November 1853; Morneweck, 2: 435–436.

16. *Pittsburgh Daily Morning Post,* 17 November 1853.

17. Foster is said to have sat only once for this bland portrait, which was not delivered to Firth, Pond and has never been satisfactorily authenticated. It now hangs in FHC, while another purported portrait by Hicks, which bears less of a likeness to Stephen Foster, is in the collection of the National Portrait Gallery in Washington. See Morneweck 2: 424–25. For Hicks, see Henry T. Tuckerman, *Book of the Artists. American Artist Life . . . ,* 2d ed. (New York: G. P. Putnam & Son, 1867), 465–66.

18. Starr, 126.

19. Quoted in H. W. Schwartz, *Bands of America* (Garden City: Doubleday, 1957), 20.

20. R. Storrs Willis, *Musical World and Times,* 19 February 1853, and Richard Hoffman, *Some Musical Recollections of Fifty Years* (New York: Scribner, 1910), 133, both quoted in Lawrence, *Strong on Music,* 2: 399, 2: 402–3 n. 80; Jeanne Behrend, introduction to Gottschalk, *Notes of a Pianist,* xvi, quoting Oscar Comettant.

21. See, for example, Locke, 37.

22. Starr, 139.

23. "The Banjo, Grotesque Fantasie, American Sketch," *Piano Music of Louis Moreau Gottschalk: 26 Complete Pieces from Original Editions,* ed. Richard Jackson (New York: Dover, 1973), 25–38.

24. Starr, 231; Schwartz, 29.

25. Schwartz, 23; Lawrence, *Strong on Music,* 2: 359, 365.

26. *Musical World and New York Musical Times,* 19 February 1853, quoted in Howard, 206.

27. *Musical World and New York Musical Times,* 8 January 1853, quoted in Howard, 220; *Musical World and New York Musical Times,* 26 February 1853,

reprinted in Elliker, 98; P. T. Barnum to his British publisher, 27 January 1860, *Selected Letters*, 103.

28. Lawrence, *Strong on Music*, 2: 380.

29. Perry Miller, *The Raven and the Whale: The War of Words and Wit in the Era of Poe and Melville* (New York: Harvest, 1956), 132.

30. Firth, Pond made this claim in an advertisement in the 4 January 1855 *New-York Musical Review and Choral Advocate: A Journal of Sacred and Secular Music* and added that, "as a consequence of its popularity, all the military bands are playing it as a *Quick Step*" (6, no. 1, 2).

31. Burns's song begins, "The winter it is past, and the summer's come at last," and describes the singer's love as "For ever constant and true." *Robert Burns, The Poems and Songs of Robert Burns*, ed. James Kinsley (Oxford, Eng.: Oxford at the Clarendon Press, 1968), 1: 409. Foster's song starts, "The morn of life is past, / And evening comes at last. . . ." Campbell's harper is a poor Irish minstrel named (what else?) Pat, who must leave his beloved Sheelah on the banks of the Shannon but is parted only by its death from his seeing eye dog, Tray. (In a surprise ending, the last quatrain reveals that Pat is blind.) *The Complete Poetical Works of Thomas Campbell*, ed. J. Logie Robertson (London: Oxford University Press, 1907), 255.

32. Morrison Foster, 48.

33. Rose, "His Widow's Memories."

34. FHC, A348; Elliker, 99.

35. Lawrence, *Strong on Music*, 2: 345–46; James, 66; Maretzek, 159–60, 164.

36. Whitman, quoted in Kaplan, 178; Whitman, "Proud Music of the Storm," ll.75–79, *Collected Writings, Leaves of Grass*, 3: 578; Lawrence, *Strong on Music*, 2: 577, 694 n. 91.

37. Way, 349; *Pittsburgh Daily Gazette*, 28 November 1853.

38. *Dwight's Journal of Music*, 19 June 1852, reprinted in *What They Heard*, 171.

39. *The Social Orchestra* is reprinted in full in Saunders and Root, 1: 287–371, and available in a separate edition edited by H. Wiley Hitchcock (New York: Da Capo, 1973). Selections from *The Social Orchestra* may be heard on *The Europeans: Music from the Motion Picture Soundtrack*, Angel CDQ 7243 5 55102 2 8, and Paula Robison, *By the Old Pine Tree: Flute Music by Stephen Foster and Sidney Lanier*, Arabesque Z6679. Austin identifies "Old Folks at Home" as the source of "Anadolia" (259), but Deane Root argues persuasively for "Massa" (interview by author, 23 May 1996).

40. Saunders and Root, 1: 482.

41. *Musical World and New York Musical Times*, 22 April 1854, 181–82, quoted in Lawrence, *Strong on Music*, 2: 444; *Musical World and New York Musical Times* 8, no. 8 (25 February 1854): 89.

42. No copy of this contract survives, but some of its provisions can be surmised from Foster's subsequent 21 December 1854 contract with Firth, Pond.

43. Starr, 211.

Chapter 22: "Heard Anything from Stephen Lately?"

1. *Foster Hall Bulletin*, no. 10 (May 1934): 23; Stephen Foster to Morrison Foster, 8 July 1853 (FHC, A348; Elliker, 99); James, 40.

2. *The Autobiography of Mark Twain*, 94; James, 98; Pike, *Catching the Tune*, 8; Frankenstein, 79, 91; Kaplan, 179–83; David S. Reynolds, *Walter Whitman's America: A Cultural Biography* (New York: Knopf, 1995), 302.

3. The manuscript is in FHC and described in Saunders and Root, 1: 467.

4. James, 41; Stephen Foster to Morrison Foster, 8 July 1853.

5. Stephen Foster to Morrison Foster, 8 July 1853.

6. *The Musical World and New York Musical Times* 8, no. 5 (4 February 1854): 53.

7. Austin points out these echoes (174).

8. I am grateful to graphologist Louise Erpelding for sharing her insights about Foster's handwriting.

9. *Christy's Plantation Melodies*. The $110 is noted in Stephen Foster's account book.

10. *The Musical World and New York Musical Times* 9, no. 7 (17 June 1854): 84.

11. Lawrence, *Strong on Music*, 2: 642 and 642 n. 161, quoting the 12 October 1855 *New York Herald*; "The Colored Fancy Ball," *Christy's Panorama Songster; containing the Songs as sung by The Christy, Campbell, Pierce's Minstrels, and Sable Brothers* (New York: William H. Murphy, n.d.), 72–73; Austin, 215 18.

12. Dunning Foster to Morrison Foster, 3 March 1854 (FHC, C539).

13. The prayer book (New York: D. Appleton, 1854) is in FHC.

14. Milligan, 74. Dating this anecdote is difficult. When Jessie Welsh Rose originally related it in "His Widow's Memories . . ." in the 4 July 1926 *Pittsburgh Post*, the phrase "when they had not yet gone to housekeeping" and her mention of "the fifties" seemed clearly to refer to the family's New York sojourn in 1853–54. But when she revised her article for the May 1934 *Foster Hall Bulletin*, where it ran under the title "My Grandmother's Memories," she wrote that afterward they "spent a happy year or so boarding in the comfortable home of Mrs. Stewart" (13)—with whom they didn't lodge until 1860–61. Rose could easily have scrambled events that occurred well before her birth. An 1853–54 date seems more likely, because 1) Rose retained the "housekeeping" reference in her revision, and the Fosters never kept a house in the 1860s; and 2) there's no reason to suppose they boarded elsewhere before lodging in 1860 with Mrs. Stewart.

15. Daniel E. Gavit, *Combined Directories of Jersey City, Hoboken, and Hudson, 1854–55* (Jersey City, 1854), 102, 110; Frances Trollope, 303; Nathan, 215–16; "Jim Crow" (New York: E. Riley, n.d.); Whitman, "Song of Myself," 1.751, *Collected Writings, Leaves of Grass*, 1: 46.

16. Gavit, Appendix, 41; T. W. Whitley, *A Guide to Hoboken, the Elysian Fields, and Weehawken* (no publisher or place of publication, but Whitley was editor of the *Hoboken City Gazette*; June, 1858), unpaginated.

17. Eliza C. Foster to Morrison Foster, 19 October 1854 (FHC, C543).

18. James Buchanan to Edward Young Buchanan, 26 October 1854 (FHC, typescript).

19. Ibid., 15 November 1854 (FHC, typescript).

20. Ibid., 15 December 1854 (FHC, typescript).

CHAPTER 23: HARD TIMES

1. Lorant, 545; James Buchanan to Edward Young Buchanan, 15 December 1854 (FHC, typescript); Bernstein, 5; George Templeton Strong, *The Diary of George Templeton Strong*, ed. Allan Nevins and Milton Halsey Thomas, vol. 2, *The Turbulent Fifties: 1850–1854* (New York: Macmillan, 1952), 203.

2. *New-York Musical Review and Choral Advocate: A Journal of Sacred and Secular Music* 6, no. 5 (1 March 1855): 73, 80.

3. Charles Dickens, *Hard Times* (London: Oxford University Press, 1955; reprint, 1963), 22, 11.

4. Morrison Foster, 36.

5. Francis Couvares, "Plebeian Society and Plebeian Culture: Pittsburgh in the Iron Age," in *David Gilmour Blythe's Pittsburgh: 1850–1865*, 42. *Hard Times* is in the collection of Pittsburgh's Carnegie Museum of Art; *Street Urchins* in the collection of the Butler Institute of American Art in Youngstown, Ohio.

6. These copies of the contract are in the Library of Congress, with photocopies in FHC.

7. *The Musical World* 10, no. 11 (11 November 1854): 140.

8. Accounts of Eliza Foster's death and burial, from the 19 and 22 January 1855 Pittsburgh *Daily Union*, are preserved among Morrison Foster's clippings (FHC).

9. Morrison Foster, 44; Dunning Foster to Morrison Foster, 25 October 1854 (FHC, C544). Morrison Foster's accounting of Eliza C. Foster's funeral expenses is preserved in FHC (C548).

10. Stephen Foster to Henrietta Foster Wick Thornton, 19 March 1855 (FHC, A308; Elliker, 99–100).

11. *Dwight's Journal of Music*, 11 March 1854, 181, quoted in Lawrence, *Strong on Music*, 2: 492 n. 44; Howard, 252; Hamm, *Yesterdays*, 222; Ida Kleber Todd to Josiah Kirby Lilly, 10 April 1933 (FHC).

12. William B. Foster's scrapbook (FHC, C390).

13. Douglas, 210.

14. *Pittsburg Press*, 7 July 1895; *Musical World*, 9 December 1854.

15. My psychological speculations about Foster here and elsewhere have been stimulated by Dr. Stuart Feder, the psychoanalyst and author of *Charles Ives: "My Father's Song"—A Psychoanalytic Biography*, who generously shared his insights in a lengthy 1995 interview.

16. Stephen Foster's account book is in FHC.

17. William B. Foster's scrapbook (FHC, C390).

18. Nevin, 616. *Temperance Pledge* (ca. 1856–60) is in the collection of the Carnegie Museum of Art.

19. Morneweck, 2: 470.

20. Ibid., 1: 168–69, 2: 491; Howard, 130 n.

CHAPTER 24: POLITICS AND PUNKINS

1. Carnegie, 65; Ullman, 83–85.

2. Allan Nevins, *Frémont, Pathmarker of the West* (New York: Frederick Ungar, 1961), 2: 442, 448; Updike, *Buchanan Dying*, 219; Coleman, 91–92.

3. "The Eighteenth Presidency!," reprinted in *Walt Whitman's Workshop: A Collection of Unpublished Manuscripts*, ed. Clifton Joseph Furness (New York: Russell & Russell, 1964), 100, quoted in Kaplan, 215.

4. Updike, *Buchanan Dying*, 261–62.

5. Klein, 126, 210; Ann Eliza Foster Buchanan to Morrison Foster, 2 June 1854 (FHC, C540); Henry Foster to Morrison Foster, 12 March 1853 (FHC, C533).

6. *New York Herald*, 3 December 1856, quoted in Klein, 262.

7. Constitution and Minutes Book of the Allegheny Buchanan Glee Club (FHC, C731); "Foster Memorial," *Pittsburg Press*, 11 July 1895.

8. Fletcher Hodges, Jr., "Stephen Foster, Democrat" (*Lincoln Herald*, Lincoln Memorial University, Harrogate, Tenn., 1945; reprint, Pittsburgh: University of Pittsburgh, 1946), 12.

9. Holt, *Forging a Majority*, 210; Klein, 268, 273; undated newspaper clipping in the Margaret Scully Townsend Archives in the Historical Society of Western Pennsylvania.

10. Stephen Foster to William Hamilton, 16 January 1857 (FHC, A311; Elliker, 100).

11. Lawrence, *Strong on Music*, 2: 602; Starr, 239, 242.

12. Barnum, *Struggles and Triumphs*, 491.

13. Walters, 35.

14. John B. Russell, "Foster's Music," *Cincinnati Daily Gazette*, 22 January 1857.

15. "Who Wrote the Negro Songs" is reprinted, with no indication of its derivation from the *Cincinnati Gazette*, in *What They Heard*, 267. A slightly different version appeared in *Western Fireside* (Madison, Wisc.) on 25 April 1857 and was reprinted on 14 November 1863 in *Notes and Queries: A Medium of Inter-Communication for Literary Men, General Readers, Etc.*, Third Series—Volume Fourth (London, July–December 1863), 392.

16. Stephen Foster to John B. Russell, 28 January 1857 (Rush Rhees Library, Rochester, N.Y.; Elliker, 101–2).

17. Foster's tally is preserved in the Library of Congress, and photocopies are in FHC. A meticulous analysis of this document and also of Foster's account book appears in Howard, 265–73.

18. Carnegie, 87–88.

19. "Editor's Table," *The Knickerbocker or New York Monthly Magazine* 54, no. 6 (December 1859): 668.

20. *New York Musical Review*, 6 February 1858, cited in Tawa, *Sweet Songs*, 117.

CHAPTER 25: WHEN THE MUSE IS MISSING

1. Foster's 1858 contract is in the Library of Congress, and photocopies are in FHC.

2. *Directory of Pittsburgh & Vicinity for 1859–60*, ed. George H. Thurston (Pittsburgh: George H. Thurston, 1859).

3. *Littell's Living Age* 2, 24 (26 October 1844): 736; Kussart, 36–38.

4. Hamm, *Yesterdays*, 222–23; Stephen Foster to Morrison Foster, 22 October 1858 (FHC, A337; Elliker, 103); *The National Melodies of Scotland; United to the Songs of Robert Burns, Allan Ramsay, and Other Eminent Lyric Poets; with Symphonies and Accompaniments for the Piano Forte, by Haydn, Pleyel, Kozeluch, and Other Celebrated Composers* (London: John and Frederick Tallis, 1849); Burns, 2: 698–99.

5. Stephen Foster to Morrison Foster, 11 November 1858 (FHC, A338; Elliker, 103); Walters, 30.

6. *Pittsburg Press*, 16 July 1895.

7. *Pittsburgh Gazette*, 5 November 1858. Kussart described William H. McCarthy as "a well-known actor" (37), but it's more likely he was the William McCarthy listed as a pressman in Pittsburgh directories for 1857 through '60, even though sometimes his name appears with the middle initial "C."

8. "None Shall Weep a Tear for Me" was not copyrighted until 9 February 1860, but the cover of the sheet music, labeling it No. 42 of "Foster's Melodies," indicates that it was issued out of sequence and initially prepared for publication by Firth, Pond to follow "Fairy-Belle," No. 41, which was copyrighted 19 August 1859. See Saunders and Root, 2: 425.

9. Aubrey Starke, "Richard Henry Wilde: Some Notes and a Check-List," *The American Book Collector* 5, no. 1 (January 1934): 7–8; Edward L. Tucker, *Richard Henry Wilde: His Life and Selected Poems* (Athens: University of Georgia Press, 1966), 1, 95, 102 (quoting Poe in the December 1841 *Graham's Magazine*), 275 n.

10. "Who Writes Our Songs?" was reprinted, among other places, in the 14 May 1859 *Dwight's Journal of Music* (see *What They Heard*, 267–68) and *Cosmopolitan Art Journal* 3, no. 3 (June 1859): 125.

11. These figures differ slightly, but not significantly, from those computed by Howard (282–83, 290–91), who relied on the tallies now in the Library of Congress, while my calculations are based on Foster's account book in FHC.

12. Matilda Eliza (Lidie) Wick to Morrison Foster, 27 May 1858 (FHC, C560); Henrietta Foster Wick Thornton to Morrison Foster, 10 June 1859 (FHC, C567).

13. Stephen Foster to Morrison Foster, 13 June 1859 (FHC, A339; Elliker, 104); Morneweck, 2: 514. Both ambrotypes are in FHC.

14. The ferrotype, on black japanned iron, is in FHC.

15. *The Knickerbocker* 54, no. 6 (December 1859): 668.

16. *Godey's Lady's Book*, 40 (June 1850): 370–71, quoted in Bushman, 369.

CHAPTER 26: ALMOST A SPIRITUAL

1. Col. John A. Joyce, "Genius Is Forgotten," *Washington Post*, 9 September 1900. Morrison Foster clipped and saved the story in his scrapbook (FHC).

2. Carmichael, 57–58.

3. *A Checkered Life* (Chicago: S. P. Rounds, 1883).

4. Tawa, *Sweet Songs*, 148–49; "Stand By Your Man," by B. Sherrill and T. Wynette, on Tammy Wynette's *Tammy's Greatest Hits*, Epic BN 26486.

5. Way, 189; Morneweck, 1: 273.

6. Rollin, 85–95; Delany, *Blake*, 100–101, 105–6, 143.

7. Berndt Ostendorf, "Minstrelsy & Early Jazz," *The Massachusetts Review* 20, no. 3 (Autumn 1979): 581–82.

8. "Crow Out Shanghai," written and composed by W. H. Percival (New York: Dressler & Clayton, ca. 1855).

9. Edward A. Pollard, *Black Diamonds Gathered in the Darkey Homes of the South* (New York: Pudney & Russell, 1859), 94–95.

10. Rose, "His Widow's Memories."

11. W. E. B. Du Bois, *The Souls of Black Folk*, in *Writings*, ed. Nathan Huggins (New York: Library of America, 1986), 540. See, also, "The Negro in Literature and Art," *op. cit.*, 862.

12. James Weldon Johnson: *The Autobiography of an Ex-Colored Man*, ed. William L. Andrews (New York: Penguin, 1990), 132; James Dixon, *Personal Narrative of a Tour through a Part of the United States and Canada: With Notices of the History and Institutions of Methodism in America* (New York: Lane & Scott, 1849), 94.

CHAPTER 27: ALL IN THE FAMILY

1. Joyce described his confinement in *A Checkered Life*, 31–43.

2. William Bender Wilson, 262; Harold C. Livesay, *Andrew Carnegie and the Rise of Big Business* (Boston: Little, Brown, 1975), 35. A copy of "An Act to Incorporate the 'Foster Coal and Iron Company' " is in FHC (C725).

3. Mary Cassatt was born in Allegheny City in 1844, while the Foster family resided there. One reason Marie Lois Buchanan Cassatt was uncomfortable with her in-laws may have been that her father-in-law, Robert Cassat, was thought by some to have once been a suitor of Marie Lois's mother before he added a second "t" to his name and Ann Eliza Foster married Edward Buchanan. See Patricia T. Davis, *End of the Line: Alexander J. Cassatt and the Pennsylvania Railroad* (New York: Neale Watson Academic Publications, 1978), 10, 20, 24–26, 29–31, 41, 82, 98.

4. William Bender Wilson, 263; Carnegie, 88; Davis, 17.

5. Stephen Foster to Morrison Foster, 27 April 1860 (FHC, A341; Elliker, 105).

6. *Warren (Ohio) Daily Tribune*, 21 May 1912; Mrs. C. G. Mygatt, quoted in the *Youngstown Telegram*, 3 February 1934.

7. Stephen Foster to Morrison Foster, 31 May 1860 (FHC; Elliker, 105–6).

8. Mahon, 6.

9. Douglas, 205–6.

10. Musical Department, *Clark's School Vistor*, July 1860, reprinted in Saunders and Root, 2: 97.

11. "... [F]or the six beautiful songs written for us by Mr. Foster, our publishers paid the sum of $400...." *Clark's School Visitor*, April 1864, quoted in Howard, 324.

12. *George Christy's Essence of Old Kentucky* (New York: Dick & Fitzgerald, 1864).

13. Mahon, 4; *Pittsburg Press*, 12 September 1900; George W. Birdseye, "A Reminiscence of the late Stephen C. Foster," *The New York Musical Gazette* 1, no. 3 (January 1867): 2.

14. *Youngstown Telegram*, 3 February 1934.

CHAPTER 28: "INFERNAL *SWISH-SWISH*!"

1. Holt, "Change and Conflict: Politics in Pittsburgh, 1850–1865," in *David Gilmour Blythe's Pittsburgh*, 56; Leland Baldwin, 311–13; James M. McPherson, *The Battle Cry of Freedom: The Civil War Era* (New York: Ballantine, 1989), 226, 328; Robert Wray, "Abandonment of the Allegheny Arsenal," *The Pittsburgh Gazette*, 12 January 1902.

2. Klein, 211 (citing John W. Forney as quoted in the Jan. 24, 1860 *Philadelphia Press*) and 374 (citing, among other sources, December, 1860 letters to Lincoln from C. S. Henry and G. G. Fogg); Anthony Trollope, *North America* (Baltimore: Penguin, 1968), 28; Morneweck, 2: 531.

3. Carlyon, 259–60 (quoting the June 29 and April 20, 1861 *Clipper*), 269–74.

4. Ernest A. McKay, *The Civil War and New York City* (Syracuse, N.Y.: Syracuse University Press, 1990), 25, 33–34, 37–38; Odell, 7: 370.

5. "Eighteen Sixty-One," ll.2–4, *Drum-Taps*, in *Leaves of Grass* . . . 2: 466–67.

6. Rose, "My Grandmother's Memories," 13–14. All quotes and paraphrases of Mahon, unless otherwise noted, are drawn from his March 1877 *New York Clipper* article, "The Last Years of Stephen C. Foster," reprinted in *Foster Hall Bulletin* 10 (May 1943): 2–6.
The exact address of the Greene Street boardinghouse and the spelling of its proprietor's name are uncertain. Their granddaughter recalled that the Fosters boarded with a Mrs. Stewart (Rose, "My Grandmother's Memories," 13), and Mahon wrote that the Fosters boarded with Mr. and Mrs. Stewart at

No. 83. Between 1860 and 1865, boardinghouses were listed in New York City directories at 113 Greene (run by a Stuart, in 1859–60), 107 Greene (run by Joseph D. Stewart, in 1861), and at 97 Greene (run by Louisa Stuart, 1863–64). It makes little difference at which of these addresses the Fosters stayed, since all but one of them were on the east side of the same block, between Prince and Spring Streets, and No. 83 Greene was just one block farther south.

7. George Cooper to Vincent Milligan, 2 July 1917 (FHC).

8. Milligan, 103.

9. The composer George F. Root's Chicago firm, Root & Cady, published "Beautiful Child of Song" and "Mine Is the Mourning Heart" in 1863; Horace Waters published "Lizzie Dies To-Night" in 1862 and "The Little Ballad Girl" in 1864; and Oliver Ditson published "The Merry, Merry Month of May" in 1862. See Saunders and Root, 2: 428–30, 433.

10. McKay, 216.

11. Odell, 7: 297, 365.

12. Ibid., 7: 90–91, 183, 349, 450, 597.

13. Ibid., 7: 310–13; Deane L. Root, *American Popular Stage Music 1860–1880* (Ann Arbor, Mich.: UMI Research Press, 1981), 70–71. Although Amelia may have been a pet name for Marion, it appears nowhere else in Foster's correspondence or lyrics.

14. This and much other information about Jane Foster's family and circumstances in Lewistown and Greensburg come from Jessie Welsh Rose's July 7, 1926, letter to William H. Stevenson, and a December 7, 1971, article by Jim Canfield in the Lewistown *Sentinel*. Copies of both are at the Mifflin County Historical Society, Lewistown, Pa.

15. Robert B. Van Atta, "Wife, child of troubled Stephen Foster found untroubled home in Greensburg," Greensburg *Tribune-Review*, 11 April 1993; and Robert B. Van Atta, letter to the author, 29 August 1995.

16. Carnegie, 66–67. Determining when Jane Foster assumed her duties is complicated by an anecdote related by Foster biographer John Tasker Howard. In 1933, Howard interviewed a man who said that his Aunt Nettie had been Jane's assistant and pupil in Greensburg, and that Aunt Nettie had been sixteen or seventeen at the time—in 1859 or 1860. His aunt told him that Jane and she

worked on the night shift, and that often Stephen would come out on the midnight train, sometimes a bit worse for wear. Stephen would be talkative, and insist on distracting Jane from her work.

After this occurred a few times, Jane would send her assistant to the station platform when she heard the train coming, to see if Stephen was aboard. If he was, the assistant would run back to the telegrapher's room in time to lock the door before Stephen got there. Then, according to the story, Stephen would sit down and play the violin he carried with him until his wife and her assistant were ready to come out at the close of their working hours. (Howard, 296–97)

If this indeed happened in 1859–60, it must have been between March 11, 1859, when Andrew Carnegie put his friend Davy McCargo in charge of telegraphy and started hiring women, and April 1860, by which date (if not earlier) Jane and Stephen Foster were in Warren, Ohio. A year seems a short time in which to hire and train Maria Hogan, for her in turn to train Jane Foster, and for Jane in turn to be training someone else. And if Jane had been working then, her income might be expected to show up in Stephen's account book, or her employment to be mentioned in one of the Foster family's letters. Every account other than this story states that Jane worked as a telegrapher after returning from New York.

If Stephen harassed Jane at a later date, it opens another can of worms, since there is no record of Stephen returning to Pennsylvania after 1860. He wrote in a December 6, 1862, letter to his brother Henry that he had not been in Pittsburgh in "nearly three years" (FHC, A309; Elliker, 106). It's conceivable but extremely unlikely that he made such a trip in the last year of his life, and its lack of corroboration argues for discounting this third-hand anecdote.

17. Jane D. Foster to Morrison Foster, 30 September 1861 (FHC, C578).

18. Ibid., 10 October 1861 (FHC, C579).

19. Willard A. Heaps and Porter W. Heaps, *The Singing Sixties: The Spirit of Civil War Days Drawn from the Music of the Times* (Norman: University of Oklahoma Press, 1960), 18; Gottschalk, *Notes of a Pianist*, 181–82.

20. George Root, 152.

21. George Cooper to Vincent Milligan, 2 July 1917 (FHC).

22. *Cleveland Plain Dealer*, 28 February 1861.

23. Dailey Paskman, *Gentlemen, Be Seated: A Parade of American Minstrels*, rev. ed. (New York: Clarkson N. Potter, 1976), 147; Odell, 7: 429–30.

24. McKay, 118–19; Lorant, 138–39.

25. "Our War-Songs," *The Musical Review and Musical World* 15, no. 24 (19 November 1864): 374.

26. Heaps and Heaps, 89; Hodges, "Stephen Foster, Democrat," 24; Saunders and Root, 2: 436.

27. Robert M. Copeland, "Luther O(rlando) Emerson," *New Grove Dictionary of American Music*, 2: 45; Heaps and Heaps, 89.

28. F. Scott Fitzgerald, "Handle with Care," *The Crack-Up*, ed. Edmund Wilson (New York: New Directions, 1956), 75.

29. Jane D. Foster to Morrison Foster, 30 June 1862 (FHC, C580); Morneweck, 2: 542; Rose, "His Widow's Memories." Rose did not date this anecdote more precisely than "the latter days of [Stephen's] life." It probably occurred in the fall of 1863, when Morrison seems to have visited New York.

30. William Arms Fisher, *One Hundred and Fifty Years of Music Publishing in the United States, 1783–1933* (Boston: Oliver Ditson, 1933), 99–100; Saunders and Root, 2: 437.

31. Silcher's setting of Heine's *"Die Lorelei"* was published in America, as "Lore Lee," as early as 1851 (Boston: G. P. Reed), and widely popularized by German singing societies.

CHAPTER 29: RUM AND RELIGION

1. Stephen Foster to Henry Foster, 6 December 1862 (FHC, A309; Elliker, 106).

2. State of New York, *Report of the Select Committee appointed to examine into the condition of Tenant Houses in New-York and Brooklyn*, Assembly Doc. No. 205, 9 March 1857, 13–29, quoted in Adrian Cook, *The Armies of the Street: The New York Draft Riots of 1863* (Lexington: University of Kentucky Press, 1974), 11.

3. George G. Foster, *New York in Slices* (New York: William H. Graham, 1849), 79–83. George W. Birdseye wrote that the "old tumble-down Dutch grocery" was on the northwest corner of Chrystie and Hester (2). More likely it was Lankenau's grocery on the northeast corner of the intersection or Sieckmann's on the southwest corner, both listed in *Wilson's Business Directory of New York City* (New York: John F. Trow, 1862), 206 and 216, respectively.

4. Unless otherwise noted, all quotes of George W. Birdseye are from *The New York Musical Gazette* 1, no. 3 (January 1867): 2–3. Birdseye wrote a second installment in the March, 1867 issue of *The New York Musical Gazette* (vol. 1, no. 5: 33–34) that adds little of interest. Morrison Foster protested Birdseye's stories in a letter to the *Gazette*'s publishers. A penciled draft of that letter is C899 in FHC.

5. Virginia Ann Cross, "The Development of Sunday School Hymnody in the United States of America, 1816–1869" (Ph.D. diss., New Orleans Baptist Theological Seminary, 1985), 409–10, 417. My discussion of Waters's Sunday school hymns is indebted to Cross.

6. Thomas Hastings, *Musical Review and Choral Advocate*, May 1853, quoted in Howard, 218–19. See also Edward Wilbur Rice, *The Sunday-School Movement, 1780–1917, and the American Sunday-School Union, 1817–1917* (Philadelphia: American Sunday-School Union, 1917; reprint, New York: Arno Press and the New York Times, 1971), 149–53; and Hamm, *Music in the New World*, 231.

7. Horace Waters, introduction to *The Sabbath-School Bell* (New York: Horace Waters, 1859), 11, quoted in Cross, 409–10.

8. "Little Lessons for Little Folks," *Youth's Companion* 1, 1 May 1833, 20, quoted in Anne M. Boylan, *Sunday School: The Formation of an American Institution, 1790–1880* (New Haven: Yale University Press, 1988), 140.

9. "Last of New England's Famous Women Hymnologists," *Boston Sunday Herald*, 12 December 1905.

10. Saunders and Root, 2: 451.

11. Milligan, 101.

12. The following account of Cooper's first meeting with Foster is drawn from Cooper's own article, "Stephen C. Foster," *J. W. Pepper Piano Magazine* 4, no. 20 (May 1902): 66; and from Milligan, 104.

13. Odell, 7: 342.

14. Milligan, 104.

15. George W. Wingate, *History of the Twenty-Second Regiment of the National*

Guard of the State of New York (New York: Edwin W. Dayton, 1896), 19, 33–35, 126, 141, 146, 327, 627, 639.

16. The words to "Give This to Mother" have been attributed to one S. W. Harding. See Saunders and Root, 2: 458.

17. Heaps and Heaps, 224–26.

18. McKay, 195; *Banquet given by the members of Union League Club of 1863 and 1864, to commemorate the departure for the war of the 20th regiment of United States Colored Troops Raised by the Club* (New York: Union League Club, 1886), 214, cited in Cook, 175.

19. Morneweck, 2: 529, 542–46; Frank L. Klement, *The Limits of Dissent: Clement L. Vallandigham and the Civil War* (Lexington: University Press of Kentucky, 1970), 135; McKay, 186–89; William Armstrong, "Personal Recollections," *Cincinnati Daily Enquirer*, 20 March 1886, quoted in Klement, 243.

20. Mark Tucker, "Tony Antonio Pastor," *The New Grove Dictionary of American Music*, 3: 484; "G. Cooper, Song Writer / Author of 'Sweet Genevieve' Dies in his Sleep at Age of 89," *New York Times*, 28 September 1927, 25.

21. *Tony Pastor's New Comic Irish Songster* (New York: Dick and Fitzgerald, 1863), 42–43. See also, Saunders and Root, 2: 450.

22. Mahon, 2, 6; Odell, 7: 224, 227–30, 236–37 (citing the 6 September 1859 *New York Herald*), 568–70.

23. *New York Leader*, 19 April 1862, reprinted in *Walt Whitman and the Civil War: A Collection of Original Articles and Manuscripts*, ed. Charles I. Glicksberg (Philadelphia: University of Pennsylvania Press, 1933; reprint, New York: Perpetua/A.S. Barnes, 1963), 48. Jon W. Finson traces this breezier, less sublimated style of love song to Silas Steel and Fred Buckley's "Kiss Me Quick and Go" (1856), putting Foster's collaborations with Cooper in the context of a shift in sexual attitudes that occurred in popular music during the 1860s. See Finson's *The Voices That Are Gone: Themes in Nineteenth-Century American Popular Song* (New York: Oxford University Press, 1994), 44–46.

24. George Cooper to Robert Coster, 11 March 1916 (FHC); FHC A309, Elliker, 106.

25. Milligan, 105; George Cooper to Vincent Milligan, 2 July 1917 (FHC); George Foster, *New York in Slices*, 81.

26. Milligan, 105; George Cooper to Vincent Milligan, 2 July 1917; Saunders and Root, 2: 444.

27. Milligan, 103. A half-century later, Cooper may well have mistaken the street address, since the hotel in which Foster was lodging at the time of his death was at 30 Bowery. But an 1867 map indicates that No. 15 was also a hotel, and Foster may have patronized both. See *Insurance Maps of the City of New York*, vol. 1 (New York: Perris & Browne, 1867).

28. Bruce Chambers, *The World of David Gilmour Blythe (1815–1865)* (Washington, D.C.: Smithsonian Institution Press for the National Collection of Fine Arts, 1980), 73–75. *Art versus Law* is in the collection of the Brooklyn Museum of Art.

CHAPTER 30: LAST PALL

1. Unless otherwise noted, this account and interpretation of the Draft Riots are drawn from Bernstein and Cook, in their entireties, and from McKay, 195–215.

2. John Vance Lauderdale, *The Wounded River: The Civil War Letters of John Vance Lauderdale, M.D.*, ed. Peter Josyph (East Lansing: Michigan State University Press, 1993), 162.

3. Wall, 168–71, 189–90.

4. Wingate, 327, 332–40.

5. *The Life of Joseph Hodges Choate as Gathered Chiefly from His Letters* (New York: Scribner's, 1920), 1: 255–56, quoted in McKay, 201.

6. Fitzgerald, "Handle with Care," *The Crack-Up*, 79.

7. Starr, 311–312, 341, 345; *Piano Music of Louis Moreau Gottschalk*, 49–66; Octavia Hensel [Mary Alice Ives Seymour], *Life and Letters of Louis Moreau Gottschalk* (Boston: Oliver Ditson, 1870), 131–33, 137, 145.

8. Cooper to Milligan, 2 July 1917, Morneweck, 2: 541–42.

9. This portion of the letter was transcribed by Evelyn Foster Morneweck, who indicated in a handwritten note on file in FHC (C881) that she had sent the original letter, "of a very personal nature which I did not feel was proper to me to take upon myself to make public," to "the relative who would be most *affected* and *concerned* if it were published." Who that "relative" was (Marion Foster?), and what revelations the letter contained, are tantalizing mysteries.

10. Mahon, 6.

11. Howard, 343; *New York Leader,* 19 April 1862, reprinted in *Whitman and the Civil War,* 49–51; Nathan, 117; Henry Foster to Ann Eliza Foster Buchanan, 4 February 1864, transcript (FHC, C534).

12. Henry Foster to Susan G. Beach, 23 January 1864, transcript (FHC, C534); Henry Foster to Ann Eliza Foster Buchanan; Milligan, 106; *New York Evening Sun,* 12 October 1888.

13. Milligan, 106.

14. Milligan, 106; Lauderdale, 171, 224–25 n. 33; Howard, 342–43; Bellevue record in FHC (A364).

15. Milligan, 106; *New York Evening Sun,* 12 October 1888; George Cooper to Morrison Foster, 12 January 1864 (FHC, A361); Henry Foster to Susan G. Beach.

16. Henry Foster to Ann Eliza Foster Buchanan; Milligan, 106–7; *New York Evening Sun,* 12 October 1888; Howard, 342.

17. Lauderdale, 167–68. The circumstances of Foster's death do not appear to indicate tuberculosis, a condition from which Howard speculated that Foster suffered (69, 150, 305). I am indebted for this deathbed diagnosis to Dr. Daniel Roses of New York University Medical Center (telephone interviews by author).

18. *The Notebooks of F. Scott Fitzgerald,* ed. Matthew J. Bruccoli (New York: Harcourt Brace Jovanovich/Bruccoli Clark, 1978), 58.

19. *Broadway Journal* 1 (1 March 1845), 139, quoted in Silverman, 246. Here and elsewhere, my interpretation of Poe has been stimulated by Silverman's biography.

20. *Baudelaire on Poe*, ed. Lois and Francis E. Hyslop, Jr. (State College, Pa.: 1952), 101, quoted in Silverman, 436.

21. Henry Foster to Susan G. Beach; Milligan, 107.

22. Henry Foster to Ann Eliza Buchanan. The receipt for Stephen Foster's Bellevue expenses and the slip of paper are in FHC (A363, A322, respectively).

23. Carnegie, 75–76; Morrison Foster, 54; *Pittsburgh Gazette*, 21 January 1864; Henry Foster to Susan G. Beach; Henry Foster to Ann Eliza Buchanan; Morneweck, 2: 561; William Bender Wilson, 261–62.

24. *Pittsburgh Post*, undated clipping in Morrison Foster's scrapbook (FHC); *Pittsburgh Gazette*, 22 January 1864; *Episcopal Common Praise: Consisting of the Chants in the Morning and Evening Service of the Book of Common Prayer and the Psalms of David . . .* , ed. George E. Thrall (New York: A.S. Barnes, 1868), 477–80; William Brooks, liner notes to *The Flowering of Vocal Music in America, Volume 2*.

25. Ralph Ellison, "The Little Man at Cheraw Station," *Going to the Territory* (New York: Vintage, 1987), 24.

26. *Pittsburgh Commercial*, 22 January 1864, cited in Milligan, 107; Henry Foster to Susan G. Beach.

27. "American Popular Ballads," *The Round Table*, 117.

28. George Cooper to Morrison Foster, 2 February 1864 (FHC, C878).

29. Waters made his claim in *The Musical Review and Musical World* 15, no. 6 (12 March 1864): 104. All the other claims are culled from the published music as reproduced in Saunders and Root, vol. 2.

30. A sheet of music paper survives on which Foster jotted down the identical melody, as well as lyrics by George Birdseye. This may well have been the "memento" from which Cooper worked, providing new words of his own. Birdseye's original lyric was set to music by two other composers and published in both settings as "Down by the Gate" in 1863. See Saunders and Root, 2: 453, 455.

31. Ibid., 2: 497.

AFTERWORD

1. Kunzog, 222–23, 328, 406, 432; *Dan Rice's Great American Humorist Song Book*, 23–25, 29–31. The letter from Dan Rice is preserved in Morrison Foster's scrapbook (FHC).

2. Morneweck, 2: 630; Wall, 338–40; Carnegie, 189.

3. *Pittsburgh Gazette*, 6 December 1864; Gottschalk, *Notes*, 237, 243.

4. Starr, 378–83, 435–37; *Piano Music of Louis Moreau Gottschalk*, 257–63.

5. Rollin, 19, 166–77; Ullman, 483, 501–6; Eric Foner, *Reconstruction: America's Unfinished Revolution 1863-1877* (New York: Harper & Row, 1989), 572–74.

6. Andrew Carnegie to John Ross, 11 February 1913, Andrew Carnegie papers, Library of Congress, vol. 213, quoted in Wall, 221; Carnegie, 335–36, 341; Morneweck, 2: 423.

7. Noel B. Gerson, *Harriet Beecher Stowe: A Biography* (New York: Praeger, 1976), 107, 179, 192.

8. *Popular Songs of Nineteenth-Century America*, 282; "G. Cooper, Song Writer," *New York Times*, 28 September 1927, 25; James J. Geller, "The Thankless Muse," *Variety* 185 (2 January 1952), 228.

9. *Pittsburgh Evening Chronicle*, 29 June 1870; *The Philadelphia Age*, undated clipping in Morrison Foster's scrapbook (FHC).

10. Morneweck, 2: 569; *Directory of Pittsburgh & Allegheny Cities . . . for 1872–73* (Pittsburgh: George H. Thurston, 1872); Jesse W. Rose to William H. Stevenson; undated newspaper clipping (FHC, A300). Jane Foster's diary is in FHC.

11. Newspaper clipping, 17 January 1903 (FHC, A300).

12. Howard, 350–57.

13. Morneweck, 2: 571–72, 584.

14. Marion Foster Welch to Anna Stephenson Boggs, 2 November 1923 (FHC). Marion's preoccupation with the Lawrenceville property is documented in a 27 July 1925 letter to Boggs, one of five graciously given to FHC by her son, John Gordon Boggs, in 1993. It is corroborated by various newspaper stories. See, for example, the *Warren (Ohio) Daily Tribune*, 7 June 1909.

15. Charles Ives, *114 Songs* (Bryn Mawr, Pa: Merion, 1935), no. 43. For a discussion of "The Things Our Father Loved," see Feder, 253–56; for an excellent performance, listen to Jan DeGaetani, Gilbert Kalish, *Charles Ives Songs*, Elektra/Nonesuch 9 71325–2.

SELECTED
BIBLIOGRAPHY

Aaron, Daniel. *Cincinnati, Queen City of the West: 1819–1838*. Columbus: Ohio State University Press, 1992.

Aiken, George L., and George C. Howard. *Uncle Tom's Cabin*. Edited by Thomas Riis. Vol. 5 of *Nineteenth-Century American Musical Theater*, edited by Deane L. Root. New York: Garland, 1994.

Allen, William Francis, Charles Pickard Ware and Lucy McKim Garrison, eds. *Slave Songs of the United States*. New York: A. Simpson, 1867.

"American Popular Ballads." *The Round Table* 1, no. 8 (6 February 1864): 117.

The American Songster, Containing a Choice Selection of about One Hundred and Fifty Modern and Popular Songs. Edited by John Kenedy. Baltimore: John Kenedy, 1835.

The Anti-Slavery Harp: Collection of Songs for Anti-Slavery Meetings. Edited by William W. Brown. 3d ed. Boston: Bela Marsh, 1851.

Austin, William W. *"Susanna," "Jeanie," and "The Old Folks at Home": The Songs of Stephen C. Foster from His Time to Ours*. 2d ed. Urbana: University of Illinois Press, 1987.

Baldwin, Leland D. *Pittsburgh: The Story of a City, 1750–1865*. Pittsburgh: University of Pittsburgh Press, 1937. Reprint, Pittsburgh: University of Pittsburgh Press, 1981.

Baldwin, Neil. *Edison: Inventing the Century*. New York: Hyperion, 1995.

Barnum, P. T. *Selected Letters of P. T. Barnum*. Edited by A. H. Saxon. New York: Columbia University Press, 1983.

———. *Struggles and Triumphs; or, Forty Years' Recollections of P. T. Barnum*. Buffalo: The Courier Company, 1882.

Baynham, E. G. "The Early Development of Music in Pittsburgh." Ph.D. diss., University of Pittsburgh, 1944.

Belohlavek, John M. *George Mifflin Dallas: Jacksonian Patrician*. University Park: Pennsylvania State University Press, 1977.

Bergreen, Laurence. *As Thousands Cheer: The Life of Irving Berlin*. New York: Viking, 1990.

Berlin, Edward A. *Ragtime: A Musical and Cultural History*. Berkeley: University of California Press, 1980.

Bernstein, Iver. *The New York City Draft Riots: Their Significance for American Society and Politics in the Age of the Civil War*. New York: Oxford University Press, 1990.

Biographical Annals of Franklin County, Pennsylvania. 1905. Reprint, Chambersburg, Pa.: The Print Peddler, 1978.

Birdoff, Harry. *The World's Greatest Hit*. New York: S. F. Vanni, 1947.

Birdseye, George W. "A Reminiscence of the late Stephen C. Foster." *The New York Musical Gazette* 1, no. 3 (January 1867): 2–3.

———. "A Reminiscence of the late Stephen C. Foster—II," *The New York Musical Gazette* 1, no. 5 (March 1867): 33–34.

Blacks at Harvard: A Documentary History of African-American Experience at Harvard and Radcliffe. Edited by Werner Sollers, Caldwell Titcomb and Thomas Underwood. New York: New York University Press, 1993.

Blair, Walter, and Franklin J. Meine, eds. *Half Horse Half Alligator: The Growth of the Mike Fink Legend*. Chicago: University of Chicago Press, 1956. Reprint, New York: Arno Press, 1977.

Blockson, Charles L. *The Underground Railroad in Pennsylvania*. Jacksonville, N.C.: Flame International, 1981.

Bode, Carl. *The Anatomy of Popular Culture 1840–1861*. Berkeley: University of California Press, 1960.

The Book of Brothers, or The History of the Hutchinson Family. New York: "published by and for the Hutchinson Family," 1852.

Boskin, Joseph. *Sambo: The Rise and Demise of an American Jester*. New York: Oxford University Press, 1986.

Boylan, Anne M. *Sunday School: The Formation of an American Institution, 1790–1880*. New Haven: Yale University Press, 1988.

Brackenridge, Henry Marie. *Recollections of Persons and Places in the West*. Philadelphia: Lippincott, 1868.

Brackenridge, Hugh Henry. *Modern Chivalry: Containing the Adventures of Captain John Farrago and Teague O'Reagan, His Servant*. Edited by Lewis Leary. New Haven: College & University Press, 1965.

Bremer, Fredrika. *The Homes of the New World: Impressions of America*. 2 vols. New York: Harper Bros., 1853. Reprint, New York: Negro Universities Press, 1968.

Brink, Carol. *Harps in the Wind: The Story of the Singing Hutchinsons*. New York: Macmillan, 1947.

Brown, T. Allston. *History of the American Stage*. 1870. Reprint, New York: Benjamin Blom, 1969.

Burns, Robert. *The Poems and Songs of Robert Burns*. Edited by James Kinsley. 3 vols. Oxford, Eng.: Oxford at the Clarendon Press, 1968.

Burt, John. "The Poet of the Iron City: Charles P. Shiras (1824–1854)." *Carnegie Magazine* 67, no. 7 (January–February, 1987): 20–25.

Bushman, Richard L. *The Refinement of America: Persons, Houses, Cities.* New York: Vintage, 1993.

Campbell, Thomas. *The Complete Poetical Works of Thomas Campbell.* Edited by J. Logie Robertson. London: Oxford University Press, 1907.

Camptown Pennsylvania 1792–1975. Wyalusing, Pa.: Camptown Civic Club, 1975.

Cantwell, Robert C. *Bluegrass Breakdown: The Making of the Old Southern Sound.* Urbana: University of Illinois Press, 1984.

Capps, Randall. *The Rowan Story: From Federal Hill to My Old Kentucky Home.* Bowling Green, Ky.: Homestead Press, 1976.

Carlyon, David James. "Dan Rice's Aspirational Project: The Nineteenth-Century Circus Clown and Middle-Class Formation." Ph.D. diss., Northwestern University, 1993.

Carmichael, Hoagy with Stephen Longstreet. *Sometimes I Wonder: The Story of Hoagy Carmichael.* New York: Farrar, Straus and Giroux, 1965.

Carnegie, Andrew. *The Autobiography of Andrew Carnegie.* Boston: Houghton Mifflin, 1920. Reprint, Boston: Northeastern University Press, 1986.

Catching the Tune: Music and William Sidney Mount. Edited by Janice Gray Armstrong. Stony Brook, N.Y.: The Museums at Stony Brook, 1984.

Chambers, Bruce. *The World of David Gilmour Blythe (1815–1865).* Washington, D.C.: Smithsonian Institution Press for the National Collection of Fine Arts, 1980.

Christy, George [George N. Harrington]. *George Christy's Essence of Old Kentucky.* New York: Dick & Fitzgerald, 1864.

Christy's Panorama Songster; containing the Songs as sung by The Christy, Campbell, Pierce's Minstrels, and Sable Brothers. New York: William H. Murphy, n.d.

Christy's Plantation Melodies. 4 vols. Philadelphia: Fisher & Brother, 1854.

Cincinnati: A Guide to the Queen City and Its Neighbors. Compiled by workers of the Writers' Program of the Work Projects Administration in the State of Ohio. Cincinnati: Wiesen-Hart Press, 1943.

Cincinnati: The Queen City. Bicentennial ed. Cincinnati: The Cincinnati Historical Society, 1988.

Cist, Charles. *Cincinnati in 1841: Its Early Annals and Future Prospects.* Cincinnati: Charles Cist, 1841.

———. *Sketches and Statistics of Cincinnati in 1851.* Cincinnati: Wm. H. Moore, 1851.

Cockrell, Dale. *Demons of Disorder: Early Blackface Minstrels and Their World.* New York: Cambridge University Press, 1997.

Coffin, Levi. *Reminiscences of Levi Coffin.* 3d ed. Cincinnati: Robert Clarke, 1898. Reprint, New York: Arno Press and the New York Times, 1968.

Coleman, John F. *The Disruption of the Pennsylvania Democracy 1848–1860.* Harrisburg: The Pennsylvania Historical and Museum Commission, 1975.

The Comic Tradition in America: An Anthology of American Humor. Edited by Kenneth S. Lynn. Garden City, N.Y.: Doubleday Anchor, 1958.

Cook, Adrian. *The Armies of the Street: The New York Draft Riots of 1863.* Lexington: University of Kentucky Press, 1974.

Cooper, George. "Stephen C. Foster." *J. W. Pepper Piano Magazine* 4, 20 (May 1902): 66.

Cooper, James Fenimore. *Home as Found.* New York: Capricorn, 1961.

Cowin, Verna. *Pittsburgh Archaeological Resources and National Register.* Pittsburgh: Carnegie Museum of Natural History, Pennsylvania Historical and Museum Commission, Pittsburgh Department of City Planning, 1985.

Crockett, David. *A Narrative of the Life of David Crockett.* Philadelphia: E. L. Carey and A. Hart, 1834. Reprint, Lincoln: University of Nebraska Press, 1987.

Crockett, David [pseud.]. *An Account of Col. Crockett's Tour to the North and Down East. . . .* 10th ed. Philadelphia: E. L. Carey and A. Hart, 1837.

Crockett at Two Hundred. Edited by Michael A. Lofaro and Joe Cummings. Knoxville: University of Tennessee Press, 1989.

Crockett's Free-and-Easy Song Book: Comic, Sentimental, Amatory, Sporting, African, Scotch, Irish, Western and Texian, National, Military, Naval, and Anacreontic. . . . Philadelphia: Kay & Troutman, 1846.

Cross, Virginia Ann. "The Development of Sunday School Hymnody in the United States of America, 1816–1869." Ph.D. diss., New Orleans Baptist Theological Seminary, 1985.

Culhane, John. *The American Circus: An Illustrated History.* New York: Henry Holt/Owl, 1991.

Curry, Leonard P. *The Free Black in Urban America 1800–1850: The Shadow of the Dream.* Chicago: University of Chicago Press, 1981.

Damon, S. Foster. *Series of Old American Songs.* Providence, R.I.: Brown University Library, 1936.

David Gilmour Blythe's Pittsburgh: 1850–1865. An All-Day Public Forum Saturday, May 9, 1981. Pittsburgh: Museum of Art, Carnegie Institute, 1981.

Davis, Patricia T. *End of the Line: Alexander J. Cassatt and the Pennsylvania Railroad.* New York: Neale Watson Academic Publications, 1978.

Davis, Susan G. *Parades and Power: Street Theatre in Nineteenth-Century Philadelphia.* Philadelphia: Temple University Press, 1986.

Davy Crockett: The Man, The Legend, The Legacy, 1786–1986. Edited by Michael A. Lofaro. Knoxville: University of Tennessee Press, 1985.

DeCamp, Graydon. *The Grand Old Lady of Vine Street.* Cincinnati: Cincinnati Enquirer, 1991.

Delany, Martin R. *Blake or The Huts of America.* Edited by Floyd J. Miller. Boston: Beacon Press, 1970.

———. *The Condition, Elevation, Emigration, and Destiny of the Colored People of the United States.* Philadelphia: 1852. Reprint, New York: Arno Press and the New York Times, 1968.

———. *"Stand Still and See the Salvation": A Martin R. Delany Reader.* Edited by Robert Levine. Chapel Hill: University of North Carolina Press. In press.

Dennison, Sam. *Scandalize My Name: Black Imagery in American Popular Music*. New York: Garland, 1982.

Despard, Matilda. "Music in New York Thirty Years Ago." *Harper's New Monthly Magazine* 57, no. 237 (June 1878): 113–21.

Dickens, Charles. *American Notes for General Circulation*. Edited by Arnold Goldman and John Whitley. London: Penguin, 1989.

———. *Hard Times*. London: Oxford University Press, 1963.

———. *The Letters of Charles Dickens*. Vol. 3, *1842–1843*. Pilgrim Edition. Edited by Madeline House, Graham Story, Kathleen Tillotson; associate ed., Noel C. Peyrouton. Oxford, Eng.: Clarendon Press, 1974.

———. *The Life and Adventures of Martin Chuzzlewit*. Edited by Margaret Cantwell. Oxford, Eng.: Clarendon, 1982.

Dickinson, Emily. *The Letters of Emily Dickinson*. 3 vols. Edited by Thomas H. Johnson; associate ed., Theodora Ward. Cambridge, Mass.: Belknap/Harvard University Press, 1958.

Directory of Pittsburgh & Vicinity for 1859–'60. Edited by George H. Thurston. Pittsburgh: George H. Thurston, 1859.

Directory of Pittsburgh & Allegheny Cities . . . for 1872–73. Edited by George H. Thurston. Pittsburgh: George H. Thurston, 1872.

Dixon, James. *Personal Narrative of a Tour Through Part of the United States and Canada: With Notices of the History and Institutions of Methodism in America*. New York: Lane & Scott, 1849.

Dizikes, John. *Opera in America: A Cultural History*. New Haven: Yale University Press, 1993.

Donovan, Frank. *River Boats of America*. New York: Thomas Y. Crowell, 1966.

Dorman, James H. "The Strange Career of Jim Crow Rice." *Journal of Social History* 3, no. 2 (Winter 1969–70): 109–22.

Douglas, Ann. *The Feminization of American Culture*. New York: Knopf, 1977.

Douglass, Frederick. *The Life and Writings of Frederick Douglass*. Vol. 2, *Pre-Civil War Decade 1850–1860*. Edited by Philip S. Foner. New York: International Publishers, 1950.

———. *My Bondage and My Freedom*. New York: Miller, Orton & Mulligan, 1855. Reprint, New York: Dover, 1969.

Drago, Harry Sinclair. *Canal Days in America: The History and Romance of Old Towpaths and Waterways*. New York: Clarkson N. Potter, 1972.

Drake, Daniel. *Malaria in the Interior Valley of North America: A Selection from A Systematic Treatise, Historical, Etiological, and Practical, on the Principal Diseases of the Interior Valley of North America. . . .* Edited by Norman Levine. Cincinnati: 1850. Reprint, Urbana: University of Illinois Press, 1964.

Du Bois, W. E. B. *Writings*. Edited by Nathan Huggins. New York: Library of America, 1986.

Eaklor, Vicki Lynn. "Music in American Society, 1815–1860: An Intellectual History." Ph.D. diss., Washington University, 1982.

Elliker, Calvin. *Stephen Collins Foster: A Guide to Research*. New York: Garland, 1988.

Ellison, Ralph. *Going to the Territory.* New York: Vintage, 1987.

Ely, Melvin Patrick. *The Adventures of Amos 'n' Andy: A Social History of an American Phenomenon.* New York: Free Press, 1991.

Emerson, Ken. "Stepping Out With Stephen Foster." *New York Times,* 3 December 1995.

Emery, Lynne Fauley. *Black Dance From 1619 to Today.* 2d rev. ed. London: Dance Books, 1988.

Episcopal Common Praise: Consisting of the Chants in the Morning and Evening Service of the Book of Common Prayer and the Psalms of David. . . . Edited by George E. Thrall. New York: A. S. Barnes, 1868.

Epstein, Dena J. *Sinful Tunes and Spirituals: Black Folk Music to the Civil War.* Urbana: University of Illinois Press, 1977.

Evens, William. Scrapbooks. 5 vols. The first four are in the Carnegie Library, Pittsburgh; the fifth is in the Darlington Memorial Library, University of Pittsburgh Libraries.

Fahnestock's Pittsburgh Directory for 1850. . . . Edited by Samuel Fahnestock. Pittsburgh: George Parkin, 1850.

Feder, Stuart. *Charles Ives: "My Father's Song"—A Psychoanalytic Biography.* New Haven: Yale University Press, 1992.

Finson, Jon W. *The Voices That Are Gone: Themes in Nineteenth-Century American Popular Song.* New York: Oxford University Press, 1994.

Fisher, William Arms. *One Hundred and Fifty Years of Music Publishing in the United States, 1783–1933.* Boston: Oliver Ditson, 1933.

Fishkin, Shelley Fisher. *Was Huck Black? Mark Twain and African-American Voices.* New York: Oxford University Press, 1993.

Fitzgerald, F. Scott. *The Crack-Up.* Edited by Edmund Wilson. New York: New Directions, 1956.

———. *The Notebooks of F. Scott Fitzgerald.* Edited by Matthew J. Bruccoli. New York: Harcourt Brace Jovanovich / Bruccoli Clark, 1978.

Fletcher, Edward G. "Stephen Collins Foster, Dramatic Collaborator." *The Colophon,* new series 1, no. 1 (Summer 1935): 33–37.

Fletcher, Tom. *100 Years of the Negro in Show Business.* New York: Burdge & Co., 1954. Reprint, New York: Da Capo, 1984.

Floyd, Samuel A., Jr., and Marsha J. Reisser. "Social Dance Music of Black Composers in the Nineteenth Century and the Emergence of Classic Ragtime." *The Black Perspective in Music* 8, no. 2 (Fall 1980): 161–93.

Foner, Eric. *Reconstruction: America's Unfinished Revolution 1863–1877.* New York: Harper & Row, 1989.

Foster, Eliza C. "Sketches and Incidents." Foster Hall Collection, C386.

Foster, George G. *New York Gas-Light and Other Urban Sketches.* Edited by Stuart M. Blumin. Berkeley: University of California Press, 1990.

———. *New York in Slices.* New York: William H. Graham, 1849.

Foster, Morrison. *My Brother Stephen.* Indianapolis: Foster Hall Library, 1932. This represents the biographical portion of Morrison Foster's *Biography, Songs and Musical Compositions of Stephen Collins Foster.* Pittsburgh: Percy F. Smith, 1896.

Foster, Stephen. *The Music of Stephen Foster: A Critical Edition.* Edited by Steven Saunders and Deane L. Root. 2 vols. Washington: Smithsonian Institution Press, 1990.

———. *The Social Orchestra.* Edited by H. Wiley Hitchcock. New York: Da Capo, 1973.

"Founding Families of Allegheny County." Compiled by Frank Powelson. 4 vols. Typescript in Carnegie Library, Pittsburgh.

Frankenstein, Alfred. *William Sidney Mount.* New York: Harry N. Abrams, 1975.

Frisbee, Ellen Morgan. *Henry Sylvester Cornwell, Poet of Fancy: A Memoir.* New London, Conn.: Ellen Morgan Fisher, 1905.

Gaul, Harvey. *The Minstrel of the Alleghenies.* Pittsburgh: Friends of Harvey Gaul, 1952.

Gavit, Daniel E. *Combined Directories of Jersey City, Hoboken, and Hudson, 1854–55.* Jersey City: n.p., 1854.

Gentle Annie Melodist, nos. 1 and 2. New York: Firth, Pond, 1858–1859.

Gershwin, George. *George Gershwin's Song-book.* Special piano arrangements edited and revised by Herman Wasserman. Rev. ed. New York: Simon and Schuster, 1941.

Gerson, Noel B. *Harriet Beecher Stowe: A Biography.* New York: Praeger, 1976.

Gerson, Robert A. *Music in Philadelphia.* Philadelphia: University of Pennsylvania Press, 1940. Reprint, Westport, Conn.: Greenwood Press, 1970.

Goldman, Herbert G. *Jolson: The Legend Comes to Life.* New York: Oxford University Press, 1988.

Gordon, John Steele. "The Man Who Invented Mass Media." *Audacity* 4, no. 1 (Fall 1995): 28–41.

Gossett, Thomas F. *"Uncle Tom's Cabin" and American Culture.* Dallas, Tex.: Southern Methodist University Press, 1985.

Gottschalk, Louis Moreau. *Notes of a Pianist.* Edited by Jeanne Behrend. New York: Knopf, 1964.

———. *Piano Music of Louis Moreau Gottschalk: 26 Complete Pieces from Original Editions.* Edited by Richard Jackson. New York: Dover, 1973.

Grattan, H. P. "The Origins of the Christy's Minstrels." *The Theatre: A Monthly Review of the Drama, Music and the Fine Arts* (1 March 1882): 129–34.

Green, Alan W. C. " 'Jim Crow,' 'Zip Coon': The Northern Origins of Negro Minstrelsy." *The Massachusetts Review* 11, no. 2 (Spring 1970): 385–97.

Grigg's Southern and Western Songster: Being a Choice Collection of the Most Fashionable Songs, Many of Which Are Original. Philadelphia: J. Grigg, 1833.

Guest, Ivor. *Fanny Elssler.* Middletown, Conn.: Wesleyan University Press, 1970.

Guralnick, Peter. *Last Train to Memphis: The Rise of Elvis Presley.* Boston: Little, Brown, 1994.

Halttunen, Karen. *Confidence Men and Painted Women: A Study of Middle-Class Culture in America, 1830–1870.* New Haven: Yale University Press, 1982.

Hamm, Charles. *Music in the New World*. New York: Norton, 1983.

———. *Yesterdays: Popular Song in America*. New York: Norton, 1979.

Handy, W. C. *Father of the Blues: An Autobiography*. New York: Macmillan, 1941. Reprint, Da Capo, 1991.

Harris, Isaac. *Harris' Business Directory of the Cities of Pittsburgh & Allegheny*. Pittsburgh: A. A. Anderson, 1844.

Hasse, John Edward. *Beyond Category: The Life and Genius of Duke Ellington*. New York: Simon & Schuster, 1993.

Hawthorne, Nathaniel. *Our Old Home, and English Note-Books*. 2 vols. Boston and Cambridge, Mass.: Houghton, Mifflin/Riverside Press, 1898.

Heaps, Willard A., and Porter W. Heaps. *The Singing Sixties: The Spirit of Civil War Days Drawn from the Music of the Times*. Norman: University of Oklahoma Press, 1960.

Hedrick, Joan D. *Harriet Beecher Stowe: A Life*. New York: Oxford University Press, 1994.

Hensel, Octavia [Mary Alice Ives Seymour]. *Life and Letters of Louis Moreau Gottschalk*. Boston: Oliver Ditson, 1870.

Hewitt, John H. *Shadows on the Wall, or Glimpses of the Past: A Retrospect of the Past Fifty Years*. Baltimore: Turnbull Brothers, 1877.

Hickok, Charles Thomas. *The Negro in Ohio, 1802–1870*. Cleveland: Williams Publishing & Electric, 1896. Reprint, New York: AMS, 1975.

Hodges, Fletcher, Jr. "Stephen Foster—Cincinnatian and American." *Bulletin of the Historical and Philosophical Society of Ohio* 8, no. 2 (April 1950): 83–104.

———. "Stephen Foster, Democrat." *The Lincoln Herald*. Harrogate, Tenn.: Lincoln Memorial University, 1945. Reprint, Pittsburgh: University of Pittsburgh, 1946.

Hoffman, Charles Fenno. *A Winter in the West*. 2 vols. New York: Harper & Bros., 1835.

Holbrook, Stewart H. *The Story of American Railroads*. New York: Bonanza Books, 1947. Reprint, New York: American Legacy Press, 1981.

Holl, Herbert. "Some Versions of Pastoral in American Music." Ph.D. diss., University of Texas at Austin, 1980.

Holliday, J. S. *The World Rushed In: The California Gold Experience*. New York: Touchstone, 1983.

Holt, Michael Fitzgibbon. *Forging a Majority: The Formation of the Republican Party in Pittsburgh, 1848–1860*. New Haven: Yale University Press, 1969.

The Honest Man's Extra Almanac, No. 1 For 1813. Pittsburgh: R. & J. Patterson, 1813.

Horton, James Oliver. *Free People of Color: Inside the African American Community*. Washington, D.C.: Smithsonian Institution Press, 1993.

Howard, John Tasker. *Stephen Foster: America's Troubadour*. Rev. ed. New York: Thomas Y. Crowell, 1953.

Hulbert, Archer Butler. *Forty-Niners: The Chronicle of the California Trail*. Boston: Little, Brown, 1931.

Hunter, Louis C. with the assistance of Beatrice Jones Hunter. *Steamboats on the Western Rivers: An Economic and Technological History*. Cambridge, Mass.: Harvard University Press, 1949. Reprint, New York: Octagon, 1969.

Hutton, Laurence. *Curiosities of the American Stage*. New York: Harper & Bros., 1891.

Insurance Maps of the City of New York, vol. 1. New York: Perris & Browne, 1867.

Ireland, Joseph N. *Records of the New York Stage from 1750 to 1860*. 2 vols. New York: 1866. Reprint, New York: Benjamin Blom, 1966.

Ives, Charles. *Memos*. Edited by John Kirkpatrick. New York: Norton, 1972.

————. *114 Songs*. Bryn Mawr, Pa.: Merion, 1935.

James, Henry. *A Small Boy and Others*. In *Henry James: Autobiography*. Edited by Frederick W. Dupee. Princeton, N.J.: Princeton University Press, 1983.

Johannsen, Robert W. *To the Halls of the Montezumas: The Mexican War in the American Imagination*. New York: Oxford University Press, 1985.

Johnson, Erleen. "Writer Has No Doubts Foster Was Here." *Kentucky Standard*, 7 June 1985.

Johnson, James Weldon. *The Autobiography of an Ex-Colored Man*. New York: Penguin, 1990.

Jones, Charles K., and Lorenzo K. Greenwich II, eds. *A Choice Collection of the Works of Francis Johnson*. 2 vols. New York: Point Two Publications, 1982– 1987.

Jones, Howard Mumford. *The Harp That Once: A Chronicle of the Life of Thomas Moore*. New York: Henry Holt, 1937. Reprint, New York: Russell & Russell, 1970.

Jones, Samuel. *Pittsburgh in the Year Eighteen Hundred and Twenty-Six, Containing Sketches Topographical, Historical and Statistical. . . .* Pittsburgh: Johnston & Stockton, 1826. Reprint, New York: Arno Press and the New York Times, 1970.

Joyce, Col. John A[lexander]. *A Checkered Life*. Chicago: S.P. Rounds, 1883.

————. "Genius Is Forgotten." *Washington Post*, 9 September 1900.

Kaplan, Justin. *Mr. Clemens and Mark Twain*. New York: Simon & Schuster, 1966.

————. *Walt Whitman: A Life*. New York: Touchstone, 1986.

Kaye, Joseph. "Famous First Nights: 'Uncle Tom's Cabin.' " *Theatre Magazine* (August 1929): 26.

The Kentucky Minstrel and Jersey Warbler: Being a Choice Selection of Coon Melodies. Philadelphia: Robinson and Peterson, 1844.

Ketner, Joseph D. *The Emergence of the African-American Artist: Robert S. Duncanson, 1821–1872*. Columbia: University of Missouri Press, 1993.

Key, Susan. "Sound and Sentimentality: Nostalgia in the Songs of Stephen Foster." *American Music* 3, no. 2 (summer 1995): 145–66.

Kingsbury, A. H. "The Old Towanda Academy." *Bradford County Historical Society Annual* (Towanda, Pa.), no. 4 (1910): 15–22.

Kisch, John, and Edward Mapp. *A Separate Cinema: Fifty Years of Black-Cast Posters*. New York: Farrar, Straus and Giroux, 1992.

Klein, Philip Shriver. *President James Buchanan: A Biography*. University Park: Pennsylvania State University Press, 1962.

Klement, Frank L. *The Limits of Dissent: Clement L. Vallandigham and the Civil War*. Lexington: University Press of Kentucky, 1970.

Koza, Julia Eklund. "Music and References to Music in *Godey's Lady's Book*, 1830–77." Ph.D. diss., University of Minnesota, 1988.

Krohn, Ernest C. "Nelson Kneass: Minstrel Singer and Composer." *Yearbook for Inter-American Musical Research* 8 (1971): 17–41.

Kunhardt, Philip B., Jr., Philip B. Kunhardt III, and Peter W. Kunhardt. *P. T. Barnum: America's Greatest Showman*. New York: Knopf, 1995.

Kunzog, John C. *The One-Horse Show: The Life and Times of Dan Rice, Circus Jester and Philanthropist—A Chronicle of Early Circus Days*. Jamestown, N.Y.: John C. Kunzog, 1962.

Kussart, Sarepta. *The Early History of the Fifteenth Ward of the City of Pittsburgh*. Bellevue/Pittsburgh: Suburban Printing, 1925.

Lauderdale, John Vance. *The Wounded River: The Civil War Letters of John Vance Lauderdale, M.D.* Edited by Peter Josyph. East Lansing: Michigan State University Press, 1993.

Lawrence, Vera Brodsky. "Micah Hawkins, the Pied Piper of Catherine Slip." *The New-York Historical Society Quarterly* 62, no. 2 (1978): 138–65.

———. *Strong on Music: The New York Music Scene in the Days of George Templeton Strong*. Vol. 1, *Resonances: 1836–1850*. New York: Oxford University Press, 1988.

———. *Strong on Music: The New York Music Scene in the Days of George Templeton Strong*. Vol. 2, *Reverberations: 1850–1856*. Chicago: University of Chicago Press, 1995.

Levine, Lawrence W. *Black Culture and Black Consciousness: Afro-American Folk Thought from Slavery to Freedom*. New York: Oxford University Press, 1977.

———. *Highbrow/Lowbrow: The Emergence of Cultural Hierarchy in America*. Cambridge, Mass.: Harvard University Press, 1988.

Levine, Robert. *Martin Delany, Frederick Douglass, and the Politics of Representative Identity*. Chapel Hill: University of North Carolina Press, 1997.

Levy, Lester S. *Grace Notes in American History: Popular Sheet Music from 1820 to 1900*. Norman: University of Oklahoma Press, 1967.

Linn, Karen. *That Half-Barbaric Twang: The Banjo in American Popular Culture*. Urbana: University of Illinois Press, 1994.

Livesay, Harold C. *Andrew Carnegie and the Rise of Big Business*. Boston: Little, Brown, 1975.

Locke, Alain. *The Negro and His Music*. Washington, D.C.: The Associates in Negro Folk Education, 1936. Reprint, New York: Arno Press and the New York Times, 1969.

Lorant, Stefan. *Pittsburgh: The Story of an American City*. Rev. ed. Lenox, Mass.: Authors Edition, 1975.

Lott, Eric. *Love and Theft: Blackface Minstrelsy and the American Working Class*. New York: Oxford University Press, 1993.

Ludlow, Noah M. *Dramatic Life as I Found It*. St. Louis: 1880. Reprint, New York: Benjamin Blom, 1966.

Maass, Alfred A. "Brownsville's Steamboat *Enterprize* and Pittsburgh's Supply of General Jackson's Army." *Pittsburgh History* 77, no. 1 (Spring 1994): 22–29.

Macdonald, Cordelia Howard. "Memoirs of the Original Little Eva." *Educational Theatre Journal* 8, no. 4: 267–82.

Mahar, William J. " 'Backside Albany' and Early Blackface Minstrelsy: A Contextual Study of America's First Blackface Song." *American Music* 6, no. 1 (Spring 1988): 1–28.

Mahon, John. "Last Years of Stephen C. Foster." *New York Clipper*, 17 or 24 March 1877. Reprinted in *Foster Hall Bulletin* 10 (May 1934): 2–6.

Maretzek, Max. *Crotchets and Quavers or Revelations of an Opera Manager in America*. New York: S. French, 1855. Reprint, New York: Da Capo, 1966.

Marryat, Frederick. *A Diary in America, With Remarks on Its Institutions*. Edited by Sydney Jackman. New York: Knopf, 1962.

Martin, Scott C. "Leisure in Southwestern Pennsylvania, 1800–1850." Ph.D. diss., University of Pittsburgh, 1990.

McDowell, Robert E. "Bones and the Man: Toward a History of Bones Playing." *Journal of American Culture* 5, no. 1 (Spring 1982): 38–44.

McFeeley, William S. *Frederick Douglass*. New York: Norton, 1991.

McKay, Ernest A. *The Civil War and New York City*. Syracuse, N.Y.: Syracuse University Press, 1990.

McKnight, Robert. Diaries. 2 vols. Darlington Memorial Library, University of Pittsburgh Libraries.

McNair, James Birtley. *McNair, McNear and McNeir Genealogies: Supplement 1955*. Los Angeles: self-published, 1955.

McPherson, James M. *The Battle Cry of Freedom: The Civil War Era*. New York: Ballantine, 1989.

Mellers, Wilfrid. *Music in a New Found Land*. New York: Hillstone, 1975.

Melville, Herman. *Pierre, Israel Potter, The Piazza Tales, The Confidence-Man, Uncollected Prose, Billy Budd, Sailor*. New York: Library of America, 1984.

———. *Redburn, White-Jacket, Moby-Dick*. New York: Library of America, 1983.

Miller, Annie Clark. *Chronicles of Families, Houses and Estates of Pittsburgh and Its Environs*. Pittsburgh: n.p., 1927.

Miller, Dorothy. *The Life and Work of David G. Blythe*. Pittsburgh: University of Pittsburgh Press, 1950.

Miller, Floyd J. *The Search for a Black Nationality: Black Colonization and Emigration, 1787–1863*. Urbana: University of Illinois Press, 1975.

Miller, Perry. *The Raven and the Whale: The War of Words and Wit in the Era of Poe and Melville*. New York: Harvest, 1956.

Milligan, Harold Vincent. *Stephen Collins Foster: A Biography*. New York: G. Schirmer, 1920.

Mills, B. H. *The Temperance Manual*. St. Louis: Edwards & Bushnell, 1859.

Moore, Thomas. *Moore's Irish Melodies with Symphonies and Arrangements by Sir John Stevenson, Mus. Doc. and Sir Henry Bishop*. Dublin: M. H. Gill & Son, 1891. Reprint, Wilmington, Del.: Michael Glazier, 1981.

————. *The Journal of Thomas Moore 1818–1841*. Edited by Peter Quennell. New York: Macmillan, 1964.

Morneweck, Evelyn Foster. *Chronicles of Stephen Foster's Family*. 2 vols. Pittsburgh: University of Pittsburgh Press, 1944.

Murray, Elsie. *Stephen C. Foster at Athens: His First Composition*. Athens, Pa.: Tioga Point Museum, 1941.

Murray, Louise Welles. *A History of Old Tioga Point and Early Athens Pennsylvania*. Athens, Pa.: n.p., 1908.

Nathan, Hans. *Dan Emmett and the Rise of Early Negro Minstrelsy*. Norman: University of Oklahoma Press, 1962.

The National Melodies of Scotland; United to the Songs of Robert Burns, Allan Ramsay, and Other Eminent Lyric Poets; with Symphonies and Accompaniments for the Piano Forte, by Haydn, Pleyel, Kozeluch, and Other Celebrated Composers. London: John and Frederick Tallis, 1849.

Negro Year Book: An Annual Encyclopedia of the Negro, 1931–1932. Edited by Monroe N. Work. Tuskegee, Ala.: Tuskegee Institute, 1931.

Nevin, Robert Peebles. "Stephen C. Foster and Negro Minstrelsy." *Atlantic Monthly* 20, no. 121 (November 1867): 606–16.

Nevins, Allan. *Frémont, Pathmarker of the West*. 2 vols. New York: Frederick Ungar, 1961.

The New Grove Dictionary of American Music. Edited by H. Wiley Hitchcock and Stanley Sadie. 4 vols. London: Macmillan, 1986.

The New Grove Dictionary of Music and Musicians. Edited by Stanley Sadie. London: Macmillan, 1980.

Odell, George C. D. *Annals of the New York Stage*. 15 vols. New York: Columbia University Press, 1927–1949.

Olmsted, Frederick Law. *A Journey in the Seaboard Slave States, with Remarks on Their Economy*. New York: Dix & Edwards, 1856. Reprint, New York: Negro Universities Press, 1968.

One Hundred and Fiftieth Anniversary of the Presbyterian Congregation of Lewistown. Lewistown, Pa.: 1935.

Orr, N. Lee. "John Hill Hewitt: Bard of the Confederacy." *American Music Research Center Journal* 4 (1994): 31–75.

Ostendorf, Berndt. "Minstrelsy & Early Jazz." *Massachusetts Review* 20, no. 3 (Autumn 1979): 574–602.

Parke, Judge John E. *Recollections of Seventy Years and Historical Gleanings of Allegheny, Pennsylvania*. Boston: Rand, Avery, 1886.

The Parlour Companion, or, Polite Song Book, Comprising a Choice Selection of Fashionable and Popular Songs. . . . Vol. 1. Philadelphia: A. I. Dickinson, 1836.

Paskman, Dailey. *Gentlemen, Be Seated: A Parade of American Minstrels*. Rev. ed. New York: Clarkson N. Potter, 1976.

Pastor, Tony. *Tony Pastor's New Comic Irish Songster*. New York: Dick and Fitzgerald, 1863.

Percival, James Gates. *The Poetical Works of James Gates Percival with a Biographical Sketch*. 2 vols. Boston: Ticknor and Fields, 1859.

Peress, Maurice. "Dvorak and African-American Musicians, 1892–1895." *Black Music Research Bulletin* 12, no. 2 (Fall 1990): 26–29.

Platt, Thomas Collier. *The Autobiography of Thomas Collier Platt*. Edited by Louis J. Lang. New York: B. W. Dodge, 1910.

Poe, Edgar Allan. *Essays, Miscellanies*. Vol. 14, *The Complete Works of Edgar Allan Poe*. Edited by James A. Harrison. New York: Crowell, 1902. Reprint, New York: AMS, 1965.

———. *Poetry and Tales*. New York: Library of America, 1984.

Pollard, Edward A. *Black Diamonds Gathered in the Darkey Homes of the South*. New York: Pudney & Russell, 1859.

Popular Songs of Nineteenth-Century America. Edited by Richard Jackson. New York: Dover, 1976.

Preston, Katherine P. *Opera on the Road: Traveling Opera Troupes in the United States, 1825–60*. Urbana: University of Illinois Press, 1993.

Pursell, Carroll W., Jr. *Early Stationary Steam Engines in America: A Study in the Migration of a Technology*. Washington, D.C.: Smithsonian Institution Press, 1969.

Quillen, Frank U. *The Color Line in Ohio: A History of Race Prejudice in a Typical Northern State*. Ann Arbor: University of Michigan Press, 1913.

Quinn, Peter. *Banished Children of Eve*. New York: Viking Penguin, 1994.

Ramshaw, Molly N. "Jump, Jim Crow! A Biographical Sketch of Thomas D. Rice (1808–1860)." *The Theatre Annual* 17 (1960): 36–47.

Ransom, Teresa. *Fanny Trollope: A Remarkable Life*. New York: St. Martin's Press, 1995.

Remini, Robert V. *Henry Clay: Statesman for the Union*. New York: Norton, 1991.

Reynolds, David S. *Walter Whitman's America: A Cultural Biography*. New York: Knopf, 1995.

Rice, Dan. *Dan Rice's Great American Humorist Song Book*. N.p.: 1863.

Rice, Edward LeRoy. *Monarchs of Minstrelsy, from "Daddy" Rice to Date*. New York: Kenny, 1911.

Rice, Edward Wilbur. *The Sunday-School Movement, 1780–1917, and the American Sunday-School Union, 1817–1917*. Philadelphia: American Sunday-School Union, 1917. Reprint, New York: Arno Press and the New York Times, 1971.

Richards, Leonard L. *Gentlemen of Property and Standing: Anti-Abolition Mobs in Jacksonian America*. New York: Oxford University Press, 1971.

Riddle, James M., compiler. *The Pittsburgh Directory for 1815. Containing the Names, Professions and Residences of the Heads of Families and Persons in Business in the Borough. . . .* Pittsburgh: James M. Riddle, 1815. Reprint, Pittsburgh: Colonial Trust Company, 1905.

Riis, Thomas L. "The Music and Musicians in Nineteenth-Century Productions of *Uncle Tom's Cabin.*" *American Music* 4, no. 3 (Fall 1986): 268–86.

Rinhart, Floyd, and Marion Rinhart. *The American Daguerreotype*. Athens: University of Georgia Press, 1981.

Robinson & Jones' Cincinnati Directory, for 1846. Cincinnati: Robinson and Jones, 1846.

Roediger, David R. *The Wages of Whiteness: Race and the Making of the American Working Class*. London: Verso, 1991.

Rollin, Frank A. [Mrs. Frances E. Rollin Whipper]. *Life and Public Services of Martin R. Delany*. Boston: 1883. Reprint, New York: Arno Press and the New York Times, 1969.

Root, Deane L. *American Popular Stage Music 1860–1880*. Ann Arbor, Mich.: UMI Research Press, 1981.

Root, George F. *The Story of a Musical Life: An Autobiography*. Chicago: Root and Sons, 1891. Reprint, New York: Da Capo, 1970.

Rose, Jessie Welsh. "His Widow's Memories of Foster's Life Are Recalled by Granddaughter." *Pittsburgh Sunday Post*, 4 July 1926.

———. "My Grandmother's Memories." *Foster Hall Bulletin*, no. 10 (May 1934): 9–22.

Rosenberg, C. G. *Jenny Lind in America*. New York: Stringer & Townsend, 1851.

Rosenberg, Charles E. *The Cholera Years: The United States in 1832, 1849, and 1866*. Chicago: University of Chicago Press, 1987.

Rosenberg, Deena. *Fascinating Rhythm: The Collaboration of George and Ira Gershwin*. New York: Dutton, 1991.

Ross, Steven J. *Workers On the Edge: Work, Leisure, and Politics in Industrializing Cincinnati, 1788–1890*. New York: Columbia University Press, 1985.

Rourke, Constance. *American Humor: A Study of the National Character*. New York: Harcourt, Brace, 1931. Reprint, New York: Harvest, 1959.

———. *The Roots of American Culture and Other Essays*. Edited by Van Wyck Brooks. New York: Harcourt, Brace, 1942. Reprint, Port Washington, N.Y.: Kennikat Press, 1965.

Russell, Henry. *Cheer! Boys, Cheer! Memories of Men and Music*. London: John Macqueen, 1895.

Russell, John B. "Foster's Music." *Cincinnati Daily Gazette*, 22 January 1857.

Sacks, Howard L., and Judith Rose Sacks. *Way Up North in Dixie: A Black Family's Claim to the Confederate Anthem*. Washington, D.C.: Smithsonian Institution Press, 1993.

Saxon, A. H. *P. T. Barnum: The Legend and the Man*. New York: Columbia University Press, 1989.

Schlesinger, Arthur M., Jr. *The Age of Jackson*. Boston: Little, Brown, 1945.

Schwartz, H. W. *Bands of America*. Garden City, N.Y.: Doubleday, 1957.

Scully, Charles B. *Journal No. 6*. Darlington Memorial Library, University of Pittsburgh Libraries.

Shiras, Charles P. *The Redemption of Labor, and Other Poems*. Pittsburgh: W. H. Whitney, 1852.

Shiras, George. *Justice George Shiras Jr. of Pittsburgh: A Chronicle of his Family, Life and Times*. Edited and completed by Winfield Shiras. Pittsburgh: University of Pittsburgh Press, 1953.

Siegel, Alan A. *Out of Our Past: A History of Irvington, New Jersey*. Irvington, N.J.: Irvington Centennial Committee, 1974.

Silber, Irwin. *Songs America Voted By*. N.p., 1971. Reprint, Harrisburg, Pa.: Stackpole, 1988.

Silverman, Kenneth. *Edgar A. Poe: Mournful and Never-ending Remembrance*. New York: HarperCollins, 1991.

The Singer's Own Book: A Well-Selected Collection of the Most Popular Sentimental, Amatory, Patriotic, Naval, and Comic Songs. Philadelphia: Key & Biddle, 1832.

Southern, Eileen. *The Music of Black Americans: A History*. 2d ed. New York: Norton, 1983.

Spitzer, John. " 'Oh! Susanna': Oral Transmission and Tune Transformation." *Journal of the American Musicological Society* 47, no. 1 (1994): 90–136.

Sponholtz, Lloyd L. "Pittsburgh and Temperance, 1830–1850." *The Western Pennsylvania Magazine* 46, no. 4 (October 1963): 347–79.

Starke, Aubrey. "Richard Henry Wilde: Some Notes and a Check-List." *The American Book Collector* 5, no. 1 (January 1934): 7–10.

Starr, S. Frederick. *Bamboula! The Life and Times of Louis Moreau Gottschalk*. New York: Oxford University Press, 1995.

Stearns, Marshall, and Jean Stearns. *Jazz Dance: The Story of American Vernacular Dance*. New York: Macmillan, 1968.

Stephens, John Anthony. "Henry Russell in America: Chutzpah and Huzzah." Ph.D. diss., University of Illinois at Urbana-Champaign, 1975.

Stowe, Harriet Beecher. *Three Novels: Uncle Tom's Cabin or, Life among the Lowly, The Minister's Wooing, Oldtown Folks*. New York: Library of America, 1982.

Strong, George Templeton. *The Diary of George Templeton Strong*. Edited by Allan Nevins and Milton Halsey Thomas. 4 vols. New York: Macmillan, 1952.

"A Talk About Popular Songs." *Putnam's Monthly* 7, no. 40 (April 1856): 401–15.

Tawa, Nicholas. *A Music for the Millions: Antebellum Democratic Attitudes and the Birth of American Popular Music*. New York: Pendragon, 1984.

———. *Sweet Songs for Gentle Americans: The Parlor Song in America, 1790–1860*. Bowling Green, Ohio: Bowling Green University Popular Press, 1980.

———. Review of *"Susanna," "Jeanie," and "The Old Folks at Home": The Songs of Stephen C. Foster from His Time to Ours*, by William W. Austin. *Yearbook for Inter-American Musical Research* 11 (1975): 219–22.

Taylor, Bayard. " 'Old Zip Coon' and 'Uncle Ned' among the Arabs." *American Musical Review and Choral Advocate* 3, no. 8 (1 August 1852): 118.

Taylor, George Rogers. *The Transportation Revolution 1815–1860*. Vol. 4, *The Economic History of the United States*. New York: Holt, Rinehart and Winston, 1951.

Thomas, Jean W. "Henry Kleber: Musical Entrepreneur of Nineteenth Century Pittsburgh." Unpublished paper, Historical Society of Western Pennsylvania Library, 1991.

Thoreau, Henry David. *Walden*. Edited by J. Lyndon Shanley. Princeton: Princeton University Press, 1971.

Thurston, George H. *Allegheny County's Hundred Years*. Pittsburgh: A. A. Anderson & Son, 1888.

Toll, Robert C. *Blacking Up: The Minstrel Show in Nineteenth-Century America*. New York: Oxford University Press, 1974.

Trollope, Anthony. *North America*. Baltimore: Penguin, 1968.

Trollope, Frances. *Domestic Manners of the Americans*. London: Century, 1984.

Tucker, Edward L. *Richard Henry Wilde: His Life and Selected Poems*. Athens: University of Georgia Press, 1966.

Tuckerman, Henry T. *Book of the Artists. American Artist Life*. . . . 2d ed. New York: G. P. Putnam & Son, 1867.

Turner, Clarence Rollo. "Black Pittsburgh: A Social History, 1790–1840 (A Census Compilation prepared for the Friday Evening Urban Historians Group, Department of History, University of Pittsburgh, March 1974)."

Turner, Edward Raymond. *The Negro in Pennsylvania: Slavery—Servitude—Freedom, 1639–1861*. Washington, D.C.: 1911. Reprint, New York: Arno Press, 1969.

Twain, Mark. *The Autobiography of Mark Twain*. Edited by Charles Neider. New York: Harper Perennial, 1990.

———. *Early Tales & Sketches*, vol. 2, *1864–1865*. Edited by Edgar Marquess Branch and Robert H. Hirst. In *The Works of Mark Twain*. Berkeley: University of California Press, 1981.

———. *Mississippi Writings: The Adventures of Tom Sawyer, Life on the Mississippi, Adventures of Huckleberry Finn, Pudd'nhead Wilson*. New York: Library of America, 1982.

Tyrrell, Ian R. *Sobering Up: From Temperance to Prohibition in Antebellum America, 1800–1860*. Westport, Conn.: Greenwood Press, 1979.

Ullman, Victor. *Martin R. Delany: The Beginnings of Black Nationalism*. Boston: Beacon, 1971.

Updike, John. *Buchanan Dying: A Play*. New York: Knopf, 1974.

———. *Memories of the Ford Administration*. New York: Knopf, 1992.

Upton, William Treat. *Anthony Philip Heinrich: A Nineteenth-Century Composer in America*. New York: Columbia University Press, 1939.

Van Der Merwe, Peter. *Origins of the Popular Style: The Antecedents of Popular Music*. Oxford, Eng.: Clarendon Press, 1989.

Wade, Richard C. *The Urban Frontier: The Rise of Western Cities, 1790–1830*. Cambridge, Mass.: Harvard University Press, 1959. Reprint, reentitled *The*

Selected Bibliography

Urban Frontier: Pioneer Life in Early Pittsburgh, Cincinnati, Lexington, Louisville, and St. Louis, Chicago: University of Chicago Press Phoenix, n.d.

Waggoner, Madeline Sadler. *The Long Haul West: The Great Canal Era, 1817–1850*. New York: G. P. Putnam, 1958.

Wall, Joseph Frazier. *Andrew Carnegie*. New York: Oxford University Press, 1970. Reprint, Pittsburgh: University of Pittsburgh Press, 1989.

Waln, Robert, Jr. *The Hermit in America on a Visit to Philadelphia*. Philadelphia: M. Thomas, 1819.

Walters, Raymond. *Stephen Foster: Youth's Golden Gleam*. Princeton, N.J.: Princeton University Press, 1936.

Ware, Norman. *The Industrial Worker 1840–1860*. Boston: Houghton Mifflin, 1924. Reprint, Chicago: Quadrangle, 1964.

Warner, Susan [Elizabeth Wetherell, pseud.]. *The Wide, Wide World*. New York: G. P. Putnam, 1850. Reprint, New York: Feminist Press, 1987.

Watkins, Mel. *On the Real Side: Laughing, Lying, and Signifying—The Underground Tradition of African-American Humor That Transformed American Culture, From Slavery to Richard Pryor*. New York: Touchstone, 1995.

Way, Frederick, Jr. *Way's Packet Directory, 1848–1983*. Athens: Ohio University Press, 1983.

Welles, R. M. "The Old Athens Academy." *Bradford County Historical Society Annual* (Towanda, Pa.), no. 5 (1911): 22–36.

Wetzel, Richard D. *Frontier Musicians on the Connoquenessing, Wabash, and Ohio: A History of the Music and Musicians of George Rapp's Harmony Society, 1805–1906*. Athens: Ohio University Press, 1976.

What They Heard: Music in America, 1852–1881, From the Pages of "Dwight's Journal of Music." Edited by Irving Sablosky. Baton Rouge: Louisiana State University Press, 1986.

White, J. W. F. "The Judiciary of Allegheny County." *The Pennsylvania Magazine of History and Biography* 7 (1883): 143–93.

Whitley, T. W. *A Guide to Hoboken, the Elysian Fields, and Weehawken*. N.p.: 1858.

Whitman, Walt. *The Collected Writings of Walt Whitman*. Edited by Gay Wilson Allen and Sculley Bradley. 18 vols. New York: New York University Press, 1964–1980.

———. *Walt Whitman and the Civil War: A Collection of Original Articles and Manuscripts*. Edited by Charles I. Glicksberg. Philadelphia: University of Pennsylvania Press, 1933. Reprint, New York: Perpetua/A. S. Barnes, 1963.

Wilentz, Sean. *Chants Democratic: New York City and the Rise of the American Working Class, 1788–1850*. New York: Oxford University Press, 1984.

Williams' Cincinnati Directory and Business Advertiser, for 1849–50. Cincinnati: C. S. Williams, 1849.

[Williams, W. F.]. "Who Writes Our Songs?" New York *Evening Post*, 22 April 1859.

Wilmoth, Ann Greenwood. "Pittsburgh and the Blacks: A Short History, 1780–1875." Ph.D. diss., Pennsylvania State University, 1975.

Wilson, Erasmus. *History of Pittsburg*. Chicago: H. R. Cornell, 1898.

Wilson, William Bender. "History of the Pennsylvania Railroad Company, with Plan of Organization, Portraits of Officials and Biographical Sketches—William B. Foster, Jr." *Railroad Men's News* 9, no. 8 (August 1897): 259–65.

Wilson's Business Directory of New York City. New York: John F. Trow, 1862.

Winans, Robert B. "Early Minstrel Show Music 1843–1852." In *Musical Theater in America: Papers and Proceedings of the Conference on the Musical Theater in America*. Edited by Glenn Loney. Westport, Conn.: Greenwood Press, 1984.

Wingate, George W. *History of the Twenty-Second Regiment of the National Guard of the State of New York*. New York: Edwin W. Dayton, 1896.

Winter, Marian Hannah. "Juba and American Minstrelsy." In *Chronicles of the American Dance*. Edited by Paul Magriel. New York: Henry Holt, 1948.

Wittke, Carl. *Tambo and Bones: A History of the American Minstrel Stage*. Durham, N.C.: Duke University Press, 1930.

Wohlgemuth, E. Jay. "Stephen Foster and Harriet Beecher Stowe." *Papers of the Literary Club of Cincinnati* 56 (2 October 1933 to 25 June 1934): 464–70.

———. *Within Three Chords: The Place of Cincinnati in the Life of Stephen Collins Foster*. Indianapolis: Rough Notes Press, 1928.

Wood's Minstrels Songs: Containing a Selection of the most Popular Choruses, Quartettes, Trios, Duets, Glees, Songs, Parodies, Burlesques, Conundrums, etc., etc. New York: Dick & Fitzgerald, 1855.

Woodson, Carter G. "The Negroes of Cincinnati Prior to the Civil War." *Journal of Negro History* 1, no. 1 (January 1916): 1–22.

Wortley, Lady Emmeline Stuart. *Travels in the United States, etc., During 1849 and 1850*. 3 vols. London: Richard Bentley, 1851.

Wyrick, Charles R. "Concerts and Criticism in Cincinnati, 1840—1850." Ph.D. diss., University of Cincinnati, 1965.

Selected
Discography

Baker, LaVern. *Soul on Fire: The Best of LaVern Baker*. Atlantic CD 82311.

The Beatles. *The Beatles* (the "White Album"). Apple SWBO 101.

DeGaetani, Jan, and Gilbert Kalish. *Charles Ives Songs*. Elektra/Nonesuch 9 71325–2.

DeGaetani, Jan, Leslie Guinn and Gilbert Kalish. *Songs by Stephen Foster*. 2 vols. Elektra/Nonesuch H–71268, H–71333. All of vol. 1 and portions of vol. 2 have been reissued on Elektra/Nonesuch 9 79158–2.

Dorsey, Tommy. *The Complete Tommy Dorsey*, vol. 8, *1938–1939*. Bluebird AXM2–5586.

———. *Yes, Indeed!* Bluebird 9987–1–RB.

Dylan, Bob. *The Bootleg Series 1961–1991 (Rare and Unreleased)*, vol. 1. Columbia 47382.

———. *Good As I Been to You*. Columbia CK 53200.

Ellington, Duke, and His Orchestra. *Jubilee Stomp*. Bluebird 66038–2.

The Europeans: Music from the Motion Picture Soundtrack. Angel CDQ 7243 5 55102 2 8.

Hampson, Thomas. *American Dreamer: Songs of Stephen Foster*. Angel CDC 0777 7 54621 2 8.

Handy, W. C. *Father of the Blues*. DRG SL 5192.

Harris, Emmylou. *Emmylou Harris & the Nash Ramblers at the Ryman*. Reprise 4–26664.

The Isley Brothers. *Timeless*. T–Neck KZ2 35650.

Jackson, Clifford, and William Bolcom. *An Evening with Henry Russell*. Nonesuch H–71388.

McGarrigle, Kate and Anna, and others. *Songs of the Civil War*. Columbia CK 48607.

The Mills Brothers. *The Mills Brothers 1936–1940*. Jazz Roots CD 56072.

Robeson, Paul. *The Power and the Glory*. Columbia/Legacy CK 47337.

Robison, Paula. *By the Old Pine Tree: Flute Music by Stephen Foster & Sidney Lanier*. Arabesque Z6679.

Shocked, Michelle. *Arkansas Traveler*. Mercury 314 512 101–2.

Smith, Bessie. *The Complete Recordings,* vol. 2. Columbia/ Legacy C2K 47471.

Stills, Stephen. *Stephen Stills.* Atlantic SD 7202.

Straw, Syd. *Surprise.* Virgin Records America 7 91266–1.

There's a Good Time Coming and Other Songs of the Hutchinson Family as Performed at the Smithsonian Institution. Smithsonian Collection N020.

Travis, Randy. *No Holdin' Back.* Warner Bros. 9 25988–1.

Various artists. *The Flowering of Vocal Music in America,* vol. 2. New World Records NW 231.

Various artists. *Homespun America.* Vox Box SYBX 5309.

Waller, Fats. *Fine Arabian Stuff: Original 1939 Recordings.* Deluxe DE 601.

Williams, Larry, and others. *The Specialty Story.* Specialty 5SPCD–412–2.

Winans, Robert B., and others. *The Early Minstrel Show.* New World Records NW 338.

Wynette, Tammy. *Tammy's Greatest Hits.* Epic BN 26486.

INDEX

Index